# Poetic License

# *Poetic License:*

*Essays on Modernist and Postmodernist Lyric*

*Marjorie Perloff*

*Northwestern University Press*    *Evanston, Illinois*

Northwestern University Press
Evanston, Illinois 60201

Copyright © 1990 by Marjorie Perloff. All
rights reserved. Printed in the United States
of America.

Design by William A. Seabright

The paper used in this publication meets the minimum require-
ments of American National Standard for Information Sciences—
Permanence of Paper for Printed Library Materials, ANSI Z39.48-
1984.

**Library of Congress Cataloging-in-Publication Data**

Perloff, Marjorie.
    Poetic license : essays on modernist and postmodernist lyric /
Marjorie Perloff.
        p.  cm.
    Includes bibliographical references.
    ISBN 0-8101-0843-7. — ISBN 0-8101-0844-5 (pbk.)
        1. American poetry—20th century—History and criticism.
2. English poetry—20th century—History and criticism.
3. Postmodernism (Literature)  4. Modernism (Literature)  I. Title.
PS323.5.P465  1989
811'.040905—dc20                                            89-71136
                                                               CIP

*For Joseph*

# Contents

# Illustrations

# *Preface*

Most of the essays in this collection have been previously published (see Acknowledgments). Since they are relatively quite recent, I have made only minor adjustments, bringing them up to date only in the case of specific developments that affect a particular argument. In the case of "*Howl* and Its Enemies," for instance, I have added a few references to other favorable reviews so as not to distort the discussion of negative response to Ginsberg's work. Similar small additions and changes are made throughout.

It is a pleasure to recall the specific occasions for which some of these essays were produced. Essay #1 was the keynote address for the annual meeting of the Northeast Modern Language Association Convention in 1985; #2 was written for a Symposium on Contemporary Poetics at the City University of New York in 1986; #3 for the conference "French Writers–Foreign Texts/Foreign Writers–French Texts," held at UCLA in 1988; #4 was a plenary address on the topic "Yeats in a European Context" at the annual convention of the American Comparative Literature Association in 1989; #6 was written for the year-long lecture series "Pound among the Poets," organized by George Bornstein at the University of Michigan in Ann Arbor in the academic year 1983–84; #8 was written for the conference "Beckett Translating/Translating Beckett" at the University of Texas in Austin in 1984 and was delivered, in rather different form, at the Triennial Conference of the International Association of University Professors of English, held in York, England, in 1986; #9 was delivered at a conference "Feminism and Contemporary Poetics" at Stanford University in 1984; #10, part 2, was written for an MLA session called "*Howl* Thirty Years Later" in 1986; #13 was delivered, in an earlier version, at the 10th Anniversary Puterbaugh Conference "Spanish, French, and Anglo-American Literatures: Postwar Interrelations in Retrospect," held at the University of Oklahoma in 1985, and then, in its present form, at a conference called "Seminaries of Instruction: On the Poetry of John Ashbery," at the Humanities Center of Brooklyn College of the City of New York in 1985. I wish to thank the students and colleagues who made up the audiences on all these occasions for helpful comments and suggestions for revision.

My specific debts in this connection, not only to those who made the various lectures possible but also to the editors who published the written versions, are many, and I wish to thank the following: Peter Balbert, Gordon Ball, George Bornstein, Claus Cluver, Ralph Cohen, Patrick Coleman, L. S. Dembo, Denis Donoghue, Betsy Draine, George Economou, Edward Engelberg, Clayton Eshleman, Neil Fraistat, Leland Hickman, Ivar Ivask, Shushi Kao, Bruce Kellner, Herbert Leibowitz, Phillip Marcus, Diane Middlebrook, Charles Molesworth, Cary Nelson, Virgil Nemoianu, Jed Rasula, Michael Riffaterre, Dina Sherzer, Peter Siegenthaler, David Trotter, Jack Undank, Robert Viscusi, Arthur Vogelsang, Susanne Woods, and Marilyn Yalom.

I also wish to thank the following friends and colleagues who have, in a less official capacity, read portions of the manuscript or discussed individual essays or lectures with me, providing both advice and encouragement: Charles Altieri, David Antin, Martha Banta, Charles Bernstein, Jo Berryman, James E. B. Breslin, Ronald Bush, Ulla Dydo, Robbert Flick, Kathleen Fraser, Frederick Garber, Albert Gelpi, Andree Hayum, Susan Howe, Judd and Renée Hubert, Herbert Lindenberger, Steve McCaffery, William McPheron, Douglas Messerli, Tyrus Miller, Esteban Pujals, Susan Rankaitis, Claude Rawson, Joan Retallack, Jerome Rothenberg, Henry Sayre, Richard Sieburth, Catharine R. Stimpson, and Emily M. Wallace. I owe a special debt to Jerome J. McGann and to Michael Davidson for their discerning readings of the entire manuscript, especially for suggestions on how to organize some unwieldly material and what to leave out.

As always, my greatest debt is to Joseph K. Perloff, who resolutely refrained from interfering with the work involved and then was happy to confront the finished product, making suggestions that I have never failed to follow. By no means a "common reader," he is nevertheless the *other* reader who forces me to take those important detours and sideroads Wittgenstein talks about in the *Philosophical Investigations*. This book is dedicated to him.

Marjorie Perloff
Stanford and Pacific Palisades, California
1989

## *Acknowledgments*

For permission to include essays originally published by them, usually in slightly different form, grateful acknowledgment is made to
the following journals and university presses.

1. "Can(n)on to the Right of Us, Can(n)on to the Left of Us:
   A Plea for Difference," *New Literary History* 18, no. 3
   (Spring 1987): pp. 633–56.

2. "Canon and Loaded Gun: Feminist Poetics and the Avant-
   Garde," *American Poetry Review* 15 (July–August 1986);
   reprinted in revised form in *Stanford Literary Review* 4,
   no. 1 (Spring 1987): pp. 23–46.

5. "Lawrence's Lyric Theater: *Birds, Beasts and Flowers,*" in
   *D. H. Lawrence: A Centenary Consideration,* ed. Peter
   Balbert and Phillip Marcus (Ithaca, N.Y.: Cornell
   University Press, 1985); pp. 108–29.

6. "The Contemporary of Our Grandchildren: Ezra Pound's
   Influence," in *Pound among the Poets,* ed. George
   Bornstein (Chicago: University of Chicago Press, 1985),
   pp. 195–229.

7. "'A Fine New Kind of Realism': Six Stein Styles in Search
   of a Reader," in *A Gertrude Stein Companion,* ed. Bruce
   Kellner (New York: Greenwood Press, 1988), pp. 96–108.

8. "Une Voix pas la mienne: French/English Beckett and the
   French/English Reader," in *Beckett Translating/*
   *Translating Beckett,* ed. Alan W. Friedman, Charles
   Rossman, and Dina Sherzer (University Park:
   Pennsylvania State University Press, 1987), pp. 37–48.

**9.** "The Two *Ariels*: The (Re)Making of the Sylvia Plath Canon," in *American Poetry Review* 13 (November–December 1984); reprinted in *Poems in Their Place,* ed. Neil Fraistat (Chapel Hill: University of North Carolina Press, 1986), pp. 308–34.

**10.** "A Lion in Our Living Room: Reading Allen Ginsberg in the Eighties," Part I: "Ginsberg's *Collected Poems,*" in *American Poetry Review* 14 (March–April 1985): pp. 35–46; Part II: "'*Howl*' and Its Enemies," *Sulfur,* no. 20 (Fall 1987): pp. 132–41.

**11.** "Apocalypse Then: W. S. Merwin and the Sorrows of Literary History," in *W. S. Merwin: Essays on the Poetry,* ed. Cary Nelson (Urbana: University of Illinois Press, 1986), pp. 122–44.

**12.** "On the Other Side of the Field: The *Collected Poems* of Paul Blackburn," in *Parnassus* 14, no. 2 (Winter–Spring 1988): pp. 197–214.

**13.** "Barthes, Ashbery and the Zero Degree of Genre," in an earlier version called "Barthes and the Zero Degree of Genre," in *World Literature Today* 59 (Autumn 1985): pp. 510–16.

**14.** "'Voice Whisht through Thither Flood': Steve McCaffery's *Panopticon* and *North of Intention,*" in *Temblor* 6 (Fall 1987); pp. 130–34.

**15.** "'Collision or Collusion with History': Susan Howe's *Articulation of Sound Forms in Time,*" in *Contemporary Literature* 30, no. 4 (Winter 1989–90).

For permission to include material published by them, grateful acknowledgment is made to the following.

Atheneum Publishers, an imprint of Macmillan Publishing Company, for permission to quote from *Selected Poems* by Mark Strand, copyright © 1979, 1980 by Mark Strand.

Atheneum Publishers, an imprint of Macmillan Publishing Company, and Georges Borchardt, Inc., for permission to quote from *The Carrier of Ladders* by W. S. Merwin, copyright © 1967, 1968, 1969, 1970 by W. S. Merwin; from *Opening the Hand* by W. S. Merwin, copyright © 1983 by W. S. Merwin.

Atheneum Publishers, an imprint of Macmillan Publishing Company, and Oxford University Press, for permission to quote from

*The Changing Light at Sandover* by James Merrill, copyright © 1978 by James Merrill.

Awede Books, for permission to quote from *Articulation of Sound Forms in Time* by Susan Howe, copyright © 1987 by Susan Howe.

Georges Borchardt, Inc., for permission to quote from *The Lice* by W. S. Merwin, copyright © 1965, 1966, 1967 by W. S. Merwin; from *A Mask for Janus* by W. S. Merwin, copyright © 1952 by W. S. Merwin.

The University of California Press, for permission to quote from *Some Americans: A Personal Record* by Charles Tomlinson, copyright © 1981 by The Regents of the University of California; from *A* by Louis Zakofsky, copyright © 1979 by Celia and Louis Zukofsky.

Farrar, Straus and Giroux, Inc., for permission to quote from *The Complete Poems* by Elizabeth Bishop, copyright © 1940 and renewal © 1948 by Elizabeth Bishop.

Farrar, Straus and Giroux, Inc., and Faber and Faber, Ltd., for permission to quote from *Imitations* by Robert Lowell, copyright © 1958, 1959, 1960, 1961 by Robert Lowell; from *For Lizzie and Harriet* by Robert Lowell, copyright © 1973 by Robert Lowell.

Editions Galilee, for permission to reproduce pages from *Glas,* vol. 2, by Jacques Derrida, copyright © 1981 by Jacques Derrida.

Allen Ginsberg, for permission to quote from "Encounters with Ezra Pound: Journal Notes" in *City Lights Anthology,* copyright © 1974 by Allen Ginsberg.

Graywolf Press, for permission to quote from *Instructions to the Double* by Tess Gallagher, copyright © 1975 by Tess Gallagher.

Grove Press, for permission to quote from *Disjecta: Miscellaneous Writings and a Dramatic Fragment* by Samuel Beckett, copyright © 1984 by Samuel Beckett; from *Ill Seen Ill Said* by Samuel Beckett, copyright © 1981 by Samuel Beckett.

Hill and Wang, a division of Farrar, Straus and Giroux, Inc., and Georges Borchardt, Inc., for permission to quote from *The Grain of the Voice* by Roland Barthes, translation © 1985 by Farrar, Straus and Giroux, Inc; from *Roland Barthes* by Roland Barthes, translation © 1977 by Farrar, Straus and Giroux, Inc.; from *Writing De-*

*gree Zero* by Roland Barthes, translation © 1967 by Jonathan Cape Ltd.

Henry Holt and Company, Inc., for permission to quote from *In Winter* by Michael Ryan. Copyright © 1975, 1975, 1976, 1977, 1978, 1979, 1980, 1981.

Alfred A. Knopf, Inc., for permission to quote from *Cats of the Temple* by Brad Leithauser, copyright © 1983, 1984, 1985 by Brad Leithauser; from *The Collected Poems of Frank O'Hara,* copyright © 1960 by Maureen Granville-Smith, Administratrix of the Estate of Frank O'Hara.

Kulchur Foundation, for permission to quote from *Defenestration of Prague* by Susan Howe, copyright © 1983 by Susan Howe.

Macmillan Company, for permission to quote from *The Letters of W. B. Yeats,* edited by Allan Wade, copyright © 1953, 1954, 1982 by Anne Butler Yeats; from *The Variorum Edition of the Poems of W. B. Yeats,* edited by Peter Allt and Russell K. Alspach, copyright © 1933 by Macmillan Publishing Company, renewed 1961 by Bertha Georgie Yeats, copyright 1928 by Macmillan Publishing Company, renewed 1956 by Georgie Yeats.

The National Poetry Foundation, for permission to quote from *Basil Bunting, Man and Poet,* edited by Carroll F. Terrell, copyright © 1980 by the National Poetry Foundation.

New Directions Publishing Corporation and Faber and Faber, Ltd., for permission to quote from *Collected Poems 1912–1914* by H. D., copyright © 1982 by the Estate of Hilda Doolittle; from *The Cantos of Ezra Pound* by Ezra Pound, copyright © 1934, 1948 by Ezra Pound; from *Personae* by Ezra Pound, copyright © 1926 by Ezra Pound.

North Atlantic Books, for permission to quote from *My Emily Dickinson* by Susan Howe, copyright © 1985 by Susan Howe.

North Point Press, for permission to quote from *The Geography of the Imagination* by Guy Davenport, copyright © 1981 by Guy Davenport; from *The Granite Pail: The Selected Poems of Lorine Niedecker,* edited by Cid Corman, copyright © 1985 by North Point Press.

Naomi Shihab Nye, for permission to quote from *Hugging the Jukebox* by Naomi Shihab Nye, copyright © 1984 by Breitenbush Books, Portland, Oregon.

Oxford University Press, for permission to quote from *Collected Poems* by Basil Bunting, copyright © 1978 by Oxford University Press.

Oxford University Press, and Routledge & Kegan Paul, for permission to quote from *Ezra Pound: Poet as Sculptor* by Donald Davie, copyright © 1964 by Donald Davie.

Oyez Publishers, for permission to quote from *Selected Poems* by Larry Eigner, copyright © 1972 by Oyez Publishers.

Persea Books, Inc., for permission to quote from *The Collected Poems of Paul Blackburn,* edited by Edith Jarolim, copyright © 1985 by Joan Blackburn.

Princeton University Press, for permission to quote from *The Tale of the Tribe: Ezra Pound and the Modern Verse Epic* by Michael A. Bernstein, copyright © 1980 by Michael A. Bernstein.

Random House, Inc., for permission to quote from *Selected Writings of Gertrude Stein,* edited, with an introduction and notes, by Carl Van Vecten, copyright © 1946 by Random House, Inc.

Random House, Inc., and Faber and Faber, Ltd., for permission to quote from *The Dyer's Hand and Other Essays* by W. H. Auden. Copyright © 1968 by Random House, Inc.

Sun & Moon Press, for permission to quote from *The Sophist* by Charles Bernstein, copyright © 1987 by Charles Bernstein, Sun & Moon Press (Los Angeles).

Viking Penguin, a division of Penguin Books USA Inc., and Georges Borchardt, Inc., for permission to quote from *As We Know* by John Ashbery, copyright © 1979 by John Ashbery; from *Three Poems* by John Ashbery, copyright © 1970, 1971, 1972 by John Ashbery.

Wesleyan University Press, for permission to quote from *Events and Wisdoms* by Donald Davie, copyright © 1965 by Donald Davie; from *Country Music: Selected Early Poems* by Charles Wright, copyright © 1982 by Charles Wright.

# Introduction

li·cense (*li*-sēns) *n.* 1. a permit from the government or other authority to own or do something
or to carry on a certain trade. 2. permission.
3. disregard of rules or customs etc., lack of due
restraint in behavior. 4. a writer's or artist's
exaggeration, or disregard of rules etc., for the
sake of effect, *poetic license.*

— *Oxford American Dictionary*

*L*icense as permit, as permission from an outside authority; *license* as defiance of authority, as failure to obtain a per-mit—the poetry of our time has navigated with difficulty between these options. For unlike artists who work in such newer genres as photography or performance or video art or even the novel, lyric poets still tend to regard their "trade" as one requiring a permit from the appropriate authority, which is to say, in the case of English and American poetry, from the Great Romantics, whose terminology—"the spontaneous overflow of powerful feelings," the "esemplastic imagination," "the willing suspension of disbelief," "negative capability"—casts a shadow on virtually every attempt to Make It New. At the same time, from the eccentric numerologies used in W. B. Yeats's *A Vision* to the assault on syntax and continuity in Steve McCaffery's *Panopticon,* twentieth-century poets have also assumed the right to "disregard" the rules so as to reconceive the very nature of the poetic project.

Contemporary criticism, at least as it is practiced in the uni-versity, is similarly preoccupied with Making It New—witness such epithets as the New Historicism, the New Feminist Theory, *New Formations, New Literary History*—which is not to say that its "licenses" and those of poetic discourse are the same. For all the recent talk of *opening up the canon,* of the need to introduce non-canonical works into the classroom, to revise such textbooks as the *Norton Anthology,* to break down the division between high and low culture, and so on, in practice *opening* rarely means more than the replacement of an X by a Y, of D. H. Lawrence's *Women in Love* by Toni Morrison's *Beloved,* of Northrop Frye by Michel Foucault. In the course of such "replacement therapy," a set of new "permits" are issued and new rules codified. It has, for example, become a received piety that "High Modernist" poetry was the poetry of the "well wrought urn," the self-enclosed, autotelic, spatialized artifact. Does that definition cover the case of Brecht? Of Marinetti? Of Apollinaire? Of Gertrude Stein? Does it, for that matter, cover the case of the young T. S. Eliot, a "radical" poet if there ever was one, whose particular use of citation and collage, fragment and ellipsis turns up in such unlikely places as John Ashbery's *A Wave* and Michael Palmer's *Sun?*

The fifteen essays collected in this volume were written between 1984 and 1989; all but three have been published previously. Although they range in subject matter from W. B. Yeats and D. H. Lawrence to Susan Howe and Steve McCaffery, and although most of them were written for specific occasions or commissions, they are part of an ongoing project that I take to be a revisionist history of twentieth-century poetics. Each essay deals in some way with problems of context and canonicity; each tries to revise or reframe, in one form or another, an accepted set of axioms about a particular poet or poetic movement. Along the way, I have not avoided controversy, especially with regard to what are currently perhaps the two dominant positions on poetry and poetics. The first—and this is the view that animates most of the writing on poetry, especially in reviews and periodicals—is that poetry has an essential nature that is timeless and universal and that ergo there is no reason why the poetic structures of the 1980s should differ perceptibly from those of earlier centuries. Individual poets, by this account, are judged according to their "sensitivity" and "craftsmanship," the appeal of their subject matter and emotional range. The second, or more self-consciously theoretical position, is that poetic discourse (like the other discourses of a given culture and moment) is defined largely by what the dominant classes take it to be, that indeed there is no such thing as "inherent" poetic value, the production of poetry always being culture specific and ideologically determined. As such, our role as critics is, in the first place, to characterize the dominant discourse and then to read against it that writing it has excluded or marginalized, thus redefining the canon so as to give pride of place to the hitherto repressed.

Ironically, this stance toward poetry turns out, at least in practice, to be just as essentialist as the first. For in automatically privileging, say, the poetry of women of color over the poetry of white men, we imply that the former are, by definition, more "sensitive," more "authentic," and, in any case, more "interesting" than the latter. And further: that suffering and exclusion provide the matrix within which the poetic takes root. Indeed, the longing for the Authentic Other brings us back, full circle, to the Romantic paradigm of Common Man and Noble Savage, with their latter-day avatars like Yeats's Old Tom and Williams's Elsie.

The impasse of this particular version of a cultural poetics might, I think, be avoided by redefining the term *dominant class* as what Charles Bernstein has called "official verse culture." For increasingly, in the twentieth century, the opposition arises not from, say, a working-class "us" against a middle-class or upper-class "them" (or even from female against male, gay against straight, black against white) but from those who, whatever their actual status in the social order, refuse the norms of mainstream publishing, book reviewing, university curricula, creative writing programs, and so on.

Consider Allen Ginsberg's "Howl," a poem very much rooted in its late-fifties cold war moment—a poem oracular, hyperbolic, profoundly lyrical and yet frequently funny that, I submit, no one, not even Ginsberg himself, would write in the late eighties. Certainly "Howl" can be (and has been) viewed primarily as a cultural and historical artifact: it tells us who and how we were in mid-century America; more specifically, it encodes counterculture values and anxieties that are specifically homosexual, Jewish, and lower middle-class, as experienced in the urban New Jersey and Columbia University landscape of the postwar era.

But what makes "Howl" unique among "Beat" poems of its moment is not these values as such—values that appear, in one form or another, in any number of other works that now seem hopelessly dated, but the actual creation and use of a *language field* that implicitly calls into question the formulaic "genteel" poetics of the period, a poetics based on Eliotic irony and "objective correlative," but with none of the urgency of Eliot's own oppositional imperative. A poetics, we might further note, that was normative in the "little magazines" of the Left as well as the Right—witness the publication of Eliot's "East Coker" in the *Partisan Review*. Into this verbal arena, in any case, a strophe like

who jumped off the Brooklyn Bridge this actually happened and walked
away unknown and forgotten into the ghostly daze of Chinatown
soup alleyways & firetrucks, not even one free beer,

introduced, for better or worse, a different way of relating syntactic units, the abrupt colloquial aside of "this actually happened," for example, cutting without so much as a dash or comma into the narrative of "jumped . . . and walked."

The separability of "poetic" from "ordinary" language was, of course, the central Russian Formalist axiom—an axiom always open to attack on logical grounds (i.e., deviation theories, as Stanley Fish argued some twenty years ago, will not hold up to scrutiny because "ordinary" language will always exhibit some of the same features as its "extraordinary" counterpart) but still the best, if imperfect, way of articulating the time-honored recognition that the "poetic" is distinguished from the "transparency" of expository discourse or the language of practical communication by some form of density, some mode of "making it strange." Yet it is also true that formalism, as such critics as Tynianov and Bakhtin recognized, has no meaning except in relation to historical *difference,* the difference, however subtle and slight, that determines the location of the particular work on the larger poetry map. What does it mean, for example, to call Lawrence a "Romantic" poet, given the oddly un-Romantic free-verse articulation in his poems of a lyric voice that is hectoring, blustering, alternately rhapsodic and comic—indeed a voice closer to Marinetti's than to Wordsworth's or Keats's. Or again, how accurate is it to speak of the "postmodernity" of Charles Olson's "projective verse," when our own late-eighties postmodernity looks so very different? And if Paul Blackburn is a postmodern poet, what kind of poet is Clark Coolidge? Or Lyn Hejinian?

These are the sorts of questions I take up in the essays that follow. They fall loosely into three groups. The first deals with the more general problems of canon formation: how, for example, the "new new criticism" continues to apply "old" New Critical criteria to poetry and hence to ignore that which is really marginal and "different" ("Can(n)on to the Right of Us, Can(n)on to the Left of Us," #1), how the category known as "women's poetry" may obscure important differences between actual poets ("Canon and Loaded Gun," #2), or again, how the French understanding of our contemporary poetic canon differs from our own ("*Traduit de l'américain,*" #3). The second group contains rereadings and reframings of some notable modernists: Yeats's number-based theory of history vis-à-vis Khlebnikov's *Tables of Destiny* (#4), for example, or the relation of Stein's supposedly impenetrable texts to the "straightforward" mode of her *Alice B. Toklas* and *Paris France* (#7), or the thematic and tonal transformation of Samuel Beckett's texts produced by the author's self-translation from French to English ("'Une Voix pas la mienne,'" #8). And the third group takes up problematics of contemporary poetry and poetics: how, for example, Ted Hughes altered the contents and sequence of *Ariel* so as to produce a different volume from the one Sylvia Plath intended to publish ("The Two Ariels," #9), how Paul Blackburn, an important coterie poet of the sixties, strikes a reader of the postfeminist eighties (#12), how Susan Howe reinvents what Ezra Pound called the "poem including history" (#15).

In all probability, those who may have read, say, "Can(n)on to the Right of Us" in *New Literary History* or "French/English Beckett" in the collection *Beckett Translating Beckett* are not those who reg-

ularly read, say, *American Poetry Review* (where the essays on Ginsberg, Plath, and feminist poetics appeared), not to mention *Sulfur*
or *Temblor.* Such diversity of projected audience—what some readers may well criticize as the eclecticism of *Poetic License*—is by no
means unintentional. From the time, more than a decade ago, when
I wrote *Frank O'Hara: Poet among Painters,* I have wanted to write
criticism that might speak to poets as well as to critics, to readers
of the *Times Literary Supplement* and the *New Republic* as well as
to readers of *Critical Inquiry* and *October.*

No one, after all, "owns" poetry, no one has a "license" to
control its reception, which is, in any case, determined, as John Cage
would put it, not by ownership but by use. If one believes, as I do,
that postmodern "poetry" and "theory"—say the writing of John
Ashbery and Roland Barthes (#13)—are part of the same larger
discourse, that there is no hard and fast division between them, that,
on the contrary, some of the most interesting poetry today theorizes
its particular positions even as theory now frequently comes to us
in intensely poetic forms, the project of what we might call
"poe(t)heory" becomes a very pleasurable activity. Pleasurable, and
also difficult. For, as Wittgenstein put it, "In the actual use of expres-
sions we make detours, we go by sideroads. We see the straight
highway before us, but of course we cannot use it, because it is
permanently closed."

# Chapter One

# Can(n)on to the Right of Us,

# Can(n)on to the Left of Us:

## *A Plea for Difference*

ome months ago, the following flyer from SUNY-Buffalo appeared in my campus mailbox:

> THE BLACK MOUNTAIN II REVIEW, a student-run journal devoted to the arts, is accepting submissions for its fifth issue of poetry, short fiction, artwork . . . interviews, and film, literary, music and cultural criticism. The theme of this issue—"From Word to Sign: A Special Double Issue"—will be so-called Language-Oriented Writing, its antecedents and its future. Significant practitioners of this writing include Bruce Andrews, Charles Bernstein, Clark Coolidge and Robert Creeley. Among the antecedents of these writers may be included Gertrude Stein, John Cage, the Dadaists and William S. Burroughs. Possible articulations may be explored between this writing and the theoretical work of Jacques Derrida, Gilles Deleuze & Felix Guattari, Guy Debord and the practitioners themselves.

And then, after some practical information about mailing and deadlines, we read: "P.S. Poets and other creative writers: fear not! You

may be writing 'Language-Oriented' works without ever having
heard of half these people."

What can this wonderful disclaimer (rather like those old ads
for the Unitarian church that said "You may be a Unitarian without
knowing it!") possibly mean? What is it that "poets and other creative writers" are producing today without being fully cognizant of
its nature? Consider the following six texts:[1]

> Yesterday the sun went West and sucked
> the sea from books. My witness
> is an exoskeleton. Altruism suggestively fits.
> It's true, I like to go to the hardware store
> and browse on detail. So sociable the influence
>
> of Vuillard, so undying in disorder is order.
> Windows closed on wind in rows.
> Night lights, unrumorlike, the reserve
> for events. All day our postures were the same.
> Next day the gentleman was very depressed
> and had a headache; so much laughing
>
> had upset him he thought.

> —Lyn Hejinian, from *The Guard* (1984)

mAdness
coLd-water
fLats

Can(n)on to
the Rights of
Us, Can(n)on
to the Left
of Us

thE
braiNs
throuGh
wIth
aNd
academieS
Burning
monEy

maRijuana
niGht

After
endLess
cLoud
thE
motioNless
Green
joyrIde

suN

aShcan

Brain
drainEd of
bRilliance

niGht

—John Cage, "Writing through Howl" (1984)

*9*

Le sceptre miroitant.

**Figure 1.** Michel Leiris, "Le Sceptre miroitant," in "Glossaire,"
*Mots sans mémoire* (Paris: Mercure de France, 1969), p. 111.

Nearly nothing
in Nature so
spirits the eye
off—but off by
way of in—to
unveil detail
as minimal
as it's recep-
tive to as does
this more than true-

to life, living
family of
diminutive
replicas of
themselves. . . .

These pondered, hand-
won triumphs of
containment, come,
tentatively,
of earth-toughened
fingers, father
to son, and on
to son, so long
as the branches
hold on each side,

bid us enter-
entertain notions of
days whose hours are
shorter than ours,
(shrunken, misted. . . .

—Brad Leithauser, from "In a Bonsai Nursery,"
Part 3 of "Dainties: A Suite," *Cats of the Temple* (1986)

Did a wind come just as you got up or were you protecting me from it? I felt the abridgement of imperatives, the wave of detours, the sabre-rattling of inversion. *All lit up and no place to go.* Blinded by avenue and filled with adjacency. Arch or arched at. So there becomes bottles, hushed conductors, illustrated proclivities for puffed-up benchmarks. Morose or comatose. "Life is what you find, existence is what you repudiate." A good example of this is 'Dad pins puck.' Sometimes something sunders; in most cases, this is no more than a hall. No where to go but pianissimo (protection of market soaring).

Can(n)on to
the Rights of
Us, Can(n)on
to the Left
of Us

—Charles Bernstein, from "Dysraphism" (1984)

d'elle-même; le père de Marie m'a présenté à son grand-père. Celui qui a dit A épelle ensuite toutes les lettres de l'alphabet. Et ainsi nous nous comportons devant le monde comme des fiancés. Par ailleurs vous savez que celui qui a fondé son affaire sur la bonté des femmes — en particulier des femmes telles que celle-ci — n'a pas bâti sur le sable. [...] Nous nous sommes déjà si souvent entretenus d'Erlangen que dans notre imagination notre union et Erlangen se sont en quelque sorte fondus en un seul être, comme le mari et la femme. L'amélioration de ma situation économique est nécessaire, étant donné l'insuffisance de mes moyens, car ma chère Marie, dont le grand-père vit encore et dont le père a en dehors d'elle 7 enfants, ne peut recevoir, outre son trousseau, qu'une somme annuelle de 100 florins... » [...]
votre ami sincère Hgl. »

De l'été qui suit, à la veille du mariage, on a encore deux lettres à Marie.

« Nuremberg,

Chère Marie,
Je t'ai écrit en pensée durant presque toute la nuit. Ce n'était pas à telle ou telle circonstance particulière de nos relations que ma pensée s'attachait, mais il s'agissait nécessairement de cette pensée essentielle : nous rendrons-nous donc malheureux *(unglücklich)*? Une voix criait du plus profond de mon âme : Cela ne peut pas, cela ne doit pas être! — Cela ne sera pas! *(Dies Kann, dies soll und darf nicht sein! — Es wird nicht sein!)*
Mais ce que je t'ai dit depuis longtemps se présente à mes yeux comme un résultat : le mariage est essentiellement un lien *(Band)* religieux; l'amour a besoin pour être complété de quelque chose de plus élevé que ce qu'il est seulement en lui-même et par lui-même. La satisfaction complète — ce que l'on appelle « être heureux » *(glücklich sein)* — n'est accomplie que grâce à la religion et au sentiment du devoir, une fois seulement sont écartées toutes les particularités du moi-même *(Selbst)* temporel, qui pourraient apporter du trouble dans la réalité, laquelle reste quelque chose d'inachevé et ne peut être prise pour la chose dernière, mais en qui devrait résider ce qu'on appelle le bonheur terrestre. J'ai devant moi le brouillon des lignes que j'ai jointes à ta lettre à ma sœur; le post-scriptum, auquel tu as certainement attaché une trop grande importance, ne s'y

Cette apparence de noyau est d'ailleurs plus dénudée, mieux lue et remarquée par le relief des deux versions, celle de Poe et celle de Mallarmé. Ce qui ne veut pas dire qu'il y ait un noyau absolu et un centre dominant, le rythme ne se liant pas seulement aux mots ni surtout à la proximité du contact entre deux lettres. Néanmoins, à ignorer *Les Cloches*, Fónagy reste sourd à l'effet + L (consonne + L), non seulement dans les traductions où il n'occurre pas mais même dans celle, l'allemande, où il le fait : « Le principal objet de la traduction en prose est de traduire, par un simple mouvement de translation, le message de la langue originale vers la langue visée, en substituant à la forme *a*, empruntée à la langue de départ, une forme *b* empruntée à la langue d'arrivée. [...] C'est le contraire qui se passe, lorsque le traducteur s'attaque à la poésie. Ici, il retient et transpose certains traits de la forme *a* pour les reproduire dans la mesure du possible à l'arrivée, dans la forme *b*. Le tintement argentin des cloches dans l'air glacé de la nuit, dans le poème d'Edgar Allan Poe, se retrouve exprimé dans les traductions hongroise, allemande et italienne du poème, par la prédominance des sons *i*, et les enchaînements des nasales :
ng, nk, nt, nd.

How they tinkle, tinkle, tinkle
In the icy air of night

Halld, mind, pendül, kondul, csendül...
*(Mihály Babits)*
Wie sir klingen, klingen, klingen,
Zwinkernd sich zum Reigen schlingen...
*(Th. Etzel)*
Come tintinnano, tintinnano, tintinnano
Di una cristallina delizia...
*(Frederico Olivero).* »

**Figure 2.** Jacques Derrida, double page 221 of volume 2 of *Glas* (Paris: Denoël, 1981).

*11*

Except for the passage from Derrida's *Glas,* these texts have been explicitly presented by their authors as poems, but readers brought up on Romantic and modernist poetry may have difficulty recognizing them as such. For if, as Paul de Man puts it, "The principle of intelligibility, in lyric poetry, depends on the phenomenalization of the poetic voice,"[2] what do we make of those poems like Lyn Hejinian's or Charles Bernstein's, whose appropriation of found objects—snippets of advertising slogans, newspaper headlines, media cliché, textbook writing, or citation from other poets—works precisely to deconstruct the possibility of the formation of a coherent or consistent lyrical voice, a transcendental ego?

Again, to build one's discourse on citation is to regard language less as a means of representation than as the very object of representation. Thus, when John Cage "writes through" Allen Ginsberg's "Howl," which is to say uses chance operations to select certain words from the parent text and then arrange those words in a *mesostic* (the name ALLEN GINSBERG forms a column down the middle of the text, the rule being that a given letter in the name cannot appear between its occurrence in a given line and that of the next letter in the next line), it is difficult to know how the reader is to produce an apparently phenomenal world through the figure of voice. For whose voice do we hear in such minimalist echoes of "Howl" as "academieS / Burning / monEy / maRijuana / niGht"? Or in Michel Leiris's "Le Sceptre miroitant," whose acrostic arrangement of three closely related words suggests that "amour" and "mourir" are in fact mirror ("miroir") images of one another, even as the only letter that is not involved in the poem's complex system of duplication is the first in the alphabet, the eternal Alpha? And even in the work of a more traditional poet like Brad Leithauser, who is hardly allied with the "language" group or with French poststructuralism, the use of visual and phonemic device, specifically the verbal play generated by the two-column structure, undercuts the controlling voice, creating what John Ashbery has called "an open field of narrative possibilities," in which "diminutive" may lead (vertically) to "replicas of themselves" or (horizontally) to "days whose hours are replicas."

In a headnote to "Dysraphism," Bernstein explains his title as follows:

> "Dysraphism" is actually a word in use by specialists in congenital diseases, to mean dysfunctional fusion of embryonic parts—a birth defect. . . . "Raph" of course means "seam," so for me dysraphism is mis-seaming—a prosodic device! But it has the punch of being the same root of rhapsody (*rhaph*)—or in Skeats—"one who strings (lit. stitches) songs together, a reciter of epic poetry," cf. "ode" etc. In any case, to be simple, Dorland's [the standard U.S. medical dictionary] does define

Can(n)on to
the Rights of
Us, Can(n)on
to the Left
of Us

"dysrhafia" (if not dysraphism) as "incomplete closure of the primary neural tube; status dysraphicus"; this is just below "dysprosody" (sic): "disturbance of stress, pitch, and rhythm of speech."[3]

This exuberant analysis of etymology, analogy, and punning might almost have appeared in Derrida's *Glas;* indeed, in the right-hand column of a sample page from *Glas* (fig. 2), we find a similar rumination on "le graphique de la *mimesis,*" the materiality of the signifier as it undergoes translation into other languages. Derrida's text is Edgar Allan Poe's 1848 poem "The Bells," specifically the lines, "How they tinkle, tinkle, tinkle / In the icy air of night"), and he notes, on this particular page, that, whereas the French *cloches* picks up the *l* phoneme of "tinkle" but not its nasal phoneme /nk/, other languages like Hungarian, German, and Italian foreground the latter at the expense of the former. As Leiris puts it in his "Glossaire: J'y serre mes gloses": "By dissecting the words we like, without bothering about conforming either to the etymologies or to their accepted significations, we discover their most hidden qualities and the secret ramifications that are propagated through the whole language, channeled by associations of sounds, forms, and ideas."[4]

In Derrida's "epiphony in echoland," as Geoffrey Hartman calls *Glas,*[5] the rumination on "le tintement argentin des cloches" in the right-hand or "Genet" column is played off against the "Hegel" column on the left, specifically, in the case of our sample page, against the conclusion of an 1811 letter from Hegel to his friend Niethammer explaining the economic difficulties that still stand in the way of his marriage to his future wife Marie, and then a melodramatic letter to Marie herself in which Hegel raises the terrible question: "Nous rendrons-nous donc malheureux (*unglücklich*)?" Immediately, "Une voix criait du plus profond de mon âme: Cela ne peut pas, cela ne doit pas être—Cela ne sera pas! (*Dies kann, dies soll und darf nicht sein!—Es wird nicht sein!*)." A romantic cry of the heart that is quickly followed by a return to convention: marital happiness, Hegel tells his fiancée, can only be based on religious and moral faith and on conjugal duty.

It is a nice question whether the juxtaposition of discourses in Derrida's *Glas*—the conventionally romantic, somewhat bathetic letter to Marie set over against the practical one to Hegel's colleague, and both of these spliced with the discourse on the *glas* of Poe's bells, in its many incarnations—is any less "poetic" than the two-column "In a Bonsai Nursery" of Brad Leithauser or the mixed discourse poems of Lyn Hejinian and Charles Bernstein. Derrida's ironic insertions of the German original into the French translation, as in "nous rendrons-nous donc malheureux (*unglücklich*)," is, for that matter, a device frequently used by Cage in his portrait-lectures

*13*

on such artists as Jasper Johns or such composers as Arnold Schoenberg.

To read *Glas* or Leiris's "Glossaire" in conjunction with Cage's mesostic, Leithauser's two-column poem, and the "language" texts of Hejinian and Bernstein is, in any case, to note a curious phenomenon. *Poetry*, for these poets, has less to do with the Romantic conception of the lyric as "an intensely subjective and personal expression" (Hegel), the "utterance that is not so much heard as overheard" (John Stuart Mill), than with the original derivation of *lyric* as a composition performed on the lyre, which is to say that it is a verbal form directly related to its musical origins.[6] Thus Leithauser's "In a Bonsai Nursery" is written in intricate two-stress lines characterized by elaborate echo structure: "unveil detail / as minimal"; "fingers, father / to son, and on / to son, so long." Leithauser's use of homonyms—"days whose hours are shorter than ours"—finds its counterpart in Hejinian's punning, as in "Windows closed on wind in rows," and in Bernstein's parody rhyming of "Morose or comatose." In "Dysraphism," as in Hejinian's *The Guard*, syntactic slots are filled with words and phrases that fail to fit semantically but are phonemically appropriate, as in "Yesterday the sun went West and sucked / the sea from books," or "Blinded by avenue and filled with adjacency. Arch or arched at." Again, in Leiris's "Le Sceptre miroitant," the first syllable of "mourir" echoes the second of "amour," thus underscoring the union of love and death, even as in Cage's "Writing through Howl," it is sound that relates "suN" to "aShcan" and that convinces us that "Brain" is "drainEd of / bRilliance."

How is it that in the late twentieth century we are once again foregrounding the *sound* of lyric poetry? How has it happened that the rather flat free verse of the American mid-century, with its emphasis on delicate epiphany and personal contingency, has given way, in the eighties, to poetic language that, far from being speech based, depends upon parodic reference to a particular convention—ladies' small talk, for example, in the case of Hejinian's "I like to go to the hardware store / and browse on detail," or fin de siècle mannerism, in the case of Bernstein's "I felt the abridgement of imperatives, the wave of detours, the sabre- / rattling of inversion"?

Whatever the answers to these difficult questions, we are not, I would posit, likely to find them in the recent academic criticism of lyric poetry. Consider, for example, a prominent collection from Cornell University Press called *Lyric Poetry* (1985), based on a symposium at the University of Toronto and edited by Chaviva Hosek and Patricia Parker. Subtitled *Beyond the New Criticism, Lyric Poetry* purports to be the response of a poststructuralist "new new criticism"—what we might call the "canon to the left of us," with its loose confederation of deconstruction (here represented by Paul

Can(n)on to
the Rights of
Us, Can(n)on
to the Left
of Us

de Man, Cynthia Chase, Joel Fineman, and Barbara Johnson), reader response theory (Stanley Fish), feminism (Mary Jacobus, Mary Nyquist), and Marxism (Fredric Jameson, John Brenkman), and various hybrids of the above—to the "canon to the right of us," which is, of course, that now familiar whipping boy (with "boy" used advisedly since it was the discourse of an almost exclusively male establishment), the (old) New Criticism.

"This book," the editors inform us in their preface, ". . . is intended to appeal to students, critics, and teachers of poetry, as well as to those interested in the application of literary theory to the study of texts from several historical periods" (*LP*, 7). There are two implications here that I find troubling. First, the book is certainly not intended for poets, a species that seems to exist for no better reason than that "students, critics, and teachers of poetry" (pretty much one and the same thing) can write about their work. And second, that "literary theory" is something to be applied "to the study of texts," that is, in other words, a second-order discourse to be applied to a primary one and in any case separable from it. We should note right away that (1) this separation replicates the New Critical division between poetry and writing *about* poetry, and (2) that, ironically enough, the New Critics took this separation rather less seriously than do their new challengers, given that many of them—Allen Tate, Robert Penn Warren, Randall Jarrell, R. P. Blackmur—were themselves poets and hence quite unlikely to suggest that a book about lyric poetry is "intended to appeal primarily to students, critics, and teachers of poetry." Indeed, as Edward Said has noted, "The New Criticism, for all its elitism, was strangely populist in intention," its aim being no less than to give all educated readers the tools by means of which they might understand literary works.[7]

A well-known weakness of the New Criticism, as Patricia Parker reminds us in her introduction, is that it advocated "the program of treating the literary text as an isolated artifact or object, dismissing concern with author's intention and reader's response, and the tenet of the text's organic wholeness, its reconciliation of tension or diversity into unity" (*LP*, 12). How has poststructuralist criticism in America responded to this challenge? For organic unity and reconciliation of opposites it has substituted the "allegory of reading" with its concomitant recognition of the undecidability of poetic language. Words, phrases, and larger units are now explicated with an eye to showing that they don't mean what they seem to mean, that the readings they generate are contradictory. Yet, and this is the irony of much "new new criticism," the premise that the poem is to be treated as "an isolated artifact or object, dismissing concern with author's intention and reader's response" is hardly less operative here than it is in the case of Cleanth Brooks's *The Well Wrought Urn* or W. K. Wimsatt's *The Verbal Icon.*

Thus Cynthia Chase's examination of Keats's "Ode to a Nightingale" focuses on that poem's difficult fifth stanza ("I cannot see what flowers are at my feet . . ."), arguing, *contra* such veteran Keats scholars as Earl Wasserman, that, read intertextually, against relevant passages by Wordsworth and Milton, Keats's particular use of prosopopoeia and apostrophe points to a central "ambivalence toward the visionary mode," a "nostalgia for pre-Romantic or non-Romantic conditions" (*LP,* 224). Again, Joel Fineman brilliantly deconstructs Shakespeare's "eye"/"I" imagery, positing that Shakespeare's persona can no longer elaborate his subjectivity in accord with the ideal model of a self composed of the specular identification of the poetic ego and the poetic ego ideal, of "I" and "you"—the "eye" and the "eyed." Eleanor Cook gives a close reading of Wallace Stevens's "An Ordinary Evening at New Haven," demonstrating that it is "a purgatorial poem in the anti-apocalyptic mode" (*LP,* 302), and Mary Nyquist, in yet another essay on a single Stevens poem, this time "Peter Quince at the Clavier," contrasts the "free-floating" Susanna of part 2, the Susanna who is "free simply, erotically, to be," with the Susanna "re-represented" through the "red-eyed gaze" of the elders, who "has been arrested and fixed by the specular gaze," which is to say, "by the pornographic and patriarchal eye, the eye that assumes it has a right to possession" (*LP,* 314). The strategy of the poem, so Nyquist argues, is to transform this "violated Susanna" into the muse "whose 'music' has mothered the male poet's verbal artifact that contains her" (*LP,* 327).

Subtle and inventive as such readings are, it might be useful to consider what they do not do. The critical project, for Parker and her fellow symposiasts, is wholly hermeneutic; its aim is to explain what particular canonical poems—and I shall come back to the question of the canon in a moment—mean; its purpose is to articulate what new meanings Shakespeare's sonnets or Keats's odes or Stevens's meditative poems might yield when examined through the "new" prisms of feminist theory or deconstruction or, as I shall suggest below, an ahistorical Marxism now increasingly fashionable. In what is to my mind the most trenchant essay in the Hosek and Parker collection, Annabel Patterson remarks that "the newer criticisms . . . have not, it seems, been able to disturb the premises of the preceding dynasty with respect to lyric, or even to improve on its work." " 'Lyric,' " writes Patterson, "remains a name for an ill-assorted collection of short(er) poems; but the genre continues to be defined normatively, in ways that exclude dozens of poems that their authors once thought of as lyric. The reason for this is clear. The modernist view of lyric as an intense, imaginative form of self-

Can(n)on to
the Rights of
Us, Can(n)on
to the Left
of Us

expression or self-consciousness, the most private of all genres, is, of course, a belief derived from Romanticism" (*LP*, 151).

The genre continues to be defined normatively—it is this situation that bedevils current discourse about poetry. For nowhere in *Lyric Poetry* do we find discussion of the following questions: (1) Is "lyric" merely another word for "poetry," as the interchangeable use of the word in the collection would suggest? If so, why talk about "lyric poetry"; if not, what other kinds of poetry are there and what is their relationship to lyric? (2) How has lyric poetry changed over the centuries? Is it meaningful to talk of Ben Jonson's project in the same terms that we talk of, say, Stevens's or Pound's? How and why is lyric more prominent in some periods than in ours? And (3) since the etymology of the word *lyric* points to its musical derivation, what does it mean to write of lyric poetry as if its sound structure were wholly irrelevant, a mere externality. What, for example, does the choice of a particular meter mean? Or the choice of a particular set of linguistic strategies?

To pose these questions is another way of saying that the thrust of *Lyric Poetry: Beyond the New Criticism* is, as Jonathan Arac notes in his acute afterword, "fundamentally unhistorical, especially in its confidence about the extensive applicability of its operative terms" (*LP*, 346). Theoretical and rhetorical terms—apostrophe, allegory, the word lyric itself—are assumed to have transhistorical, typological validity. Indeed, concerned as these critics are with the changing ways of reading lyric poetry, they too often fail to take into account that the writing of lyric poetry is itself a mode of production that undergoes change. Thus the New Critical emphasis on the poem as autotelic object is ironically preserved.

This reluctance to engage the historical dimension of lyric poetry can be seen at many levels. In "Changes in the Study of Lyric," Jonathan Culler observes, as do a number of the other contributors, that recent criticism has "neglected lyric poetry in favor of narrative." Roland Barthes, for instance, "has practically nothing to say about poetry, much less a convincing or innovatory encounter with lyric" (*LP*, 41). But why, given Barthes's "broad literary tastes," should this be the case? Because, so Culler posits, Barthes associates poetry with "plentitude," with "the symbolic," and "thus sees it as the aspect of literariness" that the writers he admires—say, Brecht and Robbe-Grillet—are "trying to combat" (*LP*, 42). "Other contemporary critics," concludes Culler, "have not followed Barthes's lead, fortunately," the point being, evidently, that a working definition of poetry must be broad enough to obviate Barthes's objection to its urge toward the transcendence of language.

Or must it? What Culler misses here is that Barthes's skepticism about "The Poem" is itself historically determined, that what Barthes is telling us—and I have argued this point elsewhere[8]—is that perhaps the "poetic," in our own time, is to be found, not in the conventionally isolated lyric poem, so dear to the Romantics and Symbolists, but in texts not immediately recognizable as poetry. Thus, when Barthes tells an interviewer, "J'aime le romanesque, mais je sais que le roman est mort,"[9] he is expressing, not the desire for an excessively narrow definition of the novel, but his own inability, given his distrust of mimesis in the late twentieth century, to create or to believe in something called "character" that is distinct from its creator, his mistrust of fictionality even as he insists on the fictiveness of narrative.

No definition of the lyric poem or of the novel can, in short, be wholly transhistorical. One would think that Marxist critics would be precisely the ones to recognize this axiom, but in practice we now frequently encounter a brand of Marxist explication that, so to speak, freezes the historical, that arrests its temporality. A particularly problematic example of this kind of criticism may be found in John Brenkman's essay "The Concrete Utopia of Poetry: Blake's 'A Poison Tree.' "

Brenkman's essay opens with a minimal gesture toward historical context. Blake, we learn, "was a poet of the volatile decades of the late eighteenth and early nineteenth centuries, writing at the very point when the democratic revolutions were being institutionalized as the class rule of the bourgeoisie"; his poetry is thus to be read as a response to "the new economic order of capitalism" and as the "struggle against dominant values and institutions" (*LP,* 183).

Logically, the next step might be to take a close look at precisely those institutions and cultural formations operative when Blake wrote the *Songs of Innocence* and *Songs of Experience.* But Brenkman evidently has no use for such empiricism; on the contrary, he now turns to the "social and aesthetic theories of thinkers like Ernst Bloch and Herbert Marcuse, Walter Benjamin and T. W. Adorno"—theories with which Blake's poetry evidently "resonates" (*LP,* 183). The actual writings of the Frankfurt school, it should be said, are cited only briefly and rather perfunctorily, the references being almost exclusively to certain scattered essays that have been translated into English. The point to be extracted, in any case, is that "the first task of analysis is to dissolve the ideological shell of the work by exposing the ways it serves particular rather than general interests and legitimates the forms of domination prevalent in its own society; once this ideological shell is dissolved, the utopian kernel of the work is supposed to shine through, a radiant core of meanings and images expressing the strivings and hopes of humanity" (*LP,* 184).

How does this "utopian kernel" "shine through" the "ideological shell" of Blake's "A Poison Tree," which is the essay's test case? Brenkman's analysis begins as follows:

Can(n)on to
the Rights of
Us, Can(n)on
to the Left
of Us

Every time one reads the poem, I believe, the first stanza has
the force of a moral statement. The past tense establishes the
twin perspective of Blake's action *then* and his judgment *now.*
The danger or unhappiness of a wrath that grows, as against a
wrath that ends, establishes a set of values or preferences that
virtually goes without saying. . . . The poem reads as a kind
of confessional utterance in which Blake the speaker shares
with the reader a reflective judgment on the actions of Blake
in the past, anchored in the view that telling one's wrath is
healthy and not telling it is harmful and even self-destructive.
(*LP,* 187)

This seemingly straightforward explication demands some unmasking of its own. First, we might note that Brenkman makes no reference to the poem's textual history; he concerns himself neither
with prior Blake scholarship nor with the relation of the poem to its
illuminated plate. The fact that the Notebook version of "A Poison
Tree" bore the title "Christian Forbearance," for example, is evidently considered irrelevant to its meaning. Second, Brenkman
assumes that the lines in question have a particular meaning, and
that it is up to the critic to tell us what that meaning is. Indeed, he
assumes that "every time one reads the poem, . . . the first stanza
has the force of a moral statement," a "kind of confessional utterance in which Blake the speaker shares with the reader a reflective
judgment on the actions of Blake in the past."

But if the poem's "I" is none other than the real William Blake,
its final lines, "In the morning glad I see / My foe outstretch'd
beneath the tree," pose, so Brenkman argues, something of a conun-
drum. Blake, he comments, "has gotten his satisfaction, and his
wrath has finally been expressed, yielding the sheer delight of seeing
an enemy destroyed." As a whole, then, the poem, "far from being
a confessional utterance, is more like a set of instructions on how
to do in an enemy and feel relief, even joy." And, sounding like a
good poststructuralist, Brenkman concludes, "The poem generates
both readings. However, neither reading can account for the possibility of the other, except to declare that it is the product of mis-
reading" (*LP,* 187).

This so-called undecidability, it seems, can only be resolved by
unraveling the difficulties posed by the conceit of the poison tree,
and especially the "apple bright" of line 10. "Within the logic of the
conceit," writes Brenkman, "the image of the apple is only vaguely
motivated, as by the idea that it is the 'fruit' of his wrath. The meaning of 'apple bright' is otherwise unspecifiable from the standpoint
of the conceit itself" (*LP,* 189).

How the image of an "apple bright," appearing in a late eighteenth-century poem written in approximate hymn stanzas (iambic
tetrameter rhyming *aabb*), could be taken as "unspecifiable" or

*19*

"unmotivated" must strike the reader as a mystery. For Blake's poem appropriates, however subtly and ironically, the most basic iconography of Genesis: an "I" watering his tree and "sun[ning] it with smiles" who is clearly usurping the role of God, and a "poison tree" in a "garden," proffering temptation in the form of an "apple bright" that immediately brings to mind Satan and Eve in the Garden of Eden.

But Brenkman is impatient with such conventional topoi. The "apple bright," it turns out, is neither more nor less than the "*enviable possession* of the speaker's," and the poem's "story" thus "unveils the form of abstraction that is historically specific to capitalist society." Blake's poem is thus to be read as a scathing "critique of bourgeois society and of capitalism." "Envy," we read, "a term borrowed from the ethics of precapitalist societies, is but a name for the fundamental law of interactions in capitalist society as a whole" (*LP,* 190). And "the utopian dimension of the poem is enacted in a poetic speaking which manifests the struggle between the social conditions of the poet's speech [the contradictory narrative of stanzas 1 and 4] and the latent possibilities of speech," as figured in the trope of the "apple bright" (*LP,* 192).

The reductiveness of this reading concerns me less than the underlying assumptions that make such a reading possible. First, Brenkman's "Marxist" reading ignores the poem's actual mode of production and distribution as well as its reception. Second, it, so to speak, puts Blake's complex poem under glass, denying it access to its actual context, whether literary, historical, or political. Third, it assumes that a given poem can be said to have a specific, identifiable meaning—in this case, the critique of bourgeois society, contaminated by capitalism. And fourth, and most important, it assumes that poetic language is, quite simply, transparent, that if the poem's first line reads, "I was angry with my friend," it means that Blake was angry with his friend, even as the poem's last lines mean that it is Blake who is "glad to see his foe outstretch'd beneath the tree."

It is one of the paradoxes of recent poststructuralist criticism that, even as deconstruction has entered the mainstream of academic discourse, actual texts are once again being read as if their language were as straightforward as a verbal command to open the door or to pass the sugar. For critics like Brenkman, the "apple bright" is the nugget that, when ingested, countermands the complexity of the reading process. The real questions about Blake's great poem are thus suppressed. How, for example, does the stanzaic structure of "A Poison Tree" qualify or ironize its overt statements? Or again, what is the function of the poem's syntactic parallelism and repetition? Of its storybook language ("And into my garden stole")? In imposing a particular theory on the text, one finds, as it turns out, what one wanted to find in the first place. Brenkman's

Can(n)on to
the Rights of
Us, Can(n)on
to the Left
of Us

masters Benjamin and Adorno, it is only fair to say, had little use for such reductionist reading.

A much more sophisticated and challenging version of what we might call Brenkman's spatialized Marxism may be found in another essay in the Hosek and Parker collection, Fredric Jameson's "Baudelaire as Modernist and Postmodernist: The Dissolution of the Referent and the Artificial 'Sublime.' " Jameson argues that there are two Baudelaires. The first is the "inaugural poet of high modernism" who wrote such familiar lyrics from *Les Fleurs du mal* as "Chant d'automne," which Jameson reads, quite brilliantly, I think, as a treatment of the moment of "withdrawal of the private or the individual body from social discourse" (*LP,* 252). The second, the Baudelaire of such later poems as "La Mort des amants," on the other hand, is postmodern in his evocation of a world of pure textuality, "the world of the image, of textual free-play, the world of consumer society and its simulacra" (*LP,* 256). In the Victorian kitsch world of "La Mort des amants," Jameson suggests, a world that has eliminated all trace of humanity in its stress on objects, especially on candelabra and mirrors, we find prefigured "the junk materials of a fallen and unredeemable commodity culture," the "strange new—historically new—feeling or affective tone of late capitalism" (*LP,* 260). "It is appropriate to see in the play of mirrors and lights of the funereal chamber some striking and mysterious anticipation of a logic of the future." As such, Baudelaire is, "perhaps unfortunately for him, our contemporary" (*LP,* 263).

Jameson's is a provocative and exciting essay; it makes one want to return to Baudelaire, teasing out the threads that prefigure our own "fallen and unredeemable commodity culture." But again I am troubled by the critic's urge to erase difference. Precisely how does the capitalism of the Second Empire relate to that of late twentieth-century America? Or again, how can we explain that however anticipatory of postmodernism "La Mort des amants" may be, the poem is instantly recognizable, whether rhetorically, linguistically, tonally, or metrically, as a poem that *was not* written in the latter part of the twentieth century? Why, for that matter, do poets living in our own "late capitalist" America write so differently? And further, why does a poet of the eighties like Charles Bernstein write so differently from, say, the Beat poets of the not-quite-so-late capitalist fifties and sixties?

The reluctance, of even a Marxist theorist like Jameson, to take on the problematic of history (and, we might add, of geography and culture, a problematic that would lead us to ask whether current Marxist ideology in, say, contemporary China, has in fact erased the desire for the "junk materials of . . . commodity culture," whether in the form of rock video, automobiles, dishwashers, or spray deodorant) has produced a critical stance that, far from moving *beyond* the New Criticism, seems to be haunted by its most characteristic gestures. This is especially the case when we consider the choice of poets and poems discussed in *Lyric Poetry:*

In her introduction Parker cites "the problem of canon-formation" as one of the "major issues" confronted by the collection, and she stresses the necessity of questioning the existing canon. For example: "Can we really be certain . . . that of the two poems Browning himself thought of as a pair, 'My Last Duchess'—which is amenable to New Critical techniques of analysis—is a 'better' poem and thus more worthy of inclusion in the curriculum than 'Count Gismond,' whose inconsistencies more immediately frustrate the translation of its written characters into the characters of a psychologically coherent utterance?" Or again, "What does it reveal about the *ideology* of canon-formation that a poem such as Whitman's ode to the Paris Commune—well known to students in the socialist bloc—is rarely encountered in North American classrooms?" (*LP,* 18–19).

Browning's "Count Gismond" rather than "My Last Duchess," Whitman's ode to the Paris Commune rather than "Crossing Brooklyn Ferry"—this is about as daring a departure from the canonical norm as we are likely to find in *Lyric Poetry: Beyond the New Criticism.* If we except Eugene Vance's essay on trouvère lyric, whose focus is on the little-known poet Gace Brulé, and David Bromwich's brief study of parody, which includes discussion of contemporary versions of Donne, Milton, and Wordsworth at the hands of the Canadian poets Daryl Hyne and Jay Macpherson, we may tabulate the authors whose poems are analyzed, either in an entire essay or in a major part of an essay, as follows:

| English or American | | French | |
|---|---|---|---|
| Surrey | 1 | Hugo | 1 |
| Shakespeare | 1 | Baudelaire | 4 |
| Jonson | 2 | Mallarmé | 1 |
| Blake | 2 | | |
| Wordsworth | 4 | | |
| Keats | 1 | | |
| Shelley | 2 | | |
| Browning | 1 | | |
| Tennyson | 1 | | |
| Hardy | 1 | | |
| Stevens | 2 | | |
| Auden | 1 | | |

The index reveals further frequencies: the following poets, who are not discussed in individual essays, are referred to more than five times: Milton, Donne, Byron, Coleridge, Poe, Eliot, and Yeats.

For all its emphasis on feminist criticism, *Lyric Poetry* does not have a single essay devoted to a woman poet.[10] For all its claim that "the range of poems reflects the comparatist outlook of recent theory in contrast to the New Critics' more exclusively English canon" (*LP*, 15), the book includes discussion of only the most predictable French poets, Baudelaire and Mallarmé (Victor Hugo is cited because one of his short poems furnishes Paul de Man with an example to question the theory of Michael Riffaterre). The "new new criticism," we are told, is "increasingly cosmopolitan in its affiliations," but its canon of lyric poets is as resolutely Anglophile as Cleanth Brooks's *The Well Wrought Urn,* and much more Anglophile than, say, R. P. Blackmur's *Language as Gesture,* which included essays on Tolstoy and Dostoyevsky, along with those on Blackmur's contemporaries like Ezra Pound.

Indeed, it is the neglect of the contemporary that I find most problematic in the academic criticism of which *Lyric Poetry* is but one exemplar. The drive to move "Beyond the New Criticism" does not, it seems, prompt the desire to learn about the poetry, indeed any of the fictive discourses, of one's own world. Two essays on Stevens and a short reading of W. H. Auden—this feeble concession to modernity should be measured against the attention paid to the Romantic tradition. Like our standard "classical" concert repertoire, our poetry canon continues to privilege the nineteenth century. Indeed, critics like Jonathan Culler and Stanley Fish seem to imply that poetry is something that has already happened, that it is now safely *over.*

Hence the perplexity that greets poetic texts like the ones I introduced at the beginning of my essay, the irony being that the poems of a Charles Bernstein or a Lyn Hejinian, not to speak of Leiris or Cage, are much more consonant with the theories of Derrida and de Man, Lacan and Lyotard, Barthes and Benjamin, than are the canonical texts that are currently being ground through the poststructuralist mill. How and why poetry and theory have come together deserves to be studied. And it is also important to ask why, say, contemporary British poetry has swerved further and further away from the American norm, opting for what often looks to us like merely clever *vers de société,* even as, conversely, the poetry of Eastern Europe—especially that of Poland and Hungary—continues to deploy figures of imaginative transformation, an intense, often visionary subjectivity.

If poetic discourse is, as the "canon to the left of us" would have it, a cultural formation, we had better have a look at the culture in question. Consider, for example, the status of the famous poem that has given me my title. "Cannon to right of them, / Cannon to left of them. / Cannon in front of them / Volley'd and thunder'd"— these ringing lines once memorized and recited by every schoolchild have become, in recent years, at best a faint echo. Indeed, I would hazard the guess that readers under forty are unlikely to recognize their source, which is Tennyson's memorial poem to the British cavalry regiment that met its death at Balaclava in the Crimean War—a military disaster resulting from the tragic error of pitting a sword-bearing cavalry regiment against a Russian army that had cannon at its disposal. The poem is called "The Charge of the Light Brigade" and it begins:

> Half a league, half a league,
> Half a league onward,
> All in the valley of Death
>     Rode the six hundred.
> "Forward the Light Brigade!"
> Charge for the guns!" he said.
> Into the valley of Death
>     Rode the six hundred.

The drumbeat of Tennyson's trimeters with their insistent rhyme and hypnotic repetition, their dramatic tale of sudden death on the battlefield, is considered something of an embarrassment by our own post–World War II generation, suspicious as we are of aggressive patriotism and the Victorian celebration of military exploits. Yet our current denigration of such lyric poetry is, as Jerome J. McGann points out in an important essay, itself just as time and culture bound as is our current preference for the muted rhythms and subtle indirections of Wallace Stevens.[11] Indeed, to understand "The Charge of the Light Brigade" is "to expose the mid-Victorian ideology which informs every part of Tennyson's poem" so as to "define critically the specific shape and special quality of its humanness" (*BI*, 190). If this program sounds at first like John Brenkman's "Marxist" reading of Blake's "Poison Tree," the illusion is quickly dispelled. For whereas Brenkman talks vaguely and abstractly of "capitalist society," "possessive individualism," and "proletarian revolution," McGann studies the actual historical and political context of Tennyson's poem, its mode of production and reception.

"The Charge of the Light Brigade" took its origin from a newspaper report; it was first printed in the *Examiner* (9 December 1854) one week after Tennyson read the initial account of the Battle of Balaclava, and the poem is, as McGann notes, "in many respects a distilled interpretation of the popular reaction to the charge as that reaction was expressed in the newspapers." In reading the poem against its newspaper sources, the critic is immediately struck by the "note of puzzlement" that colors the press reports, the repeated reference to "some misunderstanding" that brought on the disastrous "annihilation of the Light Cavalry Brigade." Thus the *Times* leader of 13 November 1854 exclaims: "Even accident would have made it more tolerable. But it was a mere mistake" (cited in *BI*, 192).

Whose mistake and why did it occur? Here textual study comes into play, McGann noting that in the first printed version of the poem in the *Examiner*, lines 5–6 of the first stanza read:

"Forward, the Light Brigade!
Take the guns," Nolan said. . . .

The specificity of reference was to be expunged in the second version, but precisely for that reason it provides McGann with an interesting clue. For Nolan (Capt. Lewis Nolan), McGann discovers, "was not just another cavalry officer, but a highly respected and even celebrated figure" (*BI*, 193), whose books on the management and tactics of cavalry units evidently created a sensation in military circles. Accordingly, the immediate newspaper linkage of Capt. Nolan's name with the infamous "mere mistake" that sent the Light Brigade to its fate, a mistake to which Tennyson refers in lines 11–12—"not tho' the soldier knew / Someone had blunder'd"—presents a troubling picture of the mid-Victorian British cavalry. For how is Nolan's "blunder" to be justified?

Here, McGann suggests, we must imaginatively re-create the class status of the cavalry officer in Tennyson's England. The Light Brigade, he notes, "was in all respects like the rest of the regiments sent to the Crimea; that is to say, they were all the most socially elite units in the British army, spit-and-polish, dashing, and notoriously affected groups which had never seen a battlefield. The units had not been in action since Waterloo" (*BI*, 194–95). Indeed, the meaning of Balaclava can be understood only in the context of that earlier battle, which had been a noble victory of the English infantry, that is to say, the lower classes. To vindicate the cavalry was thus to pay tribute to the aristocratic virtues of those who, as one newspaper account put it, "risked on that day all the enjoyments that rank, wealth, good social position . . . can offer. Splendid as the event was on the Alma, yet that rugged ascent . . . was scarcely so glorious as the progress of the cavalry through and through that valley of death" (*BI*, 194).

But isn't Tennyson's tribute to the aristocratic virtues displayed at Balaclava a case of misguided sentimentality? Can we share the jingoistic mid-Victorian sympathy for what one newspaper called "a fatal display of courage which all must admire while they lament"? And how can we admire a poem that seems to share so fully the dominant ideology of its time? In tackling these difficult questions, the critic must probe the meaning of the poem's original reception, in this case, its ability to "cross class lines and speak to the nation at large" (*BI*, 197). Tennyson's strategy, McGann argues, is "hidden in the iconography of the poem. The images in 'The Charge of the Light Brigade' are drawn from the newspaper accounts of the day, but the form of those images is based upon an iconography of heroism which Tennyson appropriated. His sources are French, bourgeois, and painterly, and his use of them in his English, aristocratic, and verbal work represents another struggle with foreigners which the entire English nation could sympathize with" (*BI*, 197). Not only the content of the images but their *form*—here historical criticism becomes genuinely literary. For the critic's role is not merely to extract some ideological nugget or "apple bright" from the poet's particular narrative but rather to study that narrative's specific formal representations.

In the case of "The Charge of the Light Brigade," the first such form is metrical. "Half a league, half a league, / Half a league onward": the "inexorable rhythm" of these lines, as McGann notes, "perfectly mirrors the cavalry's implacable movement," the spell the brigade seems to be under. And we might add that the poem's pounding dactyls and trochees enact a kind of ballet, a dance of death appropriate for cavalry discipline, which demands that ranks never be broken, that closure is all.

At the same time, the poem's imagery gives this death dance an odd twist. Tennyson was well aware, McGann remarks, that although Wellington had won the battle of Waterloo, England had lost to France the ideological struggle that followed. Accordingly, he endowed the Light Brigade with French cavalry postures, appropriating the iconography of David, Gericault, and Delacroix, the representations of dazzling equestrian heroes, depicted in all their Romantic force and energy:

Flash'd all their sabres bare,
Flash'd as they turn'd in air
Sabring the gunners there
Charging an army, while
All the world wonder'd.

Here the last line may well refer, so McGann posits, to a remark made by the French general Bosquet when he heard of the tragedy at Balaclava: "C'est magnifique, mais ce n'est pas la guerre" (*BI*, 198). Tennyson's equestrian tableaux, in other words, endow the English cavalry with "the emblems of the heroism they deserved, but had never had," the emblems as they "had been defined in another, antithetical culture" (*BI*, 200).

"The Charge of the Light Brigade" is thus "grounded in a set of paradoxes, the most fundamental of which is that [the poet's] model should have been French and Romantic rather than English and Victorian. Out of this basic paradox Tennyson constructs a series of new and changed views on certain matters of real cultural importance. Most clearly he wants to show that the charge was not a military disaster but a spiritual triumph . . . [and] that the name of the 'Light Brigade' bears a meaning which transcends its technical military significance" (*BI*, 201). The pointlessness of the military maneuver thus has its own pathos, the pathos of a post-Waterloo Britain, not yet conscious of the obsolescence of its flashing sabres, confronted as they were to be by the realities of modern cannon fire.

To read "The Charge of the Light Brigade" historically is not, however, to suggest that we should share the attitudes that the poem embodies. "On the contrary," McGann argues, "the aim of the analysis is to make us aware of the ideological gulf which separates us from the human world evoked through Tennyson's poem"; it reminds us that "we too . . . intersect with our own age and experience . . . in certain specific and ideologically determined ways" (*BI*, 201–2). Indeed, the "differential" that a poem like "The Light Brigade" represents should prompt us to reconsider the forms our own postmodern lyric is assuming.

Between the England of 1854, which generated Tennyson's vivid depiction of battle—"Flash'd all their sabres bare, / Flash'd as they turn'd in air"—and the America of 1984, which is the scene of Charles Bernstein's critique, in "Dysraphism," of the contemporary dissemination of "knowledge" with its accompanying exercise of authority—"I felt the abridgment / of imperatives, the wave of detours, the sabre- / rattling of inversion"—the "ideological gulf" is obviously large. The individual heroism of members of a threatened class, the pathos of battle, the poet's emotional response to a public disaster—for Bernstein, all these become, so to speak, "illustrated proclivities for puffed- / up benchmarks." In "Dysraphism," as in Tennyson's "Charge of the Light Brigade," "Sometimes something sunders," but for Bernstein such "mis-seaming" is less the function of a particular dramatic event than of the social fabric itself. Hence the *mise en question,* in this and the other poetic texts cited at the beginning of this essay, of such fixed forms as Tennyson's rhymed balladic stanza, or set of stanzas, centered on consecutive pages and isolated for our contemplation.

Indeed, the postmodern displacement of the central and unique event, whether we mean the event referred to in the poem or the poetic event itself, calls into question the very possibility of submitting to analysis the single framed poem, the candidate for inclusion in the hypothetical anthology of canonical poems. "Anthologies are to poets," David Antin has quipped, "as the zoo is to animals."[12] The analogy is exact: not *poema* but *poiesis,* not the event but, in Lyn Hejinian's words, "the reserve / for events" is central to our lyric discourse. A "reserve" that does not privilege one page or section of *Glas* over another, even as "Writing through Howl" cannot be isolated from the other "writings through" of Ginsberg's poem.

But how do we talk about such lyric "writings"? The answer, implicit in Derrida's *Glas* as in Leiris's "Glossaire," is that language, not structure, becomes central. Indeed, recent poetic theory is reviving the notion, at the heart of Russian Formalist poetics but in bad repute throughout the sixties, that there is an inherent difference between "ordinary" and "poetic" language. If the former is instrumental and transparent, a window through which we look at the depicted world beyond the page, the latter deploys the resources of sound and multiple, often undecidable, reference so as to call attention to its own materiality.

We should note that this emphasis on the materiality of language is not quite the same thing as the Russian Futurist doctrine of *zaum* or "transrational" poetry, the Formalist stress on "orientation toward the neighboring word" and defamiliarization. For whereas Futurist poetics construed defamiliarization as essentially a *literary* transform, a revolt against the dominant aesthetic of Symbolism, our own postmodern *ostranenie* ("making strange") has more to do with the discourses of the everyday world, of politics, culture, and commerce, than with the literary model as such. Here the relevant frame is what I should like to call the technological double bind.

On the one hand, we live in a technological world in which everything we say and write is always already given—a storehouse of cliché, stock phraseology, sloganeering, a prescribed form of address, a set of formulas that govern the expression of subjectivity. Given this context, poetic discourse is that which most fully calls into question conventional writing practices and which defies the authority of the chronological linear model.[13] "Prescribed rules of grammar & spelling," says Charles Bernstein, "make language seem outside of our control. & a language, even only seemingly, wrested from our control is a world taken from us."[14] Or, as Susan Howe puts it in *My Emily Dickinson* (1985): "Who polices questions of grammar, parts of speech, connection, and connotation? Whose order is shut inside the structure of a sentence? What inner articulation releases the coils and complications of Saying's assertion?"[15]

Hence the disruption of the linguistic and syntactical order we find in Hejinian's *The Guard* or Bernstein's "Dysraphism." Hence too the heavy reliance on citation, the graft of the other, in texts like *Glas* and "Writing through Howl," as if to say that our words can no longer be our own but that it is in our power to re-present them in new, imaginative ways.

But—and this is the curious signature of postmodern poetry— the discourse of technology rejected at one level as no more than the discourse of the dominant ideology, returns in the very structure, both aural and visual, of the poetic text. The double columns of *Glas* and of Brad Leithauser's poem, the print format of Leiris's "Le Sceptre miroitant," and the acrostic "Allen Ginsberg" buried in Cage's chance-generated lines—these breaks with what Gregory Ulmer calls "the investiture of the book"[16] are themselves part of our new technologized language. Indeed, poetry is now engaging the codes of the videotape playback, the telephone answering machine, and the computer, especially in its capacity, via modem, to address other computer terminals. At this writing, David Antin has been commissioned to compose a videopoem to be viewed alternately with the news flashes and information tapes in the waiting lounge of the Miami airport.

Can(n)on to the Right of Us, Can(n)on to the Left of Us

Such experiments promise a curious literalization—delightful or sinister depending upon one's point of view—of Pound's famous aphorism, "Poetry is news that stays news." It seems in any case impossible to talk about something called "the lyric" as if the genre were a timeless and stable product to which various theoretical paradigms can be "applied" so as to tease out new meanings. "Blinded by avenue and filled with / adjacency," we find ourselves trying "to / unveil detail / as minimal / as it's recep- / tive."

"Poets and other creative writers: fear not!" we read in the flyer for the *Black Mountain II Review.* Perhaps this imperative is not so foolish after all. "You may be writing 'Language-Oriented' works without ever having heard of half these people." Form, to adapt Robert Creeley's well-known injunction, is never more than the extension of culture.

# Chapter Two

# Canon and Loaded Gun:

## *Feminist Poetics and*

## *the Avant-Garde*

A poet is never just a woman or a man. Every poet is salted with fire.

Yes, gender difference does affect our use of language, and we constantly confront issues of difference, distance, and absence, when we should write. That doesn't mean I can relegate women to what we "should" or "must" be doing. Orders suggest hierarchy and category. Categories and hierarchies suggest property. My voice formed from my life belongs to no one else. What I put into words is no longer my possession. Possibility has opened.

—Susan Howe, *My Emily Dickinson*

## I

In a lead article for the *New York Times Book Review* (9 March 1986), Alicia Ostriker presents us with a narrative about women's poetry and the canon that has gained wide acceptance in the eighties. According to this narrative, poetry, at least until the mid-sixties, was a male domain. As Ostriker describes it in her article:

When I was a student, there were six Romantic poets: Blake,
Wordsworth and Coleridge in the first generation, followed by
Byron, Shelley and Keats in the second. Then came the Victo-
rians of whom Tennyson, Browning and Matthew Arnold
were the major figures. After that, one would read Hardy perhaps, Hopkins certainly. . . . Finally there were the supernovas of the moderns: Yeats, Eliot, Frost, Stevens, Pound,
Williams. That was literary history as my professors taught it.[1]

But this is not quite literary history as our professors taught it,
at least not in the Oberlin of the mid-fifties, where, just a few years
before Ostriker attended Brandeis, I studied the Romantics with
Chester Shaver and the modernists with Andrew Hoover. For
Shaver, there were, for all practical purposes, only four Romantics,
Blake being considered too bizarre (his apotheosis came only with
the sixties), Shelley too straightforwardly didactic, too abstract, given
the yardstick of Keats's sensuous poetry. As for what was called
"Modern Poetry," our current predilection for binary oppositions, in
this case the opposition between male and female poets, should not
blind us to the difficulties that canon formation always poses when
it deals with the literature of the present. Let me therefore begin
with a few statistics.

When I was an undergraduate in the fifties, the canonical critical study of modernist poetry was Cleanth Brooks's *Modern Poetry
and the Tradition* (1939). Brooks devotes long chapters to Yeats and
to Eliot's *Waste Land;* he also discusses, under the category "Wit
and High Seriousness," the "metaphysical" poetry of Robert Penn
Warren, John Crowe Ransom, and Allen Tate, as well as that of
Frost and the early Auden. When Brooks came to revise his book
in 1965, he observed that the one omission he regretted was that of
Wallace Stevens, whose derivation from the "a-logical" structures of
Romantic poetry now seemed more significant to him than it had in
1939. But what about those other "supernovas" listed by Ostriker?
William Carlos Williams was, in Brooks's estimation, the author of
small poems like "The Red Wheelbarrow," a lyric that, as Brooks
put it, "for some of us remains quite inert. I see the white chickens
and the raindrops glazing the red paint, but I have to take on faith
the author's statement that 'so much depends' on this scene." As
for Pound, Brooks grudgingly admitted that this poet had a "central
place in the critical revolution" and deserved attention because of
"his close association with both Eliot and Yeats." On Pound's own
poetry, however, Brooks remained silent.[2]

Indeed, Pound and Williams were consistently excluded from
the canon, at least until the early seventies, the same period when,
as Ostriker observes, women's poetry came into prominence. "Modernist" poetry meant Hardy, Yeats, Frost, and Eliot. As late as 1970
the leading poetry anthology used in college classrooms, the Gerald

DeWitt Sanders, John Herbert Nelson, and M. L. Rosenthal two-volume *Chief Modern Poets of Britain and America* (Macmillan, 5th edition), gave Yeats eighty-three pages to Pound's thirty-two, Frost forty-two pages to Williams's twenty-six. More important, although the anthology includes fifteen pages of Dylan Thomas and approximately ten each of Karl Shapiro, Howard Nemerov, Randall Jarrell, and Richard Wilbur, it does not include any of the following: Allen Ginsberg, Robert Creeley, John Ashbery, Frank O'Hara, James Merrill, Louis Zukofsky, and George Oppen. The British volume, which includes William Empson, Louis MacNeice, and Thomas Kinsella, excludes Basil Bunting.

By 1970 Bunting, then seventy years old, had published both *Briggflatts* and his *Collected Poems*. Ginsberg's "Howl" was fourteen years old, Ashbery had published *Rivers and Mountains,* Merrill *Nights and Days* and *The Fire Screen,* Oppen *Of Being Numerous,* and Zukofsky twenty-one parts (approximately two-thirds) of his great long poem *"A."* Frank O'Hara had been dead for four years. Yet in the English curriculum of the supposedly radicalized sixties and early seventies, these poets were all but invisible. Such invisibility was less a matter of gender (an apparently "genteel" poet like Marianne Moore was acceptable to all parties)[3] than of poetics: Ralph J. Mills, Jr.,'s very popular Random House anthology, *Contemporary American Poetry* (1965), which did include four women poets (Elizabeth Bishop, Isabella Gardner, Denise Levertov, and Anne Sexton), contained chapters on the following men: Richard Eberhart, Stanley Kunitz, Theodore Roethke, William Everson, Karl Shapiro, Robert Lowell, Richard Wilbur, and James Wright. And even Paul Carroll's revisionist study *The Poem in Its Skin* (1968), which does include Ashbery, O'Hara, Ginsberg, and Creeley (along with James Dickey, John Logan, W. S. Merwin, W. D. Snodgrass, and again Wright and Gardner), makes no mention of Zukofsky or Oppen.

How different is the situation today? On the one hand, we are now witnessing, in avant-garde journals and anthologies, a profound interest in the poetry of the Objectivists, especially Zukofsky, in the chance-generated lyric of Jackson Mac Low and John Cage, and especially in Gertrude Stein, whose poetry was excluded from every anthology mentioned so far. The ambitious publishing program of the University of California Press, which has, over the last decade, brought out Zukofsky's *"A,"* Charles Olson's *Maximus* and *Collected Poems,* and Creeley's *Collected Poems* and *Collected Prose,* has supported what we might take to be a move toward a revised canon. On the other hand, the *Norton Anthology of American Literature,* volume 2, published in 1985, continues to ignore the very existence of these poets (Stein is represented, but primarily in her late lectures), even as it includes Wilbur, Dickey, and Richard Hugo. And in Helen Vendler's *Harvard Book of Contemporary Poetry*, published later in 1985, the significant poets of the present are understood as deriving from Stevens, not from Pound or H.D., Stein or Williams, and, accordingly, the "alternate" tradition that extends from Olson, Duncan, Creeley, and the Objectivists to the San Francisco movement of the sixties, the Ethnopoetics and performance works of the seventies, and the "language" movement of the eighties has been, quite simply, erased.

When we turn, then, to the "new women's poetry," we should bear in mind that canonicity is almost invariably the enemy of the avant-garde. The genuinely new, the revolutionary, so history teaches us, is hardly apt to be quickly enshrined by the Academy. Accordingly, we must beware of proclamations that herald the New Dispensation. In his introduction to the 1985 double issue of *Parnassus*, titled *A Celebration of Women & Poetry*, Herbert Leibowitz declares that "the most remarkable event in American poetry of the last fifteen years has been the eruption of Vesuvius: the emergence of talented women poets in unprecedented numbers," and he refers to women's poetry as "an historical movement (still unfolding) whose seismic waves have radically changed lives and literary topography."[4] But one wonders about the aptness of the earthquake metaphor, given that Leibowitz's two exemplary poets, Sylvia Plath and Adrienne Rich, were, from the very outset of their careers in the mid-fifties, singled out for extravagant praise by the poetry establishment, which was then largely male. Rich, for that matter, gets more space in the *Norton Anthology of American Literature* than any contemporary poet except Lowell; she is, moreover, the only twentieth-century poet, male or female, British or American, who is the subject of a Norton Critical Edition.

Again, one wonders about those "seismic waves" supposedly generated by the "new" women's poetry when one reads, in the back of the *Parnassus Celebration of Women & Poetry*, the announcement of the next issue (Spring–Summer 1986, guest-edited by William Harmon), which will include poetry by Robert Creeley, Donald Davie, Albert Goldbarth, O. B. Hardison, Daniel Hoffman, Robert Morgan, John Frederick Nims, Kathleen Norris, Wyatt Prunty, David Ray, M. L. Rosenthal, George Starbuck, Peter Viereck, and "others." Twelve male poets to a single female one. Unless of course "others" is a woman.

Whether or not there are more and better women poets than in previous times, there can be no doubt that, thanks to the feminist movement, more women poets than ever are getting published. In her comprehensive history of American women poets from Anne Bradstreet to the present, Alicia Ostriker argues that contemporary women's poetry "constitutes a literary movement comparable to romanticism or modernism in our literary past."[5] In making her case, she casts an admirably wide net, including a large and varied group of women poets in her discussion of such topics as "The Quest for Identity," "The Release of Anatomy," and "Anger, Violence, and Polarization." Ostriker's methodology, as she explains in her introduction, is "inductive" and "eclectic":

> I admire closed and open forms, the pungency of colloquial idiom and the play of literary puns and allusions; evocative metaphor and clean abstraction; the disparate voices of lyric cry, satiric jibe, conversational inflection, prophetic incantation. The house of poetry has many mansions, and among the attractions of the women's poetry movement is its encouragement of diversity. (*SL*, 18)

On the face of it, such catholicity of taste seems admirable, but there is something about this demand for "diversity" that gives me pause. For what can it mean to be a critic or literary historian if one does not choose between available alternatives? And isn't the choice of, say, "closed form" itself ideological, as Anthony Easthope and others have argued?[6] Or does gender in fact override all other ideological categories, as Ostriker's title, *Stealing the Language*, seems to suggest?

If women poets are indeed defined as those poets who have "stolen the language" from their male counterparts, "eclecticism" becomes, inevitably, an ideological rather than, in any sense, a literary term: the category "woman poet" will have subcategories like "black woman poet," "Chicana poet," "lesbian poet," "Asian-American poet," "working-class woman poet," "West Coast woman poet," and so on. Or again, as in the case of Ostriker's book, the categories will be determined by subject matter: for instance, "The Quest for Identity," "The Release of Anatomy," or "Anger, Violence, and Polarization." There is nothing wrong with such groupings, provided that in making them we don't, so to speak, reaestheticize the ideological. For example, in an essay on black women poets for the *Parnassus* women's poetry issue, Calvin Hernton cites the following lines by Colleen J. McElroy from her book *Queen of the Ebony Isles* (1984):

> I want to fill the space
> with fat black babies
> with the veined hands of wretched old men
> and big mamas in flowered dresses
> shying away from welfare lines

and comments: "This is no mere abstract romanticizing of black people. McElroy cries out for primal human form. . . . But her reverence is charged with social consciousness: 'shying away from welfare lines.' The impressive quality of McElroy's poetics inheres in the ease and flow of her language . . . and the melodic rhythms and

cadences seem as natural as the steady roll of water over an undu-
lating countryside" (p. 539). Here the critic's shift from ideology
("reverence . . . charged with social consciousness") to aesthetic
value ("ease and flow of her language," "melodic rhythms and cadences") seems forced: at what point, one wants to ask, does the
"natural" become the merely ordinary? And how far can we extend
the helping hand of "pluralism" and "diversity" without making
*poetry* so reductive and bland a term that its potential readership
merely loses interest?

Indeed, the myth of inclusiveness—and this, it seems to me, is
the real irony of our current drive to "open up the canon"—goes
hand in hand with the drive, unconscious as it may be, to exclude
that which is Other. Not everyone, after all, gets invited to the party,
especially if one doesn't have solid "party" credentials. The difficult
poetry of Susan Howe and Lorine Niedecker is a case in point.

## II

The genre of Susan Howe's *My Emily Dickinson* is, as the dust
jacket comments by Michael Palmer and Don Byrd suggest, not that
of "critical commentary" but that of William Carlos Williams's *In
the American Grain,* Charles Olson's *Call Me Ishmael,* and Robert
Duncan's *H. D. Book*—texts in which one poet meditates so intensely
on the work of another that the two voices imperceptibly merge.
"Howe's ear," says Kathleen Fraser, "almost becomes Dickinson's,
hearing each musical phrase *and* its hesitancy as fierce intention
and mindful resistance" (jacket copy).[7]

Howe's subject, broadly speaking, is the impingement of historical or biographical narrative on lyric consciousness, a subject she
has already made her own in her earlier books, especially in *Defenestration of Prague* (1983). The title of this book refers to a particular
event, the putsch of 1617 in which Calvinist rebels attacked a group
of Catholic officials in the Czech royal palace and threw them out
the window, thus setting in motion the religious conflict known as
the Thirty Years' War. But Howe is writing not about Prague but
about another Catholic-Protestant conflict, this one closer to home,
in Ireland, the country of her origins. History, for this poet, is "the
true story that comes to nothing," a story that must be filtered
through "mute memory vagrant memory" and re-created in the
poet's imagination.[8] The "defenestration of Prague" thus becomes
Howe's own deconstruction of Irish myth, legend, and history, her
re-creation, for example, of the "words upon a window pane," as
Yeats called them, spoken long ago by Esther Johnson ("Stella") to
Jonathan Swift or by Cordelia to her father, Lear.

In the section called "The Liberties," at the center of *Defenestration of Prague,* Howe introjects such items as an Irish postage stamp, fragments from Swift's *Journal to Stella,* poems in octosyllabic couplets about Stella by both Swift and Sheridan, Swift's epitaph for himself, and Yeats's aphoristic six-line poem by that title into a prose text called "Fragments of a Liquidation," which reads like a slightly off-key eighteenth-century memoir, for example:

> Often [Swift] used a "little language" they both understood.
> The pages are filled with chat, puns, politics, plans, gossip,
> history, dreams, advice, endearments, secrets. . . . Left out,
> was his growing entanglement with Ester Vanhomrigh
> (VANESSA). None of Stella's letters have been saved. (p. 67;
> ellipsis in original)

Or again, under the heading "STELLA'S PORTRAIT":

> Loved horses and riding, had a sharp tongue, enjoyed
> social evenings, card games, and punning . . .
> She had raven-black hair (Swift), a pale and pensive
> expression (Mrs. Delaney), was plump (Some), extremely thin
> (Others). Sickly in her childhood, she grew into perfect health
> (Swift). She seems to have had weak eyesight. (p. 67; ellipsis
> in original)

Because "no authentic portrait [of Stella] exists," Howe turns to Swift's *Journal* for evidence, then discards that evidence for another source and yet another; finally, the narrator produces her own free-verse poem ("her diary soared above her house"), followed by "THEIR Book of Stella," a poetic collage, made up largely of citations from Renaissance and eighteenth-century texts, in which Stella, Cordelia, and the poet herself come together, culminating in the lines:

> The real plot was invisible
> everything possible
> was the attempt for the finest thing
> was the attempt
> him over the bridge into the water
> her some sort of daughter
> events now led to a region
> returned in a fictional direction
> I asked where the road to the left lay
> and they named the place
> Predestination
> automaton whose veiled face
> growing wings
> or taking up arms
> must always undo or sever
> HALLUCINATION OF THE MIRROR
> (p. 84)

Allusive, philosophical, speculative as it is, Howe's collage-poem raises questions about female identity that are a good deal more challenging than, say, Erica Jong's "Aging," with its ladies' magazine speculation about "how women age / it starts around the eyes  so you can tell / a woman of 22 from one of 28 merely by / a faint scribbling near the lids" (see *SL*, 106). Amusing and wholly accessible, such versifying is easily forgotten: *subject matter*, finally, cannot save it from its one-dimensionality. By contrast, Howe's reen-actment of Stella's decision to follow Swift from her home at Moor Park to Ireland and to live there for twenty-seven years as his unac-knowledged companion (when the news of her death was brought to the Deanery, "Swift was entertaining guests. He continued the party as if nothing had happened") resonates with possibility.

A similar resonance, the language of the present charged with echoes from an earlier time, characterizes Howe's *My Emily Dick-inson*. Howe's argument—for this book does have an argument—is that Dickinson is our great poet of "subversion":

> In prose and in poetry she explored the implications of break-ing the law just short of breaking off communication with a reader. Starting from scratch, she exploded habits of standard human intercourse in her letters, as she cut across the custom-ary chronological linearity of poetry. . . . [She] conducted a skillful and ironic investigation of patriarchal authority over literary history. Who polices questions of grammar, parts of speech, connection, and connotation? Whose order is shut inside the structure of a sentence? What inner articulation releases the coils and complications of Saying's assertion? (*MED*, 11–12)

Howe is speaking, of course, not only for Emily Dickinson but for herself. To subvert authority is, for Howe, to challenge the "custom-ary chronological linearity" of patriarchal poetry, to challenge the received model on its own ground.

But, and this is where Howe's feminist reading takes issue with current criticism, Dickinson was hardly the ghostly victim of male oppression she is often taken to be. Howe cites Sandra M. Gilbert and Susan Gubar's *Madwoman in the Attic:*

> Where the stitching of suicide simply gathers the poet's scat-tered selves into the uniform snow of death, the spider artist's artful stitching connects those fragments with a single self-developed and self-developing yarn of pearl. The stitch of sui-cide is a stab or puncture. . . . The stitch of art is provident and healing. (*MED*, 14)

"Who," asks Howe, "is this Spider-Artist? Not *my* Emily Dickinson. This is poetry not life and certainly not sewing." And she adds:

The Spider-Woman spinning with yarn of pearl, whose
use of horizontal dashes instead of ordinary punctuation is
here [in *Madwoman in the Attic*] described as being "neater and
more soigné in manuscript than in type . . . tiny and clear . . .
fine thoughts joining split thoughts theme to theme," was an
artist as obsessed, solitary, and uncompromising as Cézanne.
Like him she was ignored and misunderstood by her own generation, because of the radical nature of her work. During this
Spider's lifetime there were many widely read "poetesses."
(*MED*, 14)

"A poet," that is to say, "is never just a woman or a man." Categories
and hierarchies—woman poet, for instance—"suggest property" and
foreclose "possibility." Dickinson's poetry, Howe suggests, depends
to an unusual degree upon her reading, a reading that happens to
be primarily that of male writers:

Emily Dickinson took the scraps from the separate "higher"
female education many bright women of her time were
increasingly resenting, combined them with voracious and
"unladylike" outside reading, and used the combination. She
built a new poetic form from her fractured sense of being eternally on intellectual borders, where confident masculine voices
buzzed an alluring and inaccessible discourse, backward
through history into aboriginal anagogy. (*MED*, 21)

The relationship of Dickinson's own poetic language to the
"alluring and inaccessible discourse" of male writers provides Howe
with her starting point. To place Dickinson in a hypothetical canon
of women writers, she implies, is to cut off one of the most important
dimensions of her work. More specifically, to read Dickinson against
Anne Bradstreet, because Bradstreet was the founding mother of
American women's poetry, is to ignore the fact that Dickinson herself read, not Bradstreet, but Jonathan Edwards, just as she read
voraciously James Fenimore Cooper, Charles Dickens, George Eliot,
both Robert and Elizabeth Barrett Browning, the Brontës, and
Shakespeare's history plays.

Howe's discoveries in this regard are absolutely startling. Dickinson's third "Master" Letter (L248), for example, a letter that
begins, "Oh, did I offend it—. . . Daisy—Daisy—offend it—who
bends her smaller life to his," is read against Little Em'ly's letter in
*David Copperfield*, written after eloping with Steerforth and
addressed to her family, Ham, and possibly Master Davy/David/
Daisy, which begins, "Oh, if you knew how my heart is torn" (*MED*,
26). A second source is judged to be the passage in Barrett Browning's *Aurora Leigh*, where Marian Earle describes her passion for
Romney, Dickinson's "Low at the knee that bore her once unto . . .
Daisy," echoing Browning's "She told me she had loved upon her
knees, / As others pray," and so on. Howe remarks:

Attention should be paid to Dickinson's brilliant mask-
ing and unveiling, her joy in the drama of pleading. Far from
being the hysterical jargon of a frustrated and rejected woman
to some anonymous "Master"-Lover, these three letters were
probably self-conscious exercises in prose by one writer playing with, listening to, and learning from others. (*MED*, 27)

The implication is that the making of poems—even poems as
autobiographical as Dickinson's—depends at least as much upon
textual appropriation as upon a prior subject matter or emotional
state of mind. The bulk of *My Emily Dickinson* is devoted to a reading of a single poem, "My Life had stood—a Loaded Gun—," but
"reading" is not quite the word for what takes place in the course
of Howe's genuinely learned narrative. She begins with the world of
frontier America to which this particular poem points and, as in
*Defenestration of Prague,* her method is collage: passages from Calvin's *Institutes* and Increase Mather's *History of the War with the
Indians in New England,* juxtaposed with the *Narrative of the Captivity and Restoration of Mrs. Mary Rowlandson* and with Howe's
own commentary on Rowlandson's suffering, present us with a Man-
ichaean world "based on rigid separation of race, concentrated on
abduction, communion, war, and diabolism." "Contradiction," writes
Howe, "is the book of this place" (*MED*, 45). "Dualism of visible and
invisible."

Within this context of Puritan conversion narrative and Calvinist sermon, Dickinson's first letter to her mentor-to-be, T. W.
Higginson (7 June 1862), appears in a new light: "Far from being the
misguided modesty of an oppressed female ego, it is a consummate
Calvinist gesture of self-assertion by a poet with faith to fling election
loose across the incandescent shadows of futurity" (*MED*, 49).

If the New England world of "Guns and Grace" forms the first
circle within which Dickinson's poem operates, there are many others. The Brontë circle for one, and especially the book of the other
Emily, *Wuthering Heights,* in which, as in Dickinson's poetry, "the
inhuman legalism of Calvin warred with the intellectual beauty of
Neoplatonism" (*MED*, 61). Then Browning's "Childe Roland to the
Dark Tower Came" ("Two nameless narrators in the middle of life
were set on their path to the questionable freedom of paralysis in
power by a nameless, vaguely threatening Guide/Owner," *MED*, 70),
and then Shakespeare's Henry VI cycle and James Fenimore Cooper's *The Deerslayer.* By this time, Howe has, so to speak, become
Dickinson. Here is her lyric commentary on the second stanza ("And
now We roam in Sovreign Woods— / And now We hunt the
Doe— / and every time I speak for Him— / The Mountains straight
reply—") in the light of Cooper:

Killdeer is a hunter's gun. Together We will hunt and
kill for pleasure. American frontiersmen were generally men
on the make. Land in the West was a commodity to be
exploited for profit just as land in the East had been. The
Civil War will or will not expiate Our Sin. During the first
two Removes of Emily Killdoe's Captivity Narrative of Discovery; the unmentioned sun, blazing its mythopoeic kinship
with Sovreign and shooting its rhyme, —flash of sympathy
with Gun, has been steadily declining. Dickinson, an unwed
American citizen with "-son" set forever in her name, sees
God coolly from the dark side of noon. (*MED*, 94)

Increasingly, the world of the Loaded Gun and the Sovreign Woods,
of "Vesuvian face" and "Yellow Eye," of "the power to kill, / Without—the power to die—," belongs to the contemporary poet who
re-creates it. It is impossible to read *My Emily Dickinson* without
being swept along on its powerful lyric current. Howe's aim is not
so much to "explain" Dickinson's meanings as to relive them. Hers
is a tale of possession: the "ammunition in the yellow eye of a gun
that an allegorical pilgrim will shoot straight into the quiet of Night's
frame" (*MED*, 138). "Possibility," as the poet puts it, "has opened."

### III

Possibility, however, does not, paradoxically, seem to dwell
with Diversity, much less with Eclecticism. *The Norton Anthology of
Literature by Women* includes no work by Susan Howe; indeed, the
anthologist's problem is to know what to call a work like *My Emily
Dickinson*, what Library of Congress Catalog Number to assign to
it. But even when postmodernist poetry is more recognizably linear
and stanzaic, as is the case with Lorine Niedecker, exclusion from
the canon is not uncommon. Niedecker (1903–70), whose *Complete
Writings* (1985) is dedicated by its editor, Robert J. Bertholf, to
Susan Howe, "my guide through these poems," appears neither in
the ,*Norton* nor in Ostriker's *Stealing the Language;*[9] indeed, her
marginalization by current mainstream feminist criticism parallels
the marginalization of Williams, who was a great Niedecker admirer,
by the New Criticism or that of Zukofsky, who was her mentor, by
the Yale Critics.[10] To understand why this is the case, we must begin
with a look at the poet's biography.

Lorine Niedecker lived most of her life in a remote part of
Wisconsin, on the Black Hawk Island of the turbulent Rock River
near Fort Atkinson.[11] Her father made his living seining carp out of
Lake Koshkonong and tending bar. She attended Beloit College for

two years (1922–24), but when her mother became totally deaf, Niedecker returned home to help take care of her. A brief marriage to a local boy ended in divorce. She worked, first at the public library, then at a radio station, and from 1944 to 1950 as a proofreader for *Hoard's Dairyman,* a job made difficult by her extremely poor eyesight. In 1951 her mother died, both deaf and blind; her father died three years later, leaving her with two houses that had to be foreclosed and very little money. From 1957 to 1962 she was employed by the Fort Atkinson Memorial Hospital as a cleaning woman, sterilizing the dishes and utensils in the kitchen and scrubbing the cafeteria floors. Every day she walked the five miles or so to the hospital and back again to her one-and-a-half-room cabin without plumbing on the riverbank. In 1963 at the age of fifty-nine, she married Albert Millen, a man who evidently had no idea she wrote poetry and who spent a good deal of time at the local tavern. But he also took her on trips to South Dakota and around Lake Superior and seems to have been the companion she needed at this stage of her life. She was looking forward to a period of less housework and more time to write when in 1970 she had a stroke and died.

The external life was thus isolated and grim, a life of hard and tedious work. All the while, however, Niedecker was writing poetry. Her first published poem, "Wasted Energy," was in her high school yearbook; prophetically, its subject was the erosion of language brought on by the resort to cliché and stock phraseology:

> It's amazingly queer, but from all sides we hear
> Of the "crooks" and "tough birds" in our town,
> Of "wild women," of "guys," many "I wonder why's,"
> "Juicy" tales and requests to "pipe down."
>
> (*FTC,* 3)

In February 1931 *Poetry* magazine published the "Objectivists" issue and Niedecker discovered the work of Zukofsky, who was to become this Emily Dickinson's T. W. Higginson. It took her six months to screw up her courage to write Zukofsky, but once the correspondence began, it continued until 1963. Her 1934 meeting with him was, she later told Cid Corman, one of the high points of her life.

It was, indeed, the turning point for this poet's poet. Zukofsky helped her to get poems published in *Poetry, Furioso,* and James Laughlin's New Directions annuals. She was praised by Basil Bunting ("No one is so subtle with so few words"), Gilbert Sorrentino ("remarkable poetry, as in Catullus and Emily Dickinson"), Ian Hamilton Finlay, Donald Davie, Jonathan Williams, Michael Heller, and Ed Dorn.[12] Cid Corman, who published most of the poems she wrote in the sixties in his journal *Origin,* became friend as well as editor; Niedecker's letters to Corman testify to the wide range of her reading, her knowledge of poetry, and her dry sense of humor.[13] But her relationship with Corman, like her friendships with other poets, was confined to letters: their first actual meeting ("a day o a day to be remembered") took place only three weeks before her sudden death.

As a woman poet identified primarily with the otherwise-male Objectivist movement, Niedecker has thus, not surprisingly, been excluded from the canonical anthologies, literary histories, and mainstream feminist symposia.[14] For the male poetry establishment, her work appears to be a footnote to an already marginalized "difficult" poetic movement; for editors of feminist poetry texts, on the other hand, Niedecker's is a lyric that may be perceived as excessively "male identified." She does not, that is to say, write openly about the problems or difficulties of being a woman in a patriarchal society; on the contrary, her letters suggest that what she wanted, above all else, was to please the male writers whom she admired.

Her situation thus affords a remarkable parallel to that of Dickinson. Like Dickinson, Niedecker broke her isolation to find a male poetic mentor; like Dickinson, she regarded her cloistered life and spinsterhood less as deprivation than as a necessary precondition for the writing of poetry. Again like Dickinson, she rebelled, obliquely but bitterly, against the oppressive household routines that were forced upon her, the demands made by her difficult parents. She was, as her poems make clear, hardly an "angel in the house."

But whereas feminist criticism can accept Dickinson's need for obliquity and subterfuge as essential, given her time and place, contemporary women poets are expected to take a more overtly oppositional stance. Subject matter, topicality, "theme"—these relics of an old-fashioned stance toward literature, a stance that ostensibly disappeared in the wake of poststructuralism—are now coming in by the back door. Here, for example, is Dragon Gate Press's catalog description of Joan Swift's *The Dark Path of Our Names* (Port Townsend, N.Y., 1986):

> Part Two, entitled "Testimony," is a haunting sequence
> of twelve poems, each the utterance or thought of some par-
> ticipant in a recent rape-murder trial in Oakland, California.
> Both defense and prosecution witnesses speak, as does the
> imagined voice of the victim. Finally, in a poem with the
> understated title "Another Witness," the poet, herself a pre-
> vious victim of the defendant, offers her own powerful and
> compassionate testimony.

A sequence about rape in which the dramatized speakers include both the rapist and two of his victims! How, in the face of such colorful competition, do we come to terms with the minimalism of a Lorine Niedecker?

The *Granite Pail* opens with a characteristically minimal poem, originally part of a sequence called "Mother Geese," published in the New Directions annual for 1936:

> There's a better shine
> on the pendulum
> than is on my hair
> and many times
>
> . . .
>
> I've seen it there.
>
> (*GP,* 3)

Like so many of Niedecker's "nursery rhymes," this one is a riddle. What do pendulums and hair have in common? Absolutely nothing. The "shine" on hair is a sign of youth; as for the pendulum, its "better shine" has nothing to do with its age or, indeed, its ability to function as a pendulum. So, when we read "and many times," a line followed by a space, then three dots, as if to mimic the ticking of the pendulum, then another space, and only then the casual remark "I've seen it there," we suddenly realize that this is a poem about growing old, that the poet is contemplating her move toward a death as inevitable as the next tick of the clock.

But there is no use making a fuss about such recognitions. Life, for the moment, goes on and there are decisions to make:

> My friend tree
> I sawed you down
> but I must attend
> an older friend
> the sun
>
> (*GP,* 4)

Trees are nice but sunlight is needed for survival; besides, when the sun's heat is lost in the winter, there will be need for firewood. The foreshortened last line, its approximate rhyme ("sun"/"down") not quite as robust as the generative chiming of "friend"/"attend"/ "friend," says it all. Rhyme is similarly ironic in the title poem of *The Granite Pail:*

> Remember my little granite pail?
> The handle of it was blue.
> Think what's got away in my life—
> Was enough to carry me thru.
>
> (*GP,* 7)

What could be more absurd than such sentimental remembering? What difference does it make that the poet's little pail had a blue handle? None at all and this is precisely the point. It is the memory of the trivia that get away in life which carries us through. Or again, since the syntax is elliptical (what is the subject of "Was enough"?), despite the little sentimental memories that we nurse as we grow older, there is something else that sustains us.

If these early riddling nursery rhymes resemble Zukofsky's "Twenty-Nine Songs," Niedecker's work had, from the first, a darker, more personal side as well. Thus she could write, in a poem that anticipates Sylvia Plath's "The Other," with its reference to the rival's "bad smell" emanating from her "knitting, busily / Hooking itself to itself":

> What a woman! — hooks men like rugs,
> clips as she hooks, prefers old wool, but all
> childlike, lost, houseowning or pensioned men
> her prey. She covets the gold in her husband's teeth.
> She'd sell dirt, she'd sell your eyes fried in deep grief.
>
> (*FTC*, 19)

Perhaps Niedecker didn't include this poem in *My Life by Water* because she felt it lacked aesthetic distance, because it showed the poet as having momentarily lost her cool. But even here, the parallelism of unlike adjectives—"childlike," "lost," "houseowning," "pensioned"—and the biting culinary metaphor of the final line, which brings to mind eggs, their yolks "eyes" in a white face, fried in deep grease, make this much more than a diary jotting in which one woman expresses her personal dislike for another.

In a similar vein, Niedecker is able to transform the conventional "thank you for your friendship" poem as follows:

> You are my friend —
> you bring me peaches
> and the high bush cranberry
>                   you carry
> my fishpole
>
> you water my worms
> you patch my boot
> with your mending kit
>                   nothing in it
> but my hand
>
> (*GP*, 15)

Here the friend plays the role of caretaker; he (and implicitly the addressee must be a man) brings love offerings in the form of peaches and cranberries he himself has picked; he takes her fishing, carrying her pole, watering her worms, and even patching her boot with his "mending kit." But *his* mending kit turns out to have "nothing in it" but *her* hand, a hand that is clearly a synecdoche for the self.

Bertholf's note tells us this poem was sent to Zukofsky and dated as being received "Sept 15/60," although written many years earlier. In the typescript version the poem begins, "Why do I press

it: are you my friend?" and it had a third stanza that read, "The
trouble of the boot on you, friend/your dentist fingers/an orchard
to mow/you also/paint" (*FTC*, 316–17). In the finished poem the
tone of injured innocence is expunged; clearly, however, we can
read this as an allegory in which the isolated woman poet obliquely
reproaches her mentor—a mentor who is willing to give her "peaches,"
to carry her "fishpole," and even to "mend" her work—but who will
not, so to speak, accept the hand that is proffered to him.

"You are my friend" may be profitably compared with Marge
Piercy's "The Friend" (1969), reprinted in both *The Norton Anthology of Literature by Women* and Ostriker's *Stealing the Language:*

> We sat across the table.
> he said, cut off your hands.
> they are always poking at things.
> they might touch me.
> I said yes.
>
> Food grew cold on the table.
> he said, burn your body.
> it is not clean and smells like sex.
> It rubs my mind sore.
> I said yes.
>
> I love you, I said.
> that's very nice, he said
> I like to be loved,
> that makes me happy.
> Have you cut off your hands yet?[15]

Clever as this little parable is, its message is absorbed on first reading and then wears thin. In the case of Piercy's generic couple,
woman is the victim, man the oppressor; woman is giving, man takes
all and then demands more. I am wary of such scenarios just as I
am wary of Piercy's concept of a poem as a text that is lineated
wherever the simulated speaking voice happens to pause. By contrast, Niedecker's words, indeed her very morphemes, resonate.
"Cranberry"/"carry"—the diminution of syllables in this almost-
rhyme qualifies the value of the proffered "high bush cranberry,"
even as the double rhyme "mending kit"/"nothing in it" becomes
the poem's key image. "Hand," moreover, is related by consonance
to the "friend" of line 1. Further, the extreme condensation of
charged images creates an aura of sexual tension wholly absent from
Piercy's easy polemic. Piercy writes *about* the relationship of men
and women; Niedecker makes no such claim, but in writing about
her own relationship with one particular man, she defines a rela-

tionship that is also representative. The pathos of her poem is precisely that its addressee really is her friend, that he doesn't quite know how to respond to the gift of the woman's hand in his "mending kit."

Niedecker's desire to concentrate on her art is consistently coupled with her rueful recognition that "duty" lies elsewhere. On the one hand, in a poem that gave Bertholf his title, there is her real work:

> Grandfather
> advised me:
> Learn a trade
>
> I learned
> to sit at desk
> and condense
>
> No layoff
> from this
> condensery
>
> (*GP*, 54)

"Condensery": Niedecker's coinage is modeled on nouns like *dairy, nursery, scullery, pantry*— all those settings for a particular kind of domestic work. But where is the "condensery" that is out of earshot of the call of the blind and deaf mother?

> "It's a long day since last night.
> Give me space. I need
> floors. Wash the floors, Lorine! —
> wash clothes! Weed!"
>
> (*GP*, 17)

The poet knows these commands stem from suffering, but their futility (floors to be washed and fields to be weeded that the old .woman can't see) is irritating nevertheless. As for her father, the pathos of his life, in relation to his daughter's, is presented in one of Niedecker's finest poems:

> He lived—childhood summers
> thru bare feet
> then years of money's lack
> and heat
>
> beside the river—out of flood
> came his wood, dog,
> woman, lost her, daughter—
> prologue
>
> to planting trees. He buried carp
> beneath the rose
> where grass-still
> the marsh rail goes.

To bankers on high land
  he opened his wine tank.
He wishes his only daughter
  to work in the bank

but he'd given her a source
  to sustain her—
a weedy speech,
  a marshy retainer.

*(GP, 19)*

Here the drab facts of Niedecker's childhood life are curiously inter-
jected into the fairy-tale ballad of a kind of marsh princess. The
poet's vision is wholly unsentimental: her father's childhood poverty
("years of money's lack / and heat") has made him immune to later
self-pity, but even then his fate is hard, as the curious syntax of
stanza 2—"out of flood / came his wood, dog, / woman, lost her,
daughter"—suggests. "Lost her," which does not belong in this catalog of nouns, implies, on the one hand, that the monotony of this
man's life reduces all events to the same level. On the other, it is
because he has lost his woman that the daughter takes on new
importance. And further (stanza 3), it is because he "buried carp"
in the marsh that he turns to the "bankers on high land," with whom
he begins to drink. But—and this is the poem's strategy—the flooded
river of the father's childhood carries its own legacy from the
marshes to his only child—"a source / to sustain her— / a weedy
speech, / a marshy retainer." "Retainer" has three meanings here:
it is the "fee" the father has paid to secure his daughter's continued
services to him; the legacy that keeps her from leaving her world of
marshy origins; and the dental device that distorts normal speech
and makes it "weedy."

Niedecker's autobiographical poems repeatedly engage in such
complex wordplay. The memory poem "In the great snowfall before
the bomb" recalls Niedecker's days at the *Hoard's Dairyman* print
shop:

I was Blondie
I carried my bundles of hog feeder price lists
down by Larry the Lug,
I'd never get anywhere
because I'd never had suction,
pull, you know, favor, drag,
well-oiled protection.

*(GP, 21)*

"I'd never had suction" doesn't make too much sense until we come
to "suction's" appositive, "pull," in the next line and realize that the
two are synonyms. The parenthetical "you know" brings the sixth

line to life; "favor, drag"—the "small nouns," as George Oppen might
have called these words—are further variants on "pull," the former
abstract, the second concrete. All three of the nouns in this line could
be verbs, thus contrasting with the more explicit reference to "well-
oiled protection" in line 7. And then "protection" rhymes with "suction," the hissing *t*'s and falling rhythm mimetically conveying the
poet's contempt for these things.

The verbal play I have been describing, the concept of the
poem as a small machine made out of words, the urge to avoid "the
lyrical interference of the ego"—all these, we might say, are Objectivist characteristics that don't really distinguish Niedecker from
Zukofsky or Oppen or Carl Rakosi. But Niedecker's version of Objectivism has a curiously caustic edge—a personal stringency that looks
beyond the stylistic habits of her male counterparts to the specific
problems of her own situation, problems in which gender certainly
plays a role. It is in this sense that Niedecker resembles Dickinson.
Like Dickinson, she could never quite come to terms with the codes
of her society. In a remarkable poem of the sixties, she tried to
explain to herself why, so late in life, she should have decided to
marry:

> I married
>
> in the world's black night
> for warmth
>            if not repose.
>            At the close —
> someone.
>
> I hid with him
> from the long range guns.
>            We lay leg
>            in the cupboard, head
> in closet.
>
> A slit of light
> at no bird dawn —
>            Untaught
>            I thought
> he drank
>
> too much.
> I say
>            I married
>            and lived unburied.
> I thought —

(*GP,* 93)

Here lineation, rhyme, and word placement are charged with meaning. "I married"—subject and verb set off from the rest of the text
by white space as if to emphasize the poet's curious sense of isolation

rather than union. The rhyme "repose"/"close" puns on the second word: this kind of "repose," the poem tells us, is too "close" for comfort. Evidently, the narrator, whose "thought" is largely "untaught," expected otherwise—a little "warmth" in the "black night" of old age. But the truncated lines, whose predominant sound is the dying fall of final *d*'s and *t*'s ("married," "night," "hid," "head," "slit," "light," "Untaught," "thought," "married," "lived," "unburied," "thought"), tell us she now knows that hers was no solution. Women who marry because they fear "the long range guns," she seems to say, are condemned to lie "leg / in the cupboard, head / in closet"; women who marry, in other words, in order to "live unburied" (note the consonance of "married"/"unburied"), find themselves "at no bird dawn," all but longing for the tomb. The Dickinsonian dash after the final "I thought," echoing the lines "Untaught / I thought" six lines above it, spells it out: happy marriages are not made out of "thought."

Given its intense probing of the "no bird dawn" of her marriage, Niedecker's poem seems almost designed for the sort of scrutiny applied to texts in Ostriker's *Stealing the Language* or the *Norton Anthology*. The poet is, after all, expressing the discomfort and pain she has suffered, not just as an individual, but as a woman living in a society that upholds marriage as the norm; her choices are largely dictated by her culture. But—and this is the difference between Niedecker's treatment of marriage and, say, a Marge Piercy's—the "unburied" solitude, the claustrophobia of the "closet" expressed in Niedecker's lyric, is presented less as a study in oppression or victimization than as a portrayal of what the life of ordinary people in an isolated northern farm community is like. How good, after all, do the men have it? In one of her late sequences, "Paean to Place," Niedecker imaginatively re-creates her father's state of mind in the long years of her mother's illness:

Anchored here
in the rise and sink
    of life —
        middle years' nights

he sat

    beside his shoes
    rocking his chair
        Roped not 'looped'
            in the loop
    of her hair

(*GP,* 72)

Like the poet, who must lie "leg / in the cupboard, head / in closet," her father is imaged as "anchored," "Roped . . . in the loop / of [his

wife's] hair," the rope metaphor suggesting that one's noose is the
product, not of an external force, but of love itself—in this case, the
sexual loop of a woman's hair, a loop all the more mysterious in that
it remains outside the man who sits "beside his shoes."

I have been dwelling on the actual language of Niedecker's
poetry because, as must by now be evident, I take it that poetry is,
first and foremost, the language art. In the wake of deconstruction,
one would think it no longer necessary to repeat the truism that the
verbal signifier is not equivalent to its signifieds. But the current
wave of ideologically motivated criticism has ushered in a curious
form of backsliding. When, on the one hand, we talk theory, we
continue to talk of "difference" and "erasure," of "decenteredness"
and "supplementarity." When, on the other, we engage in practical
criticism, whether of poetry or of prose, we read texts as if language
were a mere conduit to a truth beyond it. X is a poem "about" finding
one's sexual identity, Y is "about" the horrors of rape, Z is "about"
exchange value or commodity fetish. And so on.

This new deference toward the "right" subject matter is likely
to produce, not the seismic waves Herbert Leibowitz speaks of, but
the malaise that accompanies disappointed expectations. For if
poetry is merely news (not, as Ezra Pound put it, "news that stays
news"), Poet X can always be replaced by a younger, even more
marginalized, and even more "outrageous" Poet Y who is willing to
engage the topic of the moment. In the long run, however, it is only
"weedy speech," as Niedecker calls it, that has the power to "sustain," only the "urgent wave / of the verse" that has the power to
cast us on a new shore.

*Chapter Three*

# Traduit de l'américain:

## French Representations

## of the "New American Poetry"

*I*n 1981 the prominent Paris literary journal *Change* devoted a special issue to what its editors called *l'Espace Amérique*. What does that "space" look like? In the words of the opening editorial by Jean-Pierre Faye:

> La navigation dans l'océan qui nous signifie
>                      A M E R I C A
> traversera de façon successive
> et synchronique
>              l'arête du *cut up*
> la péninsule de la *New York School*
>         l'espace actif des *Performing Arts*
> l'archipel dispersé du
> *Language Poetry movement*
>              l'afflux incessant de
>         l'A F R O A M E R I Q U E
> Notre regard les relie et les disjoint.[1]

The first thing to note here—if I may continue to use Faye's slightly bombastic geographic metaphor—is that the tide of French/American poetry relations seems to have turned. No American poet today, it is safe to say, would claim, as did Ezra Pound in 1913, that "practically the whole development of the English verse-art has been achieved by steals from the French."[2] Or at least not "steals" from French poetry. The role of French theory, on the other hand, is central: filtered through American poetics it reinscribes itself on the French poetry map. It is not coincidental, after all, that what Faye calls the "marée [qui] balaye l'espace Amérique" ("the tide that sweeps the American space") is characterized as "la marée de l'é-criture."

But which American *écriture* matters in Paris? Which of our current rival poetics has made a difference? Jean-Pierre Faye reminds the readers of *Change* that the journal has already published translations by and essays about Wallace Stevens (1969), Louis Zukofsky (1973), and Gertrude Stein (1976), as well as such later poets as Jack Spicer (1973, and a whole issue in 1976), David Antin (1978), Jerome Rothenberg (in four separate issues from 1974 to 1979), Rosmarie and Keith Waldrop (1978), and a special issue on Afro-American literature (1970). As for the current number, *L'Espace Amérique* is divided into four sections: (1) *Performing Arts,* (2) *New York School,* (3) *Language Poetry,* and (4) *Afro-Amérique,* specifically Ntozake Shange and Michael Harper. The issue concludes with Jean-Jacques Lebel's interview with William Burroughs, under the title "Cut In—Cut Out"; indeed, Burroughs is a presence, perhaps the most prominent presence, in the entire volume.

The *Performing Arts* section includes translations of Robert Wilson's *Queen Victoria* and Richard Foreman's adaptation of Gertrude Stein's *Byron: A Play,* as well as discussions of the Mabou Mines production of Lee Breuer's *Red Horse,* Richard Foreman's "Ontological-Hysterical Manifesto," Merce Cunningham's notes for the choreography of *Changes,* and John Cage's first version of "Writing through *Finnegans Wake."* The Cage extract, in turn, leads into the *New York School* section, which begins with Jacques Darras's poem "Notes abruptes sur la poésie de Frank O'Hara," which contains a versified capsule history of American poetry from Mallarmé's *Coup de dés* (in Paris, always already the first great American modernist poem) to Whitman's "ivresse de la rue" and William Carlos Williams's *variable foot* "qui se décroche comme un escalier ce magnifique étagement des conversations" ("which unwinds itself like a staircase this magnificent staging of conversations," *EA,* 114), and then, via Zukofsky, Charles Olson, and Robert Creeley, to Frank O'Hara's "poème [qui] a appris marcher," the poem as "vigile des nones . . . qui passent dans la rue / épiphanie 1, épiphanie 2, épiphanie 3" (*EA,* 115). This long poem, which contains collage fragments from O'Hara interviews, from poems by Max Jacob and Pierre Reverdy, and so on, is followed by Darras's translations of three John Ashbery poems and Jacques Roubaud's and Alix Cleo's translations of poems by Paul Blackburn, Clark Coolidge, Ron Padgett, and Ted Berrigan.

But for our purposes here, the most revealing section of the *Change* issue is the third, devoted to the topic "Poésie Langage USA" (specifically, Charles Bernstein, Lyn Hejinian, Bob Perelman, Barrett Watten, Steven Benson, Ron Silliman, and Carla Harryman, with prose notes by related poets like Rae Armantrout and Steve McCaffery). The critic Nanos Valaoritis, who introduces this section, places the "Language" movement against the background of early seventies' ideologically motivated protest movements, movements that, so Valaoritis argues, "se forme[nt] sous l'égide du signifié" ("take shape under the aegis of the signified," *EA*, 159), thus downplaying *écriture* itself. In this context, the radicalism of "language poetry" is its "refus de signifier," with the concomitant "refus [du] language comme moyen de communication" and of the stable subject. In reaffirming "les droits du signifiant" ("the rights of the signifier"), the language poets, argues Valaoritis, are in the great tradition of Russian Futurism, of Stein, and of Zukofsky, with the difference that theirs is a poetry written in response to "la castration imposée par l'environnement technologique sur toute une génération de poètes qui arrivent sur la scène dans les années 70" ("the castration imposed by the technological environment on a whole generation of poets who arrived on the scene in the seventies"). And he concludes:

> Il s'agit donc sans doute d'un écart peu usuel aux USA. Une prolifération de l'expérimental, sans précédent dans les pays européens, et sans doute tributaire d'idées européenes, mais aussi profondément américaines qu'on puisse les faire, en ce moment. . . . (*EA*, 161)

> (It is certainly the case, then, of a rupture quite uncommon in the U.S. A proliferation of experimentation, without precedent in the European countries although without doubt a tributary of European ideas, but also as profoundly American as one can make those ideas at this moment. . . .)

As such, language poetry seems to carry out the program of the Cunningham–Cage–Wilson–Mabou Mines axis on the one hand and the New York school axis on the other, creating, says the *Change* commentator, "cette camaraderie des debuts qui caracterérisa les futuristes, les dadaïstes, et les surréalistes, à l'age d'or des avant-gardes" (*EA*, 161).

Is *Change* typical of the French reception of postmodern American poetry? Absolutely. When the journal *Action poétique* ran a special issue called *Poésies USA* in 1970, it featured Louis Zukofsky, Larry Eigner, Jerome Rothenberg, Jack Spicer, and a section on American Indian poetry. Volume 61 (1975) was a Gertrude Stein issue; Volume 65, entitled *La Cuisine,* included Gary Snyder's "Oysters," Harry Matthews's "Milk Plasma," John Cage's "Mushroom

Book," and again, Gertrude Stein, this time a fifteen-page section of the relevant "food" poems from *Tender Buttons*. The 1980 double issue *Avant-Garde/Poésie/Théorie* published Claude Grimal's essay "Black Mountain: Arts en tous genres" as well as poems by the "language" poets Rae Armantrout and Lyn Hejinian. Again, *Po&sie* (the ampersand in the title signifying "le *et* qui est à l'intérieur de la poésie, un *et* de diversité"), which began publication in 1977 under the editorship of Michel Deguy, Jacques Roubaud, Robert Davreu, and Alain Duault, has devoted special features to Pound, Stein, Olson, the Ethnopoetics movement of Jerome Rothenberg, and to younger poets like Michael Palmer, whose "l'enigme du simple" is praised by the translator, Robert Davreu.[3]

But it is the anthologies that are especially interesting. In 1980 Gallimard brought out a bilingual anthology called *Vingt poètes américains,* edited by the poets Michel Deguy and Jacques Roubaud. Roubaud's preface begins with the assertion that "la littérature américaine, dans la deuxième moitié du vingtième siècle, c'est la poésie, l'explosion de la poésie."[4] This is a judgment few American critics would make about their own poetry, for reasons I will come to in a moment. Roubaud, in any case, takes as his starting point 1960, the year Donald Allen published his watershed anthology *The New American Poetry* and the "explosion" to which he refers comes out of (1) Black Mountain, (2) the San Francisco renaissance, (3) the New York school, and (4) Objectivism, as these four related movements affected the work of younger poets. The editor further explains that certain poets already well known in France (Pound, Williams, Stevens, Cummings, Olson, Creeley, O'Hara, and Cage, and especially the Beats, who have always had a large French audience) are not included, but that he and Deguy have chosen to begin the selection with a precursor whose influence on poets as diverse as Antin and Ashbery has become marked only in the seventies: namely, Gertrude Stein. Deguy and Roubaud's "twenty American poets" thus include, in the order of their presentation, Gertrude Stein, Louis Zukofsky, George Oppen, Robert Duncan, Denise Levertov, James Schuyler, Cid Corman, Jack Spicer, Paul Blackburn, Charles Olson, John Ashbery, Larry Eigner, W. S. Merwin, Harry Matthews, Kenneth Koch, Jerome Rothenberg, David Antin, Rosmarie Waldrop, Clayton Eshleman, and Nathaniel Tarn. Of the poet-translators, the most notable are Roubaud and Deguy themselves, Anne-Marie Albiach (Zukofsky), Claude Royet-Journoud (Oppen), and OULIPO's Georges Perec (Matthews).

The second anthology I wish to cite—*21 + 1: Poètes américains d'aujourd'hui,* published by Delta in 1986 in a two-volume bilingual edition—may be read as something of a sequel to *Vingt poètes américains.*[5] Its editors, Emmanuel Hocquard and Claude Royet-Journoud, are, like Deguy and Roubaud, their elders by a decade, themselves prominent poet-translators, and the anthology is billed as presenting "ce qu'il y a de plus nouveau dans la poésie américaine d'aujourd'hui"; the title *21 + 1* referring to the inclusion of one English poet, Tom Raworth, along with twenty young Americans: Rae Armantrout, Paul Auster, Charles Bernstein, Mei-Mei Berssenbrugge, Clark Coolidge, Michael Davidson, Michael Gizzi, Robert Grenier, Susan Howe, Ronald Johnson, Bernadette Mayer, Michael Palmer, Bob Perelman, Frank Samperi, Leslie Scalapino, Ron Silliman, Gustaf Sobin, John Taggart, Keith Waldrop, Diane Ward, John Yau. The majority of these have affiliations with the "language" movement or, as in the case of Mayer and Yau, to the New York school, or again, as in the case of Taggart, Johnson, and Sobin, to what we might call the second-generation Olson/Creeley/Duncan axis. Tom Raworth, the one British poet included, has affinities with all three of these movements.

*Traduit de l'américain*

How shall we interpret these selections? That is to say, how do these French versions of "our" poetry compare with our own anthologies? The answer—and this will come as a surprise to those of us who assume, commonsensically enough, that what we take to be a given nation's "leading poets" *are* in fact its leading poets—is that they quite simply don't compare. Take Helen Vendler's 1984 *The Harvard Book of Contemporary American Poetry*. Like Roubaud, Vendler begins with a great precursor, but her presiding deity is hardly Gertrude Stein. Rather, she begins with Wallace Stevens, "since he flowered late and came into his own only after the 1955 publication of the *Collected Poems*" and is thus "our chief link between the earlier high modernists (Eliot, Pound, Williams, Crane, Moore) and the later poets."[6] This statement is somewhat misleading, given that the full text of Pound's *Cantos* did not appear until 1970 and is therefore not likely to have exerted an influence *before* that date. Again, how could Stevens be the "chief link" between Williams and "the later poets," given that *Paterson* was not completed until 1958, three years after Stevens's death, and *Pictures from Breughel* was not published until 1962?

But of course it depends on what "later poets" one has in mind. Stevens may well point the way to many of the other thirty-four poets included in the *Harvard Book* for the simple reason that this particular anthology systematically erases from the canon what we know as the Pound-Williams-Stein tradition. Indeed, the introduction refers to "Pound's great failed effort in the *Cantos*" (*HB*, 11), as if this failure were a matter of public record. As such, the *Harvard Book* includes none of the following: Charles Olson, Kenneth Rexroth, Robert Creeley, Robert Duncan, Denise Levertov, Louis Zukofsky, George Oppen, and Jerome Rothenberg, to mention only the most prominent omissions. The Pound-Williams line aside, even the two poets who turn up in both the Harvard and the Gallimard anthologies—John Ashbery and W. S. Merwin—are represented in very different ways, Vendler choosing the later, more "thematic" Ashbery and Merwin poems (e.g., Ashbery's "Self-Portrait in a Convex Mirror," Merwin's "The Asians Dying"), Roubaud and Deguy the more experimental ones (Ashbery's "Sunrise in Suburbia" and Merwin's gnomic epigrams like "The Dream Again").

Who then are the *Harvard Book* poets? One thing is certain: these "contemporary" poets do not constitute what Nanos Valaoritis refers to as "une camaraderie des débuts." Nine of the thirty-five are safely dead: Wallace Stevens, Langston Hughes, Theodore Roethke, Elizabeth Bishop, Robert Hayden, Randall Jarrell, John Berryman, Robert Lowell, and Frank O'Hara. That leaves, in chronological order, Howard Nemerov, Amy Clampitt, Richard Wilbur, James Dickey, A. R. Ammons, Allen Ginsberg, James Merrill, John Ashbery, W. S. Merwin, James Wright, Anne Sexton, Adrienne Rich, Gary Snyder, Sylvia Plath, Mark Strand, Charles Wright, Michael Harper, Charles Simic, Frank Bidart, Robert Pinsky, Dave Smith, Louise Gluck, Albert Goldbarth, Michael Blumenthal, Jorie Graham, and Rita Dove. It is worth noting that only the last seven poets on this list were born after 1940.

From a French perspective, this list must surely be baffling. With a few exceptions (Ginsberg, Snyder, Ashbery, O'Hara),[7] these names (many of which, like Bishop, Lowell, and Merrill, are household words in America) are not familiar. Nor is the constellation of poets in the Vendler anthology atypical. Consider *The Morrow Anthology of Younger American Poets* (1985), edited by Dave Smith (a poet well represented in the *Harvard Book*) and David Bottoms, with an introduction by Anthony Hecht.[8] The *Morrow Anthology* contains 104 poets born after 1940. All seven poets in Vendler born after that date reappear here, but not a single one of the 104 appears in the Hocquard–Royet-Journoud *21 + 1: Poètes américains d'aujourd'hui.* Not one! Surely this is an amazing state of affairs, given that both books purport to present us with *the* important younger American poets. Surely too, only in America could there be so many published and prize-winning younger poets that there is virtually *no* overlap between anthologies.

What, then, is contemporary poetry that it should be defined so variously? "The symbolic strength of poetry," writes Helen Vendler, "consists in giving presence, through linguistic signs, to absent realities, while insisting, by the very brilliance of poetic style, on the linguistic nature of its own being and the illusionistic character of its effects. The poem stands before us brilliantly photographic and brilliantly verbal at once" (*HB*, 17). It is hard to take issue with this statement, although its implicit bifurcation of content and form, the "real" and the verbal, is not one we would find in the theoretical discussions in *Change* or *Po&sie*. Then, too, Vendler's definition implies that poetry has a stable essence, that it does not change over *Traduit de l'américain* time, at least not in its essentials. True, certain features distinguish the present from the early twentieth century: the relationship with Europe, for example, is no longer as "embattled"; on the contrary, "American poetry was for poets writing after 1940 a splendid present reality" (*HB*, 10). Again, ours is, so Vendler observes, "a Freudian culture, one in which a vaguely Freudian model of the soul has replaced an older Christianized Hellenic model" (*HB*, 10). Moreover, "Physical science has replaced metaphysics as the model of the knowable"; indeed, "There is no significant poet whose work does not mirror, both formally and in its preoccupations, the absence of the transcendent" (*HB*, 11).

It goes without saying that this way of "putting it" is very different from the discussions of "les droits du signifiant" one meets in the pages of *Change* or *Action poétique*. But Smith and Bottoms go one step further: theirs is a world in which American poetry has already become what Vendler calls "a splendid present reality." "Our collection," announce the editors of the *Morrow Anthology*, "is finally one moment's judgment. . . . We have appended no critical commentary and little assertion of value that would justify our selections. As Baudelaire said, poetry exists to be poetry; we think an anthology exists to be an anthology" (*MA*, 18).

The somewhat pretentious "as Baudelaire said" motif in the above sentence suggests that the European presence may loom larger for contemporary American poets than Vendler thinks. Still, she is right about the new American sense of confidence. Here is Smith and Bottoms's characterization of the typical poet in their anthology:

> Who, then, is the younger poet here? He, frequently
> she, is born between 1940, at the onset of World War II, and
> 1955, the third of Eisenhower's smiling presidential years. A
> child of suburban parents, television, and the nuclear night-
> mare, he is often the first in his family to complete college and
> escape a life of physical labor, the first to fight in or publicly
> oppose an unpopular national war, and among the first writers
> for whom intimate and personal revelation would not result in
> obscenity prosecution. . . . He has one or more graduate
> degrees in literature or writing and teaches both in a
> college. . . . On the average, he is thirty-seven years old, mar-
> ried with children, has been or is an editor of a literary maga-
> zine, has published widely, frequently translates poems from
> the Spanish, French, Hebrew, Swedish, Polish, and Italian,
> has been awarded a grant from the National Endowment for
> the Arts or the Guggenheim Foundation, or both, and rarely
> lives where he grew up.
>
> In his poems the younger poet tends to be himself, an
> invented version of himself. He is increasingly interested in

traditional forms of verse yet tends to be discontinuous and
irregular in his formal practices, manifesting the style of open,
personal, and sometimes garrulous poetry that his senior contemporaries evolved in the seventies. . . . He is haunted by
time and death yet God seems a minor problem. He is rarely a
card-carrying group member, political or aesthetic, rarely an
expatriate or veteran or eccentric. . . . He seems to jog more
than to write literary criticism. (*MA*, 18–19)

The poet *as boy or girl next door,* cheerfully noneccentric, indeed,
willfully ignorant of such things as philosophy or literary criticism!
The poet as blithe translator, never mind that he probably knows
only a phrase or two of the language from which he translates, rely-
ing on émigré native speakers to do the footwork. And speaking of
footwork, why *not* jog rather than read abstruse texts, given the
fellowships and teaching jobs seemingly available to the "younger
poet" at every turn. Not surprisingly, this side of American poetry—
what we might call its *côté bon bourgeois*—does not translate to a
culture where the leading poets also tend to be, like Jacques Roubaud or Denis Roche or Michel Deguy, philosophers or literary the-
orists.

To read the *Morrow Anthology* against *21 + 1: Poètes américains d'aujourd'hui,* or, within our own national frame, against, say,
Ron Silliman's anthology *In the American Tree,*[9] or against such new
journals of poetry and poetics as *Sulfur* and *Temblor, ACTS* and
*How(ever),* is to become aware that ours is indeed a schizophrenic
poetry scene. Schizophrenic not in the old terms of "raw" versus
"cooked," as the sixties would have it, of "beat" versus "academic,"
"hip" versus "square." For in one sense, the *Morrow Anthology* is
more democratic, more ecumenical, certainly more tolerant than are
the various avant-gardes and minority poetries of the present; it
includes, for example, nearly as many women as men—which is
hardly the case in French poetry journals or anthologies, anthologies
that, in their publication both of native and of foreign poetry, tend
to represent a much smaller and more cohesive, elitist, and male-
dominated group than do ours. Again, one could argue that such
*Morrow Anthology* poets as Larry Levis and Christopher Gilbert are
a lot more "raw," more "natural," and more straightforward than
are such sophisticated urban "language" poets as Charles Bernstein
or Lyn Hejinian.

My own sense is that the real division today—and here the
French connection becomes important—is between an American
poetry that continues to look toward England for its forms, modes,
conventions, even its themes, and a poetry "homemade"—to use
Hugh Kenner's term—in its language and rhetoric even as it looks
toward the continent, specifically France and Germany, for its theoretical base. If French representations of American poetry all but

ignore our literary Establishment, as that Establishment is presented Traduit de<br>l'américain in Vendler's *Harvard Book* and the *Morrow Anthology*, it is probably because "la nouvelle Angleterre" and its Midwestern cognates paradoxically strike a Parisian as somehow insufficiently "American." Let's come down to cases. Here are two poems from the *Harvard Book*, the first by Robert Lowell, the second by Mark Strand:

"Harriet"

Spring moved to summer—the rude cold rain
hurries the ambitious, flowers and youth;
our flash-tones crackle for an hour, and then
we too follow nature, imperceptibly
change our mouse-brown to white lion's mane,
thin white fading to a freckled, knuckled skull,
bronzed by decay, by many, many suns. . . .
Child of ten, three quarters animal,
three years from Juliet, half Juliet
already ripened for the night on stage—
beautiful petals, what shall we hope for,
knowing one choice not two is all you're given,
health beyond measure, dangerous
to yourself, more dangerous to others?

—Robert Lowell (1973; *HB*, 105)[10]

"A Morning"

I have carried it with me each day: that morning I took
my uncle's boat from the brown water cove
and headed for Mosher Island.
Small waves splashed against the hull
and the hollow creak of oarlock and oar
rose into the woods of black pine crusted with lichen.
I moved like a dark star, drifting over the drowned
other half of the world until, by a distant prompting,
I looked over the gunwhale and saw beneath the surface
a luminous room, a light-filled grave, saw for the first time
the one clear place given to us when we are alone.

—Mark Strand (1980; *HB*, 327)[11]

Students of contemporary American poetry would take these two poems to be quite different. Lowell's gritty realism, his "confessional" psychological stance and colloquial language have often been contrasted to Strand's visionary dreamscapes, what Harold Bloom, who has regularly dismissed Lowell as the William Vaughn Moody of our age, calls Strand's "dark and radiant peripheries."[12] But from a French perspective—and, to the best of my knowledge, neither poem has been translated into French—they obviously belong together, both late English-Romantic lyrics in which a particular self meditates on the external scene and moralizes the landscape.

Indeed, the sign under which both "Harriet" and "A Morning" are written is that of Wordsworth. Lowell's poem is an unrhymed sonnet, whose leisurely iambic pentameter—"bronzed by decay, by many, many suns"; or "already ripened for the night on stage"— immediately recalls the Wordsworth of "It is a beauteous evening, calm and free" or "The world is too much with us, late and soon." "Harriet" begins with an observation—"Spring moved to summer"— with its concomitant rueful recognition that "we" (the poet and his wife) aren't getting any younger, that "imperceptibly" their "mouse-brown" is giving way "to white lion's mane," and finally "to a freckled, knuckled skull." What, then, the sonnet asks, does life hold in store for the poet's young daughter, his late-born "Child of ten," still "three quarters animal" (one thinks of the "glad animal movements" in Wordsworth's "Tintern Abbey") but paradoxically only three years younger than Juliet on her big "night on stage." And in a conclusion reminiscent of Yeats's "May she be granted beauty and yet not / Beauty to make a stranger's eye distraught" ("A Prayer for My Daughter"), the poet, having himself opted for "danger" rather than peace, wonders if sheer "health" is not the more desirable option.

Despite the convoluted syntax of the last three lines, despite some shifting of tenses and unfinished sentences, the rhetoric of "Harriet" replicates, albeit in attenuated form, the rhetoric of the Wordsworth sonnet. Its structure is circular: observation in the present—meditation mixed with memory—a return to the present with renewed moral insight. The poem's figuration makes much use of the pathetic fallacy; indeed, everything here depends upon the equation between man and nature: "the rude cold rain / hurries the ambitious, flowers and youth."

Mark Strand's "A Morning" is similarly a *paysage moralisé*. Here the Wordsworth connection is even more overt, the source of Strand's imagery as well as his narrative being the famous "Stolen Boat" incident in *The Prelude*. But here Wordsworth's understatement gives way to a somewhat strained assertiveness: "I have carried it with me each day," the poet announces in line 1, as if to make sure that what follows will be *important*, not only to himself but to the reader. The dynamic of Strand's lyric depends upon slow, stately iambic rhythms, syntactic repetition ("saw beneath the surface"/ "saw for the first time"), and pervasive sound patterning, as in "the *hollow creak of oarlock* and *oar.*" Moving out into the silent waters "like a dark star," the poet has intimations, not of immortality, but of mere death—the "light-filled grave," "the one clear place given to us when we are alone." It is the classic epiphany of Romantic poetry, but stripped of the Romantic drive toward transcendence, toward a larger view that would make this particular moment meaningful.

Lowell's and Strand's representations of Romantic selfhood— Traduit de l'américain of the sensitive and delicate response on the part of a definable "I" to the vagaries of experience—their verbal echoes of great Anglo-American poets from Wordsworth to Yeats to Stevens (e.g., Strand's "of black pine crusted with lichen," with its echo of Stevens's "of the junipers crusted with snow" ["The Snow Man"])—these representations are destined to appeal to a readership brought up on British Romantic poetry and its early modernist offshoots in both Britain and America. And indeed it is this tradition that is carried on by the "younger poets" of the *Morrow Anthology*. Open the book at random, and you can find this:

> For the first time, on the road north of Tampico
> I felt the life sliding out of me,
> a drum in the desert, harder and harder to hear.
> I was seven, I lay in the car
> watching palm trees swirl a sickening pattern past the glass.
> My stomach was a melon split wide inside my skin.
>
> —Naomi Shihab Nye, "Making a Fist" (*MA*, 472)

or this:

> At four o'clock it's dark.
> Today, looking out through dusk
> at three gray women in stretch slacks
> chatting in front of the post office,
> their steps left and right and back
> like some quick folk dance of kindness,
> I remembered the winter we spent
> crying in each other's laps.
>
> —Michael Ryan, "In Winter" (*MA*, 591)

or this:

> In the night I get up and walk
> between the slices of deep blue sky.
> After a time, I lie down on the floor
> and stare up like a child on a roof. Stars
> tug at my face. The rooms commune
> like hillsides. I think of antelope, of
> the talons of owls, of a tiger
> that has not eaten for days.
>
> —Tess Gallagher, "Skylights" (*MA*, 207)

Such poetry is, in fact, highly formulaic: note the "I-as-sensitive-register," the "direct" colloquial diction that nevertheless moves readily and inevitably in and out of metaphor, the enjambed free-verse line, the "flat" description that yields immanent meaning, and, most important, the Romantic faith in the power of ordinary, everyday experience to yield "thoughts that do often lie too deep for tears."

In France, by contrast, Romanticism in its idealist phase (Lamartine, Vigny, Musset, and above all, Hugo) has not, in the twentieth century, played the dominant role that the British Romantics continue to play for us. Rather, the place of honor belongs to *symbolisme*, as it evolved from Baudelaire's stark and disjunctive images, to the splitting of the subject in Rimbaud, to the acute problematizing of reference in the increasingly opaque poems of Mallarmé. Indeed, it is Mallarmé who is the presiding deity of contemporary French poets from Denis Roche and Michel Deguy to Claude Royet-Journoud and Anne-Marie Albiach.[13] Accordingly, a collection like *21 + 1* is likely to include poetic texts like the following:

> Bloody tigers and fang-high fences in my dreams. Horses with baggy pockets and rhymes for cast-away things. Iron laundry poles at the center of the earth. And when the mail got handed it would be warm in your hand. Nobody lived past their role in life. Movies so dark it seemed impossible you could see a thing. Or anywhere a place to think. I pretended I knew my name and they never forgot my seeming knowledge. The windows either blue, grey, or an absolute black.

> To tell the tale, to wax unrepentant, to overlook the middle for all its ends, to form all cast out on the sea a lining, to wait until the glance all sufficiently watches. He lost the key with only the first name attached, all resultant pursuits for the nonce baseless. The agent assuming the guise leadless or is it pointless. However the threading I can well imagine. Battersea Bridge in the morning star. (2:59–60)

These are the eighth and ninth paragraphs from the opening section of Clark Coolidge's *Mine: The One That Enters the Stories* (Berkeley, Calif.: The Figures, 1982). The translation into French is by Phillipe Jaworski:

> Tigres sanguinaires et barrières hautes comme des crocs dans mes rêves. Chevaux aux poches trop larges et poème pour choses au rebut. Pôles de lessive à repasser au centre de la terre. Et le courrier qu'on vous tendait était chaud dans la main. Personne ne survivait à son rôle dans la vie. Films si sombres qu'il semblait impossible d'y rien voir. Ou un endroit quelconque pour penser. Je feignais de connaitre mon nom et ils n'oubliaient pas un instant mon apparent savoir. Les fenêtres bleues, grises, ou bien d'un noir absolu.

> Narrer le conte, s'enfoncer dans l'impénitence, négliger le milieu pour toutes ses fins, former tout rejeté sur la mer une doublure, attendre que le regard tout assez regarde. Il a perdu la clef avec le seul prénom attaché, toutes pursuites consécutives pour l'occasion sans fondement. L'agent endossant l'aspect sans plomb ou serait-ce sans objet. Peu importe le fil

facile à imaginer. Le Pont des Tempêtes dans l'étoile du matin. *Traduit de l'américain*
(*Mine: Un gisement d'histoires,* 1:50–60)

The French title cannot, of course, convey the punning of Coolidge's original: the literal "mine" (the cover of The Figures edition is a photomontage of miners at work, the frontispiece photo shows train tracks entering a mine through a mountain tunnel) metaphorically suggests the mining of the imagination, the tapping of buried layers of consciousness, even as it is also the pronoun "'mine." But French provides a comparable pun in that the French word *mine* also means "appearance," "face," "look" (as in *avoir bonne mine,* "to look well"; *faire mauvaise mine,* "to scowl," etc.). The translator is thus able to re-create something of the complexity of the original, whose focus is on the dream processes (both nocturnal and waking) that mine the past, a past that is itself seen as a mine, replete with "fang-high fences" ("barrières hautes comme des crocs") and "Iron laundry poles as the center of the earth" ("Pôles de lessive à repasser au centre de la terre"). In the poet's mental mine, there is no light: "Movies so dark it seemed impossible you could see a thing. Or anywhere a place to think." When the narrator "pretends" to know his own name, he is surprised that others don't see through his "seeming knowledge." But in a world of "bloody tigers" and horses with "baggy pockets," such subterfuge is to be expected.

Indeed, *Mine: The One That Enters the Story* is, as the translator puts it, made up of "gisement[s]" (strata, layers) of aborted stories and conflicting memories, of mail that warms the hand but whose content isn't revealed, of the casting out of "all" (all what?) on the sea which, true to the proverb, has a "lining," if not necessarily a silver one. The second paragraph refers to a "he" who has "lost the key with only the first name attached," but we are not told who "he" is or how he relates to the "agent" in the next sentence. If the conclusion of this paragraph has a vaguely Conradian note (a "sea," an "agent," "Battersea Bridge," a series of misunderstandings), the reference is less to the meaning of, say, *Heart of Darkness* than to the "darkness" of its title.

In one sense, Coolidge's references to darkness, disembodiment, and loss ("Movies so dark," "'The windows either blue, grey, or an absolute black") are not unlike the images in Mark Strand's "Morning." But in Coolidge's text there is no "first time" when one sees "the one clear place given to us when we are alone," no identifiable, coherent "I," a Man Speaking to Men, whose ruminations culminate in a moment of insight. On the contrary, the norm of natural speech seems to be largely inimical to Coolidge's "writerly" meditations, whose verbal artifice—"cast-away things," "to wax unrepentant," "all resultant pursuits for the nonce baseless"—points to the inevitable disjunction between words and things, the slippage between sounds and the meanings they carry. As such, *Mine* reasserts what Nanos Valaoritis calls "les droits du signifiant"; it is, in the Derridean sense, a poem of the *trace,* the *gramme.*

We are now in a better position to understand why there is, in the France of 1988, not a single book by Robert Frost in print, even as there are ten books by Pound available, seven by Williams, and seventeen by Gertrude Stein.[14] Rightly or wrongly, contemporary French discourse privileges what the Russian Futurist poets called the *word as such* and, by extension, the *syntactic field as such.* Indeed, French poetics is consonant with French poststructuralist theory in a way that American poetics, *Harvard Book–*style, is emphatically not.

A case in point is the poet-critic Jacques Darras's new anthology (1987) called *Arpentage [Road Map] de la poésie contemporaine,* which includes fourteen poets, each introduced by a "portrait-entretien," and a postface by Darras.[15] The fourteen poets are Robert Marteau, Yves Bonnefoy, Denis Roche, Claude Royet-Journoud, Anne-Marie Albiach, Pierre Joris, Allen Ginsberg, John Ashbery, Jacques Roubaud, Michel Deguy, Pierre Oster, Marcelin Pleynet, Philippe Sollers, and David Antin.

Three Americans—Ginsberg, Ashbery, and Antin—in the company of eleven French poets: the resulting configuration is a startling one.[16] For although Helen Vendler does include Ginsberg and Ashbery in the *Harvard Book,* there is no way that she, or critics of her persuasion, would include Antin, even if their anthologies were large enough to include two hundred poets. Antin, so the argument from this particular perspective runs, merely *talks,* casually and repetitively, recording on tape his random and disorganized observations. The published versions of these "talks" are then no more than transcriptions of talk; they are not artful at all and certainly not "poetry."

What, then, is Antin doing in *Arpentage* along with Roche and Roubaud? In his essay Darras begins by repudiating Surrealism and its lingering influence on contemporary French poetry. The "chloroform" of Surrealism, its cult of the hypnotic and incantatory Image, so far removed from the discourses of history and politics, is now giving way, so Darras argues, to a recognition of the need to incorporate the *banal:* in Williams's work, for example, "L'art du poème consiste . . . à transporter [un] fragment de réel dans le langage pour l'y faire jouer avec et sur les mots" ("The art of the poem consists in transposing a fragment of reality into language so as to play against and on top of the words," JD, 267). Indeed, "l'espace est devenu partout américain" (JD, 261), which is to say, that the role of *language* itself, not the allegorical dream images it evokes, takes center stage.

But what about the absence of lineation in Antin's "talk pieces"? Here the commentary of Jacques Roubaud is important. In

*La Vieillesse d'Alexandre* (1978; see JD, 159–65), Roubaud, himself *Traduit de l'américain* a trained linguist, relates the death of the alexandrine, the staple of French verse, to the death of the French empire, arguing that in France, if not in the United States, the alexandrine's replacement in the form of *vers libre* has gone hand in hand with a rhythmic impoverishment that seriously diminishes contemporary French poetry. But the solution, Roubaud argues, is not, as it is for the "new Formalists" in the United States, a return to the old fixed forms. The alexandrine cannot simply be revived and reinstated. Rather, the question of rhythm (as opposed to meter) must be rethought, and in the introduction to *Vingt poètes américains*, Roubaud cites David Antin as "un des poètes les plus originaux et les plus provocants aujourd'hui aux Etats-Unis" (p. 28). Antin, according to Roubaud, deconstructs not only conventional free-verse lineation but also the concept of "oral poetry," the term usually referring to no more than "le seul fait de la lecture publique à haute voix" (p. 29), a recitation, as in the case of a poet like Yevtushenko, of a text already written down and hence not genuinely "oral" at all. Whereas Antin, so the argument goes, bases his poetics "sur le rythme qui nait du décalage entre l'intention de la phrase et son déroulement sans repentirs possibles" ("on the rhythm created by the slippage between the intention of the sentence and its unfolding, no allowance being made for possible afterthoughts"). This oscillation between the drive toward closure and the resistance of speech, and further, between speech and writing is, so Roubaud argues, "une des contributions récentes les plus révolutionnaires à l'évolution de la poésie" (p. 30). And Roubaud himself has written a piece called *Dire la poésie* directly modeled on Antin's *Talking at the Boundaries*. Reproduced by Darras in *Arpentage*, it begins like this:

> C'est pourquoi     alors que la diction mémorisée
> ou la diction persuasive     additionnent les gestes     les
> sincérités     ou les provocations     pour soutenir
> l'intention et la progression des fragments     la poésie
> voix s'arrête     et repart     presque avec chacun d'entre
> eux     comme aux moments insulaires de sa composition
> (JD, 167)

None of the other poets in the Darras anthology make this particular experiment. But a number of them—Robert Marteau, Denis Roche, Michel Deguy, Philippe Sollers—are represented by prose poems; indeed Roche's *Dépots de savoir & de technique* (1981) might be classified as a critical essay on the status of literary and visual representations. Here is a sample paragraph in the section on photography:

> A béance inouïe, raccourci qui fait rêver: le coup de la ca-
> verne de Platon, ne tient pas devant une planche de contacts.

Que pourrait-on encore faire de cette vieille idée qui le
monde n'est qu'une illusion quand, dans une soirée entre amis,
ou devant sa belle-soeur nue, on déclenche d'un coup sec à la
fois le flash qu'on jette sur le monde et la sortie, comme cra-
chée par l'appareil, de l'épreuve en couleur qu'on n'a plus qu'à
coller dans un album? (JD, 60)

(Toward an inconceivable rupture, a flash that makes one
dream: the trick of Plato's Cave cannot hold up when faced
with a sheet of contact prints. What could one still do with
this old idea that the world is nothing but an illusion when,
during an evening among friends, or in front of one's nude sis-
ter-in-law, one releases in one brief instant the flash that one
explodes on the world and the exit, as if spit out by the
instrument, of the color proof with which one need do no
more than paste it into an album?)

The line between this "poetic" text and, say, Roland Barthes's essay
on photography is surely a fine one. No doubt, as Claude Royet-
Journoud puts it in his interview, the motivation of such writing is
to "romp[er] définitivement avec le lyrisme wagnérien de l'Europe,"
but there are different ways of achieving this rupture, Royet-Journoud's own strategy being to deploy short, abrupt lines and broken
phrases so as to renew what he calls the "réalisme froid" of the
Objectivists. In the same vein, Anne-Marie Albiach, who has translated parts of Zukofsky's "A," submits language to the sort of dismantling we found in Clark Coolidge. Asked, for example, why the
title of her poem "Etat" has a capital *E* in italics, Albiach replies,
"Pour le rendre imprononçable, l'italique gomme le mot, c'est un
mot qui ne veut rien dire" ("To render it unpronounceable, the italic
gums up the word, it's a word that wants to say nothing"). And
further, the italic letter "déstabilise [le mot], le rend muét. . . . En
fait le E en italique le féminise un peu et le rend transparent" ("des-
tabilizes [the word], makes it mute. . . . In fact the E in italics fem-
inizes it a little and makes it transparent," JD, 89).

This fixation on the *gramme* or smallest particle of writing
testifies to the role performance poetics and "le *Language Poetry
movement*" are currently playing in France. "J'essaie d'écrire,"
writes Denis Roche, "comme un américain qui tenterait de se traduire en français" ("I try to write like an American who would try
to translate himself into French." JD, 53)—a statement worth pondering. When Roche and his fellow poets declare that they want to
write "like Americans," they do not mean, of course, like American
poets per se (and certainly not what they would dismiss as the poets
*du coté Nouvelle Angleterre*), but to the postmodern American spirit
of experimentation that makes language the arena of production
rather than representation and thus betrays its derivation, not from

*Traduit de
l'américain*

the characteristic French poetry of the sixties and seventies, with its nagging "lyrisme wagnérien" and its Surrealist phantasmagoria, but from French poststructuralist theory. To write "comme un américain qui tenterait de se traduire en français" is thus to make what we might call an American loop, which is to say the loop that allows French poetry to receive an influx of the French theory it has always already possessed but didn't quite know it wanted. Perhaps it is a case of the old truism: the longest way round is the shortest way home.

# Chapter Four

# The Pursuit of Number:

## Yeats, Khlebnikov, and the

## Mathematics of Modernism

> Rome & Greece swept Art into their maw &
> destroyed it. A Warlike State never can produce
> Art. It will Rob & Plunder & accumulate into one
> place, & Translate & Copy & Buy & Sell & Criti-
> cize, but not Make. Grecian is Mathematic Form.
> Gothic is Living Form. Mathematic Form is Eter-
> nal in the Reasoning Memory. Living Form is
> Eternal Existence.
>
> —William Blake, "On Virgil" (c. 1820)

### I

**W**hat is irksome about [Yeats's] *A Vision,*" Harold Bloom observes, "is not its 'wildness,' in the Emersonian sense of its creative freedom, but rather that it is not wild enough. Yeatsian exuberance, throughout the book, is too much curbed by what the poet himself called a 'harsh geometry.' "[1] And he goes on to compare Yeats to Blake, much to the former's disadvantage:

> Blake, unlike Yeats, took no joy in the Wheel. . . . [He] was
> set against all dualisms. . . . But Yeats, even before he read
> arcane literature and became a Rosicrucian adept, was a

natural Gnostic. He shared always the Gnostic sense of longing acutely for the soul's fortunate destiny after the body's
death, a longing that is the negation of Blake's apocalyptic
desires. . . . For Yeats, like the Gnostics, is profoundly pessi-
mistic, even as Blake, despite all horrors, is humanly hopeful.
(Bloom, 74)

Accurate as these distinctions may be, it is the valuation placed upon
them that we might question. If we assume, as does Bloom, that the
poet is by definition one who searches, not for "ultimates beyond
knowledge but self-knowledge, not a control over fate but self-con-
trol" (Bloom, 215), then Yeats can only emerge as second-best, a
Romantic *manqué*, whose intermittent imaginative power too often
fell prey to the "barren geometries" (Bloom, 76) of system building.
But suppose we read Yeats's geometries, or, more specifically, his
mathematical paradigms, with their binary oppositions, their reliance on the Four Faculties, the Twenty-Eight Phases of the Moon,
the 2,000-year Great Wheels of History, and so on, as versions, not
of a belated English Romanticism, but, on the contrary, as analogues
to European modernist works of their own period? I am thinking
specifically of the Russian avant-garde poet Velimir Khlebnikov, a
poet with whom Yeats had absolutely no contact, but who, like
Yeats, and in the very same years as Yeats, developed elaborate
mathematical formulas to diagram the events of history and to
"place" on its circuits the famous individuals who constitute it.

Indeed, in keeping with my subject, I might begin with a number: 1917, the year of the Russian Revolution, when Khlebnikov
began to work out his "Mathematical Conception of History" to be
called *The Tables of Destiny*. In March of that year, Khlebnikov
wrote to a friend, "Aryabhatta and Kepler! We see again the year
of the ancient gods, great sacred events repeating themselves after
365 years."[2] In November of the same year, Yeats began to keep the
notebooks that culminated in *A Vision* (1st ed. 1925), whose fourth
book, "The Great Year of the Ancients," similarly deals with multiples of 365. Such parallels are not, of course, fortuitous, and one
might begin by cataloging the common sources used by both poets:
Pythagoras, Plato's *Timaeus*, Renaissance Neoplatonist texts, Leib-
nitz's monadology, and especially late nineteenth-century theosoph-
ical and Hermetic literature. But source study in itself cannot answer
the question why two poets so essentially dissimilar as Yeats and
Khlebnikov should rely on the external ordering systems of "barren
geometries" rather than on the organicist metaphors provided by
their Romantic models. Or, to take the question one step further,
why was the early twentieth-century avant-garde, whether in painting (Mondrian) or architecture (Tatlin) or music (Berg), so drawn to
number symbolisms that had been largely discredited by the scientific materialism of the nineteenth century?

The picture is complicated, at least in Yeats's case, by the poet's repeated insistence that scientific *abstraction* is the enemy. In *The Trembling of a Veil,* Yeats recalls that in the late eighties, "I began to pray that my imagination might somehow be rescued from abstraction and become as preoccupied with life as had been the imagination of Chaucer. For ten or twelve years more I suffered continual remorse, and only became content when my abstractions had composed themselves into picture and dramatization."[3] And a few pages later, in defining "Unity of Being" as the "term . . . Dante used . . . when he compared beauty in the *Convito* to a perfectly proportioned human body," Yeats adds, "I thought that the enemy of this unity was abstraction, meaning by abstraction not the distinction but the isolation of occupation, or class or faculty" (p. 190). It is the *isolation* attendant on abstraction that Yeats evidently feared: by the mid-thirties, when he wrote *Dramatis Personae,* he increasingly presented himself, in his letters as in his poems, as an expansive Last Romantic, a Wild Old Wicked Man as simple and passionate as the dawn. Thus he contrasts George Moore's mind, which is "argumentative, abstract, diagrammatic," with his own "sensuous, concrete, rhythmical" one (p. 434), a characterization amusingly questioned by Dorothy Wellesley, who observes:

> I have come to the conclusion that [Yeats's] lack of
> "visualness," this lack of interest in natural beauty for its own
> sake, may originate in the fact that most of the Celtic poets
> are not concerned with nature at all. Yeats did not himself
> draw much inspiration from Nature, certainly from no details;
> only sometimes massed effects, such as a painter sees, influ-
> enced his verse. Referring to a poem of mine Yeats once said
> to me in an outburst of irritability: "Why can't you English
> poets keep flowers out of your poetry?"[4]

And speculating that Yeats's disinterest in concreteness may also have to do with "extremely poor sight," which may have made his "perspective . . . abnormal," Wellesley remarks dryly: "Sex, Philosophy, and the Occult preoccupy him. He strangely intermingles the three" (p. 174).

But of course the preoccupation with "Sex, Philosophy, and the Occult" transcends such circumstantial facts as Yeats's bad eyesight or even his Celticism. The prayer to be rescued from abstraction, to experience Unity of Being as a "natural," living "body," was essential to Yeats's conception of himself as the inheritor of the Romantics and especially of Blake, the Blake of "On Virgil" (see the epigraph to this chapter), who distinguishes between "Mathematic Form" and "Living Form," the Blake of *The Marriage of Heaven and Hell,* who declares:

The hours of folly are measured by the clock, but of wisdom
   no clock can measure.
All wholesome food is caught without a net or a trap.
Bring out number, weight & measure in a year of dearth.
No bird soars too high if he soars with his own wings.[5]

Or, as he puts it in his "Annotations to Sir Joshua Reynolds' Discourses" (c. 1808), "All Forms are Perfect in the Poet's Mind, but these are not Abstracted nor Compounded from Nature, but are from Imagination" (Blake, 618). And he adds, "God forbid that Truth should be confined to Mathematical Demonstration" (p. 621).

As such, "mathematic form" seems to be the poet's nemesis, "Conquer[ing]," as Keats put it in "Lamia," "all mysteries by rule and line." It is in this sense that Yeats prays that his "imagination might somehow be rescued from abstraction and become preoccupied with . . . life." But there is another side of mathematics that Yeats found more congenial, the side that concerns, not formal logic or deductive reasoning, but the attraction of *number* itself.[6]

Consider, to begin with, the paradoxical meaning of the noun *number*. The *OED* makes it clear that by at least 1300, *number* meant, on the one hand, "The precise sum or aggregate of any collection of individual things or persons" (I, 1), and, on the other, "That aspect of things which is involved in considering them as separate units of which one or more may be taken or distinguished" (III, 11). John Wycliffe's sermons of the 1380s supply examples of both uses: (1) "This noumbre of fishis that here weren taken bitokeneth the noumbre of seintis," and (2) "The mysteries of al the hool crafte of number." In the former example, one can substitute the specific arithmetical symbol in question: 3 fishes (or 4 or 7 or 12) betoken 3 (or 4 or 7 or 12) saints. In the latter case, such substitution is impossible: "The mysteries of al the hool crafte of" (say) 3 makes no sense because Wycliffe is here referring to the abstract concept of *number,* not the specific arithmetical symbol of number X.

The adjective *abstract,* according to the *OED,* has as its most prominent meaning "Withdrawn, drawn away, removed, separate," with the corollaries "Withdrawn from the contemplation of present objects" and "Withdrawn or separated from matter, from material embodiment, from practice, or from particular examples." In this latter sense, "abstract" is, so the *OED* tells us, "opposite to *concrete.*" "Withdrawn or separated . . . from material embodiment" here seems to be the quality of *number* inherent in the second definition above: there are no numbers in the natural world; they exist in mind not in matter.

But if number is thus, in Alfred North Whitehead's words, the "cipher of ultimate abstraction,"[7] the paradox, as I noted above, is that number, say the number 2, has an absolutely specific value when assigned to any perceptible entity. As Khlebnikov puts it, "There exist only two trees, three rocks, etc., and not two in general or three in general. The numbers are abstractions which reflect only relationships between realities, and *outside these realities they don't exist*" (*VKCW,* 165).

What then about visual representations of number? Jasper Johns's famous number paintings, which first appeared in the late fifties—beginning with "portraits" of individual numbers (see figs. 1 and 2), then of numbers in sequence (*Gray Numbers,* fig. 3) and then in superposition (*0 through 9,* 1960, fig. 4)—take the abstract/ concrete paradox of number to its extreme. As Leo Steinberg puts it:

> The position of modern anti-illusionism finds here its logical resting place. The street and the sky—they can only be *simulated* on canvas; but a flag, a target, a 5—these can be *made,* and the completed painting will represent no more than what it actually is. For no likeness of a 5 is paintable, only the thing itself.
>
> A crucial problem of twentieth-century art—how to make the painting a firsthand reality—resolves itself when the subject matter shifts from nature to culture.[8]

*From nature to culture,* from art as the representation of natural phenomena and processes to art as a self-consciously material production: this is the shift from Romanticism to modernism, to which the mathematics of early twentieth-century artists and poets provides an index. For when *number* reappears in the essentially post-Christian decades of the early twentieth century, its Pythagorean or Platonic value (e.g., the sacred tetratkys [fig. 5] consists of 1 + 2 + 3 + 4 arranged as a triangle, providing a table of the four magnitudes, the four elements, and so on, as well being the source of the "perfect" number, 10, which is the sum of its divisors exclusive of itself) functions less as an article of faith than as what we now call a *generative device,* an external rule that sets the artistic process in motion even as it provides controls. Perhaps it is this appeal of number that Coleridge had in mind when, in a note on the flyleaf of G. H. Schubert's *Allgemeine Naturgeschichte* (1826), he wrote:

> Next to that, to which there is no Near, the guilt and the avenging Daemon of my Life [i.e., opium], I must place the neglect of Mathematics, under the strongest motives, and the most favorable helps and opportunities for acquiring them. Not a week passes in which I do not regret this Oversight of my Youth with a sort of remorse that turns it to a Sin! . . . I had not the *Organ* of all Sciences that respect Space and Quantity. My Dreams were akin to Reason: but I could not awake out of my prophetic Sleep, to effectuate their objectivization—for I was ignorant of the Mathematics![9]

**Figure 1.** Jasper Johns, *Figure 1.* 1955. Encaustic and collage on canvas. 43.8 × 34.9 cm (17 1/4″ × 13 3/4″). Private Collection, New York.

**Figure 2.** Jasper Johns, *Figure 5.* 1955. Encaustic and collage on canvas. 44.5 × 35.6 cm. (17 1/″ × 14″). Collection the artist.

ure 3. Jasper Johns, *Gray Numbers*. 1958. Encaustic and collage
:anvas. 170.2 × 125.8 cm (67″ × 49 1/″).
lection Kimiko and John Powers, Colorado.

**Figure 4.** Jasper Johns, *0 through 9*. 1960. Lithograph.
76.2 × 55.9 cm. (30″ × 22″). Edition of 35.
Published by Universal Limited Art Editions.
All Johns works © Jaspar Johns/VAGA New York 1990.

.

.    .

.    .    .

.    .    .    .

## SACRED
## TETRAKTYS

**Figure 5.** *Sacred Tetratkys*, as prepared by Joseph K. Perloff.

Coleridge's reference is to Michael Faraday's acoustic experiments
in which the poet recognizes "a fond and earnest dream-project of
my own of 30 years' standing," but the implication is that the problem is much larger than Coleridge's inability to comprehend a specific invention like Faraday's microphone. Perhaps, that is to say,
the Romantic devaluation of mathematics in favor of biological and
chemical models made it increasingly difficult for the poet to control
what Henry James was to call "the terrible *fluidity* of self-revela-
tion."[10] A counterexample may be found in the poetics of Khlebnikov, to which I now turn.

## II

Velimir Khlebnikov (1885–1922) studied mathematics and
natural science, first at the University of Kazan, where Lobachevsky
had given his famous lectures on non-Euclidean geometry, and then
in 1913 at St. Petersburg, where he shifted his attentions to poetry
and began to publish. His Cubo-Futurist experiments with *zaum*
("beyonsense," in Paul Schmidt's coinage) poetry, using such linguistic devices as pun, neologism, non sequitur, sound play, and
grammatical deformation, were first described by Roman Jakobson
in *New Russian Poetry* (1921), a study that makes a strong case for
Khlebnikov as *the* major Russian avant-garde poet. The point, for
our purposes here, is that, from the first, Khlebnikov saw language
as intimately connected to number—he speaks enthusiastically of
the "number-word" (*chisloslovo*), "number-names" (*chisloimena*),
"number language" (*chislovoy yazik*), and "number-speeches" (*chis-
lorechi*)[11]—and that he regarded these "number-words" as, so to
speak, magic spells that enabled the poet to establish an objective
grounding for the vagaries of human feelings.

From the first, Khlebnikov declared himself to be "preoccupied with numbers," confiding to friends that he did "calculations
from morning till night" (*VKCW*, 83). Thus he writes to the poet
Vasily Kamensky (May 1914):

> . . . I have a business proposition for you: describe the days
> and hours of your feelings as if they moved the way the stars
> do. Yours and hers [Augusta Koktorovna Yugova, Kamen-
> sky's fiancee]. The angles, turning points, high points. And I'll
> work out the equation! I've put together the beginnings of a
> general law. (For example, the connection between our feel-
> ings and the summer and winter solstices.) You have to dis-
> cover what relates to the moon and what to the sun. The
> equinoxes, sunsets, new moons, half-moons. That way it's pos-
> sible to work out our stellar dispositions. Work out the exact

curve of feelings in waves, rings, spirals, rotations, circles,
declinations. I guarantee when it is all worked out MES will
explain it — Moon, Earth, Sun. It will be a tale told without a
single word. Newton's law will peep out between I and E
[characters in a Khlebnikov poem] and so far it's still breath-
ing. (*VKCW*, 89–90)

Many readers will no doubt dismiss this talk of equations for
human emotions as so much superstitious nonsense, the sort of low-
brow dabbling in astrology and horoscopes W. H. Auden, writing on
Yeats, dismissed as hopelessly "Southern Californian"[12]—an epithet
borne out, last year, when that famous Southern Californian Nancy
Reagan was revealed as basing major personal and public decisions
on the advice of her California astrologist. But although Khlebnikov's
root numbers are indeed derived, via Plato, Leibniz, and Kepler,
from planetary movements and the laws of astronomic periodicity,
he wholly inverts the popular occultist study of horoscopes as revelatory of the individual personality and its hopes and fears in daily
life. On the contrary, Khlebnikov's numerical calculations, like those
of his friend Tatlin, whose great Tower (*The Monument to the Third
International,* see fig. 6) is built on mathematical relationships
derived from the zodiac (figs. 7 and 8),[13] are predicated on the notion
that Romantic subjectivity is itself a cultural construction whose relevance to modernist poetics is questionable. Indeed, Khlebnikov's
sound-text poems like "Bobeobi" and the "Incantation by Laughter"
("O, rassmeites', smekhachi!"), his fictions like *Ka,* and his plays
like *Marquise Des S.,* in which time moves backward, rather as in
Harold Pinter's *Betrayal,* present a world in which meaning is constructed only *in* and *through* language, a world devoid of "character"
in the traditional sense, of psychologism and stated motivation. As
for the poet's own individual "self," we learn singularly little about
it from Khlebnikov's writings. At least not from his writings produced during and in response to the Great War and the 1917 Revolution.

That response is prefigured by Khlebnikov's reaction to the
Russo-Japanese War of 1905, a reaction recalled in *The Tables of
Destiny:*

I first resolved to search out the Laws of Time on the day
after the battle of Tsushima, when news of the battle reached
the Yaroslavl district where I was then living, in the village of
Burmakino at Kuznetsov's.
I wanted to discover the reason for all those deaths.
(*VKCW*, 418)

The relation of number to death provides a mysterious, wholly illogical framing device for Khlebnikov's study of history. It is, to begin
with, hardly coincidental that Khlebnikov's first mathematical tabulation of historical events was made in November 1914, just a few

**Figure 6.** Reconstruction of Tatlin's *Monument to the Third International,* made by Christopher Cross, Jeremy Dixon, Sven Rindl, Peter Watson, and Christopher Woodward, 1971, for the exhibition Art in Revolution, London.

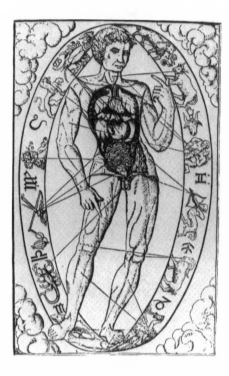

**Figure 7.** Jollat, *Zodiacal Man.* 1553. Woodcut.

**Figure 8.** *Man, Alchemy and the Cosmos,* from J. Manget, *Bibliotheca chemica curiosa,* Geneva, 1702.

months into the war, when he was home in Astrakhan, on leave from his infantry regiment. In a letter to Mikhail Matiushin, Khlebnikov appends some "Notes" that were supposed to be published in his 1914 pamphlet *A New Theory of War, Battles 1915–1917*. Here he introduces for the first time the formula: "365 ± 48 may be understood generally as $365 ± (365 + 28)$; $19^2 = 361$; the period of 28 years is connected with the lunar month of 28 days" (*VKCW*, 94). Note that 365 is the "number of numbers" because it signifies the periodicity of the annual cycle; 48 is derived from the sum of the lunar month (28 days) and the square root of 365, which is rounded off as 20. In any case, the formula provides Khlebnikov with such recurrences as the following:

> 4. Years of invention and scientific discovery sometimes fall
> into very regular patterns, like waves. Take for instance 1542,
> the date of Copernicus' Laws:
>> after 28 × 3 years,
>>> 1626: Willebrord Snell's laws of the refraction of
>>> light.
>> after 28 × 2 years,
>>> 1682: Isaac Newton's Laws of Universal Gravity
>> after 28 × 2 years,
>>> 1738: Laws of the Speed of Sound. The Academy.
>> (*VKCW*, 95)

And so on. Within a few years, Khlebnikov had developed this system, together with his *zaum* language, of which more in a moment, into what he called "The Futurian Scale": "If we conceive of all mankind as a string, then the most diligent and thorough study reveals that there is an interval of 317 years between soundings of the string. The most suitable method for determining that interval is to study similar points in time" (*VKCW*, 386). He begins by relating wars and migrations according to this interval, but then he shifts to more peculiar conjunctions:

> The scale consists of the following accords: 317 days, a
> twenty-four-hour period, 237 seconds, an infantry man's
> march step or a heart-beat (which are identical in time), a sin-
> gle vibration of the A string, and the vibration of the lowest
> sound in the alphabet *u*. . . . This string serves as the central
> axis of the art of music. If we take 70 beats per minute as the
> rate of the male heartbeat, and assuming that beat to be a
> year, for which we are to find a single day, we discover that
> day in the vibration of the same A string: in the average beat
> of the male heart it occurs 365 times. This scale forges into a
> single register wars, years, days, steps, heartbeats. . . .
> (*VKCW*, 386–87)

But of course the "single register," what Khlebnikov calls "the great sonic art of the future," exists because the poet wills it to, because he requires a map on which wars, years, days, steps, and heartbeats, male and female, can be plotted.

That map kept expanding so as to take in the whole universe. In "The Wheel of Births" (1919), Khlebnikov declares:

> It is not the planets' fault that we do not hear them. The wheel of births is in no way at fault because our hearing cannot distinguish the sound it makes, the metallic whoosh of its vanes. We may ask how it is possible to discover a general law for the births of similar individuals who champion one and the same cause if they are born in different states and as members of different nations. But humanity was long ago united by the state of lightning, which plaits the hair of all peoples into one braid. (*VKCW,* 411)

The perception of the One in the Many now takes on a mystical cast. Yet the actual placement of great men is, like Yeats's, shrewdly practical: still using 365 as his base, Khlebnikov notes:

> According to Bucke (in *Cosmic Consciousness*), Jesus was born six years before the start of the Christian era in 6 B.C., 365 years after Mencius. 365 × 4 years after Jesus in 1454, came Savonarola, "friend of the poor, scourge of the rich." 365 × 5 years after Jesus, in 1819, Walt Whitman was born, and Karl Marx in 1818. Another example: Karl Marx came 365 × 8 years after the Brahmin Buddha, according to the *Bhagavata Purana.*
>
> So Whitman is identical with Jesus, spattered by sparks from the factory workbench rather than by seaspray and the dust of the road. (*VKCW,* 411)

These reincarnations—Christ as Savonarola as Marx as Whitman, Christ as factory worker rather than humble peasant—seem to satisfy Khlebnikov's innate desire for structure. It remained to simplify the original number schemes. In *The Tables of Destiny,* completed the year of Khlebnikov's death in 1922, the 365 ± 48 scheme gives way to a system of "orderly multinomials based on three and on two," "the lowest possible even and odd numbers" (*VKCW,* 420). "I understood," writes Khlebnikov, "that the true nature of time consists in the recurrent multiplication of itself by twos and threes, and when I recalled the old Slavic belief in the powers of 'odd and even' I decided that wisdom was indeed a tree that grows from a seed. The superstition is all in the quotation marks" (*VKCW,* 420).

Given this recognition of the relativity of the contingent, "The past suddenly became transparently clear" (*VKCW,* 420). All events fall into two opposing classes: "The path of freedom, of life, of growth, lies through the power of two. The path of power, of death, of struggle, 'the closed expanse,' lies through the power of three" (p. 403). Thus, "an event upon reaching an age of 3" days changes its sign to the reverse . . . upon completion of the time sequence represented by the numerical structure $3^n$ events stands in the same relation to each other as two trains proceeding in opposite directions along the same track. . . . Thus do *yes* and *no* constantly reverse themselves" (pp. 423–24). For example:

. . . between the Moscow uprising of December 22, 1905, and
March 13, 1917 [two like events], $2^{12}$ days elapsed; between
the conquest of Siberia in 1581 and the retreat of the Russians
at Mukden in 1905 on February 25 [two opposite events],
$3^{10} + 310$ days elapsed. When the future becomes clear
thanks to these computations, the feeling of time disappears;
it's as if you were standing motionless on the deck of fore-
knowledge of the future. The feeling of time vanishes, and it
begins to resemble a field in front of you and a field behind; it
becomes a kind of space. (*VKCW*, 137)

The spatialization of time described metaphorically in that last sentence is of course characteristic, not just of Khlebnikov, but of modernist poetics in general. But the question remains *why* time should so be spatialized, why a poet as sophisticated and subtle as Khlebnikov, whose production includes plays, short stories, manifestos, librettos, critical essays, epics, and prophecies, and who was trained in linguistics and the natural sciences as well as mathematics, should want to reduce all events, from wars and battles to the footsteps and heartbeats of unnamed individuals, to the powers of two and three?

To begin with, we must take into account that Khlebnikov's *Tables of Destiny* were elaborated at a time of great national crisis—first war, then revolution, then the bloody fighting in its aftermath. In the winter of 1919, when Khlebnikov was living with his family in Kharkov, the city alternately fell into the hands of the Red and White armies. To avoid serving in the army, Khlebnikov voluntarily entered a psychiatric hospital, where he spent more than a year. But once in the hospital, he contracted typhus, a disease from which he never fully recovered. For the last two years of his life, he lived in the most extreme poverty and near-starvation. It was in Baku, on the southern front, when he was living in a maritime dormitory and working on propaganda posters for the cultural section of the Volga-Caspian fleet, that he formulated his fundamental algorithms.[14] A letter to his sister Vera (2 January 1921) is both poignant and revealing. Khlebnikov begins by telling Vera that he has finally conquered "the serpent" but that it has been a hard battle because "people remain people" and his "visions of the future," which he read as "a report at a scholarly meeting at Red Star University," fell on deaf ears:

It's true I put them through the most exquisite tor-
ments: I announced to the Marxists that I represented Marx
squared, and to those who preferred Mohammed I announced
that I was the continuation of the teachings of Mohammed,
who was henceforth silenced since the Number had now
replaced the Word. I called my report the Koran of Numbers.
Which is why those whose self-esteem goes no further
than getting a pair of boots as a reward for good behavior and
loyal thoughts have drawn away from me, and now watch me
with terrified eyes. (*VKCW*, 125)

And at the end of the letter, he remarks sadly, "I have forgotten the
world of poetry and sound, I have cast them as sacrifices into the
bonfire of numbers. But a little while longer and the sacred gift of
speech will return to me" (*VKCW*, 126)

The poet's dark mood did not last; soon he was buoyantly
telling his friends that he had discovered "the fundamental Law of
Time." But here the paradox of number enters, for Khlebnikov's
tabulations, abstract as they seem, have everything to do with his
own life. Numerical laws, he argued, "foretell the future, not through
the foaming mouths of the ancient prophets but by using cold
rational calculations." Accordingly,

we can say in all seriousness that in a certain year a certain
individual will be born, someone, let us simply say, whose
destiny will be similar to the destiny of someone born 365
years earlier. And then our attitude to death will change as
well: we stand at the threshold of a world in which we will
know the day and hour of our rebirth; we will be able to look
upon death as a temporary plunge into the waves of nonbeing.
(*VKCW*, 389)

And that, of course, is the crux. Khlebnikov came of age at a
time when "the foaming mouths of the ancient prophets" were suspect but when daily life, everywhere permeated by violence and
death, seemed to make it impossible to dwell, let us say, in a Blakean
or Wordsworthian world where the growth of a poet's soul, the
exploration of individual self-consciousness, could be regarded as
centrally important. "If," writes Khlebnikov in his 1920 essay "On
Poetry, "we consider artistic creativity as the greatest possible deviation of the string of thought from the axis of the creator's life, as a
flight from the self, then we have good reason for believing that even
poems about an assembly line will be written not by someone who
works on an assembly line, but by someone from beyond the factory
walls" (*VKCW*, 372). Distancing, what Khlebnikov calls the "strange
scientific vision . . . into the subtle life of the heart," is all. Thus the
poet's autobiography is likely to take the form of lists—lists of the
books he has written, rivers he has crossed, cities he has visited, the
kinds of blood in his veins: "The equations of my soul: I was born

October 28, 1885 $+ 3^8 + 3^8 =$ November 3, 1921; at the Red Star
in Baku I predicted the Soviet Government, December 17, 1920 $=$
$2 \times 3^8 - 317$; I was elected President of Planet Earth on $3^8 + 3^8 -$
$3^7 - 48 =$ December 20, 1915 . . ." ("From the Notebooks," *VKCW*,
402). But just when such a list is likely to lull us into inattention, the
poet abruptly breaks off and adds, "The future escapes us because
we are lazy." And he adds aphoristically, "Power, the laws of states,
is a closed body in space. The spatial yes" (p. 402). Such aphoristic
intrusions, often highly metaphoric and gnomic, give Khlebnikov's
prophetic prose its peculiar cast. A sentence like "The detonation
depends not upon force, but on measurement (exactitude)" is followed by the aphorism "The footsoldier's march step destroys the
bridge he crosses" (*VKCW*, 405), an aphorism not so un-Blakean
after all. Or again, the notion of an "armor made of numbers" does
not preclude the imperative to "spit in death's eye, no matter what
form it comes in"—an imperative that brings us full circle back to
Yeats.


### III

Like Khlebnikov's *Tables of Destiny,* Yeats's *Vision* was composed at a time of war and revolution: it was begun, by Yeats's
own account, "On the afternoon of October 24th 1917, four days
after my marriage, [when] my wife surprised me by attempting automatic writing,"[15] and the first edition was published in 1925, two
years after the bloody Irish Civil War ended. But unlike Khlebnikov,
Yeats made no attempt to invent his own numerical tables, his basic
paradigms—the Twenty-Eight Phases of the Moon, the Platonic
Year, the 2,000-year cycles of history—being drawn, quite eclecti-
cally, from his various occult and philosophical sources. Indeed,
Book I (in the 1937 edition), "The Great Wheel," buttresses its
account of the antithetical gyres with references to Empedocles,
Simplicius (as quoted by Pierre Duhem in *Le Système du monde*),
Macrobius, Plotinus, Thomas Aquinas, Giovanni Gentile, Bishop
Berkeley, Kant, Jakob Böhme, Hegel, Swedenborg, Blake, and
Flaubert—all within the space of the first six pages. As such, critics
outside the particular circle of Yeats specialists have tended to treat
*A Vision* as something of an embarrassment, a source, no doubt, of
"metaphors for poetry," as Yeats himself puts it (*AV*, 8), but hardly
a worthy successor of, say, Neoplatonic or Blakean cosmologies.
Thus Northrop Frye deplores "the absence of any sense of a demonic
world" in *A Vision*, "Visions of horror and violence . . . all [being]
rationalised and explained away as part of the necessary blood-bath
accompanying the birth of his new and repulsive Messiah."[16] And in

his excellent survey of number symbolism, Christopher Butler refers to *A Vision* as "confused," "unclear," and "idiosyncratic"—a muddled and belated version of Renaissance Neoplatonic treatises that tries "to subdue what is ultimately a vision of history to an aesthetic and astrological order" derived from Theosophy.[17]

As in the case of Khlebnikov, however, the interesting question is less whether Yeats was true to Plotinian or Blakean precepts than why he should become so obsessed with number in the first place, why, for example, he should find it satisfying to assign specific numerical points along the Great Wheel to his fellow artists and writers as well as to the "beautiful women" of his life and to historical and mythological figures. During the nineties, after all, when Yeats was composing *The Rose* and *The Wind among the Reeds,* whose poems draw at least as heavily upon occult sources as does *A Vision,* his dialectic revolved around the opposition of Rose (Kabbalistic White Woman, Helen of Troy, Ireland) and Cross, the alchemical opposition of silver and gold, and the related oppositions of the Four Elements, especially Fire and Wind. True, the magic numbers of the tetratkys, *four* and *ten* (four elements, four seasons, four times of day, four compass points; ten *Sephiroth* composing the universe and hence ten stages the adept must ascend in his movement toward union with Godhead), play a role here,[18] but what mattered in the early poetry was the question of *ascent* itself—the serpent twining around the Sephirotic tree—rather than the question of numerical system.

The turn to mathematics in the later work may be glossed by Yeats's cryptic references, in two successive letters to Olivia Shakespear (April 1926), to Whitehead's newly published *Science and the Modern World:*

> I have found a very difficult but profound person Whitehead, who seems to have reached my own conclusions about ultimate things [i.e., in *A Vision*]. He has written down the game of chess and I, like some Italian Prince, have made the pages and court ladies have it out on the lawn. Not that he would recognize his abstract triumph in my gay rabble.

And he continues a week later:

> The work of Whitehead's I have read is *Science and the Modern World.* . . . He thinks that nothing exists but "organisms," or minds—the "cones" of my book—and that there is no such thing as an object "localized in space," except the minds, and that which we call physical objects of all kinds are "aspects" or "vistas" of other "organisms"—in my book the "Body of Fate" of one's being is but the "Creative mind" of another. . . . We create each other's universe. . . . It is as though we stood in the midst of space and saw upon all sides . . . the rays of stars—but that we suppose, through a limit

placed upon our perceptions, that some stars were at our
elbow, or even between our hands. He also uses the "Quantum Theory" when speaking of minute organisms—mole-
cules—in a way that suggests "antithetical" and "primary.". . .

His packed logic, his way of saying just enough and no
more, his difficult scornful lucidity seem to me the intellectual
equivalent of my own imaginative richness of suggestion.[19]

It is doubtful that Yeats, himself a notoriously poor mathe-
matician, understood much about quantum theory, but Whitehead's
account of it in chapters 8 and 9 of *Science and the Modern World*
is entirely consonant with Yeats's own faith in interpenetration, his
conviction that "whereas subjectivity . . . tends to separate man from
man, objectivity brings us back to the mass where we begin" (*AV*,
72). Thus Whitehead insists that "a philosophy of nature as organic
must start at the opposite end to that requisite for a materialistic
philosophy. The materialistic starting point is from independently
existing substances, matter and mind"; whereas "the organic starting point is from the analysis of process as the realisation of events
disposed in an interlocked community. The event is the unit of things
real" (ANW, 218–19).[20] And further: this recognition of the universe
as one of *prehension,* each subject also functioning as an object and
vice versa in a system of interrelationships, was derived, so Whitehead says, from "my own studies in mathematics and mathematical
physics . . . [which] presumes in the first place an electromagnetic
field of activity pervading space and time." Within that field, "the
intrinsic character of the observer is merely relevant in order to fix
the self-identical individuality of the physical entities. These entities
are only considered agencies in fixing the routes in space and in
time of the life histories of enduring entities" (ANW, 220).

Here Yeats evidently found "scientific" confirmation of the
Heraclitean doctrine "Dying each other's life, living each other's
death," which provides him with his starting point in *A Vision* (*AV*,
68). A's "Creative Mind" is B's "Body of Fate" and so on: each
"event" depends on every other. "The originality of mathematics,"
writes Whitehead, "consists in the fact that in mathematical science
connections between things are exhibited which, apart from the
agency of human reason, are extremely unobvious" (ANW, 29). It
was these *unobvious* connections that the modernist poet, renounc-
ing what Whitehead called the nineteenth-century "discord between
the aesthetic intuitions of mankind and the mechanism of science"
(ANW, 127), might draw out. And mathematics provides the *modus
operandi.* Indeed, Whitehead suggests that the omission of "mathematical ideas of successive epochs" is analogous to the omission, if
not of Hamlet in the play by that title, at least of Ophelia: "For
Ophelia is quite essential to the play, she is very charming—and a
little mad. Let us grant that the pursuit of mathematics is a divine

madness of the human spirit, a refuge from the goading urgency of contingent happenings" (ANW, 31).

This notion of mathematics as "divine madness" providing a "refuge" from contingency echoes Yeats's own brashly anti-Wordsworthian formulation, expressed in the closing lines of "Meditations in Time of Civil War" (1923), that:

> The abstract joy,
> The half-read wisdom of daemonic images,
> Suffice the ageing man as once the growing boy.[21]

More important: when Yeats set out to rework the 1925 version of *A Vision,* the occult doctrine of the earlier years was buttressed by a larger concern for *series* and *system.* Consider the framing now provided by the addition, in the form of an introduction, of *A Packet for Ezra Pound,* written in 1928.

On the opening page of *A Packet,* Yeats refers to Pound as the poet "whose art is the opposite of mine, whose criticism commends what I most condemn, a man with whom I should quarrel more than with anyone else if we were not united by affection" (*AV,* 4).[22] But then he cites Pound's explanation of the form of the *Cantos,* then numbering twenty-seven:

> There will be no plot, no chronicle of events, no logic of discourse, but two themes, the Descent into Hades from Homer, a Metamorphosis from Ovid, and, mixed with these, medieval or modern historical characters. . . . He has scribbled on the back of an envelope certain sets of letters that represent emotions or archetypal events—I cannot find any adequate definition—A B C D and then J K L M, and then each set of letters repeated, and then A B C D inverted and this repeated, and then a new element X Y Z, then certain letters that never recur and then all sorts of combinations of X Y Z and J K L M and A B C D and D C B A, and all set whirling together. He has shown me upon the wall a photograph of a Cosimo Tura decoration in three compartments, in the upper the Triumph of Love and the Triumph of Chastity, in the middle Zodiacal signs, and in the lower certain events in Cosimo Tura's day. The Descent and the Metamorphosis— A B C D and J K L M—his fixed elements, took the place of the Zodiac, the archetypal persons—X Y Z—that of the Triumphs, and certain modern events—his letters that do not recur—that of those events in Cosimo Tura's day.

And having given this careful summary, Yeats comments: "I may, now that I have recovered leisure, find that the mathematical structure, when taken up into imagination, is more than mathematical, that seemingly irrelevant details fit together into a single theme" (*AV,* 4–5).

Why does Yeats dwell at such length on the "mathematical structure" hypothesized by the poet "whose art is the opposite of mine, whose criticism commends what I most condemn"?[23] Is he merely being coy? Or is his use of Pound's structural diagrams a nicely calculated move, designed to offset his skeptical reader's suspicions of his Gnostic reveries? For if a poet as different from himself as Pound can use number series generated by the alphabet to organize his "immense poem," and if a poet as antithetical as Pound can rely on the signs of the zodiac in building his structure, why not Yeats himself?

Indeed, in the letter "To Ezra Pound" that concludes the introduction of *A Vision,* having posed the question, "What if there is an arithmetic or geometry that can exactly measure the slope of a balance, the dip of a scale, and so date the coming of that something?" Yeats cites Pound's "The Return," as "giv[ing] me better words than my own" (*AV*, 29) to answer the question. Not that "The Return" makes so much as a single reference to measure, scale, or date, but Yeats evidently reads it as synecdochic for Pound's larger Vorticist poetics, as expressed especially in *Gaudier-Brzeska* (1916), where mathematical equations provide analogues to the poetic process. As Pound puts it:

> . . . we learn that the equation $(x - a)^2 + (y - b)^2 = r^2$ governs the circle. It is the circle. It is not a particular circle, it is any circle and all circles. It is nothing that is not a circle. It is the circle free of space and time limits. It is the universal, existing in perfection, in freedom from space and time. . . . in analytics we come upon a new way of dealing with form. . . . The difference between art and analytical geometry is the difference of subject-matter only.

And he adds, in an aside that must have reassured Yeats, "This statement does not interfere in the least with 'spontaneity' and 'intuition,' or with their function in art."[24]

Intuition/abstraction, spontaneous gesture/circle—here again is the central paradox of number. Yeats's Historical Cones, as diagrammed and explained in book 5: "Dove or Swan" of the 1937 edition of *A Vision,* have no counterpart in Pound's *Cantos,* and their actual calculus of the rise and fall of civilizations is closer to Oswald Spengler's *Decline of the West* than to, say, Khlebnikov's *Tables of Destiny.* Khlebnikov's significant reincarnations have to do with war and revolution, battle and conquest; Yeats's, by contrast, are those of "great" artistic civilizations: fifth-century B.C. Athenian civilization being reincarnated, a thousand years later, by fifth-century A.D. Byzantium and then—in another thousand years—by A.D. 1500 Renaissance Italy. A typical Khlebnikov chain of incarnations links the Brahmin Buddha to Jesus to Savonarola ("friend of the poor, scourge of the rich") to Karl Marx (the interval being $365^n$); a typical Yeats chain connects Phidias to a sixth-century Byzantine goldworker to Michelangelo (the interval being the thousand-year subwheel at its 15th phase). But both believe that, in Khlebnikov's words, "an event upon reaching an age of $3^n$ [or other numerical value] days changes its sign to the reverse" (*VKCW*, 423), and that, again in Khlebnikov's words, "those who have no ordinary watch, would do well to wear the great timepiece of humanity and pay heed to its regular movements, its tick-tick-tick" (*VKCW*, 425). The concept of reincarnation, even when it involves an image as ominous as Yeats's rough beast, "slouch[ing] towards Bethlehem to be born," provides what Whitehead called a "refuge from the goading urgency of contingent happenings." To put it another way: that which can be placed at a particular point on a given spectrum (e.g., Maud Gonne at Phase 14 on the Great Wheel, Mrs. Yeats at 16, Lady Gregory at 24—the female sex being assigned even numbers according to ancient tradition) is no longer threatening; the absorption into system gives it a place and habitation. It is in this sense that Yeats's "circuits of the sun and moon" have, as he puts it, "helped me to hold in a single thought reality and justice" (*AV,* 25).

## *IV*

But having opted for "mathematical structure," Yeats by no means carries the "pursuit of number" to the length we find in Khlebnikov and what was to become characteristic of postmodernism. The clue here is in Yeats's attitude toward free verse—"the American vice," as he was fond of calling it.[25] In his 1937 essay "A General Introduction to My Work," Yeats explains:

> Because I need a passionate syntax for passionate subject-matter I compel myself to accept those traditional metres that have developed with the language. Ezra Pound, Turner, Lawrence wrote admirable free verse, I could not. I would lose myself, become joyless like those mad old women. . . . If I wrote of personal love or sorrow in free verse, or in any rhythm that left it unchanged, amid all its accidence, I would be full of self-contempt because of my egotism and indiscretion, and foresee the boredom of my reader. I must choose a traditional stanza, even what I alter must seem traditional.[26]

Here is what we might call the Romantic residue in Yeats's self-imposed drive toward modernity. When it comes to verse form, the meaning of *number* Yeats adopts is the relatively late variant, first used in the Renaissance: "Metrical periods or feet; hence, lines,

verses" (*OED* 18b), the earliest example given coming from Shakespeare's *Love's Labour's Lost* (1588): "I fear these stubborn lines
lack power to move . . . These numbers will I tear and write in
prose." Number as meter, we should note, has a very different status
from number as symbol or as relational property: "Easter 1916," for
example, is written in trimeter but the poem is not built around the
meanings of 3 or of X to the third power. Again, the choice of a
particular meter raises particular reader expectations, the metrical
form (e.g., the Petrarchan iambic pentameter sonnet or ottava rima,
the tetrameter quatrain) insuring recognition *as such*. Indeed, Yeats
liked the discipline of the fixed stanza, remarking that "when I wrote
in blank verse I was dissatisfied . . . our Heroic Age went better, or
so I fancied, in the ballad metre of *The Green Helmet*" (*E & I*, 523).

Such talk of "our Heroic Age," of "a passionate syntax for
passionate subject-matter," coincides with Yeats's continued self-
presentation as the "last Romantic," the defender of "Traditional
sanctity and loveliness" ("Coole Park and Ballylee, 1931"), even as
his deeper instincts were to Make It New—witness his response to
Whitehead's discussion of quantum theory and his fascination,
against his better judgment, with the structural principles of Pound's
*Cantos.* The resulting tension between "Numbers" and Number is
pervasive in the poems of the later twenties and thirties, in which
dialectic and what we might call *trialectic* replaces the meditative,
developmental structure of, say, "The Wild Swans at Coole" or "A
Prayer for My Daughter."

Consider "At Algeciras—a Meditation upon Death," written in
response to Yeats's serious illness of October 1928 and first published in *A Packet for Ezra Pound* (1929), though not included in
the version of *A Packet* that became the introduction to *A Vision:*

> The heron-billed pale cattle-birds
> That feed on some foul parasite
> Of the Moroccan flocks and herds
> Cross the narrow Straits to light
> In the rich midnight of the garden trees
> Till the dawn break upon those mingled seas.
>
> Often at evening when a boy
> Would I carry to a friend—
> Hoping more substantial joy
> Did an older mind commend—
> Not such as are in Newton's metaphor,
> But actual shells of Rosses' level shore.
>
> Greater glory in the sun,
> An evening chill upon the air,
> Bid imagination run

Much on the Great Questioner;
What He can question, what if questioned I
Can with a fitting confidence reply.

(*VP*, 493–94)

"At Algeciras" is composed of three stanzas rhyming *a b a b c c*—
a tetrameter quatrain followed by a pentameter couplet. But this
quite conventional ballad structure is crossed by a double dialectic
between rival conceptions of number. There is first the opposition,
as stated in "Newton's metaphor" referred to in the second stanza,
between the countable "actual shells on Rosses' level shore" and
the vast ocean beyond it, between, that is to say, the pretty but petty
distractions of daily life and "the great ocean of truth [that] lay all
undiscovered before me."[27] And second, this opposition is subsumed
in the larger dialectic between the particular moment of crisis when
the old dispensation gives way to the new ("the rich midnight of the
garden trees") and the cycle of reincarnations, as imaged in the
"cross[ing of] the narrow straits" by the "heron-billed" birds, who
"light" in the trees only until "the dawn break upon those mingled
seas." This reintroduction of the reality principle—"an evening chill
upon the air"—bids "imagination run / Much on the Great Questioner," but in "At Algeciras," the Great Question elicits what is
evidently an affirmative response, given the "fitting confidence" with
which the poet replies—a confidence the reader cannot quite comprehend, given that neither question nor response are specified.

If the topos of "At Algeciras" is thus Romantic,[28] its articulation, as we have seen, is not. Quatrain structure and couplet clinch-
ing are locked in a peculiar tension with the poem's larger drive
toward abstraction, the movement whereby specific time frames—
"the rich midnight of the garden trees" and the "dawn break[ing]
upon those mingled seas"—give way to the timeless, numberless
Great Questioner. But of course the Great Questioner must be designated as 1 and so "At Algeciras" can be read as the absorption of
3 (the number of stanzas) into 1 and then of 1 into a spatialized
present. The sequential model of Romantic meditations on death—
say, Keats's "Ode to a Nightingale"—gives way to gnomic, highly
formalized utterance.

The tension between meditative flow and mathematical arrest
is something of a Yeats signature in the later poems. In "Among
School Children," for example, the linear progression from "I walk
through the long schoolroom questioning" (stanza 1) to the epiphany
of the eighth stanza is repeatedly crossed by the figure 3: the three
philosophers (Plato, Aristotle, Pythagoras), three female images
(lover, mother, nun), three qualities associated with the three kinds
of love—sexual, maternal, spiritual—presented both positively (passion, piety, and affection) and negatively ("The body . . . not bruised

to pleasure soul, / Nor beauty born of its own despair, / Nor blear-eyed wisdom out of midnight oil"), and, finally, the chestnut tree in its three aspects—leaf, blossom, and bole. These triads are complicated by the relationship of 3 to 2, 2 marking the poem's dialectic between male and female, child and man, dancer and dance, indeed "the yolk and white of the one egg." And further, the poem's ottava rima (a b a b a b c c) may be said to enact the very pull between 3 (e.g., "Are you the leaf, the blossom, or the bole?") and 2 ("How can we know the dancer from the dance?").

Such numerical structures are frequent enough in the poems of *The Tower* and *The Winding Stair*, but we should not exaggerate their role. For Yeats is reluctant to take the experiment too far, reluctant to engage in, say, Poundian experiments as when "A B C D and D C B A [are] all set whirling together" (*AV*, 5)— a case, as Yeats put it elsewhere, of "not getting all the wine into the bowl."[29] Indeed, in such late poems as "The Statues" (*VP*, 610–11), mathematics becomes overt theme—the "trac[ing of] / The lineaments of a plummet-measured face"—rather than the "hidden" form that characterizes works like Khlebnikov's "supersaga" *Zangezi*, a pageant play in which scenes are replaced by numbered "planes" from 1 to 20, the planes being defined by the mathematical multiples defined in *The Tables of Destiny*.

The future, in this respect, was to belong to Pound and Khlebnikov rather than to Yeats, but not until Romantic notions of organic unity, of plenitude, of getting all the wine into the bowl gave way to the artifice and playfulness that we think of as postmodern. In the half century since Yeats's death, *numbers* have increasingly been replaced, either by a free verse where lineation as such seems to be the only criterion for poetry, or by *number* as generative device: the artist derives his or her text from, say, the Fibonacci series (1, 2, 3, 5, 8, 13 . . .) or from a mesostic rule or from alphabet series or from lipograms (texts where one letter is proscribed), and so on.

The common wisdom is that when postmodern writers like Samuel Beckett or John Cage use such generative devices, the "spiritual" dimension inherent in Khlebnikov's or Yeats's mathematics has given way to an intentional and ironized nominalism—a desire to empty the signifier of its accrued symbolic meanings so that 5, as in Johns's elegantly painted numerals (see fig. 2), is always and only 5. But it is a good question whether the concentration on what is, after all, a pure abstraction isn't itself an example of what Khlebnikov called *zaum*, "beyonsense." Let me conclude with a brief glance at a recent exemplar of mathematical form: Georges Perec's astonishing novel *La Vie mode d'emploi* (1978).[30]

The focus of this novel is on the lives of the inhabitants of a single block of apartments at 11 Rue Simon-Crubellier in Paris. A cross-sectional plan of this block is printed as an appendix to the

| | 1 | 2 | 3 | 4 | 5 | 6 | 7 | 8 | 9 | 0 |
|---|---|---|---|---|---|---|---|---|---|---|
| 1 | 59 | 83 | 15 | 10 | 57 | 48 | 7 | 52 | 45 | 54 |
| | Hutting | | | | | | | Plassaert | | |
| 2 | 97 | 11 | 58 | 82 | 16 | 9 | 46 | 55 | 6 | 51 |
| 3 | 84 | ˒60 | Dinteville 96 | 14 | 47 | 56 | 49 | Winckler 8 | 53 | 44 |
| 4 | Réol 12 | 98 | 81 | 86 | 95 | 17 | 28 | Foulerot 43 | 50 | 5 |
| 5 | Berger 61 | 85 | Rorschach 13 | 18 | 27 | 79 | 94 | 4 | 41 | 30 |
| 6 | Bartelbooth 99 | 70 | 26 | 80 | 87 | 1 | 42 | 29 | 93 | 3 |
| 7 | Altamont 25 | 62 | 88 | 69 | 19 | 36 | 78 | Beaumont 2 | 31 | 40 |
| 8 | 71 | Moreau 65 | 20 | 23 | 89 | 68 | 34 | Louvet 37 | 77 | 92 |
| 9 | 63 | 24 | Marcia 66 | 73 | 35 | 22 | 90 | 75 | 39 | 32 |
| 0 | * | 72 | 64 | 21 | 67 | 74 | 38 | 33 | 91 | 76 |

**Figure 9.** Georges Perec, cross-section for block of flats in *La Vie mode d'emploi,* as refigured by David Bellos, in *Scripsi* 5, no. 1 (1988): 67.

novel, but since the plan is, of necessity, two-dimensional, it cannot fully represent the book's spatial puzzle-plot. Perec's English translator, David Bellos, has reproduced this plan, filling in the number divisions of the grid and the number position of the respective chapters (fig. 9), his diagram illustrating the point that Perec's fictional block of apartments is a variation on the knight's tour problem in chess.

In the game of chess the knight moves one square in one direction and two squares in a direction at right angles to the first, and the "knight's tour" is the route the knight would have to travel right around the eight-by-eight board touching every square once only. But Perec's "board" is, as he himself explains in a 1979 essay, the Greco-Roman square of ten, so that the "plot" begins on the stairs, five squares from the right and five from the bottom, and ends up in Bartlebooth's study, first on the left and five from the bottom.[31]

But the ten-by-ten grid means that there should be 100 chapters in
the book and there are only 99. As Bellos explains it:

> Perec solved the oversize Knight's Tour, then bent his solution
> with the express purpose of making the reader's puzzling pro-
> cess different from, and incommensurable with, the construc-
> tor's puzzle-making. In the bottom left-hand corner, the
> knight moves from grid square 2, 8 on the 65th move to
> square 1, 0 on the 66th, and then to 3, 9 on the 67th. The
> moves are regular but no chapter in the novel corresponds to
> that 66th move. Moves 67–100 correspond to chapters 66–99.
> This is a particularly clear instance of *clinamen* (a term which
> goes back to Lucretius' representation of the Epicurean view
> that life had its origins in a kind of error or bend). . . . the
> procedure is disguised by a deliberate imperfection.[32]

That imperfection works in a variety of ways. The number 99 (the
final chapter) unlocks what is the central mystery of the novel: to
wit, what happens to Percival Bartlebooth's grand design of spending
ten years learning to paint watercolors and then twenty years trav-
eling, painting roughly one watercolor per fortnight, five hundred
seascapes in all, which would be sent back to Paris to be pasted up
and transformed into jigsaw puzzles and stored in black boxes made
by Madame Hourcade, to await his return. As it turns out, various
events interfere with this plan and Bartlebooth falls behind sched-
ule. Chapter 99 opens with a description of Bartlebooth's study,
"lined with dark wooden bookshelves; most of them are now empty,
but 61 black boxes still remain" (Perec, 493). Why 61? Because
Bartlebooth, as we soon learn, died while working on Puzzle 439.
So much for straightforward arithmetic. But—and this is how Perec
plants his number clues—chapter 99 (see fig. 9) is located at grid
square 1, 6 or 61 reversed. And further, the timing of Bartlebooth's
death has been predicted in chapter 51, where a polymath-adven-
turer named Carel van Loorens tries to prove a mathematical conun-
drum known as Goldbach's hypothesis, which says that any number
$n$ is the sum of $K$ primes. Bellos points out that although there is
apparently no mathematical proof of this hypothesis, in the novel it
is borne out as a literary procedure. "For if $n$ be 500, and if $K$ be
set for the sake of rigour and simplicity at 2, then Bartlebooth's
position at the end of the novel . . . is a spectacular demonstration
that the arbitrary number 500 is indeed the sum of two prime numbers: $500 = 439 + 61$" (Bellos, 69).

But, someone is sure to object, what is the point of such buried
number games? And is the reader of *La Vie mode d'emploi* so much
as aware of these puzzles, given that the novel can be read as a
perfectly "realistic" tale of the lives and loves of the various inhabitants of 11 Rue Simon-Crubellier, a tale complicated by a rich
mélange of romantic stories within stories—tales of jewel thefts,

murder, unwanted pregnancies? And further, if there is no way to detect the larger numerical structure of the novel except retrospectively, what is gained by Perec's trickiness?

Perhaps such procedure is best understood as a kind of redemptive gesture, the visionary insertion, however unconscious, of the fourth dimension into the literary text.[33] When, that is to say, *number* as ec-centric foregrounding of material that "literature" usually places under erasure replaces or complements the *numbers* (e.g., the number of stresses or syllables per line or, in the case of a novel like Perec's, the ordonnance of sentences, paragraphs, chapters) that constitute its perceptible formal frame, the established contract between writer and reader breaks down. In the case of a fourteen-line poem written in iambic pentameter and rhyming *a b b a a b b a c d e c d e*, for example, the numerical contract between poet and audience is established as a given. But in the case of Khlebnikov's number "planes" or Perec's chess game, which takes place on an "imperfect" ten-by-ten grid, the authors' procedure remains mysterious and hidden until the time is, so to speak, judged ripe for the revelation that certain structures, invisible to the naked eye or ear, invisible, for that matter, to the naked intellect, have been there all along.

Think, for example, of the buried number 7, unobtrusively introduced in the small quatrain that constitutes part 4 of Yeats's "Nineteen Hundred and Nineteen"—"We who seven years ago / Talked of honor and of truth"—the magic Pythagorean and biblical number that can be construed as the missing point of rest in what is otherwise a six-part structure of unresolved and chaotic violence, culminating in the visionary coda, with its fearful image of Robert Artisson and Lady Kyteler. "I can recognize," says Yeats on the last page of "Dove or Swan," where he contemplates the influx of the antithetical gyre, "that the limit itself has become a new dimension, that this ever-hidden thing which makes us fold our hands has begun to press down upon multitudes" (*AV*, 300).

*Chapter Five*

# Lawrence's Lyric Theater:

## Birds, Beasts and Flowers

### I

*I*n September of 1920 D. H. Lawrence was staying at the Villa Canovaia in the hills above Florence. He was alone, Frieda having gone to Germany to visit her family. It is here that he wrote a dozen or so of the poems that were to be collected in what he called his "best book of poems," *Birds, Beasts and Flowers:* for example, "Pomegranate," "Figs," "Medlars and Sorb Apples," the tortoise poems, and the "Four Evangelical Beasts."[1] He was also rewriting the novel begun three years earlier that was to become *Aaron's Rod* (1922). Not surprisingly, similar motifs turn up in the novel and in the poems. I want to begin by looking at one such motif as an entrance into the world of Lawrence's poetry, a poetry I construe rather differently from the many critics who have read *Birds, Beasts and Flowers* as late versions of the Romantic quest for otherness, for the unconscious participation in natural process, the life-divine blood being.[2]

In chapter 19 of the novel Aaron Sisson takes a tram to Settignano. He feels a great need to escape all thoughts of the previous night, a night he spent with the Marquesa and his first night with a woman in many months. Although it is he who initiated the love affair, the actual physical contact leaves Aaron feeling "withered," "blasted—as if blighted by some electricity."[3] "He felt an intense resentment against the Marchesa. He felt that somehow, she had given him the scorpion." Hence the need to get away, to be alone in the Tuscan hills:

> He sat for long hours among the cypress trees of Tuscany. And never had any trees seemed so like ghosts, like soft, strange, pregnant presences. He lay and watched tall cypresses breathing and communicating, faintly moving and as it were walking in the small wind. And his soul seemed to leave him and to go far away, far back, perhaps, to where life was all different and time passed otherwise than time passes now. As in clairvoyance he perceived it: that our life is only a fragment of the shell of life. . . . In the dark, mindful silence and inflection of the cypress trees, lost races, lost languages, lost human ways of feeling and of knowing. Men have known as we can no more know, have felt as we can no more feel. Great life-realities gone into the darkness. But the cypresses commemorate. In the afternoon, Aaron felt the cypresses rising dark about him, like so many high visitants from an old, lost, lost subtle world, where men had the wonder of demons about them, the aura of demons, such as still clings to the cypresses, in Tuscany. (*AR*, 257)

The "aura of demons" clinging to the cypresses somehow reassures Aaron. "As he went home in the tram he softened," realizing that his hostility to the Marquesa had been excessive: "She had been generous, and the other thing, that he felt blasted afterwards, which was his experience, that was fate, and not her fault" (*AR*, 257).

It is true, of course, that Lawrence wants us to see the cypresses of this passage as demonic presences, visitants from the dark otherness of a chthonic divinity. But within the context of plot and character relationships, they can be seen, more accurately, as images of displacement, emblematic of Lawrence's longing, particularly acute in these years, to escape the world of threatening human sexuality. It is interesting to note, for example, that the cypresses are imaged in both male and female terms: "rising dark about him," they loom as great phallic beings, yet they are also, somewhat paradoxically, characterized as "soft, strange, pregnant presences."

As such, the cypress imagery seems to reflect Aaron's own sexual ambivalence. He has, we recall, left his wife, even though he says he still "loves" her, because he yearns for "clean and pure division, perfected singleness" (*AR*, 123). Before long, he falls under the spell of the charismatic Rawdon Lilly and becomes his disciple. After a brief fling with a girl named Josephine, he catches influenza and is nursed back to health by Lilly, who in a moment of crisis massages "the blond lower body of his patient" with camphor oil until "the spark [comes] back into the sick eyes, and the faint trace of a smile, faintly luminous, into the face" (*AR*, 91). Although Lilly and Aaron later quarrel, temporarily going their separate ways, they meet again in Florence, after the incident with the Marquesa; and in the last chapter Lilly is once again preaching the "exhaustion of the love-urge" and the need for submission to a strong male leader—in this case, himself.

In the poem "Cypresses," written at about the same time as the passage in *Aaron's Rod,* there is no such problematic narrative context. It begins:

Tuscan cypresses,
What is it?

Folded in like a dark thought
For which the language is lost,
Tuscan cypresses,
Is there a great secret?
Are our words no good?

The undeliverable secret,
Dead with a dead race and a dead speech, and yet
Darkly monumental in you,
Etruscan cypresses.[4]

By line 11 the *Tuscan* and the *Etruscan* have merged: "the undeliverable secret," it turns out, is that the cypress tree recalls the noble "subtly-smiling" Etruscan male:

Naked except for fanciful long shoes,
Going with insidious, half-smiling quietness
And some of Africa's imperturbable sang-froid
About a forgotten business.

(*CP,* 296)

In the course of the poem, the "Vicious dark cypresses . . . softly-swaying pillars of dark flame," become the "vicious, slender, tender-footed / Long-nosed men of Etruria." The poet invokes the ghosts of these "spirits of the lost," the "darkly lost." For the Etruscan consciousness, as Lawrence argues in *Etruscan Places,* expresses itself through the symbols of phallus and *arx*—"the womb of all the world, that brought forth all the creatures." And it was, so he posits, the hatred and fear of these two symbols—phallus and *arx*—on the part of the "puritan" Romans that brought about the destruction of the Etruscan world.[5]

What sort of poem is "Cypresses"? In *Birds, Beasts and Flowers,* says Joyce Carol Oates, Lawrence "honors the unknowable mysteries of other forms of life."[6] This is overtly true: certainly in "Cypresses" the poet tells us quite openly that he wants to bring back the dark secret of an alien consciousness. Yet to compare "Cypresses" with Romantic and neo-Romantic poems of communion with nature—Keats's and Shelley's odes, or, in our own time, the animistic lyrics of, say, James Wright or Galway Kinnell—is to find more difference than likeness. It is, I think, a question of tone: Lawrence's "I" is not an ecstatic, rapturous shaman, a prophet who must convey, in gnomic fragments, his mysterious vision. Rather, the voice that speaks to us is conversational, hectoring, nervous, energetic, funny, sardonic—the same voice we meet in Lawrence's remarkable letters as well as in such travel sketches as *Sea and Sardinia,* written a year after "Cypresses":

> Tuscan cypresses,
> What is it? . . .
>
> Is there a great secret?
> Are our words no good? . . .
>
> Ah, how I admire your fidelity,
> Dark cypresses!

*Einfühlung,* one might say, except that Lawrence's speaker knows very well that he is not, so to speak, alone in the room. Having addressed the cypresses as intimate friends ("Tuscan cypresses, / What is it?"), he does a kind of mental half-turn and asks, "Is it the secret of the long-nosed Etruscans?" Or again, "Were they then vicious, the slender, tender-footed / Long-nosed men of Etruria? / Or was their way only evasive and different, dark, like cypress trees in a wind?"

These questions are hardly addressed to the cypresses nor is Lawrence, on the face of it, arguing with himself. He knows, after all, how he feels about the Etruscans. No, the addressee here, as almost everywhere in the sequence, must be construed as a devoted—which is not to say a like-minded—listener, a close companion, say, or worthy antagonist, as Rawdon Lilly is to Aaron Sisson, or Gerald Crich to Rupert Birkin. Or again, we can posit the audience to be a group of friends in a café or country house, and, beyond this circle, the readership of certain books and journals that "everybody" reads.

Indeed, what makes the poems of *Birds, Beasts and Flowers* so distinctive, so wholly unlike anyone else's flower or animal poems, is, I would argue, their rhetoric, their performative stance. Whereas in the novels of the middle period, Lawrence's dialogue of self and soul belongs to a set of characters viewed in the third person—Lilly and Sisson, Lilly and Levinson, and so on—the poetry plays brilliant variations on what rhetoricians call the pathetic argument, the appeal to the audience to empathize with the speaker, to become part of the exclusive charmed circle to whom Lawrence reveals his secrets. Whereas in *Aaron's Rod* the dialogue between antagonists often seems silly and boring, in *Birds, Beasts and Flowers* Lawrence deflects "realistic" issues (should Aaron go back to his wife? should he take on a new lover? is he more attracted to men than to women?) by granting sexual power only to the vegetable and animal

kingdom (or, by fantastic analogy, to a primitive race like the Etruscans), and by making a sorb apple or an almond blossom or a fish
the vehicle for his "argument." "The fissure" to be "dared" is no
longer the "fissure" of a real woman—say, the Marchesa—but of a
pomegranate or a fig. Accordingly, sexual anxiety is deflected, at
least for the moment, and is replaced by a genial exuberance. As
W. H. Auden observes in what is, to my mind, the single best essay
written on Lawrence the poet:

> Lawrence possessed a great capacity for affection and charity,
> but he could only direct it toward non-human life. . . . When-
> ever, in his writings, he forgets about men and women with
> proper names and describes the anonymous life of stones,
> waters, forests, animals, flowers, chance traveling companions
> or passers-by, his bad temper and his dogmatism immediately
> vanish and he becomes the most enchanting companion imagi-
> nable, tender, intelligent, funny and, above all, happy.[7]

This seems to me precisely what happens in *Birds, Beasts and
Flowers.* When the scorpionlike Marquesa of *Aaron's Rod* is
replaced by the real mosquito, bat, or snake, Lawrence's outrage at
the bad faith of human beings gives way to a distancing of self or,
more precisely, a theatrical role-playing in which the poet alternately adopts the perspective of the plant or animal that happens to
be the object of his contemplation and alternately plays the dark
comedian, drawing mock lessons from his careful, almost scientific,
observations of plant or animal behavior. To compare cypresses to
Etruscan males, for example, is strictly speaking absurd, yet the "I"
of "Cypresses" convinces us that the analogy makes good sense. But
no sooner are we so convinced than the poet abruptly deflates his
own metaphor and shifts to a different angle. Indeed, despite his
repeated insistence on "the natural *lingering* of the voice according
to the feeling . . . the hidden *emotional* pattern that makes poetry,"[8]
the Lawrence of *Birds, Beasts and Flowers* was less an "emotional
realist" (A. Alvarez's term)[9] than what we now call a performance
poet; his seeming naturalness and spontaneity, his "accuracy of feeling" have a marked theatrical edge. It is this quality that I wish to
probe further.

## II

"Pomegranate," the first poem in the 1923 volume, is paradig-
matic of the whole collection:

> You tell me I am wrong.
> Who are you, who is anybody to tell me I am wrong?
> I am not wrong.

In Syracuse rock left bare by the viciousness of Greek
        women,
No doubt you have forgotten the pomegranate-trees in flower,
Oh so red, and such a lot of them.

Whereas at Venice,
Abhorrent, green, slippery city
Whose Doges were old, and had ancient eyes,
In the dense foliage of the inner garden
Pomegranates like bright green stone,
And barbed, barbed with a crown.
Oh, crown of spiked green metal
Actually growing!

Now in Tuscany,
Pomegranates to warm your hands at;
And crowns, kingly, generous, tilting crowns
Over the left eyebrow.

And, if you dare, the fissure!

Do you mean to tell me you will see no fissure?
Do you prefer to look on the plain side?

For all that, the setting suns are open.
The end cracks open with the beginning:
Rosy, tender, glittering within the fissure.

Do you mean to tell me there should be no fissure?
No glittering, compact drops of dawn?
Do you mean it is wrong, the gold-filmed skin, integument,
        shown ruptured?

For my part, I prefer my heart to be broken.
It is so lovely, dawn-kaleidoscopic within the crack.

(*CP,* 278–79)

It is customary to read this poem as a variant of the Persephone myth, Lawrence (Persephone) "daring the fissure" and eating
of the fruit that prepares him for entrance into the dark womb of
the underworld.[10] The little prose preface to "Fruits," taken from
John Burnet's *Early Greek Philosophy,*[11] gives support to this reading: "For fruits are all of them female, in them lies the seed. And so
when they break and show the seed, then we look into the womb
and see its secrets. So it is that the pomegranate is the apple of love
to the Arab, and the fig has been a catch-word for the female fissure
for ages" (*CP,* 277). However, the paragraph ends with the cryptic
sentence, "But the apples of life the dragon guards, and no woman
gives them," an aphorism to keep in mind as we read "Pomegranate." Indeed, in classical mythology, the pomegranate is not only the
fruit whose seeds Persephone fatally eats, thus being condemned to

spend part of each year in the underworld, but also the eight-petaled
scarlet anemone supposed to have sprouted from the blood of Dionysus. In related myths it refers to the tree of Tammuz or Adonis,
whose ripe fruit splits open like a wound and shows the red seeds
inside, thus symbolizing death and the promise of resurrection when
held in the hand of the goddess Hera or Persephone.[12] In this variant
of the myth, woman is the powerful and hence threatening goddess
who controls man's fate. We meet her counterpart in the opening
passage of *Sea and Sardinia,* written within a year of "Pomegranate," in which Lawrence, then living at Taormina in the shadow of
the great volcano, talks of his need to get away from "Etna, that
wicked witch, resting her thick white snow under heaven, and
slowly, slowly rolling her orange-colored smoke":

> Ah, what a mistress this Etna! with her strange winds prowl-
> ing round her like Circe's panthers, some black, some white.
> With her strange, remote communications and her terrible
> dynamic exhalations. She makes men mad. Such terrible
> vibrations of wicked and beautiful electricity she throws about
> her, like a deadly net! Nay, sometimes, verily one can feel a
> new current of her demon magnetism seize one's living tissue
> and change the peaceful life of one's active cells. She makes a
> storm in the living plasm and a new adjustment. And some-
> times it is like a madness.[13]

This passage is complemented, at the end of the novel, by the
image of a second "witch," this time the puppet witch in a mari-
onette show the narrator attends, with an all-male audience, in
Palermo:

> The old witch with her grey hair and staring eyes, succeeds in
> being ghastly. With just a touch, she would be a tall, benevo-
> lent old lady. But listen to her. Hear her horrible female voice
> with its scraping yells of evil lustfulness. Yes, she fills me with
> horror. And I am staggered to find how I believe in her as *the*
> evil principle. Beelzebub, poor devil, is only one of her
> instruments. . . . behold this image of the witch; this white,
> submerged *idea* of woman which rules from the deeps of the
> unconscious.

When the puppet finally goes up in flame, the little boys in the
audience yell with relief. "Would God," thinks Lawrence, "the symbolic act were really achieved. It is only little boys who yell. Men
merely smile at the trick. They know well enough the white image
endures" (p. 203).

In "Pomegranate," the "white image endures," at least partially, as the rock of Syracuse "left bare by the viciousness of Greek
women"—evidently an allusion to the terrible dismemberment
of Pentheus by the maenads—but, as the poet reminds his silent

auditor, the scattering of the dead man's blood on the bare-faced Sicilian rock also spells renewal: it bears the seed of the "pomegranate-trees in flower, / Oh so red, and such a lot of them."[14] And this flowering gives way, in its turn, to the unripe fruit (the "bright green stone" in the Venice garden), and then the ripe "pomegranates to warm your hands at" of Tuscany. But of course once the fruit is ripe, it must be eaten: the poem takes us, in a few quick strokes, from the flowering pomegranate trees of Syracuse to the ripe fruit of Florence, and then inside the fissure, where "the setting suns are open," where the seeds ("glittering compact drops of dawn") are inside the "Rosy, tender" pulp.

This is not to say that the pomegranate functions as a symbol of the female fruit, the womb that the male poet wishes to enter. Lawrence differs from most nature poets, both before and after his time, in allowing for no such consistency of symbolism. Moreover, the rhetorical framing, the foregrounding of the relationship between "I" and "you," makes it impossible to take the description of the fruit, accurate as it is, quite seriously.

The poem opens on a note of argument: the reader is drawn into what looks like an intense debate between the poet and a close friend, a person who, it seems, regularly engages in dialogue on such subjects—a Rawdon Lilly, say, confronting an Aaron Sisson or a Jack Calcott challenging a Lovat Somers. We can take this one step further, of course, and say that Lawrence is arguing with himself, that the "you" who tells him he is wrong is his rationalist alter ego. But "Pomegranate" is not really a convincing *débat,* for there is not the remotest possibility that the poet will be converted by the "you" or that he is even listening to what his antagonist might have to say. It is, rather, a case of buttonholing someone who has to give serious consideration to one's argument; indeed, by the time the "I" asserts loftily, in line 3, that "I am not wrong," the reader senses that this dazzling performer isn't going to let anyone—neither his friend nor, for that matter, the reader—challenge him. Thus he plays the role of playful mentor, reminding ("No doubt you have forgotten . . ."), explaining ("Whereas in Venice . . . ," "Now in Tuscany . . ."), questioning ("Do you prefer to look at the plain side?"), taunting ("Do you mean to tell me there should be no fissure?"), exulting ("For my part, I prefer . . .").

It is interesting to look at the role rhythm plays in the creation of Lawrence's performative stance. The so-called free verse of "Pomegranate" is quite unlike, say, Walt Whitman's, in which parallel rhythmic groupings, slow and stately, recur with subtle minor variations. Consider the first three lines:

> You tell me I am wrong.
> Who are you, who is anybody to tell me I am wrong?
> I am not wrong.

This is the associative rhythm of actual conversation, with its abrupt, choppy phrasing. But this speech rhythm repeatedly crosses a second, more "poetic" line, as in

> In the dense foliage of the inner garden
> Pomegranates like bright green stone,
> And barbed, barbed with a crown.
> Oh, crown of spiked green metal . . .

where heavy stresses on long open vowels cluster together, creating a movement reminiscent of Pound or certain Imagists. But when "Oh, crown of spiked green metal" is followed by the deflationary

> Actually growing!

the effect is almost parodic, as if the poet were laughing at his more bardic self. The same thing happens a few lines further down when the line

> Rosy, tender, glittering within the fissure

is followed by

> Do you mean to tell me there should be no fissure?

And again, in the final line when the hobbyhorse rhythm of

> dawn-kaleidoscopic

follows

> It is so lovely.

The delicate self-parody of the narrator's rhythms, the cosmic bullying of his tone, work, I think, to bring the reader round to the poet's point of view, to adopt his stance toward the successive versions of the pomegranate. Thus the opening image of the flowering pomegranate tree is seen to allude to the Dionysus myth, the transformation of the blood of the dying god into the scarlet flower. It is the flower of male sexuality just as the bright green stone seen in Venice is a phallic image. For Lawrence, Venice, as opposed to the Syracuse of ancient myth on the one hand and the warm, human Tuscany on the other, is always seen as an "abhorrent, green, slippery city," evidently because it is built on water.[15] It is the city of damp canals rather than of fertility; its old Doges with their "ancient eyes," saw nothing, whereas the poet can penetrate "the dense foliage of the inner garden" and discover "Pomegranates like bright green stone." These Venetian pomegranates are aggressively masculine ("barbed, barbed with a crown. / Oh, crown of spiked green metal / Actually growing!"), and even though their Tuscan counterparts are fruits "to warm your hands at," they too have "crowns, kingly, generous, tilting crowns / Over the left eyebrow."

The pomegranate is thus first linked to male sexuality. Accordingly, when Lawrence suddenly introduces the line, set off by itself,

"And, if you dare, the fissure!" he has made it impossible for us to allegorize the object, to relate it to Woman, much less to any particular woman. It is as if the poet finds in himself both aspects of pomegranatehood, the crowns of spiked green metal, "kingly, generous, tilting," and the fissure that yields up "setting suns," "glittering, compact drops of dawn." Indeed, in the end it is not the womb that is ruptured but the heart:

> For my part, I prefer my heart to be broken.
> It is so lovely, dawn-kaleidoscopic within the crack.

The ripe fruit splits open like a wound ("the gold-filmed skin . . . ruptured") and shows the red seed inside.

So tender is the poet's tone, so thoroughly familiar with the life cycle of the pomegranate, that it is easy to downplay the curious narcissism of the final lines. The poet retreats, after all, into the crack of his own ruptured heart; safe inside, he finds it "lovely" and "dawn-kaleidoscopic"—one might say, innocent, pure. But, the poem implies, its speaker has earned the right to retreat into his own heart because he has "dared" the fissure, the rupture. Just as the Lawrence of *Sea and Sardinia* must "dare" the rupture of Etna if he is going to be at one with the Sicilian landscape, so the "I" of "Pomegranate" understands that only out of intense struggle (the willingness to engage the Greek women whose viciousness almost prevents the growth of the flowering tree, the recognition of the crown of spiked green metal, the daring to look at what is "rosy, tender, glittering within the fissure") can the heart be broken and made new. One thinks immediately of Crazy Jane's aphorism, "For nothing can be sole or whole / That has not been rent"—but Lawrence does not share Yeats's drive toward Unity of Being; he is willing to accept the universe as decentered, as, of necessity, contradictory. For who, seeing the "spiked green metal" crown of the unripe pomegranate, would think that hidden *inside it* are glittering drops of dawn?

I have dwelt at what may seem to be unnecessary length on "Pomegranate" because its rhetorical mode raises issues that seem to belie our usual assumptions about Lawrence's poetry. Much has been written about Lawrence the Orphic seer, uncovering the secrets of nature or, in Ross C. Murfin's words, "expos[ing] a lost and more fundamental discourse that brings meaning into the present and future."[16] But this is to ignore the other, more "hard-boiled" or practical side of Lawrence, his stubborn insistence that a flower or animal or bird should be taken for what it *is*.

The central prose text in this connection is not the famous "Poetry of the Present" (1918), with its eloquent plea for "instant poetry," the poetry of the "incarnate moment," the *now*, but the

1927 essay called "The Nightingale," in which Lawrence contrasts his own view of the natural world to that of Keats. The fallacy of "Ode to a Nightingale," he declares with mock solemnity, is that the poet thinks he can somehow enter the world of the nightingale, a world actually wholly *other:*

> The viewless wings of Poesy carry [Keats] only into the bushes, not into the nightingale world. He is still outside.
>
> > Darkling I listen; and for many a time
> > I have been half in love with easeful death. . . .
>
> The nightingale never made any man in love with easeful death, except by contrast. The contrast between the bright flame of positive pure self-aliveness, in the bird, and the uneasy flickering of yearning selflessness, for ever yearning for something outside himself, which is Keats:
>
> > To cease upon the midnight with no pain,
> > While thou art pouring forth thy soul abroad
> > In such an ecstasy!
> > Still wouldst thou sing, and I have ears in vain,—
> > To thy high requiem become a sod.
>
> How astonished the nightingale would be if he could be made to realize what sort of answer the poet was answering to his song. He would fall off the bough with amazement. Because a nightingale, when you answer him back, only shouts and sings louder.[17]

This is Lawrence the sensible man, the same man who in real life could dust a room or bake a loaf of bread with perfect ease. He is also the comedian who delights in taking Keats's lines "Thou wast not born for death, immortal Bird! / No hungry generations tread thee down" and remarking laconically, "Not yet in Tuscany, anyhow. They are twenty to the dozen" (p. 100).

Accordingly, in "Pomegranate," flower and fruit are not the object of Romantic *Einfühlung;* they remain stubbornly *other.* Indeed, the poet is less seer than, in W. H. Auden's words, "enchanting companion . . . tender, intelligent, funny and, above all, happy." In the animal poems, such distancing of self is carried even further: in "Mosquito," for example, the address to the insect as "Monsieur" is repeatedly played off against the precise, scientific knowledge of what a mosquito is and does:

> What do you stand on such high legs for?
> Why this length of shredded shank,
> You exaltation?
>
> Is it so that you shall lift your centre of gravity upwards
> And weigh no more than air as you alight upon me

Stand upon me weightless, you phantom? . . .

Queer, with your thin wings and your streaming legs,
How you sail like a heron, or a dull clot of air,
A nothingness. . . .

Queer, how you stalk and prowl the air
In circles and evasions, enveloping me. . . .
I hate the way you lurch off sideways into air. . . .

(*CP*, 332–33)

And so on. Yet the same observer who knows the mosquito for what
it is, admits his fear of this "Winged Victory," this devil with its "evil
little aura, prowling, and casting a numbness on my mind," this
"streaky sorcerer," whose "hateful little trump" is that he "Suck[s]
live blood, / My blood."

As it unfolds, "Mosquito" can be seen to be a delicately satirical treatment of the human need to triumph over the very smallest
and most paltry creatures of the insect world. Thus the "I" alternately displays bravado—"I know your game now, streaky sorcerer"—and cajoles:

Come then, let us play at unawares . . .

Why do you do it?
Surely it is bad policy.

Or again, he waxes philosophical:

They say you can't help it.

But the most curious twist comes in the final tercet, in which we
witness man's equivocal triumph over the now-dead mosquito:

Queer, what a big stain my sucked blood makes
Beside the infinitesimal faint smear of you!
Queer, what a dim dark smudge you have disappeared into!

(*CP*, 334)

As in the case of "Pomegranate," the poem foregrounds the
rhetorical situation, the relation of "I" to "you," of manly poet to
foppish "Monsieur Mosquito," a relationship characterized by insistent questioning, exclamation, exhortation, aphorism, repetition,
and hyperbole:

Such silence, such suspended transport,
Such gorging,
Such obscenity of trespass. . . .

Away with a paean of derision,
You winged blood-drop.

Here is one man absurdly contemplating his male rival, absurdly
needing to "win in this sly game of bluff," to "out-mosquito you."
And again, the poem allows Lawrence to handle lightly and humor-

ously what is, in *Women in Love* or *Aaron's Rod,* a deadly contest between male rivals.

A darker version of "Mosquito" is found in "Bat" (September 1921), whose Tuscan setting makes it a fitting complement to "Pomegranate." It begins:

> At evening, sitting on this terrace,
> When the sun from the west, beyond Pisa, beyond the moun-
> tains of Carrara
> Departs, and the world is taken by surprise . . .
>
> When the tired flower of Florence is in gloom beneath the
> glowing
> Brown hills surrounding . . .
>
> When under the arches of the Ponte Vecchio
> A green light enters against stream, flush from the west,
> Against the current of obscure Arno . . .
>
> (*CP,* 340; ellipses in original)

This opening, with its precise setting, time of day, and concrete description of light and color, recalls such Romantic poems as Coleridge's "Aeolian Harp" or "Frost at Midnight." The suspended "when . . ." clauses follow one another with slow and stately rhythm:

> When the tíred *fló*wer of *Fló*rence is in *glóom* benéath the
> *glów*ing . . .

But this movement (a kind of slow-motion pan of the camera) is intentionally deceptive: Lawrence is setting the stage for the moment of threshold which is his subject, the sudden break between day and night, one state of consciousness and another, the moment when one becomes aware of that which the daylight had obscured. The Romantic opening is punctuated by the decidedly un-Romantic line "Look up and you see things flying."

Here the second-person address is important. Unlike the countless nature poems in which an "I" communes with the landscape ("I look up and I see . . ."), "Bat" uses phenomenology as a springboard for communication: the poet's experience can be clarified only in the course of talking about it to someone else, in making that other share his angle of vision:

> Look up, and you see things flying
> Between the day and the night;
> Swallows with spools of dark thread sewing the shadows
> together.
>
> A circle swoop, and quick parabola under the bridge arches
> Where light pushes through;
> A sudden turning upon itself of a thing in the air.
> A dip to the water.

And you think:
"The swallows are flying so late!"

Here the "you" (and, by extension, the reader) is made to share the poet's deception, his assumption that the "things flying" are swallows. Lawrence's description of the bat flight is at once minutely accurate and yet curiously enigmatic in that the geometry of flight (circle, parabola) is divorced from its source; we see, through the poet's eyes, the swoop, the turning, the dip to the water, but the bat who does the turning and dipping remains an absence. Even after the abrupt question, "Swallows?" recognition is slow to come:

Dark air-life looping
Yet missing the pure loop . . .
A twitch, a twitter, an elastic shudder in flight
And serrated wings against the sky,
Like a glove, a black glove thrown up at the light
And falling back.

This is, so to speak, the negative version of the radiant sexuality of "Pomegranate": the "dark air-life looping . . . miss[es] the pure loop"; the "elastic shudder" has neither a perceptible source nor object. Indeed, in a moment the sexually charged "elastic shudder in flight" collapses like a burst balloon; the profile of "serrated wings" gives way to the image of the inert "black glove thrown up at the light / And falling back."

Only now, twenty-five lines into the poem, is the subject of the poem called by name. It is, of course, the blindness of the bat (its flying into the light) that gives it away:

Never swallows!
Bats!
The swallows are gone.

At a wavering instant the swallows give way to bats
By the Ponte Vecchio . . .
Changing guard.

Bats, and an uneasy creeping in one's scalp
As the bats swoop overhead!
Flying madly.

So startling is the poet's sudden recognition that he must repeat the word "bat" over and over again (seven times in the last twenty-one lines), gradually distancing himself from their "circle swoops" by turning them into objects: "Little lumps that fly in air and have voices indefinite, wildly vindictive; / Wings like bits of umbrella." Transformed, mechanized, the bats are no longer a threat. The narrator

can now regard them with a measure of disdain and bemused
tolerance:

> Creatures that hang themselves up like an old rag, to sleep;
> And disgustingly upside down.
> Hanging upside down like rows of disgusting old rags
> And grinning in their sleep.
> Bats!

To call the bats "disgusting" is to neutralize their force; anyone, after
all, can deal with a set of "disgusting old rags." It is at this point
that the poet can stand up and announce, both to the friend(s) with
him on his Tuscan terrace, as well as to the reader, "In China the
bat is symbol of happiness." And the following "Not for me!" is
comically gratuitous.

Indeed, like "Pomegranate," "Bat" has a certain burlesque
element; it presents us with a speaker who is less Orphic seer than
dark comedian. Confronted by what we most fear, Lawrence seems
to be saying, we protect ourselves by metaphorizing the dreaded
object: bat becomes black glove becomes little lump, bit of umbrella,
disgusting old rag. Dismissed with a comic splutter, the bat can now
safely become the topic of polite conversation, "In China the bat is
symbol of happiness." Here, at poem's end, is Lawrence, the genial
conversationalist, the amusing companion, the delightfully candid
friend who admits that, whatever the Chinese (here synecdochic for
all that is Other) may think, he is, after all, a vulnerable Westerner.

It is interesting, in this regard, to compare Lawrence's
response to the animal kingdom with that of a later poet like Elizabeth Bishop. When we read, say, Bishop's "The Fish" against Lawrence's "Fish," we are initially struck by the thematic parallel: both
poems suggest that the otherness of the fish must be respected, that
the act of "catching" a fish bespeaks a mastery more apparent than
real. But when Bishop's "I" contemplates the fish she has just caught,
there is a clear distinction between subject and object:

> I looked into his eyes
> which were far larger than mine
> but shallower, and yellowed,
> the irises backed and packed
> with tarnished tinfoil
> seen through the lenses
> of old scratched isinglass.
> They shifted a little, but not
> to return my stare.
> —It was more like the tipping
> of an object toward the light.
> I admired his sullen face. . . .[18]

Bishop's discourse is characterized by its consistency and narrative continuity; "I looked . . . It was . . . I admired . . . then I saw." Lawrence's poem observes no such decorum; the performing self engages in impassioned conversation, sometimes directly with the fish, sometimes with a silent auditor, sometimes with himself. He shifts at will from first to second to third person, now envying the fish's freedom from human, that is to say, sexual, anxieties ("But oh, fish, that rock in water, / You lie only with the waters . . . No wistful bellies, / No loins of desire, / None," *CP*, 335), now standing back and describing the fish's attributes in rapid shorthand:

> Himself,
> And the element.
> Food, of course!
> Water-eager eyes,
> Mouth-gate open
> And strong spine urging, driving;
> And desirous belly gulping.
>
> (*CP*, 336)

Or, distancing the fish still further:

> Cats and the Neapolitans
> Sulphur sun-beasts,
> Thirst for fish as for more-than-water;
> Water-alive
> To quench their over-sulphureous lusts.
>
> (*CP*, 340)

As in "Pomegranate," Lawrence dissolves perspective: the observer is not located in any one spot, and the poet's canvas becomes, so to speak, a flickering network of multiple stresses, a field of force. Indeed, in its emphasis on the split-second transformation of the object to be examined and in the poet's performative stance vis-à-vis that object, a poem like "Fish" is perhaps closer to Italian Futurism than to the Romantic paradigm that is generally held to be its source.

In a letter to Arthur McLeod (2 June 1914) Lawrence writes:

> I have been interested in the futurists. I got a book of their poetry—a very fat book too—and book of pictures—and I read Marinetti's and Paolo Buzzi's manifestations and essays. . . . It interests me very much. I like it because it is the applying to emotions of the purging of the old forms and sentimentalities. I like it for its saying—enough of this sickly cant, let us be honest and stick by what is in us. (*CL*, 2:180)

And the following March he writes to Gordon Campbell: "Art which is lyrical can now no longer satisfy us: each work of art that is true, now, must give expression to the great collective experience, not to the individual. . . . we have accumulated enough fragmentary data of lyricism since the Renaissance" (*CL*, 2:301).

We must, of course, take such statements with a grain of salt: to express "the great collective experience," whatever that is, is surely impossible for any poet, let alone a poet of the twentieth century. Despite such hyperbole, Lawrence's perception is important; what he means is that, given the context of the Great War, of the new concepts of space and time and of the technology that so profoundly influenced the Futurists, an *individual* response to nature—the confrontation of an "I" with a skylark or a nightingale or a field of daffodils—is perhaps no longer enough. For Lawrence, there is no longer a distinction between subject and object, consciousness and the external world. Rather, the new space is one in which the mind and its objects are present in a single realm of proximity.[19] Accordingly, it is impossible to know where man ends and "fish" or "bat" or "pomegranate" begins; there is only a charged field of energies, of forces in tension. It is this theater of polarities, this performance arena that we meet in *Birds, Beasts and Flowers.*

Lawrence's debt to the Futurists has often been noted, but always with reference to his novels rather than to his poetry. The famous letter to Edward Garnett (5 June 1914) in which Lawrence cites Filippo Marinetti as the source of his new concept of character ("There is another ego, according to whose action the individual is unrecognisable, and passes through, as it were, allotropic states," *CL*, 2:183) is regularly quoted and discussed with reference to *The Rainbow* and *Women in Love*. But, ironically, Lawrence's carbon-diamond opposition, his belief that "that which is physic—non-human, in humanity, is more interesting to me than the old-fashioned human element—which causes one to conceive a character in a certain moral scheme and make him consistent" (*CL*, 2:182), a doctrine whose applications in the novels of the twenties were to become increasingly problematic, makes good sense when we turn from the fiction to the poetry.

In *Aaron's Rod*, for example, Lawrence cannot quite make up his mind whether the characters do or do not fit into what he calls "a certain moral scheme"; sometimes they behave consistently; sometimes their actions seem to be motivated by what Lawrence, following Marinetti, calls "physiology of matter." The conflict between carbon and diamond, so to speak, remains unresolved. But when, in his role as poet, Lawrence can play at being (and alternately addressing) a pomegranate or a fish, or when he can mount what we might call his "bat performance," exorcising the black demons that fly in the night, his desire to "purge" the emotions of their "old forms and sentimentalities" finds its appropriate outlet.

Perhaps we are now in a better position to understand why, for all its brilliance, a book like *Birds, Beasts and Flowers* continues to meet with indifference if not resistance on the part of historians and critics of twentieth-century poetry. In *The Modern Poetic Sequence: The Genius of Modern Poetry* (1983), for example, M. L. Rosenthal and Sally M. Gall barely mention Lawrence, even though their study covers lyric sequences from Walt Whitman and Emily Dickinson down to Ted Hughes, Sylvia Plath, Galway Kinnell, and Adrienne Rich.[20] If such exclusion of Lawrence constitutes, as I think it does, the rule rather than the exception, the reason is not far to seek. Lawrence's poetry confounds all our usual categories: Modern/Postmodern, Symbolist/Immanentist, Romantic/Realist, Confessional/Deep Imagist, and so on. If it is not easy to establish a line of precursors for Lawrence, it is even more difficult to determine the nature of his influence on later poets.

Yet there are signs that the marginal status of Lawrence's poetry is changing.[21] Today, with the erosion of the boundaries between lyric poetry and other modes of discourse, with the increasing prominence of performance art, and with the revival of interest in Dada and Futurism, we should be attuned to a poetic voice that, in a poem deceptively titled "Southern Night" (*CP,* 302), commands the moon to "Come up, thou red thing. / Come up, and be called a moon," only to become aware of "The mosquitoes . . . biting tonight / Like memories"—a "sting" that produces the characteristic Lawrentian about-face: "Call it moonrise? This red anathema?" And of course this challenge makes us want to debate the issue, to come to terms with this "red thing, / Unfold[ing] slowly upwards, blood-dark."

Again, in a poem called "The Evening Land," the poet confronts the American continent with a comically bombastic catalog of insults, for example:

> Even the winged skeleton of your bleached ideal
> Is not so frightening as that clean smooth
> Automaton of your uprisen self,
> Machine American.
> Do you wonder that I am afraid to come
> And answer the first machine-cut question from the lips of
>     your iron men?
> Put the first cents into metallic fingers of your officers
> And sit beside the steel-straight arms of your fair women,
> American?

> (*CP,* 290–91)

But then, as if it had suddenly occurred to him that he is not as detached from the American scene as he would like to think, he admits:

My soul is half-cajoled, half-cajoled,

Something in you which marries me beyond,
Yankee, Yankee,
What we call human,
Carries me where I want to be carried . . .
Or don't I?

And by the time the poem approaches its climax, the speaker is begging America's "nascent demon people / Lurking among the deeps of your industrial thicket" to "Allure me till I am beside myself, / A nympholept" (*CP*, 293).

It is a performance that might have been applauded at a *serata futurista* or at the Cabaret Voltaire. Provocation—ironic, sly, teasing—becomes the mainspring of the poetic occasion. "Would you like to throw a stone at me?" asks the speaker at the opening of "Peach" (*CP*, 279). And after soliciting the audience's active collaboration with a series of unanswerable questions ("Why so velvety, who so voluptuous heavy? . . . Why the groove?"), he concludes, "Here, you can have my peach stone." By that time, of course, we are eating out of the poet's hand.

*Chapter Six*

# The Contemporary of

# Our Grandchildren:

## *Ezra Pound and the Question of Influence*

Pound has provided a box of tools, as abundant for
this generation as those Spenser provided for the
Elizabethans, and a man who is not influenced by
Pound in this sense of trying to use at least some of
those tools, is simply not living in his own century.
(Basil Bunting)[1]

When I was living in Verona [at age twenty-three]
. . . I was told to go out to Sirmione on Lake
Garda, where the Latin poet, Catullus, supposedly
had a villa. . . . It's still one of the most beautiful
places I have ever been to, or expect to go to. Lake
Garda in front of you, the Italian Alps on three
sides of you, the ruined and beautiful villa around
you, and I read a poem that Pound had written
about the place, about Sirmione being more beautiful than Paradise, and my life was changed forever.
(Charles Wright)[2]

He was born the year of Brahms' Fourth and of
*Diana of the Crossways;* of the *Mikado* and the second
volume of *Das Kapital;* in the reigns of Grover
Cleveland and Victoria. At his death every school
of poets writing in English was under his
influence. . . . I have seen students learn Chinese

because of him, or take up medieval studies, learn
Greek, Latin, music; the power of his instigation
has not flagged.   (Guy Davenport)[3]

Question: What do you think about giving an
award to somebody who held all the positions that
Pound held?
Answer: It's irrelevant! If the award is lucky
enough to find him, God bless the award. The
award needs him—he doesn't need the award. Certainly, give him *all* the awards. It's a shame he
didn't get the Nobel and all the other awards at
once—he was the greatest poet of his age!   (Allen
Ginsberg)[4]

## *I*

*I*f these words, spoken by four very different poets, sound
extravagant—as they will to certain readers—we might
substitute for Ginsberg's nebulous "greatest" a phrase like
"most influential" and then there can barely be room for disagreement. For what poet writing in England or America since World
War II has *not* learned from Pound? In casting about for suspects,
I have come up with a few, but even those few have not escaped
the anxiety of what must be the largest poetic influence of our century. Ted Hughes, for instance, is a poet no one seems to have
claimed for the Pound tradition,[5] and yet when we read the lines

Fífteenth of Máy. ‖ Chérry blóssom. ‖ The swífts
Matèrialíze at the tóp of a lóng scréam
Of néedle—[6]

we hear, despite the un-Poundian enjambment, the rhythms and
inflections of *Cathay*—inflections guided by the Imagist credo of
"Direct treatment of the thing" as well as by the recognition that
"To break the pentameter, that was the first heave."

Or what about James Merrill, a poet who once declared that
in the *Cantos* "we find precious little unity except of the contents of
a single, very brilliant and erratic mind," and who pronounced
Pound's and Eliot's a poetry "only to react against"?[7] Merrill's own
epic *The Changing Light at Sandover* (1983) incorporates into the
text of a poem almost as long (560 pages) as the entire *Cantos*
patches of narrative and of dramatic dialogue, allusions to historical
and mythological figures, scientific documentation, personal letters,
foreign phrases, and typographical play (capital letters for messages

from the dead received via the Ouija board, phonetic spelling as in "U" for "you," "4" for "four," and "V" for "vie"). The resulting sequence, centrally different as it is from Pound's own "rag-bag," could hardly have come into being without the example of the *Cantos*. As Hugh Kenner predicted more than a decade ago in *The Pound Era*: "We can hardly distinguish what Pound instigated from what he simply saw before it was obvious. . . . He is very likely in ways controversy still hides, the contemporary of our grandchildren."[8]

Contemporary in what sense? It is usual, when talking of the Pound tradition, to draw a family tree that goes, by way of Williams, to Black Mountain, the Objectivists, and the Confessional poets. Pound and Charles Olson, Pound and Louis Zukofsky, Pound and Robert Lowell—these connections have been made often enough, and I shall not rehearse, in the short space available to me here, these individual and well-known cases.[9] Rather, I want to take up the larger question: What is it in Pound's oeuvre that has made such a difference in the poetry of the later twentieth century, a difference that transcends, in curious ways, the local differences between individual poets?

The obvious place to begin is surely with Pound's poetic, the famous obiter dicta of the critical prose. Denise Levertov probably speaks for many poets when she remarks, in her homage to Pound for the 1972 *L'Herne* (Paris) symposium:

> Reading *The Cantos* was for me until quite recently an experience which seemed to have little direct connection with the experience of studying the *ABC* and other prose. Though there was much that I responded to in *The Cantos*, all that appeared unclear and even chaotic in them seemed to me disturbingly at variance with Pound the critic's emphasis on clarity, on communication, and at the same time on music.[10]

Here Levertov may well be echoing Robert Creeley:

> For my own part I came first to the earlier poems, *Personae*, and to the various critical works, *Make It New, Pavannes and Divisions, ABC of Reading, Guide to Kulchur*, and *Polite Essays*. It was at that time the critical writing I could most clearly use, simply that my own limits made the *Cantos* a form intimidating to me.[11]

Again, Carl Rakosi, a poet who has gone so far as to declare the *Cantos* "disastrous as a model," declares that Pound's critical writing—particularly the famous "Don'ts" essay—is "an absolute foundation stone of contemporary American writing."[12] And when Donald Davie, a very different poet from the three above, writes his first book on Pound, he devotes the central chapters to the aesthetic as formulated in *Gaudier-Brzeska* and in the writings on Remy de Gourmont and Ernest Fenollosa.[13]

Whatever poets have made of the actual texture of the *Cantos*, it seems that Pound's poetic, as articulated in the famous essays, has become synonymous with modernism itself. Such axioms as "Use no superfluous word, no adjective which does not reveal something" ("A Retrospect"); "The image is not an idea. It is a radiant node or cluster from which, and through which, and into which ideas are constantly rushing" (*Gaudier-Brzeska*); "Good writers are those who keep the language efficient"; and "Poetry . . . is the most concentrated form of verbal expression" (*ABC of Reading*)[14]—these aphorisms are now embedded in our critical vocabulary. We talk of *melopoeia, phanopoeia,* and *logopoeia* as if this triad had been used by Aristotle in the *Poetics;* again, we refer to "ideogram," "vortex," and "luminous detail" as if these terms had always been applied to poetry. For Donald Davie as for Denise Levertov, for Charles Tomlinson as for Charles Wright, for Thom Gunn as for Theodore Weiss,[15] the thrust of the Poundian poetic is that poetry *matters,* that it is *important,* that if "a nation's literature declines, the nation atrophies and decays" (*ABCR,* 32). Which of us does not believe or want to believe this inspired doctrine? POETRY IS NEWS THAT STAYS NEWS. In the self-conscious eighties, when voices from all sides are expressing doubts about the future of poetry, Pound's message is the one poets want to hear.

But when we turn from the explosive poetic to the poetry itself, the question of influence becomes more complicated. There are three areas, I would suggest, in which Pound's legacy has been indisputable: (1) the drive toward precision, particularity, immediacy— *le mot juste;* (2) the "break[ing of] the pentameter" in favor of the "musical" free-verse line; and (3) the use of translation as the invention of a desired other. I shall discuss these three legacies briefly before turning to what seems to me the deeper, more lasting influence—and one that we have begun to witness only in recent years— namely, the example of the *Cantos* as "a poem including history," the new conception of the poem as "the tale of the tribe" that no longer privileges lyric over narrative (or even drama), that can incorporate the contemporary and the archaic, economics and myth, the everyday and the elevated.

1. Pound's insistence on precision, the luminous detail, the phalanx of particulars has become a rallying cry for poets as otherwise diverse as George Oppen and Frank O'Hara, poets who have wanted to avoid what John Ashbery has called the disease of "objective correlativitis."[16] Here is Basil Bunting writing to Louis Zukofsky in 1932:

> The value of Pound's preaching of Confucius does not
> lie in Confucius, whose wisdom seems to me to be mixed with

the usual quantity of bunk, some of it quite as unpleasant as anything in St. Paul: but in the fact that Pound has not isolated a set of precepts but developed a pervading stress on the immediate, the particular, the concrete; distrust of abstractions; shrinking from even the suspicion of verbalism; from the puns and polyvalencies in which mystics delight. It is not unspeculative but skeptical. It will build with facts, but declines to soar with inevitably unsteady words.[17]

Distrust of abstractions, shrinking from even the suspicion of verbalism—here Bunting seems to be speaking for a whole generation. Allen Ginsberg, calling on Pound in 1967, explains to the (nearly silent) old poet that he has been able to find certain works of art in Venice, say, a fountain or a fresco or "the casa que fue de Don Carlos," merely by following the "descriptions—of exact language composed"—the "tin flash in the sun dazzle" and "soap-smooth stone posts" of the *Cantos*. When Pound demurs, declaring that "any good [in the *Cantos*] has been spoiled by my intentions— the preoccupation with irrelevant and stupid things," Ginsberg replies: "Ah well, what I'm trying to tell you—what I came here for all this time—was to give you my blessing then, because despite your disillusion . . . my perceptions have been strengthened by a series of practical exact language models which are scattered throughout the *Cantos* like stepping stones."[18] And the next evening, sitting behind Pound in Santa Maria del Carmelo, Ginsberg tries his own hand at an "exact language model":

    Carmini, organ, apse brilliant yellow
        gilt angels, violincello,
            Byzance cross hung silhouette,
        Flowers on altar, Pillars wrapped in red velvet—
    old man sat before me,
        brown canvas shoes, one heel raised alter,
            hat and cane in hand
        Smooth woodslab resting
            under a fold in his coatback.[19]

Ginsberg's cataloging of items, his notion, one by one, of things seen is, of course, only superficially Poundian; the passage in question— and this would be true of "Howl" or "Kaddish" or "A Supermarket in California" as well—does not exhibit Pound's principle of juxtaposition, of intercut, of cultural overlayering, one image or ideogram jostling another. Nevertheless, the emphasis is on the *particular*, not as metaphor but as embodiment of a specific perception. Whitman would be the more plausible model, but Whitman was no longer alive in 1967 and Ginsberg needed Pound, even as he needed Williams, as intermediary.

The case of Zukofsky presents another variation on the fate of Pound's presentational methods. Overtly, the Objectivist creed grew out of Pound's Imagism and Vorticism: *"Impossible* to communicate anything but particulars—historic and contemporary—things, human beings as things their instrumentalities of capillaries and veins binding up and bound up with events and contingencies. The revolutionary word if it must revolve cannot escape having a reference. It is not infinite. Even the infinite is a term."[20]

But although Zukofsky makes much of "presentation in detail: the isolation of each noun so that in itself it is an image,"[21] the fact is that his poetry, like Bunting's or Oppen's or Creeley's or H.D.'s later work, abjures "direct presentation" in favor of a lyric mode that looks like this:

> Whatever makes this happening
> Is unheard
> To a third.

> Two. Where two should
> Stand. One. One.
> With the sun. In a wood.

> Tomorrow is unsought.
> No oasis of ivy to inurn
> Either foot or fern.[22]

This is, as Burton Hatlen has recently said about a related poem, a long way from the Poundian "phalanx of particulars": "Zukofsky doesn't *want* us to pass through the words of his poem, to engage directly with 'things.' . . . Rather, he wants the words themselves to become presences within the poem, simply because language is the only presence we can know. . . . the poem (deliberately I think) evokes the gap that separates words from things."[23]

Why then the repeated appeal on Zukofsky's part to Pound as the poet of precision, of "presentation in detail"? I think we must understand Objectivist doctrine—whether in Zukofsky or in Oppen or even in Creeley—less as the continuation of Imagist precision or of the "Ideogrammic Method" than as the repudiation of the Symbolist model that had dominated Anglo-American poetry at least until the Second World War.[24] "Like Williams and Pound," writes Burton Hatlen, Zukofsky "refuses the transcendental temptation, the impulse to look beyond the given world (either 'up' to God or 'within' to the human spirit) for a source of meaning."[25] Indeed, Pound's declaration in *Gaudier-Brzeska* that "the image is the poet's pigment," that "one does not want to be called a symbolist, because symbolism has usually been associated with mushy technique" (pp. 84–85), provides the impetus for the stress on precision that we meet in contemporary poetics. Asked by Charles Tomlinson whether "Pound provided a sound inoculation against the New Critics," Robert Creeley replies: "Yes . . . he warned against the muzziness that can come of a too conscious fuddling of symbolism. . . . Pound has always been intent to make a clear demarcation between a symbol which in effect exhausts references as opposed to a sign or mark of something which constantly renews its references."[26] Donald Davie similarly remarks, "Pound's repeated assertion [in *The Pisan Cantos*] that the paradisal is *real*, out there in the real world, is a conscious challenge to the whole symbolist aesthetic."[27] And the same year that he publishes his Pound book, Davie writes a poem called "In California" that begins:

> At Ventucopa, elevation
> Two-eight-nine-six the water hydrant frozen,
> Deserted or broken settlements,
> Gasoline stations closed and boarded,[28]

lines that Poundians will immediately connect to the opening of "Provincia Deserta":

> At Rochecoart,
> Where the hills part
>      in three ways
> Are three valleys, full of winding roads.[29]

Imagism as a challenge to Symbolist aesthetic—this, rather than the actual *Poundspeech* with its abrupt collage cuts and startling juxtapositions, is what comes down to so many of our poets. Indeed, the cult of exactitude, of a stubborn literalness, is likely to turn up in such unexpected places as James Merrill's *Mirabell: Book of Numbers.*

> Between our dining room and stairs
> Leading to the future studio
> From long before our time, was this ill-lit
> Shoebox of a parlor where we'd sit
> Faute de mieux, when not asleep or eating.
> It had been papered by the original people—
> Blue-on-eggshell foliage touchingly
> Mottled or torn in places.[30]

"Blue-on-eggshell foliage . . . / Mottled or torn"—the phrasing is Poundian although Pound would have omitted the word "touchingly." Tell it straight, he would have argued, and the reader will be touched, all right.

2. "I scarcely know," John Berryman wrote in 1949, "what to say of Pound's ear. Fifteen years of listening has not taught me that it is inferior to the ear of *Twelfth Night*."[31] High praise indeed, if a bit stilted. But compare it to the response of a British poet who had barely heard of Pound when he went up to Cambridge in 1945. In his memoir *Some Americans,* Charles Tomlinson recalls:

While still at grammar school, I had invested half a crown . . .
in a copy of the Sesame Books selection of Ezra Pound. . . .
Puzzled, I read it through many times, tried to scan the opening lines of "E.P. Ode Pour L'Election de Son Sepulchre";
tried the same with "The River-Merchant's Wife." Evidently it
couldn't be done. This was a naive discovery, no doubt. Scan-
sion had figured prominently in one's education—in English,
French, and Latin, I am grateful that it did. But here its only
use was to point the difference, to suggest, with the Mauberley extract, that perhaps some type of syncopation was at
work. . . . It was a sense of cleanliness of the phrasing that
drew me, still puzzled, to Canto 2, toward the end of the
book. I returned many times to

> Lithe turning of water,
> > sinews of Poseidon,
> Black azure and hyaline,
> > glass wave over Tyro. . . .

The canto closed on the word "And. . . ." That was also
something to think about.[32]

What was it that made Pound's prosody seem so revolutionary? Writing of the breaking of the pentameter that first occurs in
the *Cathay* poems, Donald Davie explains:

> It is important to understand what is involved. From
> Edmund Spenser onwards in English verse the finest art was
> employed in running over the verse line so as to build up
> larger units of movement such as the strophe, the Miltonic
> verse paragraph, or, in Shakespearean and other theatrical
> poetry, the sustained dramatic speech. . . . the grammatical
> unit, the sentence, is draped over the metrical unit, the
> line. . . . This is not to "break" the pentameter (or more gen-
> erally the verse-line of whatever length), but rather to sub-
> merge it, by incorporating the line into the building of larger
> and more intricate rhythmical units. . . . It was only when the
> line was considered as the unit of composition, as it was by
> Pound in *Cathay*, that there emerged the possibility of "break-
> ing" the line, of disrupting it from within.[33]

Here Davie perceives, quite rightly I think, that Pound's great con-
tribution to modern prosody was his focus on the line, rather than
the larger stanzaic block, "as the unit of composition." Whitman,
one might object, had already done the same thing, but the Whitman
free-verse line is still inherently iambic (or anapestic):

> I belíeve a léaf of gráss is nô léss than the joúrney-wórk of the
> > stárs, ‖
> And the písmîe is équally pérfect, | and a gráin of sánd, and
> > the égg of the wrén, ‖
> And the trée-toâd is a chêf-d'oéuvre for the híghest, ‖

And the rúnning bláckbêrry would adórn the párlors of
   heáven ‖[54]

In contrast, Pound's line repeatedly violates the iambic norm, which
is to say that it goes counter to the stress pattern inherent in English:

Tórches mélt in the gláre ‖
   sét fláme of the córner cóok-stâll ‖
Blúe ágate cásing the ský (as at Goúrdon thât time) ‖
   the spútter of résin, ‖
Sáffron sándal so pétals the nárrow fóot:   Hỳmenáeus Íô! ‖
   Hýmen, | Íô Hỳmenáee! ‖ Ârúnculéia! ‖
Óne scárlet flówer is cást on the blánch-whîte stóne. ‖[55]

This particular habit of lineating, with its heavy stressing, its
spondaic, amphibrachic, and cretic feet, its long sonorous vowels in
assonant patterns, was taken over by a score of poets, for example:

Bunting:

Swírl sléeping in the wáterfâll! ‖
On mótionlèss póols scúm appéaring ‖
   dísappéaring! ‖

Eáves fórmal on the zénith, ‖
   lófty cíty Kyótò, ‖
wéalthy, withóut antíquitiès! ‖[56]

H.D. in her early poetry:

Crásh on crásh of the séa, ‖
   stráining to wréck mén, séa-bôards, cóntinènts, ‖
ráging agaínst the wórld, ‖ fúriòus, ‖
stáy at lást, | for agaínst your fúry ‖
and yôur mád flíght, ‖
   the líne of héroes stánds, gód-lîke ‖[57]

And in her late:

Ô ébony ísland, | Ô táll cýprèss-trées, ‖
nów I am bléssed anéw as my dárk véils →
clíng clóse and clóse and máke an ímage of mé ‖[58]

Charles Wright:

Caráfe, | còmpotiér, | séa shêll, | váse: ‖
Blánk spáces, | whíte óbjects; ‖
Lúminoùs knóts alóng the bláck rôpe. ‖[59]

Larry Eigner:

fláke díamond of →
               the séa ‖
the shímmering sánd ‖
   dilátion | shádow in ráin ‖[40]

*127*

Interestingly, many poets who have praised Pound's music, like Robert Duncan or Allen Ginsberg, do not follow his two cardinal rules: (1) use the end-stopped line as a unit, and (2) avoid conventional iambic rhythm. Duncan's "A Poem Beginning with a Line by Pindar," for example, begins with a line one might find in Pound—"The light foot hears you and the brightness begins"—and follows Pindar's line with the Poundian "God-step at the margins of thought, / Quick adulterous tread at the heart." But these Poundian inflections soon give way to Duncan's own characteristic rhythm:

> In Góya's cánvas Cúpid and Psýche →
> have a húrt volúptuous gráce →
> brúised by redémption. ‖ The cópper líght →
> fálling upón the brówn bóy's slîght bódy →
> is cárnal fáte that sénds the soúl wáiling →
> úp from blínd ínnocènce, | ensnáred →
>     by dímness  ínto the déprivátions of desíring síght. ‖[41]

Here the consistent enjambment coupled with light, irregular stressing (chiefly anapestic) creates what is almost a prose rhythm, although alliteration and assonance are marked. The effect is carried even further in Zukofsky's "A":

> When we dréam that we spéak ‖
> We thínk we spéak →
> From frée decísion of the mínd; ‖
> Yet we dó nôt spéak, or íf we dó; ‖
> This decísion thóught to be frée
> is imáginátion | — or mémory; ‖
> Is nóthing bùt the accórd →
> An idéa invólves. ‖
> A suspénsion of júdgement →
> Àpprehénds, is nôt frée. ‖
> In dréams álso we dréam that we dréam ‖
> I gránt nó ône is decéived →
> In sô fár as hé percéives. ‖
> The imáginátions of the mínd
>              in thèmsélves
> Invólve no érror, ‖
> But Í dený that a mán →
>        affírms nóthing →
> In sô fár as hé percéives.[42]

Zukofsky's predominantly three-stress lines, sometimes run-over, sometimes pausing, are visual rather than auditory units; the rhythm pushes us forward from line to line, sound structure depending upon the very subtle pattern of word repetition—*dream, speak, free, perceives*—all with the same vowel sound and occasionally rhyming ("deceived"/"perceives"), but recurring in different contexts.

It is interesting that Allen Ginsberg, who has written extensively on Pound's "lovely stress syncopation," his "lines that could
be chanted rhythmically without violating human common sense,"
his breaking of the pentameter as "no less than the whole alteration
of human consciousness,"[43] himself uses the repetitive, bardic, oracular, loosely iambic free-verse line of Whitman rather than Pound's
more classically "musical" one; in "Howl," for that matter, the linear
unit is often stretched out into small paragraphs:

> who jumped off the Brooklyn Bridge this actually happened
> and walked away unknown and forgotten into the ghostly
> daze of Chinatown soup alleyways & firetrucks, not even
> one free beer,
> who sang out of their windows in despair, fell out of the sub-
> way window, jumped in the filthy Passaic, leaped on
> negroes, cried all over the street, danced on broken wine-
> glasses barefoot smashed phonograph records of nostalgic
> European 1930's German jazz finished the whiskey and
> threw up groaning into the bloody toilet, moans in their
> ears and the blast of colossal steamwhistles[44]

Indeed, to talk about the legacy of Pound's rhythm is to realize that
there is finally as much metrical difference as likeness. For who can
really imitate this sort of thing?

> "Búk!" | said the Sécond Báronèt, | "éh . . .
> "Tháss a fúnny lóokin' búk" | saíd the Báronèt
> Loóking at Báyle, | fólío, | 4 vóls. | in gílt léather, | "Áh . . .
>
> *(Cantos, 139)*

Here the language is alternately slangy and formal—"Buk" and
"Thass" side by side with "Looking at Bayle" and "in gilt leather."
Few poets writing today move as easily between these two poles;
few would invent a line like the third, with its fourteen syllables
carrying eight stresses and its three caesuras, the slow and broken
rhythm appearing to be "free" until we realize that it can be scanned
as follows:

> / x x /     / x /     / /     x / / x          /
> choriambus   cretic   spondee  antispast   monosyllable

In its intricacy, Pound's is a rhythm that has given *les jeunes* a goal
to aim toward, the "musical phrase," *not* the sequence of the
metronome.

3. "In my opinion," wrote Basil Bunting in 1932, " 'Propertius' was
the most important poem of our times, surpassing alike 'Mauberley'
and 'The Waste Land.' " And he explains:

> The question of the relation of Pound's poem with
> the book of Propertius' elegies does not arise, except for the

literary historian. There is no claim that this is a translation. The correspondence, the interpenetration of ancient and modern is Pound's, not Propertius's. . . .

The beautiful step of the verse, the cogent movement of thought and feeling throughout, the sensitive perception of the little balanced in the great and their mutual dependence, the extraordinary directness, here and there quite naked, achieved in spite of the complexity of the whole conception; a poem that is a society and an age, that of Rome as well as that of London. (*BBMP*, 254)

What Bunting, like so many other twentieth-century poets, learned from Pound was that "translation" should not suffer from what Peter Quartermain nicely calls "the archeological fallacy that the experience the original audience had of the poem can be replicated" (in *BBMP*, 150). In the same year that he praised *Propertius*, Bunting published his version of Horace's Ode 1.13, compressing the original twenty lines into twelve, remarkable for their curious—and quite un-Horatian—conjunction of guttural north Umbrian monosyllables, archaisms, and modern slang:

Please stop gushing about his pink
neck smooth arms and so forth, Dulcie; it makes me sick,
badtempered, silly: makes me blush.
Dribbling sweat on my chops proves I'm on tenterhooks.
—White skin bruised in a boozing bout,
ungovernable cub certain to bite out a
permanent memorandum on
those lips. Take my advice, better not count on your
tough guy's mumbling your pretty mouth
always. Only the thrice blest are in love for life,
we others are divorced at heart
soon, soon torn apart by wretched bickerings.[45]

Horace with an Anglo-Saxon overlay—the mode is identifiably Poundian. Think, for that matter, of Canto 1, whose mode Guy Davenport characterizes as follows:

It is a translation of the most archaic part of the *Odyssey:* the descent of Odysseus into Hades, a motif that goes all the way back to the Gilgamesh epic. And how does Pound translate it? Not from the Greek, but from the Latin of Andreas Divus, the first Renaissance translator of Homer, thereby working another archaic fact into his symbol. And into what kind of English does he translate it? Into the rhythms and diction of *The Seafarer* and *The Wanderer:* archaic English.[46]

Such "daedalian art"[47] sets the stage for all those twentieth-century "translations," like Bunting's version of Horace, that use the "archaic," the "classical," the historically or geographically remote culture as a source of invention. Pound's influence in this sphere has been so enormous that there is no measuring it, and one would have to discuss at some length the poetry of Olson and Duncan, of H.D. and Zukofsky, to understand even its rudiments. Pick up any poetry magazine today—say, the eclectic *American Poetry Review*—and you will find scores of "translations" that are in fact free versions of this or that Persian or Indian or Hungarian poet. Again, the movement called Ethnopoetics has made what its founder Jerome Rothenberg calls Pound's "pivotal breakthrough in translation"[48] the cornerstone of its re-creation of tribal and sacred texts from "primitive" and ancient cultures: a journal like *Alcheringa* carries into new realms (the Mayan, the Somali, the Polynesian) Pound's "invention of China," as Eliot called it, or his invention of Rome and Provence.

This is not to say that the results of the modern translation-as-invention fever have always been happy. In the introduction to his *Imitations* (1961), Robert Lowell writes:

> This book is partly self-sufficient and separate from its sources, and should be first read as a sequence, one voice running through many personalities, contrasts, and repetitions. . . . I have been reckless with literal meaning, and labored hard to get the tone. Most often this has been *a* tone, for *the* tone is something that will always more or less escape transference to another language and cultural moment. I have tried to write alive English and to do what my authors might have done if they were writing their poems now and in America.[49]

It sounds, for all the world, like Pound declaring in 1931 that *Propertius* "presents certain emotions as vital to me in 1917, faced with the infinite and ineffable imbecility of the British Empire, as they were to Propertius some centuries earlier, when faced with the infinite and ineffable imbecility of the Roman Empire."[50] Indeed, asked by Frederick Seidel about his own adaptation of a Propertius poem (see "The Ghost [After Sextus Propertius]" in *Lord Weary's Castle*), Lowell replies:

> I got him through Pound. When I read him in Latin I found a kind of Propertius you don't get in Pound at all. Pound's Propertius is a rather Ovidian figure with a great deal of Pound's fluency and humor and irony. The actual Propertius is a very excited, tense poet, rather desperate; his line is much more like parts of Marlowe's *Faustus*. And he's of all the Roman poets the most like a desperate Christian. His experiences, his love affair with Cynthia, are absolutely rending, destroying.[51]

Propertius, that is to say, becomes a mirror image of Robert Lowell.

But the transference cannot always be willed. In a stinging review of *Imitations*, John Simon argues:

The begetter of Lowell's imitations is, without question, Pound, and particularly the Pound of the versions of Propertius. . . . But it is precisely because Pound was able to ignore his original so sublimely, and because Pound is a great enough poet in his own right, that the damage to Sextus Propertius becomes an homage to Ezra Pound and English free verse. Lowell, however, is not that free from his models, nor has his free verse the energy and variety of Pound's. It is the neither-fish-nor-fowlness of Lowell's imitations, plus all the red herring they contain, that makes them perverse as translation and unpalatable as poetry.[52]

We need not agree with this harsh judgment in order to see the problems a "free" or "creative" translation à la Pound may raise. Take, for example, Lowell's "imitation" of the late Heine lyric "Mein Tag war Heiter":

Mein Tag war heiter, glücklich meine Nacht.
Mir jauchzte stets mein Volk, wenn ich die Leier
Der Dicktkunst schlug. Mein Lied war Lust und Feuer,
Hat manche schöne Gluten angefacht.[53]

In literal English:

My day was merry, happy was my night.
The people cheered me on whenever I smote
The lyre of poetry. My song was joy and fire,
It kindled many a lovely blaze.[54]

And in Lowell's version:

My zenith was luckily happier than my night:
whenever I touched the lyre of inspiration, I smote
the Chosen People. Often — all sex and thunder —
I pierced those overblown and summer clouds.[55]

Heine, suffering on his "mattress-grave," remembers a time when both his days *and* his nights were happy; he remembers how his poetry moved the people ("mein Volk"), what fiery power his song could have. Lowell changes all this: "Mein Tag" is now equated with the poet's youth, "meine Nacht" with his old age. The poet's song "smote" not "mein Volk" but, in an allusion to the Jewish poet's radicalism and youthful atheism, "the Chosen People." "Lust" is mistranslated as "sex" (i.e., "lust"), and the poet recalls himself as quintessential rebel, "piercing those overblown and summer clouds" of ordinary life with his sexual anger.[56] Heine's concern for the lyric imagination is thus reduced to a set of references to the poet's youthful rebellion; it can be related to Lowell's own poem by that name.

But suppose we forget about the Heine original and read Lowell's poem as his own version of German Romanticism even as we read the *Homage* as Pound's invention of Propertius. In this case, we have Lowell-Heine solemnly announcing that his youth ("zenith") was happier than his "night." Not a very arresting statement. Again, the "lyre of inspiration" is now viewed as some sort of irritant, a way of shaking up Lowell's own "Chosen People," which is to say the Lowells and Winslows of Boston. We know from *Life Studies* that Lowell as a young man was "all sex and thunder," but in what sense could he pierce the "overblown and summer clouds" (of New England?) with his angry sexuality? Are we to assume that New England responded to his clarion call? And, if so, what is his role now that his "zenith" has passed?

It is hard to take these questions seriously and indeed the poem only treats its material as gesture. Heine's particular sense of loss—the loss experienced by one who was once the poet of the people—evaporates and there is nothing that quite fills the gap. It is a problem by no means unique to Lowell, the point being that Poundian "translation" is a very difficult process, depending finally upon the poet's ability to make the past present. As Guy Davenport has put it:

> What is most modern in our time frequently turns out
> to be the most archaic. The sculpture of Brancusi belongs to
> the art of the Cyclades in the ninth century B.C. Corbusier's
> buildings in their cubist phase look like the white clay houses
> of Anatolia and Malta. . . . in *Finnegans Wake* [Joyce] writes
> across the fact of the Indo-European origin of European lan-
> guages, seeing in the kinship of tongues the great archeologi-
> cal midden of history, the tragic incomprehensibility of which
> provides him with a picture of the funeral of Western culture.
> (*GOI*, 21)

## II

I turn now to what seems to me the most interesting side of the Pound legacy: namely, the poet's canto structure. In a review of Stanley Burnshaw's *The Seamless Web* (1970), Davenport remarks:

> For all his careful inspection of the kinds of voice with which
> poems speak, Mr. Burnshaw sees *the poem* as a particular kind
> of poetry to the exclusion of other kinds. Poetry for him is
> lyric or elegiac almost wholly, and I think what moves him is
> *song*, the rich surge of emotion, the radiant glory of speech in
> flight. This is splendid, of course, but it tends toward a puri-
> tanism that diminishes our taste for the comic, the satiric, the
> grotesque, the narrative poem, the wholesome and drab. (*GOI*,
> 213)

*An epic is a poem including history.* Perhaps Pound's chief gift to the contemporary poet, we are now beginning to see, is his recovery for poetry of "the comic, the satiric, the grotesque, the narrative," his move beyond the isolated lyric poem (*poema*) valorized by New Critics like Stanley Burnshaw, the poem as embodiment of "the radiant glory of speech in flight," of crystallized emotion, toward a larger, more capacious poetic form (*poesis*) that could once again accommodate various levels of discourse.

This is the point made in the opening chapters of Michael A. Bernstein's *The Tale of the Tribe*. One of Pound's main motives in the *Cantos*, Bernstein argues, is to challenge the dominance the novel had achieved by the end of the nineteenth century as *the* genre that could engage political, economic, historical, and social realities. The *Cantos* attempt to reappropriate these "realities" and to absorb them into the lyric fabric; the "Inductive or Ideogrammic Method" is combined with "Confucian Historiography":

> The seemingly unobtrusive moment in Canto VIII, when the first series of historical letters is introduced into *The Cantos* and the personality of Sigismundo is shown by juxtaposing his prose instruction concerning a painter he wishes to engage with a lyric poem he writes for Isotta degli Atti *without privileging either medium*, represents one of the decisive turning-points in modern poetics, opening for verse the capacity to include domains of experience long since considered alien territory.[57]

The recovery of such "alien territory" occurs most obviously, among Pound's heirs, in Williams's *Paterson* and Olson's *Maximus*. The connections between these poems and the *Cantos* have been made frequently, not least by Bernstein himself, who takes up the knotty problem of the relationship between the historical and mythological codes, between symbol and rupture in these works. Other critics have traced a lineage from the *Cantos* via *Paterson* to the long poetic sequences of Lowell and Berryman. *The Dream Songs*, for example, has been called "Poundian" in its range and allusiveness, its shifting from humor to pathos, from high style to black slang.[58] But neither Berryman nor Lowell, nor for that matter Ginsberg or Bunting, violates the lyric frame as do such other Poundian poets as Zukofsky and, in their different ways, Guy Davenport and Jerome Rothenberg. A few examples must suffice here.

Zukofsky's "*A*"-12 (1950–51) takes up 138 of the 800-odd pages that constitute "*A*," the long poem written over the half century between 1928 and 1974, when "*A*"-23 was completed. Following hard upon the two-page "*A*"-11, which is a formal love song for the poet's wife, Celia, and his son, Paul, "*A*"-12 begins on a musical note that takes us back to the opening line of "*A*"-1, "A /Round of fiddles playing Bach," with the lines:

> *Out of deep need*
> Four trombones and the organ in the nave
> A torch surged—

Timed the theme Bach's name
Dark larch and ridge, night.

Not only is the subject here music, but the lines have an intricate sound pattern: "ti*m*ed"/"the*m*e"/"na*m*e"; "*D*ark"/"*l*arch"; "lar*ch*"/ "rid*ge*." The musical motif comes back again and again, in references to Paul's violin playing, to "H—playing / The Turkish Concerto / By Mozart" ("A," p. 161), and so on. But Bach is also viewed as a father, and throughout "A"-12 we find interwoven stories of fathers and sons: Odysseus and Telemachus; the physician Nichomaeus and Aristotle ("A," p. 236); the groaning old father of Gertrude Stein's *The Making of Americans,* who protests to his son, who is dragging him through his own orchard, "Stop! I did not drag my father beyond this tree" ("A," p. 168); and, centrally, Zukofsky's own father and grandfather in their relationships to him and his own relationship to Paul as well as to the "Poor Pay Pfc. Jackie," neighborhood kid and surrogate son, who is sent off to fight in the Korean War and writes a series of letters (in slangy, nonorthographic prose) to the poet.

Reading fragment after fragment about the poet's childhood on the Lower East Side and then about Paul's childhood, one realizes that the germ of a whole novel is contained in the pages of "A"-12. But the narrative cannot be linear because for Zukofsky, as for Pound in less extreme form, experience is regarded as unfinished, indeed always only potential—moving toward something that never quite happens. There is no unifying principle in "A"-12, no Supreme Fiction that will bring all the fragments together, because, in Don Byrd's words, "the structure of history is not to be found in logic or mythologic . . . but in language and the complex web by which language is involved with perception."[59] And because language is so central, straight prose—the medium of the novel, however alogical its structure—cannot be sufficient. Rather, the literary pastiches and borrowings (e.g., the dialogue between Titania and Bottom on pp. 133–34, the speech of Stephen Dedalus on Aristotle on p. 142, or the condensed version of a Reznikoff narrative on pp. 208–10)[60] are arranged in a verbal-visual structure that accords with Zukofsky's declaration:

I'll tell you.
About my *poetics* —

music
∫
speech

An integral
Lower limit speech
Upper limit music

*("A," p. 138)*

Between these "limits" we find pictograms like the valentine on page
129:

or the playful graph on pages 163–64, which begins

MAN → EARTH → WORLDS

Thus the discourses of commerce (the greeting card) or of science
(the graph) are absorbed into the fabric of the poem. Again, "A"-12
follows the example of the *Cantos* in juxtaposing the found object
to the moment of metamorphosis; Zukofsky's father, for example,
becomes for the boy Paul the image of Aristotle:

> P.Z. remembers the day "Aristotle" died,
> Still owns his snowshoes
> Indispensable in Macedonia.
> I bought him two balloons:
> "Plato" and "Aristotle."
> Filled with air they had faces
> Mounted on snowshoes
> As expected
> "Plato" and "Aristotle."
> "Aristotle" —
> Carus, to Paul, it was sad.
>
> ("*A*," p. 164)

Such moments occur against the backdrop of historical events:
"the first John Jacob Astor / Landing in Baltimore / With $25 and
seven flutes to sell" ("*A*," p. 190), within ever-shifting political and
geographic frames. The "upper limit / Music" appears in odal
hymns, chants, and sonnets; the "lower limit / Speech" in the conversations of the poet with Paul or with his father or with the poet
Lorine Niedecker.

To what voice can we attribute all this heterogeneous material? Of Pound's voice in the *Cantos*, Michael Bernstein writes:

Pound's authorial "voice," I think, is often implicitly and theo-
retically definable as that unspoken "marginal presence" which
silently articulates (makes sense out of) the gaps in the printed
text, a voice we only really discover in the process of "speak-
king it" ourselves. . . . He wanted the text to give the impression of the tribe's own heritage narrating itself, of the different
historical voices addressing us as if without the mediation of
one unique narrator or controlling author. It is almost as
though the texture of *The Cantos* were designed to illustrate
Karl Popper's idea of an "epistemology without a knowing
subject," of information objectively existing and available for
communal use without necessarily being fully realized in any
single individual's competence.[61]

This abandonment of the "speaking subject" is carried a step
further in Zukofsky's "*A*." In the *Cantos,* after all, the "ideogrammic
method" allows us to move from image to image, following a particular thread (mythological, historical, economic, etc.), whereas in
"*A*" such binding devices are rare and accordingly the reader must
tease out, even more extensively than in Pound, the "repeat in history." Indeed, the status of history in these poems is curious. As Guy
Davenport, himself a great inventor of collage-texts,[62] puts it:

To say that *The Cantos* is "a voyage in time" is to be blind to
the poem altogether. We miss immediately the achievement
upon which the success of the poem depends, its rendering
time transparent and negligible, its dismissing the supposed
corridors and perspectives *down* which the historian invites us
to look. . . . In Pound's spatial sense of time, the past is here,
now; its invisibility is our blindness, not its absence.[63]

This is also true of a poem like "*A*"-12, in which the time of
Roosevelt and Wilkie coexists with "1313. Rabbi Hacen Ben Sal-
omo— / (Great One Singer Son of Peace— / Taught Spanish
Christians / To dance in a church" ("*A*," p. 186). But in "*A*," as in a
work like John Ashbery's *Litany,* these "events" are not only spatialized; they are, as such "language" poets as Ron Silliman have
argued, subordinated to the play of language itself: "Each line &/or
stanza a study in balance, silence (peace) proposed as maximum
stress in all directions, thus active. This never-to-be resolved equi-
librium of the spoken within the written within the spoken etc. is
for him the motivating center of craft."[64]
Zukofsky thus carries further Pound's program for a poem
including history, a poem that no longer privileges the lyric over,
say, the found object (actual letter received, newspaper passage,
document), a poem in which the single startling epiphany gives way
to collage, which is to say to the juxtaposition of disparate materials
without commitment to explicit syntactical relations between elements and without a consistent authorial voice as ordering principle.

This notion of collage is taken even further in the work of Jerome Rothenberg, not so much in his lyric poems as in the unique anthologies that began to appear in 1968 with the publication of *Technicians of the Sacred.*

Rothenberg has regularly praised what he calls "the collage composition of the *Cantos*" and is fond of quoting Pound's statement that "*all* ages are contemporaneous *in the mind.*"[65] In the "Pre-Face" to *Revolution of the Word: The Avant-Garde, 1914–45,* in which he presents us with an alternative tradition to the accepted modernist canon, Rothenberg writes:

> When Pound writes (1915) of a basic poetic process that involves "a rush of experience into the vortex" (i.e., the mind), he is talking about a condition that has become newly critical. . . . where the ideas truly "rush," the process no longer links event to event in good straight lines. In the face of multiple chronologies, many poets turn to synchronicity (the simultaneous existence of all places & times) as a basic organizing principle. As a method, a process of making the poem, this becomes "collage."[66]

How does this purpose work in a Rothenberg anthology? In an essay called "On Anthologies" (1978), Rothenberg begins:

> It seems to me that I've been making anthologies for as long as I've been making poems *per se.* . . . As a kid I inherited a large desk with a sheet of glass on top, beneath which I would slip in pages of poems—my own & others'—& pictures, etc. that I had been coming across in the stuff I was reading. I used to arrange them to form "shows" of works that seemed, by juxtaposition, to inform each other. I also typed up poems from different places & times & kept them in a series of folders marked *anthology.* That was from high school days & stopped sometime in college, when I started to *buy* books & be deceived by other people's arrangements.[67]

What the poet recognizes here is that it is by *juxtaposition* that works "inform each other." Or, as Pound points out in the *ABC of Reading,* the word "red" can only be defined by putting together such words as

| | |
|---|---|
| ROSE | CHERRY |
| IRON RUST | FLAMINGO |

(*ABCR,* 22)

To put an anthology together thus means to assemble seemingly diverse particulars: "I've felt," says Rothenberg, "a sense of the book as poem, a large composition operating by assemblage or collage: my own voice emerging sometimes as translator, sometimes as commentator, but still obedient to the other voices, whether 'out there' or 'in here.' "[68] Notice that this takes us back to Bernstein's account of voice in the *Cantos* as "unspoken marginal presence," as "information objectively existing and available for communal use without necessarily being fully realized in any single individual's competence."[69]

*America a Prophecy,* assembled in 1973 with the collaboration of George Quasha, begins with Pound's dictum that poetry is "language charged with meaning to the utmost degree" and outlines four sources upon which the anthology draws: (1) "the aboriginal poetry of the American continent"; (2) "other traditions, usually relegated to the status of 'folklore,' notably Afro-American oral poetry"; (3) "an ongoing meditative and visionary tradition, European in origin"; and (4) a "meta-poetry" or "expansion of verbal possibilities" that includes diaries, letters, notebooks, scientific writing, visual and ritual media, modern experimental poetry, and so on.[70] In arranging texts from these four sources, the emphasis is to be on "the interplay of myth and history," following the injunctions of Emerson, Thoreau, and Whitman, and especially those of Pound.

Let us look at a particular unit: the section called "Image-Making" under the category "Map Four: Renewals" (pp. 403–52). Image-making, so the editors' headnote tells us, "includes such concepts as hieroglyphics, emblem poems, symbol, visualization, image, imagism, ideogram, phanopoiea, vortex, cubism, surrealism, frottage, hypnologues, photoheliograph, metaphor, objectivism, dialectic, concrete poetry, projectivism, deep image, chance imagery, and mudra" (p. 401). This dizzying catalog of nonparallel items (some refer to trope, others to genre or mode or movement; some, like *cubism,* are familiar terms; others, like *hypnologues,* are coinages; still others, like *mudra,* refer to a specific religious practice)[71] interestingly includes a number of Poundian items (imagism, ideogram, vortex, phanopoeia), and indeed Pound's presence provides a point of reference for the entire text. Thus the section opens with a statement about the thaumaturgic power of the written word, taken from Boris de Rachewiltz's (then Pound's son-in-law) essay "Pagan and Magic Elements in Ezra Pound's Works." This passage is followed on later pages by such Pound items as an italicized section from "A Retrospect" (p. 409); an extract from Fenollosa's *Chinese Written Character,* prefaced by Hugh Kenner's biographical note on Fenollosa in *The Pound Era* (p. 415); Rothenberg's own account of the Vortex, again quoting Kenner (pp. 417–18); the entire "Seven Lakes Canto" (Canto 49, on pp. 418–20); a passage about "ideogrammic structure" quoting *Guide to Kulchur* (p. 420); and a note on Pound and the Objectivists (p. 430).

These Pound references function, so to speak, as metapoetic signposts. The "poem" itself begins with (1) ten lines from Longfellow's *Hiawatha;* (2) a frame from the Dresden Codex, one of the Mayan books containing history, prophecy, song, science, and genealogy, "written on long strips of bark paper, folded like screens and covered with gesso" (p. 404); (3) a pictograph from the mural of Tlalocan at Teotihuacán, which depicts a Toltec paradise; "the sexual motif," according to the end note, "appears to inform the imagery of the ritual, reminding us of the Tibetan Tantric link between sexuality and higher consciousness"; (4) the image of the "torsion-form," which is, according to Wilhelm Reich, the "basic form" of the "sexual embrace"; (5) two emblem poems written by the Shakers between 1844 and 1859, "visionary drawings . . . really spiritual messages in pictorial form," felt to be controlled by supernatural agencies. (See fig. 1.) The drawings, according to Edward Deming Andrews (*The Gift to Be Simple*), "often contained poems inscribed in a circle, heart or perhaps a scroll carried by a dove or angel" (p. 407). Since these ink drawings are hard to decipher, the editors helpfully transcribe the poems written around and within the leaf: "Ho ho ho (Shout) / Now while my love is flowing / You are not forgotten," and so on. This transcription is followed by the italicized sentence:

> "*It is wonderful how a handwriting which is illegible can be read, oh yes it can.*" (Gertrude Stein, from *The Geographical History of America [1936]*).

Here the conjunction of Shaker emblem poem and Stein aphorism seems to me precisely the sort of thing we find in the *Cantos*, for we suddenly realize that the "illegible" (to us) handwriting on the left can be read, oh yes it can, since the editors have supplied us with the printed version on the right and a commentary beneath it. If a text is illegible, the collaging of writing and print implies, wait and before long it will reveal its secret.

A few pages later, under the heading "The Standard of Clarity," Rothenberg introduces us to a text by Louis Agassiz, "acknowledged as a master of the art of scientific description by Emerson, Thoreau, and William James. Ezra Pound claimed him as a model" (p. 411). "The art of Agassiz," says Rothenberg, "consists in revealing the Minute Particular as Luminous Detail; or, in Pound's phrase, the natural object is always the adequate symbol." What follows is a minute description of *Cyanea arctica* that begins, "Seen floating in the water Cyanea Arctica exhibits a large circular disk, of a substance not unlike jelly, thick in the centre, and suddenly thinning out towards the edge, which presents several indentations" (p. 411). As Agassiz continues, he introduces a series of metaphors—tentacles as "floating tresses of hair," organs as "bunches of grapes," "four masses of folds, hanging like rich curtains, loosely waving to and fro," the "disk" of the animal opening and closing like an umbrella (p. 412). Ironically, the "scientific" description by Agassiz is more heavily metaphoric than the poem to which it is juxtaposed, Emily Dickinson's "Banish Air from Air," which takes its terms—the notion of "banish[ing] Air from Air," of dividing light—quite literally.

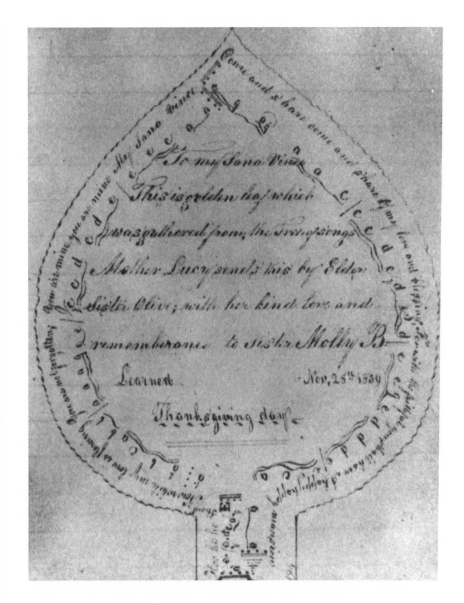

**Figure 1.** From Edward D. Andrews, *The Gift to be Simple: Songs, Dances, and Rituals of the American Shakers* (New York: Dover Publications, 1940), p. 36.

Moreover, the "Three Definitions from *Sharp Eyes*" by the naturalist
William Hamilton Gibson that are printed directly beneath Dickinson's lyric look like perfect haiku:

*Poppies*
Flowers closed like two clam-shells;
inner petals coiled.

*Lupine*
The wheel-like leaf closes
downward against the stem
at its center,
like a closed umbrella,
or rises
in the form of a goblet.

And Rothenberg concludes: the texts "combine accurate observation
and sharp descriptive language with a post-Transcendentalist sense
of immanent power in all living things. [Gibson's] illustrations of his
own text suggest both Blake's illuminations and later uses of photomontage" (p. 413). Thus a strong case is made for the proximity of
scientific and poetic discourse: the collage suggests that Gibson is a
poet, the author of delicate haiku-like utterance, even as Dickinson,
wedged between Agassiz and Gibson, turns into something of a sci-
entist: "While Cubes in a Drop / Or Pellets of Shape / Fit / Films
cannot annul. . . ."

To find, at the center of "Image-Making," Pound's "Seven
Lakes Canto" is to see the collage principle of the *Cantos* at work.
For Canto 49 is itself a collage, consisting, so Hugh Kenner tells us,
of "(1) [eight] anonymous poems much rearranged; (2) the Emper-
or's poem; (3) a folk song; (4) a terminal Poundian distich and four
interpolated Poundian lines."[72] Sanehide Kodama has identified the
source of the poems as "eight famous paintings of scenes along a
river in China which pours into Lake Dotei. Ezra Pound's parents
owned an old Japanese manuscript book which contained the eight
Chinese and eight Japanese poems illustrated by the paintings. The
book is entitled *Sho-Sho* [the river] *Hakkei.*"[73] So the first six lines
of the canto, evidently based on the sixth painting or scene, go like
this:

For the seven lakes, and by no man these verses:
Rain; empty river; a voyage,
Fire from frozen cloud, heavy rain in the twilight
Under the cabin roof was one lantern.
The reeds are heavy; bent;
and the bamboos speak as if weeping.

(p. 418)

We read this passage quite differently in *America a Prophecy*
than we would if we met it in the normal sequence of the *Cantos*.

For one thing, lines like "Fire from frozen cloud, heavy rain in the twilight," and later, "sharp long spikes of the cinnamon" remind us of William Hamilton Gibson's "the wheel-like leaf closes / downward against the stem / at its center, / like a closed umbrella." For another, Rothenberg's "framing"—the account of Vortex preceding the canto and of ideogrammic structure following, the latter leading into Wylie Sypher's discussion of the synchronization of time sense in modern art, "corresponding to cinematic montage or juxtaposition of elements"—such framing foregrounds the imagistic, perceptual quality of Pound's collage, itself made up of so many fragments, rather than its references to money and banking ("State by creating riches shd. thereby get into debt?"), which connect it to the neighboring cantos in the Adams sequence. The metatexts, in other words, "inform" one another even as the analogies to Agassiz or to Gibson or to Gertrude Stein provide a sense of ongoing process, of beginning again and again. To cut up and rearrange texts, the anthology implies, is to see familiar works in quite a new way. How seriously, for example, can we take Pound's "Sun up; work / sundown, to rest / dig well and drink of the water," when we read it against Stein's "Question and butter. / I find the butter very good / Lifting belly is so kind. / Lifting belly fattily" (p. 422)?

As we make our way through "Image-Making," Pound's Canto is further "informed" by texts written by the poet's followers—Williams, Oppen, Zukofsky—and by contemporary analogues—for example, to Dada and Surrealist works—as well as by later texts, partially belonging to the Pound tradition but also standing apart from it—a John Cage parable, of which more in a moment, a Jackson Mac Low "Light Poem" (1962), a series of concrete poems, and finally Bernadette Mayer's "Fiction," which deploys Steinian language, syntax, and "naive" storytelling devices to invent a kind of antipoem including history.

"Image-Making" can thus be read as a poetic sequence about different solutions to the question of the thaumaturgic power of the image, the point being that, as different as Stein's *Tender Buttons* is from the mural of Tlalocan, as different as Emmet Williams's concrete poem "Like Attacks Like" (p. 43) is from the Shaker emblem poems, these works are addressing themselves to related questions: (1) How do we perceive? (2) How do we record our perceptions? And (3) what do we take these perceptions to mean? Since it is often difficult to know where a given text ends and the editors' commentary begins, or again, at what point that commentary blurs into a commentary by some other critic or scholar, the collage anthology becomes, in an ironic sense, the "seamless web" Stanley Burnshaw describes. Consider the place, in the larger scheme of things, of the following anecdote told by John Cage, which is printed just a few pages after the "Seven Lakes Canto":

Translating Basho's Haiku

*Text: Japanese*
Matasutake ya
shiranu ko-no-ha no
hebaritsuku
        Basho, 1644–1694

*English transliteration*
Mushroom;
ignorance; leaf of tree
adhesiveness

*Versions:*

*R.B. Blythe translates Basho's haiku as follows:*
The leaf of some unknown tree sticking on the mushroom.
*I showed this translation to a Japanese composer friend. He said
he did not find it very interesting. I said, "How would you translate
it?" Two days later he brought me the following:*
Mushroom does not know that leaf is sticking on it.
*Getting the idea, I made during the next three years, the following:*
That that's unknown brings mushroom and leaf together.
*And the one I prefer?*
What leaf? What mushroom?

(p. 437)

What leaf, what mushroom? Pound is not likely to have posed
this Zen question: he is too assertive, too passionately didactic to
allow for an "opening of the field" quite as self-surrendering as this
one. But Rothenberg, standing apart from both, can see the obvious
connections between Cage's anecdote and the sequence of Japanese
"stills" in the "Seven Lakes Canto." Or again, between the Basho
haiku and the William Hamilton Gibson naturalist descriptions of
flora and fauna.

"To know the season," Guy Davenport observes, "we must
understand metamorphosis, for things are never still, and never
wear the same mask from age to age. The contemporary is without
meaning while it is happening: it is a vortex, a whirlpool of action.
It is a labyrinth. . . . *The Cantos* . . . are labyrinthine in structure, a
zigzag of subject, modifying and illuminating each other by proximity,
treating time as if it were a space over which one can move in
any direction" (*GOI*, 56). As the lessons of Pound's "poem including
history" come home to us, we will witness more such "labyrinthine
structures." Anthologies like *America a Prophecy*, "short stories"
like Davenport's *Tatlin!*, performance works like David Antin's *Tuning*, and long poems like Zukofsky's *"A,"* or, in its very different way,
James Merrill's "Ouija board" trilogy—these give testimony to the
vitality of the "daedalian art" of the *Cantos*.

# Chapter Seven

# "A Fine New Kind

# of Realism":

## Six Stein Styles in

## Search of a Reader

A grammar relates to not liking to see again
those you used to know.
—Gertrude Stein, *How to Write*

**W**e usually think of Gertrude Stein's writings as falling into
two broad categories: on the one hand, the public, accessible, "transparent," and more or less straightforward
mode of *The Autobiography of Alice B. Toklas* or of such well-known
essays as "Portraits and Repetition"; on the other, the opaque, private, experimental, "difficult" mode that ranges from *Tender Buttons* (1914) to *Mrs. Reynolds* (1941–42) and beyond.[1] Obvious as
this basic distinction may be, it doesn't get us very far. For is the
device of repetition in, say, Stein's portrait of Matisse in fact dupli-
cated in a work like "Patriarchal Poetry"? And is the so-called plain
style of the *Autobiography* equivalent to the plain style of *Wars I
Have Seen?* What, moreover, about chronology: does Stein's work
chart some sort of progress from an early experimentalism to a
mature directness or is it the other way around? Or neither, given

that *Stanzas in Meditation* (1929–33), one of Stein's most difficult and obscure works, dates precisely from the period in which she wrote "Alice's" autobiography?

My own view is that there are at least six basic variations on the famous Stein signature, which is to say, at least half a dozen permutations of the familiar model, "Very fine is my valentine. Very fine and very mine," or "Toasted susie is my ice-cream." To examine the larger spectrum of Stein's styles may help us to dispel two still-popular myths about her work. First, that her fabled "difficulty," like her rarer clarity, is all of a piece. And second, that her "easy" works avoid the stylization of her difficult ones and hence do not demand the same reading strategies. I want to suggest that, on the contrary, Stein's texts, whatever their date of composition or their hypothetical genre, must be read strenuously in keeping with her own notion that, whatever else a literary text may be, its central unit is always the sentence, that verbal unit that encompasses what Stein calls "Resemble assemble reply."[2]

1. Consider, to begin with, the status of description and narration in what is surely one of Stein's most transparent and seemingly innocent texts: *Paris France,* the short memoir she wrote at Bilignin in the early months of World War II. Here is the opening:

> PARIS, FRANCE is exciting and peaceful.
> I was only four years old when I was first in Paris and talked french there and was photographed there and went to school there, and ate soup for early breakfast and had leg of mutton and spinach for lunch, I always liked spinach, and a black cat jumped on my mother's back. That was more exciting than peaceful. I do not mind cats but I do not like them to jump on my back. There are lots of cats in Paris and in France and they can do what they like, sit on the vegetables or among the groceries, stay in or go out. It is extraordinary that they fight so little among themselves considering how many cats there are. There are two things that french animals do not do, cats do not fight much and do not howl much and chickens do not get flustered running across the road, if they start to cross the road they keep on going which is what french people do too.[3]

Generically, this account of French life recalls nothing so much as a fourth- or fifth-grade reader; indeed, Stein's simple declarative sentences probably do not contain a single word that a schoolgirl of her day would not have known. Nor do the sentences in this "reader" seem in any way remarkable, conveying as they do ordinary observations about what is perceived ("There are lots of cats in Paris") and remembered ("I always liked spinach"). The phrasal repetition for which Stein is best known, for that matter, is kept to a minimum, and even syntactic parallelism (for example, "talked french there and was photographed there and went to school there") is not especially prominent.

But the reference to "Paris, France" is redundant even for a grade-school child, and of course no primer written for children would contain the sentence, "Paris, France is exciting and peaceful," the second adjective contradicting the first and making it all but impossible for Stein's reader to formulate an image of place. The semantic contradiction is reinforced by the syntactic one at the end of the first sentence, where the coordinating conjunction "and" joins a clause referring to a specific incident ("a black cat jumped on my mother's back") to a preceding "when" clause with its cataloging of habitual actions. Normal usage would require a period after "spinach," followed by a temporal marker like "one day."

Why then does Stein ignore the basic distinction between perfect and imperfect verb forms and draw the clause in question into the larger parataxis of her composition? Perhaps because even in as seemingly transparent a text as *Paris France,* her urge is to minimize temporal distinctions, to present us with a spatial figure, a synchronicity, analogous to the flat or planar landscape of a Cézanne or Picasso. As Lyn Hejinian observes, "One of the characteristics of Stein's writing is that elements coexist with alternatives in the work; phrase or sentence A is not obliterated when it appears, slightly altered perhaps, as phrase or sentence B."[4] Indeed Stein must, so to speak, draw the black cat out of her verbal hat so as to confirm the exciting/peaceful paradox of her opening sentence. "I do not mind cats but I do not like them to jump on my back. There are lots of cats in Paris and in France and they can do what they like. . . ." The two sentences are placed side by side without a linking adverb that might explain their relationship, but the positioning makes a sense of its own. Insofar as they jump, "french cats" (the lower case *f* designating that nationality is merely an attribute, rather like size or color) are exciting; insofar as they do as they like, they are peaceful. Indeed, we now learn, "french animals" in general are peaceful: "chickens do not get flustered running across the road." And from chickens it is only one step to human beings: "if they [chickens] start to cross the road they keep on going which is what french people do too."

End of paragraph. The "lesson" is as inexorable as that of any schoolbook. "Paris, France is exciting and peaceful." How is it exciting and peaceful? Its animals and hence people are very lively and always in motion but "they keep on going" without getting "flustered." Stein's "argument," wholly devoid of logic or empirical evidence as it is, carries us along by the sheer force of its relational syntax. Accordingly, the text remains peculiarly impervious to explication. When Richard Bridgman suggests that Stein's optimistic portrait of a France forty years into the twentieth century and hence ready to "settle down to middle age and a pleasant life and the enjoyment of ordinary living" (*PF*, 119) is "pitifully unrealistic,"[5] he is assuming that the mode of *Paris France* is essentially expository. But as Stein herself points out, hers is intentionally an external, and therefore an idealized, view of her adopted country:

> After all everybody, that is, everybody who writes is interested in living inside themselves in order to tell what is inside themselves. That is why writers have to have two countries, the one where they belong and the one in which they live really. The second one is romantic, it is separate from themselves, it is not real but it is really there. (*PF*, 2)

Which is to say that the "France" of jumping cats and docile chickens is not "real" (indeed, one of the central ironies of the book is that Paris itself, the urban environment, is, so to speak, under erasure, the focus throughout being on country life), even as, within the synchronic field of the text itself, the exciting/peaceful realm called France is "really there."

The paradox, then, is that Stein practices what William James called, with reference to *Three Lives*, "a fine new kind of realism,"[6] even as she resolutely opposes mimesis, the notion that the verbal or visual construct can replicate the external world of nature. *Paris France* tells us precious little about French history or geography, but in its particular focus on, say, the village girl Helen Button and her dog, William, or on the proper preparation of *quenelles,* it creates a verbal space we come to recognize as *Stein France*. In the same vein, the anecdotes about famous artists that fill the pages of *The Autobiography of Alice B. Toklas* are notable less for their informational content than for their attention to the principle that, as Stein put it about Cézanne, "in composition one thing was as important as another thing."[7]

2. The "transparent" style of the *Autobiography* is, of course, more complex than that of *Paris France,* given its fictional premise that Toklas rather than Stein tells the story. Like the later memoir, however, the *Autobiography* purports to tell its story quite literally, with a minimum of fuss. Here is "Alice Toklas's" account of the famous first night of Stravinsky's *Sacre du printemps:*

> Nijinsky did not dance in the Sacre du Printemps but he created the dance of those who did dance.
>
> We arrived in the box and sat down in the three front chairs leaving one chair behind. Just in front of us in the seats below was Guillaume Apollinaire. He was dressed in evening clothes and he was industriously kissing various important looking ladies' hands. He was the first one of his crowd to come out into the great world wearing evening clothes and kissing hands. We were very amused and very pleased to see him do it. It was the first time we had seen him

doing it. After the war they all did these things but he was the only one to commence before the war.

Just before the performance began the fourth chair in our box was occupied. We looked around and there was a tall well-built young man, he might have been a dutchman, a scandinavian or an american and he wore a soft evening shirt with the tiniest pleats all over the front of it. It was impressive, we had never even heard that they were wearing evening shirts like that. That evening when we got home Gertrude Stein did a portrait of the unknown called a Portrait of One.

The performance began. No sooner had it commenced when the excitement began. The scene now so well known with its brilliantly coloured background now not at all extraordinary, outraged the Paris audience. No sooner did the music begin and the dancing than they began to hiss. The defenders began to applaud. We could hear nothing, as a matter of fact. I never did hear any of the music of the Sacre du Printemps because it was the only time I ever saw it and one literally could not, throughout the whole performance, hear the sound of music.[8]

Here the narrator seems to be doing nothing but recording, as faithfully as possible, what happened at the first night even as a child might report it. Nijinsky "did not dance . . . but he created the dance of those who did dance," "We . . . sat down in the three front chairs leaving one chair behind," and so on. No metaphor, no symbolism, no learned allusions, no background information about the Ballet Russe or Diaghilev, no biographical sketch of Stravinsky, and, most important, no word as to Gertrude Stein's judgment on the music or the ballet. Instead, we are treated by the "naive" Alice Toklas to an account of Apollinaire's hand-kissing habits and a description of the pleated evening shirt worn by the unknown "'tall well-built young man" who becomes the subject (dressed "in the best most silk and water much, in the best most silk") of Stein's portrait "One."[9]

Why the shift of focus from purported subject to ancillary detail? Like a Cubist collage, Stein's composition creates its effect, not by representing the external event but by, so to speak, pasting up metonymically related items that, as in the case of *Paris France*, spatialize the narrative and make it what Stein calls a "continuous present."[10] Thus Apollinaire's outrageous hand-kissing ritual ("He was the first one of his crowd to come out into the great world wearing evening clothes and kissing hands") ironically parallels Stravinsky's "rite of spring." "After the war," Toklas tells us, "they all did these things but he was the only one to commence before the war." The comic miniature version of the avant-garde ballet makes the latter accessible to us. We know that this is an important evening, an evening to remember—"the first time we had seen him doing it."

In the same vein, the never-before-seen "soft evening shirt with the tiniest pleats all over the front of it," an evening shirt worn by a man who "might have been a dutchman, a scandinavian or an american," is a portent of things to come: "we had never even heard," says Toklas, "that they were wearing evening shirts like that." The portrait Stein produces that night is appropriately called "One" because the evening shirt is a "first," even as Apollinaire's hand-kissing routine is a first. In this context the actual performance of Stravinsky becomes a kind of anticlimax, even as a Picasso collage may place its "subject" in the corner and place primary emphasis on a calling card or a newspaper page.

The *Autobiography* describes neither the music nor the dancing; the "anecdote," which is thus quite unlike the anecdotes found in the typical biography or autobiography, is all the more telling. What the reader comes to see is that (1) the first night of *Sacre du printemps* is a watershed for the arts, prefiguring the watershed soon to be created by the war; (2) Stein herself is part of the magic circle of artists which includes Nijinsky, Apollinaire, and Stravinsky in that the "well-built young man" (Carl Van Vechten) becomes the occasion for her own artistic composition, the portrait "One"; and (3) the neutral and nonjudgmental voice of Alice Toklas, herself neither artist nor critic but merely someone who is alternately "amused" and "astonished" by the furor in the theater, serves to highlight the brilliance of a Nijinsky, an Apollinaire—and of course of Gertrude Stein herself.

The compositional strategy of the *Autobiography* is thus one of metonymic deflection. Readers who know Stein's work primarily through James Mellow's biography or Marty Martin's play *Gertrude Stein Gertrude Stein Gertrude Stein* or through the countless memoirs of Stein and Toklas in Paris assume that Stein's own autobiography is "colorful," a series of juicy stories about the French/American avant-garde. But in fact the style of the *Autobiography* is not especially imagistic, its descriptions less than concrete, the emphasis being on such pronoun-copula units as "He was, "We were," "We looked," "when we got home," "We could hear nothing." Nijinsky, for example, is defined as he who "created the dance of those who did dance." Period.

3. "The dance of those who did dance." Incremental repetition is not especially notable in the *Autobiography*, but such locutions as "We were very amused and very pleased to see him do it. It was the first time we had seen him doing it" recall those Stein texts, from *Three Lives* to *Lectures in America*, in which repetition is the central device. I want next to consider the two poles of this more "difficult" Stein compositional mode, a mode that puts off many

potential readers who equate excessive repetition with boredom. But once we understand the syntactic habits of the *Autobiography*, Stein's experiments in repetition will seem much less eccentric. Here, as my example of a third "style in search of a reader," is the opening of the short story "Miss Furr and Miss Skeene" (1908):

> Helen Furr had quite a pleasant home. Mrs. Furr was quite a pleasant woman. Mr. Furr was quite a pleasant man. Helen Furr had quite a pleasant voice a voice quite worth cultivating. She did not mind working. She worked to cultivate her voice. She did not find it gay living in the same place where she had always been living. She went to a place where some were cultivating something, voices and other things needing cultivating. She met Georgine Skeene there who was cultivating her voice which some thought was quite a pleasant one. Helen Furr and Georgine Skeene lived together then. Georgine Skeene liked travelling. Helen Furr did not care about travelling, she liked to stay in one place and be gay there. They were together then and travelled to another place and stayed there and were gay there. (*SW*, 563)

The key to the repetition-permutation pattern in this rather unusual love story may be found in a comment Stein made in "A Transatlantic Interview—1946" on the subject of her own earlier *Tender Buttons*, specifically, "A Piece of Coffee," which contains the sentence "Dirty is yellow." Stein, who was not exactly someone given to frequent self-criticism, here tells Robert Bartlett Haas, "Dirty has an association and is a word I would not use now. I would not use words that have definite associations."[11] Which is to say that the best words, from Stein's perspective, are those whose meanings remain equivocal and hence able to take on slightly different shading at each reappearance.

Take "pleasant," as in "Helen Furr had quite a pleasant home." Unlike "dirty," "pleasant," and especially "quite a pleasant," provides us with what John Ashbery has called "an open field of narrative possibilities."[12] "Quite a pleasant" can connote anything from "very nice, very comfortable" to "barely tolerable." "Mrs. Furr was quite a pleasant woman. Mr. Furr was quite a pleasant man." Again, all we know is that Helen Furr was living with her parents, two people defined only by their indefinability. They are, one supposes, neither better nor worse than most parents—but then, even this supposition cannot be proved or disproved. In the fourth sentence, the phrase "quite a pleasant" is now transferred from persons to Helen Furr's voice, a transfer that makes that voice seem no more interesting than her "quite pleasant" home. "A pleasant voice a voice quite worth cultivating"—it is this bit of exposition that sets Stein's "plot" in motion. For it is Helen's decision to "cultivate her voice" that provides her with the motive she needs to leave home

and go to a place where "some were cultivating something, voices
and other things needing cultivating."

In between these two references to "cultivating," the seventh
sentence introduces the key word of the story: *gay*. At the time Stein
wrote "Miss Furr and Miss Skeene," the definition "gay" as "homo-
osexual" had not yet entered the vocabulary even as an underground
or coterie term, but surely "gay" means more than "happy,"
"merry," or "blithe" (its dictionary meanings) in Stein's private lexicon.[13] Thus its introduction in the sentence "She did not find it gay
living in the same place where she had always been living" strikes
us as at first as meaning no more than that Helen Furr is somehow
bored at home. Not until "gay" begins to undergo its series of permutations does its other or latent meaning (inevitably prominent for
the contemporary reader) come into prominence.

"She did not find it gay living in the same place where she had
always been living." How does the repetition of "living" work here?
Why can't Stein simply say, "She did not find it gay living at home"
or "in her pleasant home"? The locution "living in the same place
where she had always been living" emphasizes the duration of Helen
Furr's existence before her meeting with Georgine Skeene; it is the
persistence of her prior "living" that will make the change that now
occurs all the more important. In the same vein, the repetition of
"cultivating" in "She went to a place where some were cultivating
something, voices and other things needing cultivating" is wittily
deflationary, its second appearance, modifying "voices and other
things needing," suggesting that "cultivating" has less to do with
"work" than with some sort of group "gay" activity.

Indeed Helen Furr's new association with a fellow "cultivator"
named Georgine Skeene (the punning names relate fur and skin,
even as Georgine Skeene's rhyming name gives her an air of absurdity) suggests that "cultivating" is no more than an excuse for estab-
lishing a sexual relationship. But this relationship is already
threatened by difference: "Georgine Skeene liked travelling. Helen
Furr did not care about travelling, she liked to stay in one place and
be gay there." This simple distinction casts doubt on the paragraph's
final sentence, "They were together then and travelled to another
place and stayed there and were gay there." For it is "travelling"
that will produce the split between the two women.

Verbal and phrasal repetition, in this context, is neither orna-
mental nor, as for many poets, a form of intensification. Rather,
repetition generates meaning. For even as the narrative seems to
occur in a continuous present ("They stayed there and were gay
there, not very gay there, just gay there"), the situation gradually
and inevitably changes. By the end, Helen Furr is left alone, but she
has learned to be "regular in being gay" and "telling about little

ways one could be learning to use in being gay, and later was telling them quite often, telling them again and again" (*SW*, 568).

Who are "they" and what is Helen Furr telling them again and again? Such information is intentionally withheld. "Miss Furr and Miss Skeene" is curiously nonmimetic even as its "realism" is intense. The two women are given no motives; indeed, we know almost nothing about them. There is no explanation of their mutual attraction or of the activity in which they were engaging when they were "regularly" going "somewhere" with the "men who were dark and heavy" or with the men "who were not so dark" and those "who were not so heavy." The mystery of their being is thus left intact. To say that Stein's is a story of how a girl from a nice home comes out of the closet, has a brief fling with a less nice girl, and thus gains the experience to carry on with her "gay" life is to reduce Stein's enormously subtle work to a cartoon. The text itself remains impervious to such easy reading for it never allows us to make secure judgments about character and action. How "pleasant" is a pleasant home? What does being "regularly gay" entail? If we interpret "gay" as homosexual, what are Helen Furr and Georgine Skeene doing when they "sit regularly" with the dark and heavy men? And in the final standoff between Helen and Georgine, whose side are we on?

Repetition, variation, permutation, the minuscule transfer of a given word from one syntactic slot to another, one part of speech to another, creates a compositional field that remains in constant motion, that prevents closure from taking place. *Pleasant, gay, work, cultivate, regularly, somewhere*—these permutating counters make up a dense network of narrative possibilities without ever coalescing into a definable story line. But indeterminacy does not imply, as readers often assume, that Stein's story has no meaning. On the contrary, its meanings are multiple. Stein is describing a woman who moves out from the "quite a pleasant" home of her quite pleasant parents into a larger world where people are "cultivating" some-thing. In the course of her "cultivation" and her "being gay" with another woman and "sitting" with men of all descriptions, Helen Furr learns to be "gay every day" and "learning other ways in being gay" that she can "tell" others about. By the end of this five-page story, Helen Furr is a different person. And it is the coming about of this difference that "Miss Furr and Miss Skeene" charts.

4. Many of Stein's best-known texts—*The Making of Ameri-cans, Melanctha*, "Composition as Explanation," the first Picasso portrait—employ the mode of repetition used in "Miss Furr and Miss Skeene." But what of the many compositions that carry repetition to what seems to be a point of no return? Here, for example, is Part 26 of Stein's improvisation on George Hugnet's poem "Enfances," which she called *Before the Flowers of Friendship Faded Friendship Faded* (1931):

Little by little two go if two go three go if three go four go if
four go they go. It is known as does he go he goes if they go
they go and they know they know best and most of whether
he will go. He is to go. They will not have vanilla and say so.
To go Jenny go, Ivy go Gaby go any come and go is go and
come and go and leave to go. Who has to hold it while they
go who has to who has had it held and have them come to go.
He went and came and had to go. No one has had to say he
had to go come here to go go there to go go go to come to
come to go to go and come and go.[14]

Even as enthusiastic an advocate of Stein's "experimental writing"
as Marianne DeKoven refers to the poetic sequence in which this
text appears as a "travesty."[15] But if we think of Stein's series of
permutations on a small corpus of words and phrases as her verbal
equivalent to the nonrepresentational landscape of her painter contemporaries, we begin to discern patterns not unlike the exciting/
peaceful clusters in *Paris France.*

"A sentence," as Stein puts it, "is an interval in which there is
finally forward and back" (*HTW,* 133). The "forward and back"
in this case is the buried phrase "to and fro." "Little by little two
go"—the narrative begins normally enough in the vein of a children's
book, even as *Paris France* contains sentences like "There are lots
of cats in Paris and in France." Again, the logic of "If two go three
go if three go four go" sounds like a jingle in the Dr. Seuss books or
a nursery rhyme. But Stein never quite lets the "child's play" continue, so she ends this first sentence with the twist "if four go they
go."

Successive sentences provide us with further examples of this
ambivalence between instinct and knowledge, the perspective of the
child ("To go Jenny go Ivy go Gaby go"—a kind of jump-rope rhyme)
and that of the grown-up ("It is known"; "they know best and most
of whether he will go"; "no one has had to say"). Within this framework, embedded in the sound chiming of "come and go" and "go
go go," a single word stands out, rather like a white flag in an otherwise black field—"They will not have vanilla and say so." "Vanilla"
is the only three-syllable word in the entire composition (for that
matter, out of 144 words, there are only 6 that have two syllables,
and 3 of those are proper names); it is the only noun, and the only
concrete image referring to a particular sense impression.

What does it mean thus to embed *vanilla* in the field of *come/*
*go, two/go, he/they, who/no one, if/of?* Perhaps no more nor less
than that the mind tries to center its little verbal steps on something
concrete and tangible, something one might see or taste or touch.
But "Who has to hold it"? No sooner does the noun appear than it
disappears again, obliterated by the march of "go go go." As in a
Dada collage, "vanilla" is the absurd "pasted paper" that momen-

tarily attracts the eye by its evident difference only to be reabsorbed into the dominant field of formal relationships. And in this sense, Stein's composition does have meaning: it suggests that the authority vested in "vanilla" is rejected ("They will not have vanilla and say so") in the interest of the "two [who] go," who "come to come" and "go to go."

5. An enigma text like this one demands, of course, a great deal from the reader; indeed, many readers will find the demand excessive. But even at her most "repetitious," Stein is not just indulging, as some critics have supposed, in automatic writing. And at their best her enigma texts present us with a formidable challenge. I turn now to the most difficult of the Stein styles: first, the fragmented, nonreferential mode of *Tender Buttons* and then the "sound poetry" of such texts as "Lipschitz," "Jean Cocteau," and "Pink Melon Joy."

Like the great realists of the nineteenth century who were her precursors, Stein believed that the domain of literature is the real rather than the ideal, the ordinary rather than the unusual, the everyday rather than the fantastic. But, as Lyn Hejinian observes, "realism" can be an attitude toward language itself rather than only toward the objects to which language refers:

> Perhaps it was the discovery that language is an order of reality itself and not a mere mediating medium—that it is possible and even likely that one can have a confrontation with a phrase that is as significant as a confrontation with a tree, chair, cone, dog, bishop, piano, vineyard, door, or penny, etc.—which replaced [Stein's] commitment to a medical career with a commitment to a literary career.[16]

Which is not to say that references to tree, chair, cone, or dog are not also obliquely present. In *Tender Buttons* (1914) Stein presents us with a series of objects, food items, body parts, and enclosures, naming each item only to set into motion a kind of riddle. "COLD CLIMATE," we read, and then the single enigmatic sentence, "A season in yellow sold extra strings makes lying places" (*SW*, 471). Does this mean that the title is pure nonsense, having nothing to do with the "description" that follows? Or can we relate the "cold climate" to the "season in yellow" (November? autumn? the time of fog?) and consider the possibilities raised by the suggestion that "extra strings" (for a blanket, a pillow, a lap robe) are sold at this time of year so as to make "lying places" more comfortable?

In such instances language is certainly not "a mere mediating medium," but neither is it, as Stein's detractors often suggest, purely nonreferential. If what Hejinian calls the "confrontation with a [verbal] phrase" becomes as important as the confrontation with an event, it can only be because we have to be peculiarly attentive so as to uncover the connection between the two. Here is "A Waist":

A star glide, a single frantic sullenness, a single financial
grass greediness.
    Object that is in wood. Hold the pine, hold the dark, hold
in the rush, make the bottom.
    A piece of crystal. A change, in a change that is remarkable
there is no reason to say that there was a time.
    A woolen object gilded. A country climb is the best dis-
grace, a couple of practices any of them in order is so left.
    (*SW*, 471–72)

Unlike my third and fourth examples, "A Waist" does not rely upon
repetition as a form of defamiliarization. Neither is the characteristic
sentence a simple declarative one. Rather, Stein here makes use of
both synecdoche and pun, these figures being embedded in what
tend to be short noun phrases and sentence fragments.

The first thing to notice is that "waist" has as its homonym
"waste," and that both words generate what follows. "A star
glide"—one immediately conjures up a dancer gliding into the room,
a graceful person with a delicate, tiny waist. But pinching the waist
has its problems: "A single frantic sullenness" suggests that the waist
has been laced too tightly, that it hurts. To force the dancer into this
role is perhaps a "financial . . . greediness," the desire not to "waste"
anything. "Grass" suggests envy on someone's part; it also recalls
"glass" and hence refers back phonemically to "glide" and to the
image of a "single" graceful movement of the waist. The repetition
of the phonemes /gl/, /gr/, and /l/ reinforces this image of fragility
and gliding motion.

But in the second "stanza," Stein abruptly shifts to an entirely
different image: "Object that is in wood." Perhaps the "waist" is
now that of a carved wooden statuette or idol. Someone is carving
a figure and "mak[ing] the bottom," but to talk of waists is, of course,
also to talk of hips and bottoms. In the third paragraph the object
is explicitly defined as a "piece of crystal," and the image is that
of the sort of little glass figurine one finds in display cases. The
"change" that turns a bit of wood or glass into a sculpture is so great
that "there is no reason to say that there was a time" (i.e., when it
was not yet "made"). And now, in the fourth paragraph or "stanza,"
"glide" is metathesized to "gilded," and the "object" has become
woolen. Is the statuette dressed in wool? Or is Stein shifting from
artwork to real life and to the benefit waists receive from "a country
climb" or related "practices" occurring in some sort of "order"?
What is "so left," then, is finally an image of tiny waists delicately
moving, not wasting any motion, of an artist's carving, whether in
glass or in wood, that creates a definite change.

Each item in *Tender Buttons* has a place on this larger continuum of change and transformation. Like *Paris France* that is exciting
and peaceful, buttons can be tender and a carafe that is a blind glass

can be a spectacle. If, in her later work, Stein provides us with more connectives, the basic impulse, which is to "define" things as they really occur, not as if they are to be pigeonholed or seen from one angle only, is to force us to think about the subject—in this case, to come to terms with the word "waist."

6. In thus "confronting" a group of words as if it were an event in the external world, Stein also pays close attention to sound. Indeed, her corpus includes the first experiments with what we now call "sound poetry." Here is the opening of the 1926 portrait called "Jean Cocteau":

> Needs be needs be needs be near.
> Needs be needs be needs be.
> This is where they have their land astray.
>   Two say.
> This is where they have their land astray
> Two say.
> Needs be needs be needs be
> Needs be needs be needs be near.
>   Second time.[17]

No doubt, this is Gertrude Stein at her most "non-sensical," her most opaque. We know neither the subject nor the object of the locution "needs be," nor can we be sure whether the verb is indicative or conditional ("if need be . . ."). Again, we can't pinpoint the meaning of the pun on "Two say" ("to say") or the effect of the rhyme "say"/"astray," any more than we can establish the reference in line 5 to "their land astray."

But read aloud, the poem has a particular rhythmic figure, specifically, the ballad rhythm of songs like "Skip to My Lou," with its refrain lines (three per stanza) like "I'll take another one, prettier than you," or "Fly's in the buttermilk, shoo fly shoo." Just so, the first line of "Jean Cocteau," "Needs be needs be needs be near," introduces what sounds like the kind of song children sing during circle games; indeed, the refrain "Second time" suggests that the physical movement (skipping? jumping? clapping?) associated with the incantation is to be repeated.

But just as *Paris France* is a parody schoolbook, so "Jean Cocteau" is a parody nursery rhyme or jump-rope song. For "needs be" is also a pun on "kneads bee" and the reference, "This is where they have their land astray," refers to the world of grown-ups, not children. And knowing that Stein admired the young Cocteau, who had praised her work but who never quite seemed to find the time to participate in her salon and become one of her *fidèles,* the "land astray" and "needs be" begin to make more sense. Stein regards her literary situation as one in which Cocteau "needs be near," since he regularly flatters and encourages her. But because their primarily epistolary friendship is more assumed than real, Cocteau never quite having time for Stein, she presents herself and the exotic young French writer ("Two say") as two fellow artists whose "land" or common artistic property has gone "astray." Still, the need continues and, as she says in the final line cited above, "It may be nearer than two say." "We" may, that is to say, have more in common than even "we" think.

The highly charged phonemic and rhythmic pattern of "Jean Cocteau" is so close to pure chant, to a kind of Sitwellian nonsense verse, that readers may well conclude that this is no portrait at all, only an elaborate sound game. Wendy Steiner, for example, writes: "Relieved of specific reference, the words in this portrait have nothing more than their pale dictionary meanings, and even these are made ambiguous through the variations in context. Words thus are almost pure phonological quanta."[18] But what "Jean Cocteau" "says" is that there is something that "needs be," that there is a mutual "land" that has gone "astray," and that, for the "second time," there are "Two [who] say." Indeed, once we have gotten the hang of finding the excited/peaceful configuration in *Paris France* or the metonymic account of the first night at Stravinsky's *Sacre du printemps* in the *Autobiography*, we will find that even the most abstruse of Stein's sound poems or synecdochic riddles do refer, however obliquely, to the events of her extraverbal universe.

To recapitulate. Stein's oeuvre gives evidence of at least six different styles: (1) seemingly "straight" reportage (*Paris France*), (2) autobiographical narrative as ironized by presenting a fictional narrator who tells the story, as in *The Autobiography of Alice B. Toklas,* (3) narrative-as-permutation of phrasal repetitions, each reappearance of the word or phrase giving us a new view, as in "Miss Furr and Miss Skeene; (4) "abstract" repetition of words and phonemes, as in *Before the Flowers of Friendship Faded Friendship Faded,* where the "action" is less a matter of incident than of verbal event; (5) the synecdochic riddling poetry of *Tender Buttons,* where a given title is the impetus for the creation of its "Cubist" equivalent, and (6) sound poetry, as in "Jean Cocteau."

One might, of course, refine these distinctions; the mode of repetition in *Lectures in America,* for instance, falls somewhere between the repetition-as-narrative of "Miss Furr and Miss Skeene" and the abstraction of *Before the Flowers.* Or again, the fragments of *Stanzas in Meditation* are at once similar to, and yet also recognizably different from, the concrete texts in *Tender Buttons.* But the issue is less whether there are six distinguishable modes—or five or eight—than it is to define the differences *within* Stein's oeuvre, not just the more obvious differences *between* Stein and other modernist writers.

Stein herself was well aware of the possibilities her writing might engage. It was not just a matter of writing "simply" so that everyone could understand her, or "obscurely" so that no one could. Nor was it—as is now often posited—primarily a case of dismantling "patriarchal" discourse, of challenging what Julia Kristeva calls the Symbolic by letting the presymbolic feminine Other, the Semiotic, come into play.[19] Perhaps the greatest difficulty Stein's writing presents to her readers is that it is not finally typical or characteristic of any one thing—neither characteristically "feminist" nor "lesbian" nor "expatriate" nor "Jewish" nor "Cubist" nor "American," nor even characteristically "pre-postmodern," although it is the *côté postmoderne* of Gertrude Stein I personally find most intriguing. As a writer rather than as a "character," Stein, like her own Melanctha or Helen Furr, refuses definition. As she herself puts it in "Arthur a Grammar":

> I am a grammarian. I believe in duplicates.
> Duplicated means having it be twice. It is duplicated. . . .
> Think well of this. You cannot repeat a duplicate you can duplicate. Now think of the difference of repeat and of duplicate. I am a grammarian. I think of the differences there are. . . .
> Oh grammar is so fine.
> Think of duplicate as mine.
> It stops because you stop. Think of that. You stop because you have made other arrangements.
> Changes.
> Grammar in relation to a tree and two horses.
>
> (*HTW*, 111)

# Chapter Eight

# "Une Voix pas la mienne":

## *French/English Beckett*

## *and the French/English Reader*

### *I*

*I*n conversation with Richard Coe, some twenty years ago, Beckett remarked that he was afraid of English because "you couldn't help writing poetry in it."[1] This is not, I think, a facetious remark designed to put off the prying critic. English, for Beckett, is, after all, the language of his childhood, more specifically, the canonical language of "English literature" as taught to a schoolboy at the Portora Royal School in the Northern Ireland of the early twenties. Such a schoolboy would of course have been subjected to heavy doses of Shakespeare and Elizabethan poetry, of Milton, and, more immediately, of the great Romantic and Victorian poets. Like it or not, the iambic pentameters of Keats's odes, or again, the quatrains of Tennyson's *In Memoriam,* must have been engraved in some corner of Beckett's mind. Thus, when the "I" of "Enough" says "I see the flowers at my feet," the English-speaking reader remembers the poet of "Ode to a Nightingale" exclaiming ecstatically:

> I cannot see what flowers are at my feet
> Nor what soft incense hangs upon the boughs. . . .

Beckett's irony is that for the disillusioned speaker of "Enough," there is no such vision: "I see the flowers at my feet and it's the others I see. Those we trod down with equal step. It is true they are the same."[2] It is an irony lost on the French reader of *Assez*, for whom the sentence "Je vois les fleurs à mes pieds et ce sont les autres que je vois" contains no such buried allusion.

Accordingly, when Beckett tells Niklaus Gessner that "in French it is easier to write without style," when he remarks to Herbert Blau that French "had the right weakening effect,"[3] he is referring, however obliquely, to a certain kind of poetic diction. "Without style" means without, or rather outside, the style of his great English and Irish precursors: Joyce is the most obvious example, but by extension, the "style" Beckett wants to be "without" is also that of Milton or Coleridge, Keats or Swinburne. "The right weakening effect" is one that "weakens" or neutralizes the heavy weight of the Anglo-Irish tradition, which is to say the poetry memorized and recited, as Yeats puts it, "among school children."

In a letter to his German friend Axel Kaun, written in 1937 almost a decade before he became a French writer, Beckett remarks:

> It is indeed becoming more and more difficult, even senseless, for me to write an official English. And more and more my own language appears to me like a veil that must be torn apart in order to get at the things (or the Nothingness) behind it. Grammar and Style. To me they seem to have become as irrelevant as a Victorian bathing suit or the imperturbability of a true gentleman. A mask. Let us hope the time will come, thank God that in certain circles it has already come, when language is most efficiently used where it is being most efficiently misused. . . . Is there any reason why that terrible materiality of the word surface should not be capable of being dissolved?

And he adds, "Perhaps the logographs of Gertrude Stein are . . . what I have in mind. At least the texture of language has become porous."[4]

To dissolve the "terrible materiality of the word surface" so as to create the "literature of the unword," as Beckett calls it in this same letter, became the task of Beckett's great French period, the period of the *Trilogy, Godot, Endgame*. Between the writing of *Molloy* in 1947 and *Company* in 1979, all of Beckett's fiction, with the exception of *From an Abandoned Work* (1957), was written first in French, then translated by the author into English. The longing to "write without style," without "'poetry," must, of course, be understood as part of Beckett's larger longing to escape from the oppressive world of his bourgeois, suburban childhood, especially the painful love-hate relationship with his mother. Add to this, as Vivian

Mercier points out, the dilemma of the Protestant Anglo-Irish writer who can never be wholly English or wholly Irish, a dilemma Beckett resolved by exiling himself from both and adopting French as his language.[5] Further, as Katharine Worth has suggested, Beckett's shift to French may well have been a natural consequence of his work in the French Resistance: forced to play the role of Frenchman in the tense and terrible years of subterfuge and hiding during the war, he reemerged afterward as, so to speak, a French writer.[6]

But of course the Anglo-Irish literary past could not be erased. "What I would do," Beckett wrote Cyril Cusack in 1956, "is give the whole unupsettable applecart for a sup of the Hawk's Well, or the Saints', or a whiff of Juno to go no further."[7] Yeats, Synge, O'Casey: these are not writers usually associated with the spare and austere Beckett. But in Beckett's recent fictions, an interesting phenomenon is at work. Increasingly, in the prose of his old age, the Anglo-Irish schoolroom of the writer's youth is coming in by the back door—which is to say, the door of translation. When, for example, Beckett translates *Mal vu mal dit* (1981) into English (*Ill Seen Ill Said*),[8] he inserts into the interstices of the text a network of parodic allusions to what we might call the Eng. Lit. canon. Given this particular subtext, the English version demands a rather different reading from the French original. Indeed, if French readings of this and related Beckett texts have, as I shall suggest later, been rather different from those in English, surely the critical difference is prompted, not only by the different cultural and literary predispositions of Francophone and Anglophone readers, but by the simple practical fact that the two groups are reading *different* texts.

What happens when Beckett's translation is from English to French? *Company* (1980) is less allusive than *Ill Seen Ill Said*, but it resembles the latter in reinstating the poetic rhythms and echoes Beckett had spent so many years purging.[9] Here is a typical passage: "By the voice a faint light is shed. Dark lightens while it sounds. Deepens when it ebbs. Lightens with flow back to faint full. Is whole again when it ceases. You are on your back in the dark. Had the eyes been open then they would have marked a change."[10] The ambiguous syntax of the first sentence (Does the voice shed light or is the light shed next to ["by"] it?) gives way to a cadence reminiscent of Dylan Thomas (e.g., "Light sounds where no sun shines"), to the flatness of the declarative "You are on your back in the dark," and then, in the next paragraph, to the archaizing language of "Whence the shadowy light?" The French translation flattens out these effects: "La voix émet une lueur. Le noir s'éclaircit le temps qu'elle parle. S'épaissit quand elle reflue. S'éclaircit quand elle revient à son faible maximum. Se rétablit quand elle se tait. Tu es sur le dos dans le noir. Là s'ils avaient été ouverts tes yeux auraient vu un changement."[11] The passive construction of the first sentence becomes active and unambiguous, the literary echoes don't operate, the lilting "flow back to faint full" becomes the more denotative "revient à son faible maximum," even as the poetic construction "Whence the shadowy light?" becomes simply "D'où le demi-jour?" Indeed, as Brian Fitch has noted, *Compagnie* is a reductive version of the English original: whole sentences are removed, references erased, and literary epithets like "cankerous" are purged.[12]

But of course such reduction functions precisely in the same way as do the additions made when Beckett translates *Mal vu mal dit*. In either case, the Beckett of the recent fiction has reintroduced the long-dormant question of national identity. To put it another way: once the "sans style"—the dissolution of the "terrible materiality of the word surface"—had been achieved, the return to literary origins became a desirable possibility. Provided, of course, that those origins could be sufficiently disguised. Let me begin by examining the double venture of *Mal vu mal dit/Ill Seen Ill Said*.

## II

The language of *Ill Seen Ill Said* has, to begin with, a curiously Pre-Raphaelite or Yellow Nineties cast. On the first page we read, "She sits on erect and rigid in the deepening gloom" ("Droite et raide elle reste là dans l'ombre croissante"), and a few pages later, "Watches all night for the least glimmer" ("Guette en vain la nuit la moindre lueur"). "Gloom" and "glimmer": these alliterating nouns appear in poem after poem written by, among others, the young Yeats: "crimson meteors hang in the gloom," "midnight's all a glimmer, and noon a purple glow." The "Shadowy Horses" have eyes that are "glimmering white," and the "Polar Dragon's" "heavy rings" uncoil "from glimmering deep to deep." In *Ill Seen Ill Said*, as in the poetry of the early Yeats or of Ernest Dowson or Arthur Symons, gloom and glimmer are related to "withered flowers" (p. 15), "slow wavering way" (p. 15), "cold comfort" (p. 26), "Black night fallen" (p. 47), "the westering sun" (p. 48), "olden kisses" (p. 49), "dim the light of day" (p. 51), "Toward unbroken night." Beckett's old woman is seen by her dark window "For long pacing to and fro in the gloom" (p. 47) even as the father in Yeats's "A Prayer for My Daughter" tells us that "And for an hour I have walked and prayed / Because of the great gloom that is in my mind."

The voice that "ill sees, ill says" the story of the old woman who sits by the black window, waiting for Venus to rise, is steeped not only in the vocabulary but also in the meters of the nineties. Indeed, what sound like little rhyming stanzas are introduced at odd junctures: for example,

Rigid with face and hands
against the pane she stands
and marvels long—

"Une Voix
pas la
mienne"

which recalls such poems as Arthur Symons's "The Obscure Night of the Soul" ("All things I then forgot . . . All ceased, and I was not") or Oscar Wilde's "Requiescat" ("All my life's buried here") in its use of trimeter lines that begin and end with heavy stresses. Such rhythmic figuration is absent from the French text ("Raide debout visage et mains appuyés contre la vitre longuement elle s'émerveille"), which subordinates rhythmic recurrence to syntactic progression, the adjectival modifiers pushing on toward the main verb "s'émerveille," which provides semantic closure.

At the level of word or phrase, then, the tone of *Ill Seen Ill Said* (but not of *Mal vu mal dit*) can be characterized as a kind of parody fin de siècle, abrupt speech rhythms regularly punctuating the elegant variations on Wildean or Paterian discourse:

> But see she suddenly no longer there. Where suddenly
> fled. Quick then the chair before she reappears. At length.
> Every angle. With what one word conveys its change? Care-
> ful. Less. Ah the sweet one word. Less. It is less. The same
> but less. Whencesoever the glare. (p. 52)

> Mais voilà soudain qu'elle n'est plus là. Où soudain
> elle fut laissée. Vite donc la chaise avant qu'elle reparaisse.
> Longuement. Tous les angles. De quel seul mot en dire le
> changement? Attention. Moindre. Ah le beau seul mot. Elle est
> moindre. La même mais moindre. D'où que l'oeil s'y acharne.
> (p. 66)

Note especially the difference in the final sentence fragment: as in the passage from *Company* cited above, the almost comic archaism of "Whenceover" has no counterpart in the sober French of "D'où que."

Against this background of late Victorian bric-a-brac, we find intricately jumbled allusions to earlier and later English writers. Here is a partial tabulation:

1. *L'herbe la plus mauvaise s'y fait toujours plus rare.* (p. 9)
   Ever scanter even the rankest weed. (p. 8)
   —A predominantly trochaic pentameter line whose sound structure alludes parodically to Milton's "Lycidas" (e.g., "As killing as the canker to the rose"), even as its imagery recalls *Hamlet:*

> . . . 'tis an unweeded garden
> That grows to seed. Things rank and gross in nature
> Possess it merely. (2.1)

or

And do not spread the compost on the weeds,
To make them ranker. (3.4)

2. *Mer invisible quoique proche. Inaudible.* (p. 11)
   Invisible nearby sea. Inaudible. (p. 10)
   —Joyce, *Ulysses,* opening of the "Proteus" chapter: "Ineluctable modality of the visible . . . seaspawn and seawrack . . . ineluctable modality of the audible."

3. *Sans pâtre ils divaguent à leur guise.* (p. 11)
   Unshepherded they stray as they list. (p. 10)
   —Burlesque of St. Peter's speech in "Lycidas": "Of other care they little reck'ning make, / Than how to scramble at the shearers' feast. . . . And when they list, their lean and flashy songs / Grate on their Scannel Pipes of wretched straw."

4. *Fait baisser le regard dans l'acte d'appréhender. Incrimine l'acquis. Retient de deviner.* (p. 19)
   Averts the intent gaze. Incriminates the dearly won. Forbids divining her. (p. 16)
   —These tightly woven three-stress lines recall Satan's first view of Eve in *Paradise Lost,* 4: "When Satan still in gaze, as first he stood. . . ."

5. *La folle du logis s'en donne à coeur chagrin.* (p. 21)
   Imagination at wit's end spreads its sad wings. (p. 17)
   —A burlesque of Gerard Manley Hopkins's "God's Grandeur": "Because the Holy Ghost over the bent / World broods with warm breast and with ah! bright wings."

6. *Comme si la terre tremblait sans cesse à cet endroit.* (p. 21)
   As if here without cease the earth faintly quaked. (p. 18)
   —A collusion of the King James Bible ("world without end") and Yeats's *The Wind among the Reeds* (e.g., "I hear the Shadowy Horses").

7. *Choses et chimères.* (p. 24)
   Things and imaginings. (p. 20)
   —Yeats, "The Tower," 3: "I have prepared my peace / With learned Italian things / And the proud stones of Greece, / Poet's imaginings. . . ."

8. *Cette vielle si mourante.* (p. 24)
   This old so dying woman. (p. 20)
   —The syntactic oddity of the English phrase ("old so dying"), which is not present in its French counterpart, is standard Irish ballad diction and turns up in both Yeats and Joyce.

9. *Fermés les yeux ne livrent pas leurs prunelles. L'avenir les dira cernées d'un bleu delavé.* (p. 30)
   The lids occult the longed-for eyes. Time will tell them washen blue. (p. 25)

—Tennyson, *In Memoriam* (e.g., 67: "And closing eaves of wearied eyes"; 80: "And dropt the dust on tearless eyes") plus a parody-ballad refrain. The first sentence also recalls Swinburne, "Atalanta in Calydon," 4: "Yet thine heart shall wax heavy with sighs and thine eyelids with tears."

"Une Voix pas la mienne"

10. *L'oeil reviendra sur les lieux de ses trahisons. En congé séculaire de là où gèlent les larmes.* (p. 32)

The eye will return to the scene of its betrayals. On centennial leave from where tears freeze. (p. 27)

—Perhaps an amalgam of Shakespeare, *Antony and Cleopatra,* 4.12 ("Betrayed I am. / O this false soul of Egypt! this grave charm, / Whose eye becked forth my wars and called them home"); Wordsworth, "Tintern Abbey" ("Knowing that Nature never did betray / The heart that loved her"); and Tennyson's "Tears Idle Tears." Note that the second sentence is a perfect Swinburnian anapestic pentameter.

11. *Passée panique la suite.* (p. 38)

Panic past pass on. (p. 31)

—Nursery rhyme like "Pease porridge cold."

12. *Sentent-elles seulement la chair sous l'étoffe? La chair sous l'étoffe les sent-elle? Ne vont-ils donc jamais frémir?* (p. 40)

Do they as much as feel the clad flesh? Does the clad flesh feel them? Will they then never quiver? (p. 32)

—A kind of Swinburnian tongue twister, playing on such poems as "Atalanta in Calydon" (e.g., "Come with bows bent and with emptying of quivers, / Maiden most perfect, lady of light." The touch of "clad flesh" is a frequent motif in Swinburne, especially in "The Triumph of Time" and "Laus Veneris."

13. *Immortel jour qui agonise encore.* (p. 49)

Death again of deathless day. (p. 40)

—Poetic diction, with characteristic Pre-Raphaelite rhythm.

14. *Partie sans fin gagnée perdue. Inaperçue.* (p. 49)

Day without end won and lost. Unseen. (p. 40)

—King James Bible.

15. *La chaise squelettique s'y dresse plus blafarde que nature.* (p. 51)

Stark the skeleton chair death-paler than life. (p. 41)

—Keats, "La Belle Dame sans Merci": "Pale warriors, death-pale were they all."

16. *Ombre d'un ancien sourire souri.* (p. 62)

Ghost of an ancient smile. (p. 49)

—Play on Pound's "The Return": "host of an ancient people."

17. *Refermé l'oeil las à cet effet ou rouvert ou laissé en l'état quel qu'il fût.* (p. 67)

Closed again to that end the vile jelly or opened again or left as it was however that was. (p. 52).

—Shakespeare, *King Lear:* Cornwall blinding the old Gloucester: "Out vile jelly. Where is thy lustre now?" The allusion gives the sentence in question a sardonic edge that is not found in the French.

18. *Jusqu'au moment pour l'heure lointain ou les manteaux vont manquer aux fenêtres et au clou le tire-bouton.* (p. 71)
Far ahead to the instant when the coats will have gone from their rods and the button-hook from its nail. (p. 56)

—Ecclesiastes in the King James Bible. A note of bathos is introduced by the placement in the key nominal slot of the word "button-hook," this trivial object functioning as a central motif in the old woman's meditation.

19. *Puis noir parfait avant-glas tout bas adorable son top départ de l'arrivée.* (p. 75)
Then in that perfect dark foreknell darling sound pip for end begun. (p. 59)

—Keats, "Ode to a Nightingale." Beckett's sentence is an elaborate spoof on the opening of the last stanza: "Forlorn! the very word is like a bell / To toll me back from thee to my sole self!" The "perfect dark" alludes to the "embalmed darkness" of stanza 5; "darling" is a play on "Darkling I listen" in stanza 6.

20. *Plus miette de charogne nulle part.* (p. 76)
Not another crumb of carrion left. (p. 59)

—The allusion is to Hopkins's "Carrion Comfort":

> Not, I'll not, carrion comfort, Despair, not feast on thee;
> Not untwist—slack they may be—these last strands of man
> In me or, most weary, cry *I can no more.* I can;
> Can something, hope, wish day come, not choose not to be.

Here, in the final paragraph of *Ill Seen Ill Said,* the allusions to Keats and Hopkins are intricately bound up in the meaning of Beckett's text. In the coda the speaking voice alludes first to Beckett's own earlier work: "For the last time at last for to end yet again what the wrong word?"—and then takes its final stance in the face of "the last wisps of day when the curtain closes." Like Keats's "Adieu! Adieu!" the words "Farewell to farewell" bring the Beckettian speaker back to the realization that "the fancy cannot cheat so well as she was wont to do" and to the acceptance of the fact that one must "Lick chops and basta" that, in Hopkins's words, "I can; / Can something, hope, wish day come, not choose not to be."

Ironically, the Hopkins allusion is a perfectly literal translation from the French. Indeed, the concluding words of *Mal vu mal dit* are rendered in their precise English equivalent even if the syntax is slightly altered:

> Goulûment seconde par seconde. Ciel terre et tout le bataclan.
> Plus miette de charogne nulle part. Lechées babines baste.

Non. Encore une seconde. Rien qu'une. Le temps d'aspirer ce
vide. Connaître le bonheur.

"Une Voix
pas la
mienne"

Moment by glutton moment. Sky earth the whole kit and boo-
dle. Not another crumb of carrion left. Lick chops and basta.
No. One moment more. One last. Grace to breathe that void.
Know happiness.

The English version "says" exactly what the French does, but the
Keatsian and Hopkinsian references give the passage a parodic edge,
an edge underscored by such archaisms as "Moment by glutton
moment" (where a literal translation would be "Gluttonously,
moment by moment").[13] Such phrasing qualifies the Romantic idealism of Beckett's conclusion, an idealism that one reviewer has
called "a thumping C major chord," "too glib [in its] way of phrasing
a refusal to mourn."[14] But neither the French text, with its comic
inflections like "Lechées babines baste," and certainly not the English, with its sardonic allusions to Keats and Hopkins, is "glib" in
this sense. In reading Beckett, contextualization is always necessary.

## III

What, then, do we make of the elaborate web of poetic references that inform the text of *Ill Seen Ill Said?* For one thing, their
frequency seems to be Beckett's way of saying that we must be
cautious in reading the French and English versions of a given text
as if they were quite simply identical. And here we may observe a
curious phenomenon. Whereas Beckett's early critics—Ruby Cohn,
Martin Esslin, John Fletcher, Hugh Kenner, Ludovic Janvier—were
very aware of Beckett's bilingualism, perhaps because Beckett's turn
to French in *Molloy* was such a novelty, recent discussions, even
those that deal closely with stylistics, seem to assume that the Beckett text is a stable and unitary entity.[15]

Thus David Read's discussion of the theme of "consciousness
of being [as] tertium quid of the interplay between experience and
abstinence" in *Company* and *Ill Seen Ill Said* makes no allusion
whatever to the textual problem.[16] Or again, when the difference
between the French and English versions is noted, the tendency is
to assume that the text in one's own language is the "real" one.
Judith E. Dearlove, for example, in her otherwise exemplary stylistic
study *Accommodating the Chaos: Samuel Beckett's Nonrelational
Art* (1982), writes of *Ping* (in French, *Bing*), "Indeed, Beckett's revi-
sions show a movement toward briefer, more ephemeral sounds
from 'paf' to 'hop' to 'bing.'" In the English text Beckett alters even
the voiced 'b' of 'bing' to the voiceless and hence even slighter 'p'

of 'ping.'"[17] Here the French is regarded, not as an alternate, but as an earlier, hence less finished, version, the title word being made appropriately slight in the text's "final," which is to say, its perfected stage.

Needless to say, the French reader of the French text will see it the other way around: Jude Stefan, reviewing *Mal vu mal dit* for the *Nouvelle revue française*, reads Beckett's fiction as an existentialist document, as a "cri reduit de la poésie en fin de siècle," the cry of a voice that is powerful but "vigilante jusqu'au soupir final."[18] But when the "soupir final" includes the phrases "Sky earth the whole kit and boodle" and "Lick chops and basta," its comic and robust edge suggests that this sigh may not be so final after all.

It is interesting, in this connection, to compare the early French reviews of Beckett's work to their English counterparts. "[Beckett's] language," wrote Maurice Nadeau in one of the first reviews of *Molloy*, "dissolves into nothingness (annihilates itself) as soon as it is established, erases instantly its faintest traces." And further, "Beckett settles us in the world of the Nothing where some nothings which are men move about for nothing. The absurdity of the world and the meaninglessness of our condition are conveyed in an absurd and deliberately insignificant fashion."[19] These motifs—the absurdity of the human condition and the consequent dissolution of language, its refusal to signify—are echoed in the Beckett commentaries of Georges Bataille and Maurice Blanchot. Bataille writes:

> Language is what determines this regulated world, whose significations provide the foundation for our cultures, our activities and our relations, but it does so in so far as it is reduced to a means of these cultures, activities and relations; freed from these servitudes, it is nothing more than a deserted castle whose gaping cracks let in the wind and rain: it is no longer the signifying word, but the defenseless expression death wears as a disguise.

And he suggests that the epigraph for *Molloy* could be "Lasciate ogni speranza voi qu'entrate."[20] Similarly, Blanchot observes:

> "The Unnamable" is precisely an experiment conducted, an experience lived under the threat of the impersonal, the approach of a neutral voice that is raised of its own accord, that penetrates the man who hears it, that is without intimacy, that excludes all intimacy, that cannot be made to stop, that is the incessant, the *interminable*. . . . The man who writes is already no longer Samuel Beckett but the necessity which has surrendered him to whatever is outside himself, which has made him a nameless being, the Unnamable, a being without being . . . the empty site in which an empty voice is raised without effect, masked, for better or worse by a porous and agonizing *I*.[21]

Compare to these representations of Beckett, Donald Davie's assertion, made with reference to the radio play *All That Fall,* written in English for the BBC, that "Beckett is a comic writer. He has yet to write a book that is not a funny book." Having illustrated this thesis by citing snatches of dialogue between Mr. and Mrs. Rooney, Davie comments on the parodic function of Beckett's syntax: "Though language may betray the speaker in a Joycean pun ( 'Nip some young doom in the bud'), more often for Beckett it does so by syntactical over-elegance." And as for the "bleak pessimism about the human person and human destiny" of which Beckett stands accused, Davie argues: "[Beckett's pessimism] could equally well be explained as an attempt, like Wordsworth's in his progress from articulate men through peasants and children to idiots and lunatics, to strip from the human being all attributes save precisely that of being—a common ground on which (who knows?) Beckett might stand, as Wordsworth did, to utter a hurrah for the human race."[22]

Is Davie talking about the same writer as are Bataille and Blanchot? Is he merely being insensitive? Here is the opening of Hugh Kenner's *Samuel Beckett* (1968):

> Mr. Beckett's patient concern with bicycles, amputees, battered hats, and the letter M; his connoisseurship of the immobilized hero; his preoccupation with footling questions which there isn't sufficient evidence to resolve; his humor of the short sentence; his Houdini-like virtuosity (by preference chained hand and foot, deprived of story, dialogue, locale): these constitute a unique comic repertoire like a European clown's. The antecedents of his plays are not in literature but—to take a rare American example—in Emmett Kelly's solemn determination to sweep a circle of light into a dustpan. . . . The milieu of his novels bears a moral resemblance to that of the circus.[23]

From the vestibule of hell (Bataille) to the circus: the difference in emphasis between Bataille and Blanchot on the one hand and Davie and Kenner on the other cannot, of course, be accounted for simply by the differences between the French and English texts. Nor have all French critics lined up in the former camp, and British or American ones in the latter.[24] To understand the difference, one would have to study the contrasting cultural formations of postwar Paris and postwar Britain/America, beginning with the profound malaise of the Occupation, a malaise surely inconceivable for British and especially for American critics, for whom war is always, so to speak, somewhere else.

Beckett, whose day-to-day life during the years of Occupation and Resistance was one of constant threat, subterfuge, hiding, and reinvention, was very much the poet of silence and dissolution defined by Blanchot and Nadeau, even as he retained the urge toward comedy, clowning, wordplay, and buffoonery that had already manifested itself in his first two novels, *Murphy* and *Watt*. His work thus bears out Kenner's reading as well as Bataille's, Davie's as well as Nadeau's. For our purposes, in any case, the important thing is that these two sides of Beckett are reflected in his French/English texts as early as *Molloy*. To give just one example, here is Molloy ruminating on his inability to remember names, even the name of the town in which he was born and where his mother lives:

> Oui, même à cette époque, où tout s'estompait déjà, ondes et particules, la condition de l'objet était d'être sans nom, et inversement.
>
> Yes, even then, when already all was fading, waves and particles, there could be no things but nameless things, no names but thingless names.[25]

The English translation begins by following the French closely, but with the articulation of the main clause, the two diverge. A literal translation of the French would give us, "The condition of the object was to be without a name, and vice-versa," or "The state of the thing was to be . . ." or, more colloquially, "It was the condition of the thing to be. . . ." But Beckett colloquializes —"there could be no things but nameless things"—even as he then embellishes: the terse "et inversement" gives way to wordplay, "no things but nameless things, no names but thingless names."

Try to think of a thingless name, a name that does not refer to anything, and you will see that Beckett's Molloy is having a bit of fun. Slight as the difference here and throughout the text may be, the English has a playful edge not present in the French. Again, the English phrasing often takes on a familiar Anglo-Irish verse rhythm as when "la petite nuit où des taches claires naissent, flamboient, s'éteignent, tantôt vides, tantôt peuplées, comme d'ordures de saints la flamme" (p. 36) becomes "the little night and its little lights, faint at first, then flaming and extinguished, now ravening, now fed, as fire by filth and martyrs" (p. 28), or when "Tout cela à travers une poussière étincelante et bientot à travers cette bruine aussi" (p. 37) becomes "all that through a glittering dust and soon through that mist too" (p. 29), a phrase that could be lineated and scanned so as to fit comfortably into a nineties ballad:

> áll thât thróugh a glíttering dúst
> and sóon thrôugh thât míst tôo.

Which version is the "real" or the "better" one? Obviously both and neither. The scene of Beckett's writing exists somewhere between the two, a space where neither French nor English has autonomy. The slippage of language, its drive toward self-erasure and retracing, takes place not only within the text, as Nadeau and

Blanchot observed, but intertextually as well. More and more, in the late work, it is a slippage back into the world of Beckett's youth; the "porous" linguistic texture brings to the surface images and motifs that had been carefully suppressed. "Language," as Beckett put it in the letter to Axel Kaun, "is most efficiently used where it is being most efficiently misused." Or as the voice of *Ill Seen Ill Said* puts it, "The eye must return to the scene of its betrayals."

"Une Voix
pas la
mienne"

*Chapter Nine*

# The Two *Ariel*s:

## *The (Re)Making of the*

## *Sylvia Plath Canon*

### I

*T*he reception of a slim book of poems called *Ariel* (published in London in 1965 and in New York in the early summer of 1966) is by now legendary. The foreword was by none other than Robert Lowell and it was printed, not just inside the book as anyone might reasonably expect, but, tantalizingly, on the front cover, in italics:

> *From the introduction by ROBERT LOWELL*
> *"In these poems, written in the last months of her life, and often rushed out at the rate of two or three a day, Sylvia Plath becomes herself, bcomes something imaginary, newly, wildly and subtly created. . . ."*[1]

And a purple arrow points us toward the inside, where, after the title page and table of contents, we continue to read Lowell's characterization of Sylvia Plath as "hardly a person at all, or a woman, certainly not another 'poetess,' but one of those super-real hypnotic, great classical heroines." Referring to the title poem, Lowell observes that "dangerous, more powerful than man, machinelike from hard training, she herself is a little like a racehorse, galloping relentlessly with risked, outstretched neck, death hurdle after death hurdle topped." And, in a sentence that was to be much cited, he concludes, "These poems are playing Russian roulette with six cartridges in the cylinder, a game of 'chicken,' the wheels of both cars locked and unable to swerve" (A, x).

So began the myth of the "literary dragon who . . . breathed a burning river of bale across the literary landscape" (*Time*, 10 June 1966), the "infirm prophet," whose poems exhibit "the madness within" as "the ultimate term of the objectivity and narrowness of the lyric poem" (Irving Feldman in *Book Week*, 19 June 1966), the "extremist poet" (A. Alvarez's term) par excellence.[2] Whether *Ariel* was to be read, in George Steiner's words, as "representative of our present tone of emotional life,"[3] or whether, as Stephen Spender observed in a review called "Warnings from the Grave" (the *New Republic*, 18 June 1966), Plath's "landscape is an entirely interior, mental one, Keatsian in its intensity,"[4] the consensus of the late sixties was that this was a poetry of great "risk-taking," a poetry anguished, demonic, feverish, obsessed, violent, and tragic.[5]

In the seventies revisionary readings began to appear, readings that tried to place Plath more firmly in the poetic mainstream: I myself gave one such early reading, making the case for her poetry as a lyric of process in the Lawrentian tradition, oscillating between the poles of angst and animism.[6] M. L. Rosenthal grouped Plath with the confessional poets (Lowell, John Berryman, Anne Sexton), and Judith Kroll submitted her poetry to an archetypal analysis based largely on Robert Graves's myth of the White Goddess, arguing that the poet's oeuvre exhibits a "vision which is complete, self-contained, and whole, a vision of a mythic totality."[7] Other critics began to make a case for the earlier poetry, suggesting that *The Colossus* (1960) was remarkable not so much for its "controlled hallucination" (Lowell's phrase for *Ariel*) as for its careful craftsmanship and brilliant imagery.[8] And feminist critics began to take a closer look at the repressed anger at patriarchy expressed in *The Bell Jar* as well as at the role gender plays in the poetry.[9]

At the same time, no one doubted that *Ariel* was indeed *Ariel*; no one, that is, raised the issue of whether or not Plath's book, as published by Faber and Faber in London and Harper and Row in New York, reflected the poet's own stated wishes. It was generally assumed that Plath's estranged husband, Ted Hughes (whose name appears neither on the title page of *Ariel* nor in Lowell's foreword), had put together a collection of the poems written in Plath's final year.[10] The publication in 1971 of *Crossing the Water* (a volume of "transitional poems" written between *The Colossus* and *Ariel*) and in 1972 of *Winter Trees*, a slim volume of previously unpublished or uncollected poems from the *Ariel* period, did little to change the assumption that *Ariel* was all of a piece. A *Collected Poems* was, of course, projected, but for reasons the publishers never made clear, it did not appear until 1981, almost twenty years after Plath's death.

By this time, of course, the literary landscape had changed and interest in Plath's poetry had appreciably declined. She was, after all, only thirty-one when she died and so her oeuvre is, of necessity, limited in scope. More important: the question of mental illness, of consuming interest to a generation brought up on R. D. Laing's *The Divided Self*, is now regarded either as a disease to be controlled biochemically or as part of a larger cultural phenomenon: Lacanian criticism, for instance, is more interested in unmasking the verbal strategies of "sane" discourse than in dealing with individual psychosis. Again, the feminist movement, only in its infancy in Plath's lifetime, has put the "marriage plus career" problem at the center of Plath's life and writing in a rather different perspective: it is not that the problem has been solved, but Plath's stated desire to have "millions of babies" and her scorn for the "spinster bluestockings" of Cambridge and Smith College is not likely to strike a sympathetic chord in young women today. Most important: Plath's rhetoric, at least the rhetoric of the earlier poems, now seems anything but revolutionary. Her controlled stanzas, heavy with assonance and consonance, her elaborate syntax with its inversions and subordinate clauses, her ingenious metaphors—all these now look, to a generation of younger poets, almost genteel, almost Victorian. In the famous debate over the "raw" versus the "cooked," a debate that has been with us since the forties, Plath's "Russian roulette," as Lowell called it, now seems more "cooked" than "raw." After all, doesn't Woody Allen's Annie Hall, hardly an avant-garde reader, have a copy of *Ariel* on her bookshelf?

Not surprisingly, then, the response to the *Collected Poems*, as to *The Journals of Sylvia Plath* (1982), for which Ted Hughes served as consulting editor, has been polite and dutiful rather than partisan or polemic. True, reviewers expressed some dismay over Hughes's admission, in the foreword to the *Journals*, that he destroyed the notebook that covers the last months of Plath's life "because I did not want her children to have to read it (in those days I regarded forgetfulness as an essential part of survival)."[11] In an acute review Nancy Milford pointed out that even the earlier journals have been, in Hughes's own words, "curtailed." "The question about these Journals," writes Milford, "is always the same: who is doing the cutting? And why?"[12]

But the same question applies even more urgently to *Ariel*, and yet it has not been asked.[13] In Hughes's introduction to the *Collected Poems*, we read:

> [For Plath] a poem was always "a book poem" or "not a book poem." . . . Some time around Christmas 1962, she gathered

most of what are now known as the "Ariel" poems in a black
spring binder, and arranged them in a careful sequence. (At
the time, she pointed out that it began with the word "Love"
and ended with the word "Spring." . . .)

The *Ariel* eventually published in 1965 was a somewhat
different volume from the one she had planned. It incorpo-
rated most of the dozen or so poems she had gone on to write
in 1963, though she herself, recognizing the different inspiration of these new pieces, regarded them as the beginnings of a
third book. It omitted some of the more personally aggressive
poems from 1962, and might have omitted one or two more if
she had not already published them herself in magazines—so
that by 1965 they were widely known. The collection that
appeared was my eventual compromise between publishing a
large bulk of her work—including much of the post-*Colossus*
and pre-*Ariel* verse—and introducing her late work more cautiously, printing perhaps only twenty poems to begin with.
(Several advisers had felt that the violent contradictory feelings expressed in those pieces might prove hard for the reading public to take. In one sense, as it turned out, this
apprehension showed some insight.) (*CP*, 14–15)

On a first reading this sounds reasonable enough: the addition
of the 1963 poems, the exclusion of "the more personally aggressive"
ones—presumably because they failed to formalize or distance
Plath's experience—and the respect for the "reading public" which,
so "several advisers had felt" was not ready for "the violent contradictory feelings" expressed in certain poems. The fact remains that
Plath herself had arranged the future *Ariel* poems "in a careful
sequence," plotting out every detail including the first and last words
of the volume. In the notes to the *Collected Poems*, we find the list
of poems to be included and their exact order. To compare what
we may call Plath's *Ariel* to the book that actually appeared—which
is to say, to Hughes's construction of *Ariel*—turns out to be something of a shock. For both *Ariel 1* and *Ariel 2*, as I shall call them,
have a plot, but the two plots are so different that we cannot help
wondering what it means to reconstruct a poetic sequence after
the fact.

## II

The *Ariel* manuscript contains forty-one poems. In the following list, reprinted from the *Collected Poems* (p. 295), I have placed
in parentheses the dates of composition as Hughes gives them in the
text. Unless otherwise noted, all the poems date from 1962.

*Ariel 1* (Plath MS)

  1. Morning Song (19 February 1961)
  2. The Couriers (4 November)

3. The Rabbit Catcher (21 May)
4. Thalidomide (8 November)
5. The Applicant (11 October)
6. Barren Woman (21 February 1961)
7. Lady Lazarus (23–29 October)
8. Tulips (18 March 1961)
9. A Secret (10 October)
10. The Jailer (17 October)
11. Cut (29 October)
12. Elm (19 April)
13. The Night Dances (6 November)
14. The Detective (1 October)
15. Ariel (27 October)
16. Death & Co. (14 November)
17. Magi (1960)
18. Lesbos (18 October)
19. The Other (2 July)
20. Stopped Dead (19 October)
21. Poppies in October (27 October)
22. The Courage of Shutting Up (2 October)
23. Nick and the Candlestick (29 October)
24. Berck-Plage (30 June)
25. Gulliver (6 November)
26. Getting There (6 November)
27. Medusa (16 October)
28. Purdah (29 October)
29. The Moon and the Yew Tree (22 October 1961)
30. A Birthday Present (2 October)
31. Letter in November (11 November)
32. Amnesiac (21 October)
33. The Rival (July 1961)
34. Daddy (12 October)
35. You're (January/February 1960)
36. Fever 103° (20 October)
37. The Bee Meeting (3 October)
38. The Arrival of the Bee Box (4 October)
39. Stings (6 October)
40. The Swarm (7 October)
41. Wintering (9 October)

Note that, with the exception of seven poems, all the *Ariel* poems were written between 19 April and 14 November 1962—a mere seven-month span. Even more remarkable: twenty-three, or more than half, were written in a single month—October—and there are six more for November but none at all for August or September. I shall come back to this curious gap later.

The second list presents the poems as they appeared in *Ariel* as published by Harper and Row in 1966; the date of composition, as recorded by Ted Hughes in the *Collected Poems,* is again enclosed in parentheses.

*Ariel 2* (Hughes MS)
1. Morning Song (19 February 1961)
2. The Couriers (4 November)
3. Sheep in Fog (2 December/28 January 1963)
4. The Applicant (11 October)
5. Lady Lazarus (23–29 October)
6. Tulips (18 March 1961)
7. Cut (29 October)
8. Elm (19 April)
9. The Night Dances (6 November)
10. Poppies in October (27 October)
11. Berck-Plage (30 June)
12. Ariel (27 October)
13. Death & Co. (14 November)
14. Lesbos (18 October)
15. Nick and the Candlestick (29 October)
16. Gulliver (6 November)
17. Getting There (6 November)
18. Medusa (16 October)
19. The Moon and the Yew Tree (22 October 1961)
20. A Birthday Present (2 October)
21. Mary's Song (19 November)
22. Letter in November (11 November)
23. The Rival (July 1961)
24. Daddy (12 October)
25. You're (January/February 1960)
26. Fever 103° (20 October)
27. The Bee Meeting (3 October)
28. The Arrival of the Bee Box (4 October)
29. Stings (6 October)
30. The Swarm (7 October)
31. Wintering (9 October)
32. The Hanging Man (27 June 1960)
33. Little Fugue (2 April)
34. Years (16 November)
35. The Munich Mannequins (28 January 1963)
36. Totem (28 January 1963)
37. Paralytic (29 January 1963)
38. Balloons (5 February 1963)
39. Poppies in July (20 July)

40. Kindness (1 February 1963)
41. Contusion (4 February 1963)
42. Edge (5 February 1963)
43. Words (1 February 1963)

In putting together his version of *Ariel,* Hughes has eliminated eleven of the forty-one poems on Plath's own list, eight of them dating from the period October–November 1962. Further, he adds nine poems from the last six weeks of Plath's life in 1963. The result is that the volume is skewed in quite a different direction. What Hughes himself calls Plath's "careful sequence" has, I shall argue, a particular narrative structure: it begins with the birth of Frieda (hence the inclusion of the earlier poem "Morning Song") and moves through the despair Plath evidently experienced when she learned, in April 1962, that Hughes was having an affair with another woman; to the period of rage and misogyny that followed upon his actual desertion in mid-September, a rage best expressed in "Purdah" (a poem missing from *Ariel 2*); and then to a ritual death and a move toward rebirth, as chronicled in what many critics consider to be her finest poems, the Bee Sequence. The last stanza of "Wintering" goes like this:

Will the hive survive, will the gladiolas
Succeed in banking their fires
To enter another year?
What will they taste of, the Christmas roses?
The bees are flying. They taste the spring.

*Ariel 1* thus ends on a note of hope. In *Ariel 2*, on the other hand, the poems that make only too clear that Hughes's desertion was the immediate cause of Plath's depression are expunged; instead, the volume now culminates in ten death poems, poems, as it were, written from beyond rage, by someone who no longer blames anyone for her condition and reconciles herself to death:

The heart shuts,
The sea slides back,
The mirrors are sheeted.

("Contusion")

The woman is perfected.
Her dead
Body wears the smile of accomplishment. . . .

("Edge")

Words dry and riderless. . . .

("Words")

Indeed, the arrangement of *Ariel 2* implies that Plath's suicide was inevitable ("I have done it again"), that it was brought on, not by her actual circumstances, but by her essential and seemingly incurable schizophrenia. Or so the critics have generally viewed it. The classic interpretation of Plath's "problem" is probably that of Murray M. Schwartz and Christopher Bollas in a psychoanalytic essay called "The Absence at the Center: Sylvia Plath and Suicide."[14] Schwartz and Bollas confirm what early critics like Alvarez and Steiner had surmised: that "when her father died [when she was only eight years old] the erotic component of Plath's identity, her sexuality as a woman, remained unconfirmed. The good libidinal attachment to the father could not realize itself and her subsequent fantasized relations with men confirm instead both her ambivalence toward her father's loss and her struggle against that loss" (GL, 186). And again, "Plath's response to her father's death was to become like her father. The compulsive aspect of Plath's ritual of self-destruction mirrors the strongly obsessional nature of her personality. . . . Unable to find daddy in the outside world, she will get back to him by dying" (GL, 187, 189).

Not only does this account underplay the crucial—and very peculiar—role Sylvia Plath's mother played in this drama, a role I have discussed elsewhere,[15] it also ignores the reality of what actually happened to Plath in 1962. Schwartz and Bollas do suggest that "the precipitating factor in her final self-destructive journey was [Plath's] feeling of having been abandoned by Ted Hughes" (GL, 198). The implication is that Plath *felt* abandoned, not that she really *had been* abandoned. Indeed, Schwartz and Bollas tell the story as follows:

> [The] crisis of motherhood seems gradually to have overwhelmed Plath's resources. Her daughter was born in April 1960. By April 1961 she was in the midst of writing *The Bell Jar*. In 1961 she suffered a miscarriage, an appendectomy and became pregnant again. . . . In January 1962, her son was born, and like her own mother she now had a daughter and a son. The birth of her son seems to have provided her both with new confidence and new access to her own rage. In the summer of 1962 she suffered flu and high fevers, and in June she was involved in a driving accident that she described to A. Alvarez as a suicide attempt. In the fall of 1962 she moved herself and her children from Devon to London, where she rented a house once occupied by Yeats. The move was probably a response to a triangular situation in which she felt abandoned by Ted Hughes. Early in the mornings, before the children awakened, she wrote at amazing speed many of the poems in *Ariel*. (GL, 198)

This account was written before the publication of *Letters Home* (1975) or Edward Butscher's biography (1976); it is based,

moreover, only on a reading of *The Colossus* and *Ariel*, no reference
being made to *Crossing the Water* (1971) or *Winter Trees* (1972),
and certainly not to the poems of 1962 published for the first time
in the *Collected Poems*.[16] Now that we have access to these materials
as well as to the Plath papers in the Lilly Library (Indiana University), a very different story begins to emerge.

In April 1962, just three months after the birth of her second
child, Nicholas, Plath found out that her husband was having an
affair with Assia Wevill; the discovery is documented in her unpublished letters as well as in the poem "The Rabbit Catcher," which
Plath put in *Ariel 1*, and in an even more explicit poem, which she
chose not to include, called "Words Heard, by Accident, over the
Phone," with its pun on Assia's name, "Now the room is ahiss. The
instrument / Withdraws its tentacle" (*CP*, 202–3).[17]

The import of such an overheard telephone conversation can
be understood only against the background of Plath's total devotion
to and dependency upon her husband; indeed, it is not too much to
say that she worshipped him. When, for example, Hughes's *The
Hawk in the Rain* won the first Harper's publication contest (February 1957), Plath wrote in her journal: "I am so glad Ted is first.
All my pat theories against marrying a writer dissolve with Ted: his
rejections more than double my sorrow & his acceptances rejoice
me more than mine—it is as if he is the perfect male counterpart
to my own self: each of us giving the other an extension of the life
we believe in living" (*J*, 154). And a year later, when they were both
teaching at Smith, we read in the journal:

> Woke as usual, feeling sick and half-dead, eyes stuck together,
> a taste of winding sheets on my tongue after a horrible dream
> involving, among other things, Warren [Sylvia's brother]
> being blown to death by a rocket. Ted, my saviour, emerging
> out of the *néant* with a tall mug of hot coffee which, sip by
> sip, rallied me to the day as he sat at the foot of the bed
> dressed for teaching. About to drive off—I blink every time I
> see him afresh. . . . he is unbelievable and the more so
> because he is my husband and I somehow love cooking for
> him (made a lemon layer cake last night) and being secretary,
> and all. And, riffling through all the other men in the world
> who bore me with their partialness, the only one. (*J*, 221)

"Sylvia Plath," Hughes reminds us in the foreword to the *Journals*, "was a person of many masks, both in her personal life and in
her writings. Some were camouflage cliché facades, defensive mechanisms involuntary. And some were deliberate poses, attempts to
find the keys to one style or another" (*J*, xii). But even if we surmise
that Plath is never quite "herself," even in her own private journals,
it is clear that, at least with respect to the "selves" that functioned

in the world, Ted Hughes was her idol. There is, accordingly, no reason to doubt her plaintive statement, made in a letter to her patroness, Olive Higgins Prouty (20 November 1962), that the novel she wanted to write after *The Bell Jar* was to be about "a wife whose husband turns out to be a deserter and philanderer although she had thought he was wonderful and perfect."[18]

The man held to be "wonderful and perfect," moreover, was having a secret affair with the wife of a mutual friend; the couple had been houseguests of the Hugheses in Devon just weeks before. When we bear in mind that Nick was only four months old at the time and demanded regular night feedings, that Frieda was just two, and that Plath, who had feverishly remodeled the old Devon farmhouse, had not yet regained her strength, we can sense how devastating her discovery must have been. Hence the "flu and high fevers" and the "driving accident" of the summer of 1962, mentioned so matter-of-factly by Schwartz and Bollas. Toward the end of that summer, there seems to have been some attempt at reconciliation: indeed, on September 11, the Hugheses left the children with a nanny and set off on a trip to Ireland. It was there that Hughes told Plath he was leaving her; he departed the next day for London, where he took a flat and began divorce proceedings.[19]

August and September are thus the months of crisis, and there are no extant poems from this period. The bitter and explicit poems of October that follow are omitted from *Ariel 2*, and so critics like Schwartz and Bollas misinterpret what happened. "In the fall of 1962," they write, "she moved herself and her children from Devon to London." It sounds tame enough: "the move was *probably* a response to a triangular situation in which she *felt* abandoned by Ted Hughes" (my italics). The fact that she *was* quite literally abandoned is never confronted. Indeed, more attention has been paid to the unusually bitter cold January 1963 in London, of the frozen pipes and the breakdown of central heating, than to the simple fact that Sylvia Plath, who had been "abandoned" by her father when she was eight, now found herself, at thirty, abandoned by the man who was supposed to take his place. She had two children under the age of three, very little money, and no close friends or relatives in England. Given these circumstances, a much more stable woman than Plath was might easily have become despondent. If Plath was, as *Ariel 2* presents her, an "Electra on the Azalea Path," she was also, and perhaps more notably, a Medea, the betrayed and vengeful wife. For a brief time, in the fall of 1962, vengeance and rage found their outlet in a set of remarkable poems.

Both versions of *Ariel* open with "Morning Song," a poem of acute ambivalence about motherhood. In Plath's later poetry, as I have suggested elsewhere,[20] childbirth is regarded as the greatest of gifts but it is also the source of severe anxiety. For if carrying a child gives the poet a sense of being, of having weight, of inhabiting her own body, the separation of the child's body from her own is regarded as a frightening state in which one feels weightless, empty, disembodied. The point is made more baldly in "Barren Woman," written two days after "Morning Song" and not included in *Ariel 2:* "Empty, I echo to the least footfall, / Museum without statues," a museum in which "Marble lilies / Exhale their pallor like scent" (*CP,* 157).

The imagery of disembodiment and petrifaction ("New statue. / In a drafty museum, your nakedness / Shadows our safety") has been noted often enough, but in the framework of *Ariel 1,* "Morning Song" is juxtaposed to the last poem in the volume, "Wintering," where the potential for rebirth is conveyed by the image of the flower bulb:

> Will the hive survive, will the gladiolas
> Succeed in banking their fires?
> To enter another year?
>
> (*CP,* 219)

But here what is in question is not the birth of one's child but the birth into selfhood, the forging of a separate identity. That identity is symbolized by the queen bee:

> The bees are all women,
> Maids and the long royal lady.
> They have got rid of the men,
>
> The blunt, clumsy stumblers, the boors.
> Winter is for women. . . .
>
> (*CP,* 218–19)

Read against this text, the earlier "Morning Song" (one of only six poems from the period before 1962 included in the volume) takes on an ironic edge. If it is "Love" that set Plath's baby going "like a fat gold watch," the six jars of honey she has produced with the help of "the midwife's extractor" belong only to her. "Love"—the sexual act—can, in other words, produce a "bald cry . . . among the elements," a "new statue" whose mother and father "stand round blankly like walls." But there is another love, so "Wintering" implies, that can produce a poem: note the assertive tone of "I have my honey, Six jars of it, / Six cat's eyes in the wine cellar."

Between these two poles—the pole of the "Love" for a man
that produces babies and the pole of rebirth as an isolate self, a
rebirth that produces the honey of poetry—the narrative of *Ariel 1*
unfolds. The note of distrust of the male is introduced in what is the
second poem in both versions of *Ariel,* "The Couriers":

The word of a snail on the plate of a leaf?
It is not mine. Do not accept it.

And, more explicitly in the third couplet:

A ring of gold with the sun in it?
Lies. Lies and a grief.

This "disturbance in mirrors," the failure in vision that characterized
the poet's marriage, is made quite explicit in the next poem, "The
Rabbit Catcher," which seems to be the first poem Plath wrote after
she found out about Hughes's infidelity.[21] Here the speaker identifies
with the rabbits for whom her husband has set traps: "it was a place
of force—/the wind gagging my mouth with my own blown hair,/
Tearing off my voice" (*CP,* 193). The rabbit traps are insidious, for
they cannot be easily detected: "the snares almost effaced themselves— / Zeros, shutting on nothing, / Set close, like birth pangs."
The reference is, of course, to Plath's recent labor and the birth of
Nick, a birth that should never have occurred in this context. Here
are the last two stanzas of "The Rabbit Catcher":

I felt a still busyness, an intent.
I felt hands round a tea mug, dull, blunt,
Ringing the white china.
How they awaited him, those little deaths!
They waited like sweethearts. They excited him.

And we, too, had a relationship—
Tight wires between us,
Pegs too deep to uproot, and a mind like a ring
Sliding shut on some quick thing,
The constriction killing me also.

(*CP,* 194)

In her fevered vision, the poet confutes the rabbit snare with the
male hand squeezing the white china tea mug and, by extension, the
throat of the woman who serves him his tea. The parent text here
is D. H. Lawrence's "Love on the Farm," but whereas in Lawrence,
the caress of "his fingers that still smell grim / of the rabbit's fur"
produces instant sexual arousal, in Plath, the same image spells only
death: indeed, the man's hand can caress only an inanimate object,
while his mind is like a steel ring "Sliding shut on some quick thing."

It can be argued that Hughes omitted this poem from *Ariel*
because it is too "personally aggressive," but, with the possible

exception of the bald line "And we, too, had a relationship," it is no
more Gothic, no more sensational than, say, "Lady Lazarus" or even
the famous "Daddy." No, the "fault" of "The Rabbit Catcher" seems
to be its explicit reference to the broken marriage: not surprisingly,
Hughes replaces it with "Sheep in Fog," a much less personal lyric
that belongs to the cycle of death poems of January–February 1963.
Notice that the poet's anger is now internalized and that she speaks
of her fate as inevitable:

> The hills step off into whiteness.
> People or stars
> Regard me sadly, I disappoint them.
>
> (*CP,* 262)

The "dolorous bells" toll for the poet who partly longs, partly fears
the "dark water" beyond the "heaven / Starless and fatherless." She
is beyond anger, which is to say, beyond life.

Touching as such poems are, they are not the poems Plath
intended to publish in *Ariel.* "Sheep in Fog" is not on her list; rather,
"The Rabbit Catcher" is followed by "Thalidomide" (not in *Ariel 2*),
and "The Applicant." The former, despite its ostensible subject,
refers indirectly to Hughes in such phrases as "The lopped / Blood-
caul of absences," and "White spit / Of indifference!"; in the last
lines, the image of the broken mirror, regularly associated with the
betraying male, recurs: "The glass cracks across, / The image / Flees
and aborts like dropped mercury."

The latter poem, "The Applicant," extends this imagery, but
in the context of *Ariel 2,* where it follows "Sheep in Fog," it has
been read primarily as a blistering attack on modern advertising
techniques. Thus Richard Allen Blessing talks of its "language that
mocks itself while mocking the consumer and the product"; the
"chauvinistic applicant," argues Blessing, must be seen, as he is
by the poet, for the "abomination" he is.[22] Such interpretations are
in accord with Plath's own explanation, prepared for a BBC broad-
cast, that "the speaker is an executive, a sort of exacting super-
salesman. He wants to be sure the applicant for his marvelous product really needs it and will treat it right" (see *CP,* 293).

But who is this applicant anyway? He is told to open his hand
and, when it is revealed to be empty, he is promised "a hand / To
fill it and willing / To bring teacups and roll away headaches / And
do whatever you tell it. / Will you marry it?" Marriage, in other
words, demands of the woman that she turn herself into a mindless
robot, administering to the comforts of the man in the "waterproof,
shatterproof" suit. This man is promised a "sweetie," who is rolled
out of the closet, "Naked as paper to start":

> But in twenty-five years she'll be silver,
> In fifty, gold.

A living doll, everywhere you look.
It can sew, it can cook,
It can talk, talk, talk.

It works, there is nothing wrong with it.
You have a hole, it's a poultice.
You have an eye, it's an image.
My boy, it's your last resort.
Will you marry it, marry it, marry it.

(*CP*, 221–22)

In the context of *Ariel 1* this is a sardonic indictment of the traditional marriage that had been Sylvia Plath's. If the husband is to
blame for his demands, so is the wife for her acquiescence to them,
for her willingness to be "A living doll," an "it" that can sew and
cook, that acts as a "poultice" for his "hole," an image or mirror
reflection of what is in his eye. The phrasal repetitions and harsh
ballad rhythms of the poem also act to cast a spell on the Other
Woman, the one who is going to be put in the doll's house and asked
to "bring teacups and roll away headaches," to sew and to cook and
to apply the "poultice." "My boy, it's your last resort" thus has the
force of a veiled threat: in marrying this "it" (Ted marrying Assia),
the "applicant" is contemptuously dismissed to the realm of the
"Empty," a realm of "Rubber breasts or a rubber crotch," that can
no longer threaten the poet in her splendid isolation and superiority.
Reborn as "Lady Lazarus" in the next poem, she sheds "A cake of
soap, / A wedding ring, / A gold filling," and, rising above "The
peanut-crunching crowd," becomes a red-haired demon who can
"eat men like air."

The voice of "Lady Lazarus" is still that of outrage: the poet
cannot yet transcend the sense of personal loss and the need for
vengeance expressed in such tercets as

Dying
is an art, like everything else.
I do it exceptionally well.

I do it so it feels like hell.
I do it so it feels real.
I guess you could say I've a call.

(*CP*, 245)

These famous lines may now strike us as merely overwrought:
"Naked negation," as Hugh Kenner put it, "spilling down the sides
of improvised vessels" (GL, 42). More poignant, I think, is the tension between the death wish and the longing for life expressed in
the poems that follow "Lady Lazarus" in *Ariel 1:* first in "Tulips,"
written in March 1961, when Plath was recovering in the hospital
from an appendectomy,[23] and then in two poems that were omitted

from Hughes's *Ariel 2:* "A Secret" and "The Jailer." Both date from the same week of October 1962 as "The Applicant."

"A Secret" avoids the Gothic trappings of "Lady Lazarus" by locating the betrayal of the husband-father within the familiar and seemingly cozy world of the baby's nursery, with its colorful wallpaper, quilts, and coverlets. The threatening "you" thus becomes "blue and huge, a traffic policeman, / Holding up one palm," a figure in a child's picture book, whose presence is almost obscured by "the African giraffe in its Edeny greenery" (notice the purposely foolish rhyme) and the "Moroccan hippopotamus," both of whom "stare from a square, stiff frill." Silhouettes on the baby's coverlet or the canopy of the crib, these friendly creatures turn threatening, for they cannot help embodying the "secret" of the husband-father, even if it is only a "Faint, undulant watermark," which the poet, who has "one eye" (blindness) as compared with his two, has failed to decipher. So terrible is the "secret" that the speaker now perceives her baby as "illegitimate," a rotten apple stuck in the bureau drawer under the lingerie. Illegitimate because its father has disowned it, because his secret wish is to "Do away with the bastard." In the hallucinatory vision of the last four stanzas, the unwanted baby is seen as emerging from its hiding place in a sudden and violent rush that recalls the stampede on the Place de la Concorde when the traffic light changes ("My god, there goes the stopper!"). The cars suddenly pour out even as a bottle of stout explodes, "Slack foam in the lap." The infant leaps out from its mother's lap, a "Dwarf baby, / The knife in your back." The father has "killed" the child even as the mother has given it birth. The poem concludes with this terrifying "delivery":

'I feel weak.'
The secret is out.

*(CP,* 220)

"The Jailer" presents the next phase in this family drama. Once "The secret is out," man and wife becomes jailer and jailed:

My night sweats grease his breakfast plate.
The same placard of blue fog is wheeled into position
With the same trees and headstones.
Is that all he can come up with,
The rattler of keys?

*(CP,* 226)

The nursery is now replaced by the graveyard, the sex act by the "rape" of the sleeping pill, the only escape being "the black sack" of oblivion, where the poet can ironically "relax" by fueling, not her husband's real, but only "his wet dreams." But the sleeping pill wears off:

O little gimlets—
What holes this papery day is already full of!
He has been burning me with cigarettes,
Pretending I am a negress with pink paws.
I am myself. That is not enough.

The recognition of the last line is especially poignant in its irony: for the poet has no stable self, and the "self" that she projects is therefore not enough. Accordingly, she can get through the day only by "gluing my church of burnt matchsticks," trying to exorcise the image of the powerful male who has put her in this position ("How did I get here?"). The victim is now beginning to question the victimizer:

I imagine him
Impotent as distant thunder
In whose shadow I have eaten my ghost ration.

Here the "ghost ration" is, of course, Plath's own poetry, a poetry she had always regarded as taking second place to Hughes's own. The poem moves toward the recognition that the dependency has perhaps been mutual, that the jailer needs to have someone in his jail:

What would the dark
Do without fevers to eat?
What would the light
Do without eyes to knife, what would he
Do, do, do without me?

(*CP*, 227)

Once the context set up by poems like "The Rabbit Catcher," "A Secret," and "The Jailer" has been established, images in Plath's best-known *Ariel* poems take on a somewhat different edge. In "Cut" (which originally followed "The Jailer"), the strange detachment whereby the speaker can watch her own blood gushing from her cut thumb, gives way, in the seventh quatrain, to the bitter recollection of the "Saboteur" or "Kamikaze man" who has brought her to this pass, who has turned her into a "Trepanned veteran," even though the actual kitchen accident has nothing to do with the absent husband.[24] In "Elm":

Love is a shadow.
How you lie and cry after it.
Listen: these are its hooves: it has gone off, like a horse.

In "The Night Dances," she must convince herself that "Their [the father and son's] flesh bears no relation," that the father's "Cold folds of ego" cannot touch the "small breath" of the baby. In the famous title poem, the "Dead hands, dead stringencies" that the "White Godiva" "unpeel[s]" are identical to "the smell of years burning, here in the kitchen" that the speaker of "The Detective" (see *Ariel 1*, where this poem comes between "The Night Dances" and "Ariel") must destroy. And in "Lesbos," the "widow's frizz" applies not only to the "Coy paper strips for doors" but to her own condition.

In *Ariel 1* "Lesbos" is followed by "The Other" and "Stopped Dead." In all three, the poet's rage is now directed, not at her husband, but at other women and their children. "Lesbos" was the fruit of a visit, in late October 1962, to a couple in Cornwall whom the Hugheses had befriended; the visit, far from comforting Plath, evidently enhanced her sense of isolation and separate destiny. No longer is the infant seen as a "new statue in a drafty museum"; rather "there's a stink of fat and baby crap," and the poet's own little girl is seen as a "Little unstrung puppet, kicking to disappear."[25] "The Other" (written in July) is more explicitly addressed to Assia:

> You come in late, wiping your lips.
> What did I leave untouched in the doorstep —
> White Nike,
> Streaming between my walls?
>
> (*CP*, 201)

In the nightmare vision of the speaker, the victorious woman destroys everything: the very air motes become "corpuscles"; the handbag opens to give off a bad smell, the "knitting [is] busily hooking itself to itself" like "sticky candies." Yet the once-subdued, despairing poet can now triumph over her adversary: "The Other," ironically, is sterile: "the fornications / Circle a womb of marble." She is no more than "a cold glass," and so her attempt to "insert" herself "Between myself and myself" fails.

Indeed, the poet's triumph over the sterile "Other"—a Victory who is, after all, only a "White Nike"—is fueled by her fierce devotion to her infant. In "Nick and the Candlestick" and "Gulliver," the baby, no longer associated in her mind with his father ("O love, how did you get here?"), becomes her sole love object:

> Love, love,
> I have hung our cave with roses,
> With soft rugs —
>
> (*CP*, 241)

And finally the Christ child:

> You are the one
> Solid the spaces lean on, envious.
> You are the baby in the barn.

"Nick and the Candlestick," whose concluding lines these are, was written on 29 October. On the same day, Plath wrote what is generally considered to be one of her finest poems, "Purdah," not found in *Ariel 2* but published in *Poetry* in August 1963 (Plath herself had submitted it before her death) and then in *Winter Trees*. Written in condensed, elliptical tercets with elaborate sound patterning (e.g., "Jade"/"side"/"agonized" modulating into "Side"/"Adam"/ "Smile"), "Purdah" presents the transformation of a prelapsarian Eve into Clytemnestra. At the outset the "I" is no more than a piece of jade, a "Stone of the / Side of green Adam." If she "gleam[s] like a mirror," the "bridegroom" is "Lord of the mirrors"; she knows that "I am his. / Even in his / Absence." "Purdah" is associated, in this fierce poem, not with the eroticism of the harem but with the "cancerous pallors" of the moon, the same "cold and planetary" blue moon that we meet in the next poem, "The Moon and the Yew Tree." But whereas the latter poem posits only "blackness and silence," "Purdah" posits the possibility of escape from the bride- groom: first the unloosing of "One feather," then "One note / Shattering / The chandelier / of air," and finally:

> And at his next step
> I shall unloose
>
> I shall unloose—
> From the small jeweled
> Doll he guards like a heart—
>
> The lioness,
> The shriek in the bath,
> The cloak of holes.

> (*CP*, 243–44)

Here is the move toward rebirth that finds its culmination in the Bee poems. The reference, as Margaret Dickie Uroff points out, is to the two lioness-goddesses of Egyptian mythology. "One is Sekh- met, the terrible goddess of war and battle, whose name means 'the Powerful.' Claiming that her heart rejoiced in killing, she attacked men with such fury that the sun-god, fearing the extinction of the human race, appeased her with a magic potion. The other is Bast, whose origin as a lioness-goddess personified the fertilizing warmth of the sun. Goddess of pleasure, she loved music and dance. Plath's conception embraces both goddesses."[26]

"Purdah" is thus one of Plath's most forceful statements about power—the power to assume a new identity, to shed the "veil" of harem wife and destroy her former persona as "small jeweled / Doll." But in *Ariel 2*, Plath as Sekhmet-Bast or as Clytemnestra ("The shriek in the bath") is replaced by Plath as the Mother of God: "Mary's Song" (19 November), a poem Plath chose not to include in *Ariel*, emphasizes the role of the poet as war victim, a Mary whose Jewish son finds his fate in the glowing ovens of Poland. Indeed, in foregrounding what have always struck me as rather empty and hence histrionic references to the Nazis, the gas cham- bers, and the holocaust (see *CP*, 257), Hughes presents us with a

Sylvia Plath who is victimized by her time and place rather than by a specific personal betrayal.

My own guess is that Plath omitted "Mary's Song" from *Ariel* because she was less than satisfied with the bathos of lines like "O golden child the world will kill and eat." In reinstating it, Hughes, so to speak, gives Lady Lazarus a motive and disguises the fact that Lady Lazarus is really the destructive-creative lioness of "Purdah." Again, he uses the poem to set the stage for "Daddy," a poem that is read quite differently in the context of "The Jailer" and "Purdah" than it is in the war-holocaust context of "Getting There" and "Mary's Song."

As in the case of "The Applicant," Sylvia Plath's explanation of "Daddy" in her BBC script is purposely evasive. "The poem," she says, "is spoken by a girl with an Electra complex. Her father died while she thought he was God. Her case is complicated by the fact that her father was also a Nazi and her mother very possibly part Jewish. In the daughter the two strains marry and paralyze each other—she has to act out the awful little allegory once before she is free of it."[27] As such, "Daddy" has been extravagantly praised for its ability "to elevate private facts into public myth," for dramatizing the "schizophrenic situation that gives the poem its terrifying but balanced polarity"—polarity, that is to say, between the hatred and the love the "I" feels for the image of the father/lover.[28]

But after what we might call its initial "Guernica effect"[29] had worn off somewhat, "Daddy" was also subjected to some hard questions as critics began to wonder whether its satanic imagery is meaningful,[30] whether, for example, lines like "With your Luftwaffe, your gobbledygoo" or "Not God but a swastika / So black no sky could squeak through" are more than fairly cheap shots, demanding a stock response from the reader. Indeed, both the Nazi allegory and the Freudian drama of trying to die so as to "get back, back, back to you" can now be seen as devices designed to camouflage the real thrust of the poem, which is, like "Purdah," a call for revenge against the deceiving husband. For the real enemy is less Daddy ("I was ten when they buried you")—a Daddy who, in real life, had not the slightest Nazi connection—than the model made by the poet herself in her father's image:

I made a model of you,
A man in black with a Meinkampf look

And a love of the rack and the screw.
And I said I do, I do.
So daddy, I'm finally through.
The black telephone's off at the root,
The voices just can't worm through.

(*CP*, 224)

The image of the telephone is one that Plath's early admirers like George Steiner or Stephen Spender simply ignored, but with the hindsight a reading of the *Collected Poems* gives us, we recognize it, of course, as the dreaded "many-holed earpiece," the "muck funnel" of "Words heard, by accident, over the phone." And indeed, the next stanza refers to the "vampire" who "drank my blood for a year, / Seven years if you want to know." This is a precise reference to the length of time Sylvia Plath had known Ted Hughes when she wrote "Daddy"—precise as opposed to the imaginary references to Plath's father as "panzer-man" and "Fascist."

A curiously autobiographical poem, then, whose topical trappings ("Luftwaffe," "swastika," "Dachau, Auschwitz, Belsen") have distracted the attention of a generation of readers from the poem's real theme. Ironically, "Daddy" is a "safe" poem—and hence Hughes publishes it—because no one can chide Plath for her Electra complex, her longing to get back to the father who died so prematurely, whereas the hatred of Hughes ("There's a stake in your fat black heart") is much more problematic. The Age Demanded a universal theme—the rejection not only of the "real" father but also of the Nazi Father Of Us All—hence the label "the *Guernica* of modern poetry" applied to "Daddy" by George Steiner. But the image of a black telephone that must be torn from the wall—this, so the critics of the sixties would have held, is not a sufficient objective correlative for the poet's despairing vision. The planting of the stake in the "fat black heart" is, in any case, a final farewell to the ceremony of marriage ("And I said I do, I do"). What follows is "Fever 103°" and the metamorphosis of self that occurs in the Bee poems.

The first of these, "The Bee Meeting," is a dream sequence in which the poet finds herself a victim, unprotected in her "sleeveless summery dress" from the "gloved," "covered," and veiled presences of the villagers. In the initiation ritual that now takes place, there are two dreaded male figures: the "man in black" (cf. the "fat black heart" in "Daddy") and the "surgeon my neighbors are waiting for, / This apparition in a green helmet, / Shining gloves and white suit." Neither the black man nor his white counterpart are named: indeed, the poet asks: "Is it the butcher, the grocer, the postman, someone I know?" She cannot, in any case, run away:

> I could not run without having to run forever.
> The white hive is snug as a virgin,
> Sealing off her brood cells, her honey, and quietly humming.

The virginal white hive now becomes the source of new life for the poet, identifying, as she does, with the queen bee: "Is she hiding, is she eating honey? She is very clever. / She is old, old, old, she must live another year, and she knows it." "Exhausted," she can

finally contemplate the "long white box in the grove" which is both
coffin and hive. She is "the magician's girl who does not flinch."

In the next poem, "The Arrival of the Bee Box," the "dangerous" box of bees becomes a challenge that is desired: "I have to live
with it overnight / And I can't keep away from it." The poet is now
tapping her own subconscious powers; at the end of "Stings" we
read:

> They thought death was worth it, but I
> Have a self to recover, a queen.
> Is she dead, is she sleeping?
> Where has she been,
> With her lion-red body, her wings of glass?
>
> Now she is flying
> More terrible than she ever was, red
> Scar in the sky, red comet
> Over the engine that killed her—
> The mausoleum, the wax house.
>
> (*CP*, 215)

"I have a self to recover, a queen": here is the lioness of "Purdah,"
the avenging goddess, triumphing "Over the engine that killed her,"
just as the "swarm" in the next poem must evade "The smile of a
man of business, intensely practical," a man "with grey hands" that
"would have killed *me*." In the final poem, "Wintering," this male
figure is no longer present. "Daddy," the man in black, the rector,
the surgeon—all have disappeared:

> The bees are all women,
> Maids and the long royal lady.
> They have got rid of the men,
>
> The blunt, clumsy stumblers, the boors.
> Winter is for women—
> The woman, still at her knitting,
> At the cradle of Spanish walnut,
> Her body a bulb in the cold and too dumb to think.
>
> Will the hive survive, will the gladiolas
> Succeed in banking their fires
> To enter another year?
> What will they taste of, the Christmas roses?
> The bees are flying. They taste the spring.
>
> (*CP*, 218–19)

With this parable of hibernation, a hibernation that makes way
for rebirth and continuity ("The bees are flying"), *Ariel* was to have
concluded. But Hughes, not content to leave it at that, added eleven
poems, all of which concern, not the possibilities of renewal, but, on
the contrary, death. Thus "Wintering" is immediately and oddly
followed by a poem of 1960 called "The Hanging Man," which

presents the poet as possessed by "some god," a kind of "desert prophet," and ends ominously with the line, "If he were I, he would do what I did" (*CP*, 142). "The Hanging Man" serves as kind of prelude for the January 1963 poems that follow, poems in which the inevitability of death is everywhere foregrounded. No longer does the poet look forward to the "Years"; her thoughts turn on "greenness, darkness so pure / They freeze and are" (*A*, 72). In "Paralytic," "all / Wants, desire [are] Falling from me like rings / Hugging their lights" (*A*, 78); in "Contusion," "The heart shuts, / The sea slides back, / The mirrors are sheeted" (*A*, 83). Finally, in "Edge" (dated 5 February 1963, six days before her suicide), Plath imagines herself in death:

> The woman is perfected.
> Her dead
> Body wears the smile of accomplishment,
> The illusion of a Greek necessity
>
> Flows in the scrolls of her toga,
> Her bare
>
> Feet seem to be saying:
> We have come so far, it is over.

> (*A*, 84)

And the final poem, "Words" (1 February 1963), is despairing in its sense that the poet's "words" become "dry and riderless," that they are no longer connected to the poet who gave them birth. The connection between self and language has been severed: there is only fate in the form of the "fixed stars" that "From the bottom of the pool . . . Govern a life."

One can argue, of course, that Hughes is simply completing Plath's own story, carrying it to its final conclusion, where "Each dead child coiled, a white serpent" has been folded back into the woman's body, where the "Words" are entirely cut off from the poet who created them. But it is also possible that, in taking advantage of a brief spell of depression and despair, when death seemed the only solution, Hughes makes the motif of inevitability larger than it really is. "The woman is perfected" in more ways than one.

## IV

In any collection of poems, ordering is significant, but surely *Ariel* presents us with an especially problematic case. For two decades we have been reading it as a text in which, as Charles Newman puts it, "expression and extinction [are] indivisible,"[31] a text that culminates in the almost peaceful resignation of "Years" or "Edge." The poems of *Ariel* culminate in a sense of finality, all passion spent.

*Ariel 1* establishes quite different perimeters. Plath's arrangement emphasizes, not death, but struggle and revenge, the outrage that follows the recognition that the beloved is also the betrayer, that the shrine at which one worships is also the tomb. Indeed, one could argue that the very poems Hughes dismissed as being too "personally aggressive" are, in an odd way, more "mainstream," that is to say more broadly based, than such "headline" poems as "The Munich Mannequins" or "Totem," with its "butcher's guillotine that whispers: 'How's this, how's this?' " (*A*, 75). For, as long as the poet can struggle, as long as she still tries to defy her fate, as she does in "The Jailer" or "The Other" or "Purdah," the reader identifies with her situation: the "Cut thumb" is not only Plath's but ours.

Perhaps Sylvia Plath's publishers will eventually give us the original *Ariel*. But it is not likely, given the publication of the *Collected Poems,* which now becomes our definitive text. How ironic, in any case, that the publication of Plath's poems has depended, and continues to depend, on the very man who is, in one guise or another, their subject. In a poem not included in *Ariel* called "Burning the Letters" (*CP*, 204–5), the poet decides to do away with the hated love letters, with "the eyes and times of the postmarks":

> here is an end to the writing,
> The spry hooks that bend and cringe, and the smiles, the
>     smiles.
> And at least it will be a good place now, the attic.

But the attic was soon invaded, the dangerous notebooks were destroyed, and the poems that were permitted to enter the literary world had to get past the Censor. The words of the dead woman, to paraphrase W. H. Auden, were modified in the guts of the living. Only now, some twenty-five years after her death, can we begin to assess her oeuvre. But then, as Plath herself put it in a poem written during the last week of her life:

> The blood jet is poetry,
> There is no stopping it.

# Chapter Ten

# A Lion in Our

# Living Room:

## *Reading Allen Ginsberg*

## *in the Eighties*

### *THE* COLLECTED POEMS *(1985)*

### *I*

I saw the best minds of my generation destroyed by
    madness, starving hysterical naked,
dragging themselves through the negro streets at dawn
    looking for an angry fix.[1]

In the New York of the late fifties, Frank O'Hara, hearing Allen Ginsberg declaim the now classic opening of "Howl," turned, so the story goes, to his neighbor and whispered, "I wonder who Allen has in mind?"

The question is not mere camp. What O'Hara meant, no doubt, is that, despite the universalizing gesture, the roll call of "best minds . . . destroyed by madness," the real hero of "Howl," the "angel-headed hipster"

who poverty and tatters and hollow-eyed and high sat up
smoking in the supernatural darkness of cold-water flats
floating across the tops of cities contemplating jazz,

(*CP*, 126)

was a single, lonely, and bookish young man named Allen Ginsberg,
writing, like the François Villon of "The Testament," in the thirtieth
year of his life, when he felt himself to be beyond shame. "Howl,"
that is to say, is less Ginsberg's "Ode to the Confederate Dead" or
his elegy for Carl Solomon (institutionalized, like Ginsberg's own
mother, Naomi, in a mental hospital) than it is the most harrowing
as well as the funniest of autobiographies.

To put it more accurately: "Howl" is one link in the larger
autobiographical chain that constitutes Allen Ginsberg's poetry. In
the "Author's Preface, Reader's Manual" that opens his canonical
800-page *Collected Poems* (an elegant edition by Harper and Row,
whose back cover bears the photograph of a charmingly rabbinical
Allen Ginsberg, holding a packet of the seven small black-and-white
City Lights volumes in which the bulk of his poetry has appeared
from 1956 to the present), Ginsberg announces, "Herein author has
assembled all his poetry books published to date rearranged in
straight chronological order to compose an autobiography" (*CP*, xix).
Indeed, the *Collected Poems* has an index of proper names so that
the reader can trace the evolving relationship of Ginsberg and, say,
Neal Cassady or can look up what the poet said about his grandmother, Rebecca Ginsberg (four references).

The "straight chronological" arrangement gives a startling new
shape to a life we have so far perceived only in bits and pieces. Thus
the "youthful poetries" (1945–52) originally published in *The Gates
of Wrath* (1972) and *Empty Mirror* (1961) are now combined, the
"imperfect literary rhymes" of the former interspersed with the
"raw-sketch practice poems" of the latter so that "disparate simultaneous early styles juxtaposed [will] aid recognition of a grounded
mode of writing encouraged by Dr. Williams, 'No ideas but in
things.' " Again, Ginsberg has arranged the volume so that the
"Travel poems Calcutta-Saigon-Angkor Wat-Japan, 1963, mixed
through three separate books, now cohere in sequence," and he
takes pains to alert us to the continuity of the "Cross-country Auto
Poesy chronicle [that] starts 1965 at Northwest border." The ten
sections of the book, we are told, "roughly indicat[e] time, geography, and motif or 'season' of experience"; the book as a whole is
meant to portray "poetic energy as cyclic, the continuum a panorama
of valleys and plateaus with peaks of inspiration every few years"
(*CP*, xx).

These brief hints are not just rationalizations, designed to
"make it cohere." To read Ginsberg's *Collected Poems* in 1985 is

something of a shock—a *frisson* of pure pleasure. Was our poetry really this energetic, this powerful and immediate just a few short decades ago? Did the poet really dream of a "Green Automobile," in which he could take his lover "riding / over the Rockies . . . riding / all night long until dawn" (*CP*, 86)? At a time when so much of our poetry wears white gloves, when the main precept often seems to be "Proceed with caution!" Ginsberg's poetic trajectory is a marvel to behold. Vortex, as Ginsberg's mentor Ezra Pound put it, is ENERGY!

This energy has not always been appreciated. The more theoretical studies of postmodern poetry and poetics—Charles Altieri's *Enlarging the Temple,* Hugh Kenner's *A Homemade World,* Robert von Hallberg's *American Poetry and Culture, 1945–1980,* and, for that matter, my own *Poetics of Indeterminacy*—have tended to ignore, if not deprecate, Ginsberg's achievement, partly, perhaps, in reaction to the journalistic overkill devoted to the Beat Generation.[2] "In 'A Supermarket in California,' " says Denis Donoghue, "Ginsberg had done everything that is required of a poet except the one essential thing—to write his poem."[3] And in an essay called "The Sorrows of American-Jewish Poetry," Harold Bloom declares:

> The chanter of *Howl, Kaddish,* and many lesser litanies is as much beyond the reach of criticism as Norman Mailer; both have been raised to that bad eminence where every fresh failure is certain of acclaim as an event, something that has happened and so is news, like floods, fires, and other stimulating disasters. The genuine painfulness of reading through *Kaddish* is not an *imaginative* suffering for the reader, but is precisely akin to the agony we sustain when we are compelled to watch the hysteria of strangers.[4]

The charge of formlessness, of poetry as mere rant, will no doubt continue to haunt Ginsberg, but the publication of his *Collected Poems* should do much to dispel it. Indeed, to read one's way through the "valleys and plateaus" of these 800 pages is to be reminded how fatuous are the legends that have grown up around Allen Ginsberg, legends for which the poet's own *ex cathedra* pronouncements have been at least partially responsible.

The first such myth is that Ginsberg's poetry is a straight transcription of visionary speech. As he himself insists in the preface, " 'First thought, best thought.' Spontaneous insight—the sequence of thought-forms passing naturally through ordinary mind—was always motif and method of these compositions" (*CP*, xx). Ginsberg has been making this claim for years: in the *Paris Review* interview with Tom Clark (1965), he explains:

> We all talk among ourselves and we have common understandings, and we say anything we want to say. . . . So

then—what happens if you make a distinction between what
you tell your friends and what you tell your Muse? The problem is to break down that distinction: when you approach the
Muse to talk as frankly as you would talk with yourself or
with your friends. . . . That meant . . . a complete revision of
what literature was supposed to be. . . . It's the ability to com-
mit to writing, to *write*, the same way that you are![5]

Such comments have often been taken at face value. In a study of
the Beats called *Naked Angels* (1976), John Tytell commends Ginsberg's *Paris Review* commentary for its "great clarity" and remarks:

Prematurely conscious of the potentials for lying on a national
scale, the Beats raised the standard of honesty no matter what
the artistic consequences. . . . [They] passionately embraced
the extreme of uncontained release and denounced superim-
posed and confining forms. . . . The desire to remove the literary superego was a sign of how the Beats would struggle with
the conditioning influences of language; in many ways it represented a fulfillment of the romantic credo as formulated in
the preface to the *Lyrical Ballads* in which Coleridge and
Wordsworth promised to use the language of ordinary men.[6]

"Uncontained release"? The removal of "the literary super-
ego"? Here is a little diary-poem of 1955 called "A Strange New
Cottage in Berkeley," originally designed as a prelude to the famous
"A Supermarket in California" and now restored to its proper place:

All afternoon cutting bramble blackberries off a totter-
ing brown fence
under a low branch with its rotten old apricots miscellaneous under the leaves,
fixing the drip in the intricate gut machinery of a new
toilet;
found a good coffeepot in the vines by the porch, rolled
a big tire out of the scarlet bushes, hid my marijuana;
wet the flowers, playing the sunlit water each to each,
returning for godly extra drops for the stringbeans and
daisies;
three times walked around the grass and sighed
absently:
my reward, when the garden fed me its plums from the
form of a small tree in the corner,
an angel thoughtful of my stomach, and my dry and
lovelorn tongue.

(*CP*, 135)

Perhaps the first thing to notice here is that "the sequence of
thought-forms passing naturally through ordinary mind" would not
include the title, "A Strange New Cottage in Berkeley," a title that
serves as the focal point for the catalog that follows. For it is, of

course, the poet who is "strange" and "new" to his surroundings
and hence lonely in his solitude, even as he senses himself to be on
the brink of something "new" that he longs for. Ginsberg in conversation with William Burroughs or Jack Kerouac or Gregory Corso
might talk about the same activities—cutting brambles from the
fence, fixing the toilet, watering the flowers—but hardly in the
sequence found in the poem, a sequence that moves carefully from
the ordinary to the strange and that culminates in the high style of
"an angel thoughtful of my stomach, and my dry and lovelorn
tongue."

The sequence of images moves from without to within, from
the bramble blackberries on the fence to the "dry and lovelorn
tongue" that craves the fruit of the garden. The first three lines
present images that seem to be in accord with the great American
work ethic, the natural desire to "fix up the place," to create order.
But Ginsberg as boy scout imperceptibly gives way to Ginsberg the
resourceful tramp, finding "a good coffeepot in the vines by the
porch, roll[ing] a big tire out of the scarlet bushes," and then Ginsberg the bad Beat boy, hiding his marijuana in anticipation of the
times to come. The pragmatic and the visionary here go hand in
hand: to "wet the flowers, playing the sunlit water each to each,"
becomes a rite of initiation, a rite confirmed in the line "three times
walked round the garden and sighed absently."

This self-portrayal makes us smile. The poet as lord of the
manor surveying his domain is, of course, a scared young man,
"absently" dreaming of lost and future love. But "absence" also
paves the way for the influx of spirit, for the vision of the plum tree
in the corner of the garden as "an angel thoughtful of my stomach,
and my dry and lovelorn tongue."

Such wry conjunctions of the ordinary and the "strange," of
grubby fact and vision, are typical of Ginsberg. There is a touch of
the Jewish clown in the makeup of this poet-prophet. In the appendix to the *Collected Poems* we find a photograph of Naomi, Allen,
and Louis Ginsberg taken at the New York World's Fair on 15 June
1940 (fig. 1). The bespectacled adolescent looks like nothing so much
as a nice Jewish boy on an outing with his respectable parents,
although even here Naomi's expression beneath her rakish black
hat is decidedly odd, and Louis, holding a neat umbrella, has the
smile of the insecure. The homely urban kid with glasses is, in any
case, still very much a part of the bardic young poet who arrives in
Berkeley looking for freedom and love. The ethos of rehabilitating
the "good coffeepot" found in the vines and the automobile tire
beneath the burning bush is still the ethos of the Paterson, New
Jersey, streets, indeed, of the Lower East Side, where Louis and
Naomi grew up. The poet's angel, it seems, is ready to be "thoughtful

**Figure 1.** Naomi, Allen, and Louis Ginsberg, New York World's Fair, 15 June 1940, on p. 764 of the *Collected Poems*. By permission of the author.

of [his] stomach," because he has not wasted his material substance.
Waste not, as it were, want not.

"Waste not, want not" is, for that matter, the adage that comes to mind as one reads Ginsberg's early poems and journals. A second common Ginsberg myth dispelled by a reading of the *Collected Poems* is that the conventional verse forms of the poet's youth were, at best, a false start, a kind of straitjacket he had to shed in order to find his "real self" in the long, loose sweeping line of "Howl"—a line purportedly derived from Blake, Whitman, and the Bible. In his famous letter of 1949 to his mentor, William Carlos Williams (the letter reproduced by Williams in *Paterson* V), Ginsberg writes: "I do not know if you will like my poetry or not—that is how far your own inventive persistence excludes less independent or youthful attempts to perfect, renew, transfigure, and make contemporarily real an old style of lyric machinery, which I use to record the struggle with imagination of the clouds."[7] Williams, who had little tolerance for fixed verse forms, replied with the terse comment, "In this mode perfection is basic." Ginsberg took the hint: the poems of *Empty Mirror* (1952) abandon verse forms completely: the new line is created by breaking the prose of his journals into lines of verse.[8] This time Williams responded enthusiastically. In his introduction to *Empty Mirror,* he writes: "The lines are superbly all alike. Most people, most critics would call them prose—they have an infinite variety, perfectly regular; they are all alike and yet none is like the other. It is like the monotony of our lives that is made up of the front pages of newspapers and the first (aging) 3 lines of the *Inferno"* (*CP,* 809).

And from here, so the story usually goes, it was just a short step to the "breath unit" of "Howl," the long jazz-inspired line first heard in Ginsberg's reading at the Six Gallery in San Francisco in 1956, a line the poet himself has described as moving according to "natural inspiration of the moment . . . disparate thinks put down together, shorthand notations of visual imagery, juxtapositions of hydrogen juke-box. . . . Mind is shapely, Art is shapely."[9]

Hip as this sounds, the fact is that Ginsberg has always been the most careful of prosodists and that the metrical forms of the *Gates of Wrath* have never been entirely abandoned.[10] Indeed, by the late seventies Ginsberg was once again writing ballad quatrains like the following:

Lack Love

Love wears down to bare truth
My heart hurt me much in youth
Now I hear my real heart beat
Strong and hollow thump of meat

I felt my heart wrong as an ache
Sore in dreams and raw awake
I'd kiss each new love on the chest
Trembling hug him breast to breast

Kiss his belly, kiss his eye
Kiss his ruddy boyish thigh
Kiss his feet kiss his pink cheek
Kiss behind him naked meek. . . .

(*CP*, 693)

This harks back thirty years to such poems as "A Western Ballad":

When I died, love, when I died
My heart was broken in your care;
I never suffered love so fair
as now I suffer and abide
when I died, love, when I died. . . .

(*CP*, 13)

Or to the even earlier "An Eastern Ballad," dated 1945–49:

I speak of love that comes to mind:
The moon is faithful, although blind;
She moves in thought she cannot speak.
Perfect care has made her bleak. . . .

(*CP*, 18)

It could (and has) been argued that Ginsberg's recent return to the "simple" ballad form of his repressed youth marks a loss of poetic power, a retreat into the pleasant and easy. But since the circular arrangement of the *Collected Poems* is Ginsberg's own, we can take it to signify that, for this poet, as for Pound before him, "poetry withers and 'dries out' when it leaves music . . . too far behind it."[11] Consider lines 3–4 of "An Eastern Ballad," one of the first poems Ginsberg wrote and preserved:

She móves in thóught ‖ she cánnot spéak.
Pérfect cáre has máde her bléak.

The twenty-year-old poet who placed the caesura in the third line and who foreshortened the fourth, beginning, in Blakean fashion, with a trochee, was already a very accomplished poet. The consonance of "per"/"care"/"her," the alliteration of "has"/"her," the assonance of *e*'s and *a*'s—all culminating in the rhyme "speak"/ "bleak"—this is a poetic debut that bears watching, no matter how hackneyed the image of the blind moon and the theme of lost love. Side by side with such songs, we find "prosaic" poems like "Paterson" (1949), which begins:

What do I want in these rooms papered with visions of
money?

How much can I make by cutting my hair? If I put new heels
	on my shoes,
bathe my body reeking of masturbation and sweat, layer upon
	layer of excrement. . . .

(*CP*, 40)

This jaunty self-mocking opening immediately brings to mind Frank
O'Hara, who was still an undergraduate at Harvard and quite
unknown to Ginsberg in 1949. After listing all the Establishment
institutions to be rejected ("employment bureaus," "statistical cubi-
cles," "cloakrooms of the smiling gods of psychiatry," and so on),
Ginsberg launches into a long catalog of what he would rather be
doing:

> rather jar my body down the road, crying by a diner in the
> 	Western sun;
> rather crawl on my naked belly over the tincans of Cincinnati;
> rather drag a rotten railroad tie to a Golgotha in the Rockies;
> rather, crowned with thorns in Galveston, nailed hand and foot
> 	in Los Angeles, raised up to die in Denver,
> pierced in the side in Chicago, perished and tombed in New
> 	Orleans and resurrected in 1958 somewhere on Garret
> 	Mountain,
> come down roaring in a blaze of hot cars and garbage,
> streetcorner Evangel in front of City Hall, surrounded by
> 	statues of agonized lions,
> with a mouthful of shit, and the hair rising on my scalp,
> screaming and dancing in praise of Eternity annihilating the
> 	sidewalk, annihilating reality,
> screaming and dancing against the orchestra in the destructible
> 	ballroom of the world,
> blood streaming from my belly and shoulders
> flooding the city with its hideous ecstasy, rolling over the
> 	pavements and highways
> by the bayoux and forests and derricks leaving my flesh and
> 	my bones hanging on the trees.

(*CP*, 40–41)

Here, seven years before the performance of "Howl" in San Francisco, is the Ginsberg mode in embryo: the long anapestic line built
on the anaphora of "rather" (as the "Howl" line builds on the anaphora of "who"), the cataloging of American place names, the reference to ugly reality ("the tincans of Cincinnati," "a rotten railroad
tie," "hot cars and garbage"), the conjunction of the physical
("mouthful of shit") and the spiritual ("hair rising on my scalp, /
screaming and dancing in praise of Eternity). Indeed, some of the
phrasing of "Paterson" (e.g., "to die in Denver") reappears almost
verbatim in "Howl."

But toward the close, "Paterson" goes somewhat limp. Such phrases as "the destructible ballroom of the world" and "hideous ecstasy" are hackneyed, and the Whitmanian conclusion, "by the bayoux and forests and derricks leaving my flesh and my bones hanging on the trees," has not quite been earned by the preceding catalog: the speaker is too angry at the world to become a seer, too preoccupied with himself to enter the life of the bayoux and forests and derricks.

Indeed, the feat of "Howl" is that it pays homage to Whitman and Williams even as it transforms their characteristic rhythms and images. Consider the following sequence:

> who júmped ôff the Bróoklyn Brídge ‖ thîs áctually háppened ‖
> and wálked aẃay ûnknówn and forgótten into the
> ghóstly dáze of Chínatôwn sóup álleywâys & fíretrûcks, ‖
> nót êven óne frêe béer,
> who sáng oût of their wíndows in despáir, ‖ féll oût of the
> súbway wíndow, ‖ júmped in the fílthy Passáic, ‖ leáped
> on négroes, ‖ críed áll óver the stréet, ‖ dánced on
> bróken wíneglâsses bárefôot ‖ smáshed phónogrâph
> récords of nostálgic Eúropéan 1930s Gérman jázz ‖
> fínished the whískey and thréw ûp gróaning into the
> blóody toílet, ‖ móans in their eárs and the blást of
> colóssal stéamwhístles,
> who bárreled dówn the híghwâys of the pást joúrneying to eâch
> óther's hótrôd- ‖ Gólgôtha ‖ jáil- ‖ sólitude ‖ wátch ‖ or
> Bírminghâm jázz incârnátion.
>
> (*CP*, 129)

Compare this to Whitman's "Song of Myself":

> Wálking the páth wórn in the gráss and béat through the léaves
> of the brúsh,
> Where the quáil is whístling betwixt the wóods and the whéat-
> lôt,
> Where the bát flíes in the Séventh-mónth éve, ‖ where the
> gréat góldbûg dróps through the dárk,
> Where the bróok puts oút of the róots of the óld trée and flóws
> to the méadow. . . .[12]

Whitman's rhythm is characterized by its flow, its forward thrust. Phrase succeeds parallel phrase with only the slightest of pauses between them, and the predominant anapests and amphibraches are linked by alliteration and assonance. In contrast, Ginsberg's line moves forward only to go into reverse. His mode is a curious amalgam of graphic realistic reference and surrealist image, a mix, so to speak, of Williams ("No ideas but in things," as Ginsberg repeatedly tells us) and the high style of the Great (English) Tradition, learned from Mark Van Doren and other professors at Columbia University and filtered through Hart Crane. "The ghostly daze of Chinatown," "the highways of the past," "moans in their ears"—

such phrases could and did appear in *The Gates of Wrath*, as could such poetic diction as "unknown and forgotten," "in despair," "journeying," and "solitude." But in "Howl," this elegant language quickly modulates into parenthetical statements like "this actually happened" or "not even one free beer." Here is the speech base we hear so much about, but notice that Ginsberg's clotted catalogs— "Chinatown soup alleyways & firetrucks" or "each other's hotrod-Golgotha jail-solitude watch" are closer to Apollinaire or Blaise Cendrars's proto-Dada style than to Whitman. The rhythmic contour of such phrases is one of intentional clash:

éach óther's hótrôd- ‖ Gólgôtha ‖ jáil- ‖ sólitude ‖ wátch

where the opposition of voiced and voiceless stop ($d + g$) or liquid and spirant ($l + s$) forces the reader to pause and draw breath.

Throughout "Howl" we hear this oppositional rhythm, a bumping and grinding that vocalizes the poet's feverish intensity. But in the "Footnote to 'Howl,' " written some time after the completion of the poem, the clash of energies gives way to something much more predictable:

> Holy the solitudes of skyscrapers and pavements! Holy the
> cafeterias filled with the millions! Holy the
> mysterious rivers of tears under the streets!
>
> (*CP*, 134)

Evidently Ginsberg added the "Footnote" to counter the criticism (made, among others, by his father) that the poem propounded no positive values.[13] But the "Holy! Holy! Holy!" conclusion (set over against the "Moloch" litany of the preceding section) has an air of willed assertion: everything is too easily and too inexplicably "holy" and beautiful. The long lines now consist of no more than a series of neatly parallel phrases ("Holy New York Holy San Francisco Holy Peoria"), phrases that have none of the bite of such earlier sequences as "Peyote solidities of halls, backyard green tree cemetery dawns, wine drunkenness over the rooftops, storefront boroughs of teahead joyride neon blinking traffic light, sun and moon and tree vibrations"). I mention this because poems like the "Footnote to 'Howl' " have been imitated by countless Ginsberg disciples, whereas the linear structure of "Howl" itself is all but inimitable in its density.

The question of density brings me to a third myth, which has to do with the interpretation of the poet's voice. Simply put, this is the myth that, from "Howl" onward, Ginsberg writes a poetry of vatic inspiration coupled with a searing denunciation of modern capitalist society as the embodiment of the spiritual death brought on by a culture bent on "visions of money." Only the transformation of consciousness, whether induced by drugs or poetry or Buddhist meditation, can bring the poet to a cosmic vision of the essence of things. Ginsberg, according to this myth, is a poet-prophet in the tradition of Plotinus, Blake, and Mahayana Tibetan Buddhism. The negative side of this myth (and we hear this often too) is that Ginsberg's claim to vision is dubious, that his drug-induced poems or Buddhist mantras make pretentious claims for what is in fact no more than free association, and that his political ideology is at best naive and at worst irresponsible, as when he insists that there is some kind of connection not only between Carry Nation's Wichita temperance movement and the "defoliat[ion] of the Mekong Delta" but that Carry Nation began the "vortex of hatred" that "murdered my mother / who died of the communist anticommunist psychosis / in the madhouse" ("Wichita Vortex Sutra," *CP*, 410).[14]

Interestingly, the controversy over the value of Ginsberg's prophetic mode generally tends to bypass the role of the comic, the absurd in his poetry. What the *Collected Poems* show us is that Ginsberg is, finally, a very *funny* poet. To read "Howl" as a serious indictment of American culture, a culture that denies the possibility of spiritual illumination, is to ignore the poet's self-deprecatory humor, his ability to laugh at himself and at his friends. When, in a 1976 reading of the poem at the Naropa Institute in Boulder, Colorado, Ginsberg came to the line

> who reappeared on the West Coast investigating the FBI in
> beards and shorts with big pacifist eyes sexy in their
> dark skin passing out incomprehensible leaflets
>
> (*CP*, 127)

the audience laughed delightedly, no doubt at the non sequitur of referring to "the big pacifist eyes" as "sexy," as well as to the open question of what those "incomprehensible leaflets" did, in fact, contain.[15] Or again, the line "who cut their wrists three times successively unsuccessfully, gave up and were forced to open antique stores where they thought they were growing old and cried" is playful in its insinuation that the youthful slitting of the wrists was all bravado, a Chaplinesque gesture designed to protect the "best minds of my generation" from the middle-class boredom that turned out to be precisely their fate.

"Howl" is replete with images of young men who thought "the cosmos instinctively vibrated at their feet in Kansas," who were dragged off roofs "waving genitals and manuscripts," who furnished their rooms with "orange crates of theology," who jumped off the Brooklyn Bridge only to walk away "unknown and forgotten" and be rewarded with "not even one free beer," who made "harlequin speech[es] of suicide, demanding instantaneous lobotomy," and "who were given instead the concrete void of insulin Metrazol electricity hydrotherapy psychotherapy occupational therapy pingpong

& amnesia." It is in many ways an elegy for the poet's youth, to the time when opposition was all, when taking risks was daily fun, designed to *épater* one's parents and teachers. Part 1 of "Howl" presents Ginsberg in the role of urban Jewish Huck Finn, the street-wise kid who refuses to obey those boring, hypocritical grown-ups. The same voice speaks to us in "A Supermarket in California," where we find "Aisles full of husbands! Wives in the avocados, babies in the tomatoes!" (*CP*, 136). Or again, in "America," where the poet exclaims, "America after all it is you and I who are perfect not the next world," but then admits, "There must be some other way to settle this argument" (*CP*, 146).

The other side of such clowning is, as in a Chaplin film, a terrible sadness, the emptiness of having no one for whom to perform. Consider the opening of "Transcription of Organ Music," written in Berkeley in 1955:

The flower in the glass peanut bottle formerly in the kitchen crooked to take
    a place in the light,
the closet door opened because I used it before, it kindly stayed open waiting
    for me, its owner.

I began to feel my misery in pallet on floor, listening to music, my misery,
    that's why I want to sing.
The room closed down on me, I expected the presence of the Creator, I saw
    my gray painted walls and ceiling, they contained my room, they
    contained me
as the sky contained my garden,
I opened my door

    The rambler vine climbed up the cottage post, the leaves in the night
still where the day had placed them, the animal heads of the flowers where
they had arisen
    to think at the sun

                    (*CP*, 140)

Here the poet is himself the "flower in the glass peanut bottle" straining crookedly "to take a place in the light." Nothing happens. Like the young men of "Howl" who "cowered in unshaven rooms in underwear," the "I" finds himself in a room that "closed down on me," and opening the door leads to no influx of spirit. Everything remains exactly as it was: rambler vine, leaves, flowers, and, inside the house, "My books . . . waiting in space where I placed them . . . my words piled up, my texts, my manuscripts, my loves."

In the lines that follow, the lonely poet attempts to cheer himself up by contemplating "the red blossoms in the night light" of a bush "peering in the window." In a moment of Lawrentian communion he tries to assume the position of the leaves "upturned top float to the sky to receive." But Ginsberg's is a sensibility that communes with people, not with flowers (unless, of course, a Jack

Kerouac is sitting close by, as in "Sunflower Sutra"), and so nothing changes. "The light socket is crudely attached to the ceiling, after the house was built, to receive a plug which sticks in it allright, and serves my phonograph now." Indeed, "There are unused electricity plugs all over my house if I ever need them." And worst, for a poet who needs friends and lovers, "The telephone—sad to relate—sits on the floor—I haven't the money to get it connected."

In *The Visionary Poetics of Allen Ginsberg*, Paul Portuges argues that "Transcription of Organ Music" records a "transcendental, prophetic experience," that the poet "masterfully uses his physical surroundings to force himself into a visionary state" (p. 76). True, the poem ends with the lines:

> I want people to bow as they see me and say he is
> gifted with poetry, he has seen the presence of the Creator.
>     And the Creator gave me a shot of his presence to grat-
> ify my wish, so as not to cheat me of my yearning for him.

> (*CP*, 141)

But in the context of the unused electric plugs, unconnected telephone, and the masturbatory fantasy about the kitchen door as "hole [that] will admit me," the telling thing is that the poet wants "people to bow as they see me," he wants *others* to *know* that "he is gifted with poetry," that "he has seen the presence of the Creator." Like the Lawrence of *Birds, Beasts and Flowers*, Ginsberg has a strong sense of theater. Even at his most introspective, he does not forget to play to the stands.

The Chaplinesque mode with its rapid shifts from sadness to laughter and back again is brought to perfection in such poems of the late fifties as "In the Baggage Room at Greyhound," which culminates in the lines:

> A swarm of baggage sitting by the counter as the
>     transcontinental bus pulls in.
> The clock registering 12:15 A.M., May 9, 1956, the second
>     hand moving forward, red.
> Getting ready to load my last bus. — Farewell, Walnut Creek
>     Richmond Vallejo Portland Pacific Highway
> Fleet-footed Quicksilver, god of transience.
> One last package sits lone at midnight sticking up out of
>     the Coast rack high as the dusty fluorescent light.
>
> The wage they pay is too low to live on. Tragedy reduced to
>     numbers.
> This for the poor shepherds. I am a communist.
>
> Farewell ye Greyhound where I suffered so much,
> hurt my knee and scraped my hand and built my pectoral
>     muscles big as vagina.

> (*CP*, 154)

Here is the Ginsberg signature: the careful location of the self in place and time, the roll call of place names as if the very naming process could conjure up godhead, the sudden political gesture ("The wage they pay is too low to live on. . . . I am a communist")—all finally giving way to the burlesque of the tough-guy boast about "pectoral muscles big as vagina."

## II

Ginsberg's autobiography takes him from these exquisite anatomies of loneliness to the more public (and sometimes strident) pronouncements of *Planet News* (1968) and *The Fall of America* (1973). Between these two modes there is "Kaddish" (1961), at once Ginsberg's most highly praised and his least typical poem. So close is the poet of "Kaddish" to the story he tells about his mother Naomi's mental breakdowns and remissions, her "mad" episodes, her relationship with her weak husband and her adolescent son, that we respond to his terrible disclosures with a certain astonished embarrassment, embarrassment that any man would be willing to describe his own mother as follows:

> One night, sudden attack—her noise in the bathroom—
> like croaking up her soul—convulsions and red vomit coming
> out of her mouth—diarrhea water exploding from her
> behind—on all fours in front of the toilet—urine running
> between her legs—left retching on the tile floor smeared with
> her black feces—unfainted—
>   At forty, varicosed, nude, fat, doomed, hiding outside
> the apartment door near the elevator calling Police, yelling for
> her girlfriend Rose to help. . . .
>                                        (*CP*, 218)

How the twelve-year-old Allen Ginsberg coped with this situation, how years later Naomi no longer recognized him when he visited her on the mental ward, and how, "2 days after her death," he found a letter from her saying, "The key is in the window, the key is in the sunlight at the window—I have the key—Get married Allen don't take drugs—the key is in the bars, in the sunlight in the window"—these tales are moving, even harrowing, but no one would wish this portion of Ginsberg's autobiography any longer. On the contrary, it seems that the Ginsberg of "Kaddish" is writing somewhat against the grain. He had, no doubt, to get the Freudian drama off his chest, but in his best and most characteristic poems, the "family" is that of male comrades, the band of brothers whose lives intersect with his. With the exception of Naomi and Aunt Rose, women play no role in Ginsberg's poetry. Indeed, Woman is the absence that haunts the poet's worst moments. In "This Form of Life Need Sex" (1961), we read:

> I will have to accept women
> > if I want to continue the race,
> > kiss breasts, accept
> > strange hairy lips behind
> > > buttocks,
> Look in questioning womanly eyes
> > answer soft cheeks. . . .

And because he cannot in fact accept women in any sense:

> Between me and oblivion an unknown
> > woman stands;
> Not the Muse but living meat-phantom,
> a mystery scary as my fanged god. . . .
>
> (*CP*, 284)

This is Ginsberg at his least attractive: his equation of Woman and Death, his references to "the one hole that repelled me 1937 on," call into question, it seems to me, his protest poems about the oppressive "Fathers in office in these industries" ("War Profit Litany," *CP*, 486), his references to the "Corporate voices [that] jabber on electric networks building / body-pain, chemical ataxia, physical slavery" ("Pentagon Exorcism," *CP*, 483). For Ginsberg does not reject the patriarchal world; he merely wants to replace one set of fathers with a more congenial one, for example, the "peasant manhoods [of Vietnam, who] burn in black & white forest" on the TV screen. One of the low points in the volume is a poem of 1970 called "Ecologue," which begins:

> In a thousand years, if there's History
> America'll be remembered as a nasty little Country
> full of Pricks, thorny hothouse rose
> Cultivated by the Yellow Gardeners.
> "Chairman Mao" for all his politics, head of a Billion
> > folk, important old & huge
> > > Nixon a dude, specialized on his industrial
> > > > Island, a clean paranoiac Mechanic. . . .
>
> (*CP*, 542)

Our "nasty little Country" is metaphorized as the female rose; it is the rose that is, in an all-too-obvious pun, "full of Pricks." In this context, the homage to Chairman Mao as "head of a Billion / folk, important old & huge" has a macho ring: it brings to mind Ezra Pound's adulation of "old Muss" (Mussolini). Today, in the reign of

Mao's enemy Comrade Deng, Ginsberg's simpleminded opposition
of the good Mao to the bad Nixon is hardly compelling.

What is compelling in the later (and, on the whole, lesser)
poems is Ginsberg's extraordinary sense of the moment, of being,
so to speak, at the center of the vortex. Read as an autobiography,
the *Collected Poems* is a kind of ironic Horatio Alger story. The hero
of this narrative learns how to take every liability of his childhood
and turn it into an asset. The homely little kid with glasses becomes
a bearded, exotically attractive guru figure; and then, just when
everyone expects him to appear in Indian dress and beads, he dons
suit and tie, cuts his hair, and looks for all the world like everyone's
cuddly Jewish uncle. The dreary lower-middle-class setting of Paterson, New Jersey, gives way to the cross-country and cross-continent
journeys that take the poet to Big Sur and Benares, to Calcutta and
Kathmandu. Yet these travels have never produced, as they have
for so many writers and artists, a scorn for one's native place: Ginsberg is just as celebratory of Wichita, Kansas, as of Machu Picchu,
just as attentive to the sights and sounds on the New York subway
as on the Patna-Benares express. Again, his homosexuality, surely a
source of guilt and shame for a Jewish boy growing up in America
in the forties, becomes, by the time of "Howl" and *Planet News,* the
source of a newfound strength: it allows Ginsberg to play a double
role. On the one hand, his sexual otherness calls into question the
complacent "masculinity" of the straight men who are in power. On
the other, it is a source of vulnerability, bringing the "famous poet"
down to the reader's level. For, despite all his celebrity, here is a
man whose lovers continue to leave him, who can never get enough
sex, who, in his mid-fifties, can still complain:

Rarer and rarer
Boys give me favor
Older and older
Love grows bolder.

(*CP,* 722)

Or:

It's not the most romantic
dream to be so frantic
for young men's bodies,
a fine sugar daddy
blest respected known
but left to bed alone.

(*CP,* 723)

If love is often a failure, there is consolation in friendship. Like
the Yeats of "The Municipal Gallery Revisited," Ginsberg might well
declare, "Say that the glory was I had such friends." The poor and

lonely Columbia undergraduate, masturbating in his Harlem room, grows up to count among his friends Jack Kerouac and William Burroughs, Gary Snyder and Robert Creeley, Frank O'Hara and John Ashbery. Having made a convert of Williams at the outset of his career, twenty years later Ginsberg takes on Pound. Calling on the Great Poet in Venice at a time when Pound no longer speaks, Ginsberg cajoles the old man into commenting on the *Cantos* ("It's all tags and patches") and introduces his attentive listener to songs by Dylan and the Beatles.

A great deal of fuss has been made about the role of drugs in Ginsberg's work: he himself has conscientiously noted which poem was written on which drug—part 2 of "Howl" on peyote, "Kaddish" on Methedrine, "Wales Visitation" on LSD, and so on. But here again, Ginsberg's history, as presented in the *Collected Poems*, is a kind of Fortunate Fall. As a child, we learn in "Kaddish," his response to the food prepared by his mother was one of disgust:

> Serving me meanwhile, a plate of cold fish—chopped
> raw cabbage dript with tapwater—smelly tomatoes—week-old
> health food—grated beets & carrots with leaky juice, warm—
> more and more disconsolate food—I can't eat it for nausea
> sometimes—the Charity of her hands stinking with Manhat-
> tan, madness, desire to please me, cold undercooked fish—
> pale red near the bones. Her smells—and often naked in the
> room, so that I stare ahead, or turn a book ignoring her.
>
> (*CP*, 219)

To escape from this world is, at first, to go West, to the "Supermarket in California" with its "peaches and . . . penumbras," its avocados and giant melons, so unlike the "grated beets & carrots with leaky juice" of his childhood. In poems like "Sunflower Sutra" and "Sather Gate Illumination," the poet's new "mad locomotive riverbank sunset Frisco hilly tincan evening sitdown vision" (*CP*, 139) is, at least in part, induced by the ingestion of exotic food and drugs. "Float[ing] on the sweetened scene of trees & humans" at Berkeley, he exclaims:

> My stomach is light, I relax, new sentences spring forth
> out of the scene to describe spontaneous forms of Time—
> trees, sleeping dogs, airplanes wandering thru the air, negroes
> with the lunch books of anxiety, apples and sandwiches,
> lunchtime, icecream, Timeless.—
>
> (*CP*, 143)

Apples, sandwiches, ice cream under the trees—it is a far cry from the "cold undercooked fish" his mother fed him. "Kaddish" is followed, not coincidentally, I think, by the three drug poems, "Mescaline," "Lysergic Acid," and "I Beg You Come Back & Be Cheerful," as if to say that, with the death of his mother, he is now free to do as he pleases.

But not quite. Unlike Kerouac or Neal Cassady, unlike the countless Beat poets who OD'd or drank themselves to death, Ginsberg emerges in the *Collected Poems* as the ultimate survivor. There is something of the professor (and also of the once good boy who ate his chicken soup) in his disciplined experimentation with drugs, the careful accounts made in his journals of his precise physical reactions. By the early seventies the fascination with drugs had largely given way to the absorption in the discipline of Buddhist meditation.

And here again, Ginsberg has responded to the challenge with a certain pragmatism. If Buddhism has been useful to him, he has not exactly retired to a monastery. In conversation with Paul Portuges, he is candid about his inability to follow fully the Tibetan doctrine of nonattachment to the ego. As he puts it, "[Buddhist practice] is just a question of learning a sharper, more experienced way of recognizing and appreciating what's already in your head. It doesn't require a big breakthrough or anything like that."[16]

So in the seventies we find the poet returning more frequently to the scene of the crime, to the old neighborhood on New York's Lower East Side where Naomi once walked. In a charming poem called "Mugging" (1974), which begins:

> Tonite I walked out of my red apartment door on East tenth
> street's dusk —

we see Ginsberg strolling down his familiar street, calmly observing the local sights and sounds, when something happens:

> Walked past a taxicab controlling the bottle strewn curb —
> past young fellows with their umbrella handles & canes
>     leaning against a ravaged Buick
> — and as I looked at the crowd of kids on the stoop — a boy
>     stepped up, put his arm around my neck
> tenderly I thought for a moment, squeezed harder, his
>     umbrella handle against my skull,
> and his friends took my arm, a young brown companion tripped
>     his foot 'gainst my ankle —
> as I went down shouting Om Ah Hum to gangs of lovers on the
>     stoop watching
> slowly appreciating, why this is a raid, these strangers
>     mean strange business
> with what — my pockets, bald head, broken-healed-bone leg, my
>     softshoes, my heart —
> Have they knives? Om Ah Hum — Have they sharp metal wood to
>     shove in eye ear ass? Om Ah Hum. . . .

> (*CP*, 625)

The spectacle of Ginsberg, once himself the hoodlum suspended from Columbia for writing "Butler has no balls" on his dorm window, now middle-aged and bald, wearing "a neat orlon shirt" and carrying a "woolen bag of poetry address calendar & Leary-lawyer notes," the spectacle of this man suddenly being knocked down by a gang of slum kids and trying to calm himself by chanting a mantra, is both funny and touching. For the irony is that the once wild poet has become a member of the Establishment and he knows it. His "snakeskin wallet" ("actually plastic," he explains apologetically) contains "70 dollars" as well as "dreary plastic contents—Amex card & Manf. Hanover Trust Credit too—business card from Mr. Spears British Home Minister Drug Squad—my draft card—membership ACLU & Naropa Institute Instructor's identification."

The metamorphosis the poet has undergone is rather like the metamorphosis of the little black-and-white City Lights pocket books into the big fat *Collected Poems* selling for $27.50. But so good-humored is Ginsberg about his new role as "sixty-year old smiling public man" that we can only smile too. As he rises from "the cardboard mattress" where the boys have thrown him, having carried off his wallet and Seiko Hong Kong wristwatch, he remarks ruefully: "Om ah Hum didn't stop em enough, / the tone of voice too loud." And there is the further irony that they took his "valuables," but "my shoulder bag with 10,000 dollars full of poetry left on the broken floor."

So much for being a poet. He gets up, picks up his glasses from the step where he had the good sense to deposit them even as he was dragged into the store, and surveys the now wholly defamiliarized scene:

> Whole street a bombed-out face, building rows' eyes & teeth
>   missing
> burned apartments half the long block, gutted cellars,
>   hallways' charred beams. . . .

The chanting of "Om Ah Hum" now gives way to a more Western jeremiad: "O hopeless city of idiots empty eyed staring afraid." In the poet's imagination, the "honking neighborhood" is transformed into a surreal and frozen landscape: the poem's final image is of an "old lady with frayed paper bags / sitting in the tin-boarded doorframe of a dead house."

"Mugging" may be read as an elegy for the lost New York of the fifties, a New York in which people still spoke to their neighbors and chatted on their tenement steps. But it avoids sentimentality by turning the poet's situation into comedy. The image of Ginsberg, down on the ground and deprived of his glasses, trying to chant Buddhist mantras so as to pacify his teen-age assailants, carries on the tradition of "Howl."

In recent years, as I noted earlier, Ginsberg has returned to the short ballad stanzas of his youth. Having written so expansively for decades, he now shows a penchant for the minimal, as in a poem called "For Creeley's Ear," which begins with the stanza:

> The whole
> weight of
> everything
> too much.

> (*CP,* 663)

Such minimal lyrics may be profitably read against a recent text by John Cage called "Writing through Howl" and subtitled "for A. G. on his Sixtieth Birthday." Commissioned for a birthday fest-schrift,[17] "Writing through Howl," which is dated, Ginsberg style, "through Asia and home to New York, January–April 1984," functions as a fascinating commentary on its parent text, even as it creates a new poetic construct of a very different sort.

"Writing through Howl" is what Cage calls a *mesostic,* which is to say that the acrostic "ALLEN GINSBERG" runs down the middle of the page rather than at the left margin. "Howl" is subjected to I Ching chance operations, and the mesostic follows the rule that "a given letter capitalized does not occur between it and the preceding or following capitalized letter."[18] Thus the word "saw" ("I saw") gives us the first letter of "Allen," and the second letter, *l,* is taken from "themselves," the "l" of "hysterical" not counting because the word also contains an *a.* When the "writing through" is completed, the process begins again, this time using what Cage calls the "rubble," that is, the words that were not used the first time around. So the first word containing an *a* is "madness," and the first *l* that qualifies comes in "cold-water flats." By the ninth and last time of "writing through," we have the tiny mesostic "Allen"—

> Angry
> soLidities
> battaLion
> thE
> aNd—

which nicely characterizes Ginsberg's stance: the "lion" ready to spring from the larger "battaLion," and "the end" that becomes, for Ginsberg, "the aNd," in keeping with his faith in the rhetoric of accumulation. But—and here is where Cage is so interesting—Ginsberg himself would never use such a phrase any more than he would use so abstract a designation as "Angry soLidities." "Starry dynamo," "unshaven rooms," "incomparable blind streets"—with Ginsberg, we still know where we are.

"Writing through Howl" begins like this:

saw
themseLves
Looking for
hipstErs

starry dyNamo

hiGh sat
theIr
heaveN

Saw
puBlishing
odEs on
Rooms

listeninG to the terror

beArds returning through
Laredo

beLt
for nEw york
iN
druGs
wIth
alcohol aNd
ballS

Blind
in thE mind
towaRd
illuminatinG
dAwns
bLinking
Light

thE
wiNter
liGht

endless rIde

Here Ginsberg's dense, clotted, overwrought line gives way to stark
reduction, a reduction that leaves a great deal to the reader's imagination. We don't know, for example, who it is that is "Looking for /
hipstErs," for we are given only flashes of a "starry dyNamo," of a
Miltonic "hiGh sat / theIr / heaveN," of "beArds returning through /
Laredo." Ginsberg's snowballing and sonorous chant here becomes
the trill of "Blind / in thE mind / towaRd / illuminatinG / dAwns /
bLinking / Light," a trill followed by the echo "thE / wiNter / liGht,"
and then a kind of breath pause and the addition "endless rIde."

Further on, we get such stanzas as

> visionAry
> onLy
> supernaturaL
> Ecstasy
> iN
> streetliGht

Or:

> Gaunt
> waItresses
> loNely petticoat
> eSpecially
> Blood
> on thE snowbank docks
> foR
> floodliGht

By the time we get to the third writing through, we get little fragments like:

> stArving
> fLoating
> contempLating jazz

Or:

> theIr
> bloNde
> loSt
> loveBoys
> thE
> thRee

Cage's stanzas leave a good deal open (e.g., who are "the three"?) but they are by no means to be taken as non-sensical. When, for example, the "loNely petticoat" or the "Gaunt / waItresses" is metonymically related to "Blood / on thE snowbank docks," a new narrative possibility is suggested. Think of the promising plots that might contain these elements! Or again, when we read "incomprehensibLe / capitaLism / distributEd / iN / deliGht," we are struck by the realization that the stanza provides a playful commentary on Ginsberg's own wholesale diatribes against the System.

Emblematically, "Howl" and "Writing through Howl" provide us with two interesting poetic alternatives. Gingsberg's is a mode of continuity: however surrealist, jarring, hilarious, horrendous his conjunction of images may be, he regards the poem as a living *whole* with, somewhat surprisingly, a beginning, middle, and end. "Howl" moves from the "I saw . . ." sequence to the diatribe against Moloch (part 2) to the resolution of "Carl Solomon! I'm with you in Rockland" (part 3), with the footnote "Holy! Holy! Holy!" as an even

more elaborate (and I think unnecessary) coda. Similarly, "Sunflower Sutra" moves from the despair of "I walked" to the final
"evening sitdown vision," and "America" ends on the triumphant
assertion "America, I'm putting my queer shoulder to the wheel."
Ginsberg, we may conclude, is never the poet of collage, of
fragment, of layering and splicing. As such, his poetry now looks,
for all its references to "cock" and "balls," reassuringly traditional.
This may well be what Cage is implying in his gently ironic mesostics,
featuring as they do the primacy of the word over its referent. But
Cage's poetic text is also an act of homage, in that it isolates key
words and phrases like "in the goldhorn shadow" so as to make us
more aware of their peculiar density. "Writing through Howl" is
thus a fitting tribute to the author of the Collected Poems, which is
itself an homage to America at mid-century.

## "HOWL" AND ITS ENEMIES: THE
## GENTEEL REACTION (1987)

In the December 1984 issue of the Boston Review, Allen Ginsberg's Collected Poems received the following mini-review from
Richard Howard: "The MacPherson de nos jours, this gathered
assortment, fragments shored, limbs remembered, adds up to an
astonishing confession: it may not be poetry at all, it is always testimony, a kind of processional martyrology—in that martyrs are wit-
nesses to the truth."[19] Period. Which is to say, with a dismissive
wave of the hand, that Ginsberg's oeuvre, like James MacPherson's
invention of the Celtic bard Ossian, whose pseudoprimitive epics
delighted his eighteenth-century audience, is no more than inspired
fakery. "It may not be poetry at all."
To those of us who have followed Ginsberg's career from its
inception, Howard's bemused dismissal has an air of déjà vu. It
recalls the now notorious and much reprinted 1957 review of Howl
and Other Poems by Ginsberg's fellow Columbia student and poet-
friend John Hollander. To wit:

> It is only fair to Allen Ginsberg . . . to remark on the utter
> lack of decorum of any kind in this dreadful little volume. I
> believe that the title of his long poem "Howl," is meant to be
> a noun, but I can't help taking it as an imperative. . . . Howl
> seems to have emerged under the influence of a kind of liter-
> ary Festspiel held at frequent intervals on the West Coast, in
> the course of which various poets, "with radiant cool eyes,"
> undoubtedly, read their works before audiences of writhing
> and adoring youths.[20]

Again, the argument is that *Howl* is fake, hype, media event—anything, in short, but Poetry with a capital P.

In the thirty-year span between Hollander's reference to that "dreadful little volume" called *Howl* and Howard's dismissal of the whole *Collected Poems* as "the MacPherson *de nos jours*," "Howl" has become one of the best known poems in the world. In the sixties and seventies, for that matter, Ginsberg's poetry gained wide acceptance in the Academy, critics, scholars, and fellow poets taking pains to demonstrate that the so-called confessional rant was by no means formless, that indeed Beat poetry, Ginsberg-style, was remarkable for its polyglot learning, for the complexity of its derivations and intertexts.

In recent years, however, a curious reaction has set in. We can attribute a certain measure of the current hostility to Ginsberg on the part of newspaper and journal reviewers to what is called the New Conservatism or the Age of Reagan, but this is only part of the story, since most of the reviewers who have dismissed the *Collected Poems* came of age in the wake of the Vietnam War and espouse the left-wing politics now *de rigueur* in English departments across the country.[21] No, what I should like to call here the Neo-New, where New refers to the New Criticism, has a more complex derivation.

Reviewing the *Collected Poems* for the *New Criterion*, Bruce Bawer, himself a poet and the author of a book on the Robert Lowell circle called *The Middle Generation* (Archon, 1986), writes:

> To read such poems as these back-to-back . . . is to be stunned by the oversimplification, the repetition, the self-indulgence, the egocentrism, the utter inability to develop a theme. Doesn't [Ginsberg] ever, one wonders, get sick of reiterating these banalities? Doesn't he ever yearn to get beyond the surface cliché, to develop a more sophisticated view of the world, and to express it in more memorable and meticulously chosen words?[22]

The "utter inability to develop a theme" or to "express it in . . . meticulously chosen words," the inability, as Bawer later puts it, to produce "a finely turned phrase"—inherent in such strictures is a curiously prestructuralist faith in language as vehicle, as a conduit that leads directly from the speaking subject to a meaning above and outside the signifier. One should have, so it seems, a "view of the world" that is sufficiently "sophisticated"; one then explores, as Bawer says, "the complexities that make the actual world interesting and frustrating and *real*," assuming, of course, that one knows what reality is.

A similar charge is made by Roger Rosenblatt in the *New Republic:* "If one makes comparisons with Eliot, Pound, Lowell,

Stevens, or even with Ransom or Robert Penn Warren, the collected Ginsberg does not stand a chance. . . . the bulk of [Ginsberg's] work shows no philosophical growth . . . and rarely any depth. [As for "Howl"], it is a poem worth rereading, especially if one deluded oneself into liking it when it made its loud debut."[23] No philosophical growth, rarely any depth—here again is the dismay at the poet's "utter inability to develop a theme." Rosenblatt's complaint is echoed by Lachlan Mackinnon's suggestion, in his *Times Literary Supplement* review, that Ginsberg can write only out of his personal life because he lacks "a true culture."[24] But perhaps the "Neo-New" case against Ginsberg is presented most forcefully by the poet Mark Jarman in an omnibus review for the *Hudson Review*. This piece covers thirteen American poets born between 1900 and 1960, ranging from Elder Olson and Shirley Kaufman to Jarman's contemporaries, Gary Soto, Eric Pankey, and Sharona Ben-Tov. In this eclectic context, Ginsberg's *Collected Poems* gets short shrift (less than a page), Jarman observing that "Ginsberg was not a promising young poet nor has he become a mature older poet. But for about ten years, from 1955 to 1965, his writing anticipated American life, especially the youth subculture built around music and drugs and the now waning fascination with Eastern religions."[25]

The poetry, that is to say, is judged thematically, and since the "themes" are, so Jarman argues, now passé, so is much of Ginsberg's poetry:

> We know that sexuality is as various as American life is supposed to be. We know our government's abuse of its immense military power is madness. Drugs have been sources of insight rather than simply recreational. A spiritual alternative to western religion exists in the orient. The list sounds dismissive only because to mention these themes of Ginsberg is to realize, unfortunately, how ironic they have become, how much a source of parody. (p. 331)

A source of parody is precisely what these so-called themes have become: witness Christopher Buckley and Paul Slansky's "Yowl: For Jay McInerney," which is printed in the 8 December 1986 issue of the *New Republic* as a commemorative offering "On the 30th anniversary of 'Howl.' " I shall come back to this parody in a moment, but first it might be helpful to look at a few poems by those who do, according to Jarman and his colleagues, have the "ability" to "develop a theme" or invent what Bruce Bawer calls "a finely turned phrase," those poets who are evidently not guilty of self-indulgence or oversimplification, concentrating as they do on the "complexities" that, in Bawer's words, "make the actual world interesting and frustrating and *real.*"

One such poet is Eric Pankey, last year's winner of the Walt Whitman Award for a book called *For the New Year* (Atheneum). A Pankey poem called "Tending the Garden" is praised by Jarman for its complex dramatic strategies: "Pankey imagines Horatio at Elsinore, speaks in the voice of Cain, addresses Vallejo, and assumes the characters of a railroad bull and a survivor of a Nazi death camp." "The latter," remarks Jarman, "may seem an overworked subject, but I would argue that Pankey's clarity makes the poem exceptional," and he cites the following passage:

> The other prisoners were envious
> of our duty. It was, at times, hard work,
> but the work, it seems, promoted our health.
> I was determined to stay well, to last
> through the coming winter and not end up
> face up in a grave my own hands had dug.

And Jarman comments: "In writing of such apparent simplicity, words like *duty, promoted, determined,* and *health* resonate with their special meaning, and the cunning word play of 'end up / face up' is nearly subliminal. Frankly, I admire this, for the narrative poem as such might seem to have no time for these effects" (p. 339).

Such a reading recalls nothing so much as those Brooks-and-Warren exercises where the student would learn to identify the speaker (never, according to Rule 1, the poet himself but always a persona!) and comment on the poem's way of saying one thing but meaning another—which is to say, its irony (Rule 2). To call the torturous task of the death-camp survivor "the work," to use the casual "end up" as a lead-in to "face up"—this, one surmises, is to provide us with "meticulously chosen words." Except that the real New Criticism, as opposed to its "neo" version, would have recognized this passage from the ironically entitled "Tending the Garden" (get it?) as pure contrivance. Allen Tate, for one, would have asked some hard questions about the function of the iambic pentameter in this poem.

Another poem Jarman singles out for praise is Dick Allen's "Overnight in the Guest House of the Mystic," which contains these lines:

> I dream
> of histories ahead, the quasars flowering
> upon the edge of space; odd specks of light
> like fireflies in the pines, the first
> new cities of another galaxy.
>
> Which marks me of my time—which turns
> almost helplessly between
> huge shadows and the drifting stars,
> a boat upon a boat at sea

floating in a bottle, each uplifted sail
raised to catch a wind that cannot be.

"Allen's expression of hope in what lies beyond," comments the
reviewer, "is finally an integrated one . . . for he knows the limitation
of his subject matter. . . . His dream does indeed mark him of his
time, as it does many another, yet the wisdom of the statement—
the admission—is rare" (p. 333).

Note the classic New Critical terminology—"integrated," "limitation," "wisdom of the statement," an "admission" that is "rare."
Thematics are all, blinding the reader to the real "limitation" of this
little poem, which is its inability to convince us that any conceivable
voice is actually saying the things in question. One doesn't in fact
"dream / of histories ahead" but only of a specific historical event;
again, it is hard to conceive of a dream in which "odd specks of
light" are viewed as being, in the most reasonable of tried-and-true
similes, "like fireflies in the pines." But even these images are not
as bathetic as the moralizing statement of the second stanza: "Which
marks me of my time. . . ." A latter-day William Vaughan Moody,
this melancholy speaker is "helplessly" positioned "between / huge
shadows and the drifting stars." Stars have been poetically "drifting"
from Wordsworth's *Lyrical Ballads* on down; it is reassuring, I suppose, to know that even quasars can't change these Romantic veri-
ties. And then Allen sees himself as "a boat upon a boat at sea"—
there's an original metaphor—a boat, moreover, "floating in a bottle." And now, with the click of a spring, comes the final recognition
that "each uplifted sail / raised to catch a wind that cannot be."
"Sea"/"be"—the perfect closural rhyme underscores the poet's
mournful conclusion.

"The wisdom of the statement," says Jarman, "the admission—is rare." But what is it that is being admitted? Does Allen
know anything we don't know about galaxies and quasars? Is his
point of view in any way special? Do those who are "of their time"
usually tell us they are so? And if the poet is so uncertain about the
future, how does he know, with such metrical and rhyming certainty,
that the "uplifted sail [is] raised to catch a wind that cannot be"?

These questions do not occur to Jarman because his central
postulate is the bifurcation of form and content. The poet, it is
implied, first chooses his subject matter—something that is important, serious, and of its time—and then "expresses" it using as many
"finely turned phrases" (Bruce Bawer's term) as possible. "Knowing
the limitation of [one's] subject matter" thus becomes the cardinal
virtue. And, given this aesthetic stance, a poem like "Howl" is perceived as nothing but a loose, baggy monster. "*Howl*, once effective
as counter-culture manifesto," writes R. Z. Sheppard in *Time* magazine, "is now an unconvincing historical oddity."[26] But "Howl" was

never a counterculture or any other kind of manifesto, and mistaking
Ginsberg's brilliant Dada/Surrealist autobiographical poem, with its
particular blend of the comic and the serious, the everyday and the
visionary, the pedestrian and the fantastic for something as pat as a
"counter-culture manifesto" leads to the writing of such "clever"
parodies as the Buckley-Slansky "Yowl," to which I now turn.

Like *The Waste Land,* "Howl" has a stylistic signature so singular that nothing is easier than to parody it. Buckley's satire, which
purports to take on both Ginsberg's vatic excesses and eighties yuppiedom, opens as follows:

> I saw the best minds of my generation destroyed by stress
>     frazzled overtired burnt-out
> jogging through suburban streets at dawn
>     as suggested by the late James Fixx,
> career-minded yupsters burning for an Amstel Light
>     watching Stupid Pet Tricks,
> who upwardly mobile and designer'd and bright-eyed and high
>     sat up working in the track-lit glow of the Tribeca loft
>     skimming through the Day Timer while padding the expense
>     account. . . .
> who ate chocolate croissants in outdoor cafes and drank
>     blush wine on Columbus Avenue washed down with a little
>     Percodan with Dove bars with Diet Coke with Lean Cuisine.[27]

The authors of "Yowl" are obviously having a good time finding
substitutions for Ginsberg's images: the "angry fix" of the "angel-
headed hipsters" becoming, in a nice little joke, the late James Fixx
of jogging fame, or the "stale beer" of "Howl" becoming the Diet
Coke of "Yowl." But the one-dimensional exposé of the "upwardly
mobile and designer'd and bright-eyed" yuppie, who "sat up working in the track-lit glow of the Tribeca loft," only serves to put into
bold relief the very real complexities of "Howl."

Take that famous opening line, "I saw the best minds of my
generation destroyed by madness, starving hysterical naked." In the
first draft, the three adjectives were "starving mystical naked," and
surely Ginsberg is not exaggerating when he says, in the notes for
the Harper Facsimile Edition (1986), that this is a "crucial revision,"
"hysterical" providing "a key to the tone of the poem." He observes,
"Tho the initial idealistic impulse of the line went one way, after-
thought noticed bathos, and common sense dictated 'hysteria.' . . .
The poem's tone is in this mixture of empathy and shrewdness."[28]
Which is to say that the connotations of "hysterical" more or less
throw the poem's gear into reverse, calling into question the purported darkness of the poet's vision.

Indeed, "Howl" is itself much funnier—and much more subtly
satiric—than is its 1986 parody. Take the strophe

who vanished into nowhere Zen New Jersey leaving a trail of
        ambiguous picture postcards of Atlantic City Hall

Those who complain of the poem's repetitiveness, its seemingly endless cataloging of "who" clauses ("This continues," declares John
Hollander, "sponging on one's toleration, for pages and pages"),[29]
fail to recognize what is actually a marked condensation. The first
draft of the strophe above reads:

who vanished into the New Jersies of amnesia
        posting cryptic picture postcards
            of Belmar City Hall and last years sharks
                (*HODF,* 13)

And Ginsberg's note tells us that this is a "composite image of a few
post-college 'career failures' characteristic of 1950s, including
author's own two-year sojourn in Paterson 1950–51 on leaving
Columbia Psychiatric Institute. Author's family spent many 1930s
summers at the shore in Belmar—'Atlantic City,' final draft. 'Sharks'
ref. recurrent seaside newspaper reports and souvenir postcards"
(*HODF,* 126).

The note testifies to the autobiographical source of this and
almost every image in "Howl"; it also counters Ginsberg's own pro-
fessed aesthetic of "First thought, best thought," of "spontaneous
insight" as "motif and method" of composition (*CP,* xx). For when
"the New Jersies of amnesia" become the "nowhere Zen New Jersey," the bleak memory of Paterson summers gives way to a teasing
oxymoron: a "nowhere" New Jersey that is also "Zen" can't be all
bad, can it? Again, the specificity of "sharks" as a local term for the
waste paper products of the area gives way to the comic image of
the postcard trail, left behind by the poet and his friends. Are they
dirty pictures? Threats to City Hall? The poem opens possibilities
that will now be picked up in the account of the "bop kabbalah"
that is its métier.

The notion of "bop kabbalah" also defines the syntactic drive
of "Howl." Ginsberg's syntax typically puts parts of speech into
"incorrect" slots so as to make us rethink their relationship. Thus
we read:

who poverty and tatters and hollow-eyed and high sat up
        smoking in the supernatural darkness of cold-water flats
            floating across the tops of cities contemplating jazz[30]

where the placement of the heavily stressed nouns "poverty" and
"tatters" in adjective slots creates the very jazz syncopation the poet
is describing, even as the participle "floating" can refer to the "flats"
as well as the relative pronoun "who," and even as the syntax suggests that it is the "cities" that are "contemplating jazz." The heavily
alliterative, aggressively grinding and "difficult" rhythm ("of cold-

water flats floating across the tops of cities contemplating jazz") is wholly flattened out in "Yowl":

who hollow-eyed and febrile read the theater reviews in
unread issues of the *New Yorker* yes the *New Yorker*

a locution that suggests to me a wholly one-dimensional reading of the parent text. Thus, when a critic like Lachlan Mackinnon announces that Ginsberg "has been too lazy to shape his material as it, like any material, demands," one wonders whether "lazy" doesn't apply to the reader rather than to the poet.

By the time "Yowl" winds up its "I'm with you" litany with the final couplet, "I'm with you on the Upper East Side / looking for myself in *People* magazine," it has become clear that yuppiedom is being satirized by those who are themselves its charter members. The clever knowingness of the parody, like Lachlan Mackinnon's reference to the "cultural sterility" of Ginsberg's *Collected Poems*, or Roger Rosenblatt's patronizing dismissal of "Howl" ("One can grow giggly learning that 'the best minds' of the poet's generation 'copulated ecstatic and insatiate with a bottle of beer.' . . . It makes you wonder what the second best minds were doing") point to the curious paradox inherent in what I have called the Neo-New movement in letters—the paradox that, for all the talk of culture and complexity, for all the outcry against the formlessness, the simplification, the self-indulgence, and the "laziness" of Ginsberg's poetry, the younger critics who are now casting the stones are quite simply not very good readers.

Why should this be the case? My own hunch—and I can do no more here than make tentative suggestions—is that the emphasis on theory in the "English" and "Comparative Literature" curriculum of the past decade or so has produced a curious split. On the one hand, we now train students to follow, say, Paul de Man's most arcane arguments, to watch and understand as deconstructionist criticism uncovers the hidden place where a given text unravels and reveals its real workings. Or again, we train students in Marxist theory, teaching them how to determine the covert power relations in Shakespeare's comedies or to define the role of exchange value in Emily Dickinson. It is a case of *reading for* rather than *reading*, and hence the exemplary texts are likely to be the safe ones—the texts everyone *knows* to be "great literature" so that we can get down to the business of submitting them to this or that theoretical paradigm.

On the other side of the academic fence, we find the Poetry Writing Workshop, that last bastion of those who want to have nothing to do with what they take to be the arid and abstract discourse of the theoreticians. In the writing workshop, "understanding poetry," as Brooks and Warren called it in their famous book by

that title, is still considered a worthwhile exercise: questions of voice, meter, metaphor, and structure, questions now denigrated by the theory camp as "mere" formalism, continue to be asked. But the difficulty—and there was no real precedent for this in the era of *Understanding Poetry*—is that today's workshop poet is likely not to read anything *but* poetry, which is to say, given our elaborate system of grants, fellowships, summer workshops, and mini-seminars, primarily the poetry of his fellow poets. As such, the practice and reception of poetry becomes increasingly a kind of cottage industry, a middlebrow pastime no more likely to produce widespread enthusiasm than it is likely to disturb anyone.

Given this climate, the bardic-comic voice of an Allen Ginsberg can hardly help being perceived as some sort of irrelevancy. For if poetry is a middlebrow pastime, its watchwords become safety, respectability, correctness, and "interesting" subject matter well put: "What oft was thought but ne'er so well express'd." Moreover— and here the politics of poetry reviewing comes in—young poet-critic X must be careful to say nice things about poets Y and Z for by next week they will be reviewing his or her own new book. Ginsberg, on the other hand, is sure to review neither X, Y, nor Z, and so there isn't much incentive to be polite.

As such, Ginsberg's now immortal "Rockland," where "we are great writers on the same dreadful typewriter," has become, in the late eighties, the Upper East Side of "Yowl," where "I'm with you . . . pricing modems." But not quite. For in a curious sense, it is "Howl" that has the last word, containing as it does its own parody of its future parodists, which is to say of all the Sad Young Men "who were burned alive in their innocent flannel suits on Madison Avenue / amid blasts of leaden verse & the tanked-up clatter of the iron regiments of fashion . . . & the mustard gas of sinister intelligent editors." All that gas, after all, "crowned" as it is "with flame under the tubercular sky," is bound to burn away, leaving behind, in the words of "Howl," "a variable measure and a vibrating plane."

*Chapter Eleven*

# Apocalypse Then:

## W. S. Merwin and the

## Sorrows of Literary History

### *I*

W. S. Merwin's sixth book of poems, *The Lice*, appeared in 1967 at the height of the war in Vietnam. Reviewing the book for the *Yale Review*, Laurence Lieberman declared:

> If there is any book today that has perfectly captured the peculiar spiritual agony of our time, the agony of a generation which knows itself to be the last, and has transformed that agony into great art, it is W. S. Merwin's *The Lice*. To read these poems is an act of self-purification. Every poem in the book pronounces a judgment against modern man — the gravest sentence the poetic imagination can conceive for man's withered and wasted conscience: our sweep of history adds up to one thing only, a moral vacuity that is absolute and irrevocable. This book is a testament of betrayals; we have betrayed all beings that had power to save us: the forests, the animals, the gods, the dead, the spirit in us, the words. Now, in our last moments alive, they return to haunt us.[1]

Extreme claims, these, especially now that a younger generation is proclaiming that *it* is the last, even as its poets are writing in a "cool" mode, very different from Merwin's.[2] The apocalyptic consciousness of the sixties had no use for the lessons of history: to write, as Merwin presumably did, about what Charles Altieri calls "the other side of despair," to "make loss itself the ground for numinous awareness that might suffice for the attentive imagination"[3]—this, it was assumed, was to write "the New Poetry," or "Poetry in Open Forms" or "Postmodern Poetry"—a radical poetry that questioned the assumptions of modernism. Thus Merwin holds a place of honor in Stephen Berg and Robert Mezey's 1969 anthology, *Naked Poetry,* an anthology that grew out of "the firm conviction that the strongest and most alive poetry in America had abandoned or at least broken the grip of traditional meters and had set out, once again, into 'the wilderness of unopened life.' "[4] In his own statement for *Naked Poetry,* "On Open Form," Merwin himself insisted, "I am a formalist, in the most strict and orthodox sense," but that statement could be—and was—safely ignored, for on the same page the poet remarked, "In an age when time and technique encroach hourly . . . on the source itself of poetry, it seems as though what is needed for any particular nebulous unwritten hope that may become a poem is not a manipulable, more or less predictably recurring pattern, but an unduplicatable resonance, something that would be like an echo except that it is repeating no sound" (p. 271).

I find this statement puzzling: if ours is indeed "an age when time and technique encroach hourly on the source itself of poetry," how can any poem claim to produce an "unduplicatable resonance"? Never mind: Merwin's "echo . . . repeating no sound" became, for "the generation which knows itself to be the last," a kind of *nouveau frisson.* Reviewing *The Carrier of Ladders* (1970), Richard Howard, whose *Alone with America* devotes more space to Merwin than to any of its other forty poets, declared that "the real goal of these poems . . . [is] a quality of life which used to be called visionary, and which must be characterized by its negatives, by what it is not, for what it is cannot be spoken."[5] And in a very different study, Paul Carroll's *Poem in Its Skin* (1968), a book that submits to close reading ten new poems by "the generation of 1962," a generation which Carroll refers to as "Barbarians inside the City Gates" and which includes Allen Ginsberg, Frank O'Hara, Robert Creeley, and John Ashbery, Merwin is called "the prince of the new poets": "In many of his most recent lyrics, one feels as if taken into a country where all is poetry—pristine, totally natural, miracles everywhere. . . . the poet finds himself gazing into the eternal."[6]

Merwin as New Visionary—this view was codified by Karl Malkoff in his *Crowell's Handbook of Contemporary American Poetry* (1973). Again Merwin gets more space than any other poet of his generation (the only two poets who receive more are Robert Lowell and Theodore Roethke) and is called "the representative poet of his time, having gone through a process that is not only common to many of his contemporaries, but a microcosm of the history of modern verse as well."[7] That history, as Malkoff sees it, is the movement "from the formal to the free, from the traditional to the innovative." The poems of *A Mask for Janus* (1952) are "monuments to orderly vision," but by the time he wrote the final section of *The Drunk in the Furnace* (1960), with its more realistic family poems, somewhat in the vein of Lowell, Merwin had emerged "as a practitioner of open form": "The syntax is frequently fragmented, the language is less precious, less archaic, and much tougher" (p. 213). The "new spareness" of the sixties poems, a "language . . . simple but capable of bearing much weight" (p. 215), paradoxically brings Merwin back to the beginnings of his career: "It is as if he had not developed his style by metamorphosis, but rather by a stripping down, so that what we have now in the later poems are the bare elements of his earliest verse reduced to their essential forms" (p. 216). A similar case was made by Cary Nelson in a challenging essay called "The Resources of Failure: W. S. Merwin's Deconstructive Career" (1977): "[Merwin's] recent work offers us what remained after he rigorously pruned the excesses of his first poems and then turned what was left back on itself. The result has been a poetry of extraordinary force, a poetry that inherits the despair of the century but gives it a prophetic new form, a form that ruthlessly deconstructs its own accomplishments."[8]

But even as Merwin's "prophetic new form" was being hailed by the critics, dissenting voices were beginning to question it: Nelson himself, for that matter, remarks that "Merwin's desolate landscapes are pervaded with a sense of uneasy expectation. The apocalypse in our past survives only as a kind of vague dread, as if it were only about to occur" (*MEOP*, 104). The same point was made more emphatically by Harold Bloom in a 1973 essay called "The New Transcendentalism: The Visionary Strain in Merwin, Ashbery, and Ammons." Like Malkoff, Carroll, and Howard, Bloom calls Merwin "the indubitably representative poet of my generation," but although he admires Merwin's attempt to make himself into "an American visionary poet," he concludes that "Merwin's predicament . . . is that he has no Transcendental vision, and yet feels impelled to prophesy":

> The poignance of his current phase is the constant attempt at self-reliance, in the conviction that only thus will the poet *see*. Merwin's true precursors are three honorable, civilized representative poets: Longfellow and MacLeish and Wilbur, none of whom attempted to speak a Word that was his own Word only. In another time, Merwin would have gone on with the cultivation of a more continuous idiom, as he did in his early volumes, and as Longfellow did even in the Age of Emerson. The pressures of the quasi-apocalyptic nineteen-sixties have

made of Merwin an American Orphic bard despite the sorrow
that his poetic temperament is not at home in suffering the
Native Strain. No poet legitimately speaks a Word whose burden is that his generation will be the very last. Merwin's litanies of denudation will read very oddly when a fresh generation proclaims nearly the same dilemma, and then yet another
generation trumpets finality.[9]

One may want to quarrel with Bloom's list of legitimate precursors, but his prediction that the poet's "litanies of denudation"
would read oddly to the next generation has already come true:
indeed, the same year that Bloom published his essay, two young
poet-critics, both political activists, submitted the premises of poems
like "The Asians Dying" to severe questioning. In an essay called
"Language against Itself: The Middle Generation of Contemporary
Poets," Alan Williamson argued that poets like Merwin, Galway
Kinnell, James Wright, and Gary Snyder had turned the search for
poetic vision into a kind of "ecological survival technique."[10] As "the
first generation to confront concentration camps and the atomic
bomb, the fully revealed destructiveness of civilized man, while still
in the process of growing up," this generation of poets, so Williamson argues, turned inward, concentrating on "the lessons to be
learned from animals, Indians, primitive or peasant cultures, the
wilderness as well as simple Wordsworthian solitary works; and
thus a whole new repertory of characteristic subjects is created"
(pp. 56–57). Merwin and Kinnell, Bly and Wright have a "shared
penchant for putting the 'I' in the simplest of possible sentence structures, pronoun/active or linking verb, with no modifiers before or
between. The 'I' becomes numb, neutral, universal: a transparency
through which we look directly to the state of being or feeling"
(p. 58). Indeed, Merwin, by Williamson's account, denies his natural
sensibility, which is ethereal rather than "concrete or earthly," forc-
ing his poetry to "develop toward the same tactics as his contemporaries' (the simple, quasi-narrative sentence, the isolated word,
the numb 'I'), toward the same loyalties, political and symbolic, and
above all, toward the same stress on the inadequacy of language"
(p. 65). And Williamson quotes three lines from "The Gods":

> My blind neighbor has required of me
> A description of darkness
> And I begin I begin but. . . .[11]

James Atlas's essay, published in the same collection, is called
"Diminishing Returns: The Writings of W. S. Merwin." Like Williamson, Atlas objects to the poet's "disembodied voice, addressing
some unknown Other," to his excessive use of animism (e.g., "the
horizon / Climbs down from its tree"), which imbues the poems
with "Surrealist confusion."[12] What Lieberman calls "a testament of

betrayals" is considered by Atlas to be a curious withdrawal from the meaning of political experience. For although Merwin may follow writers like Roland Barthes in believing that only a language of disruption can measure our current history, he "still resists the real significance of what he practices; the disruption of language is no more than a device in *The Lice* (1967) and *The Carrier of Ladders* (1970). Monotonous, interminable, self-imitative, each poem exudes unbearable exhaustion; none supports a close analysis" (p. 78). And Atlas submits "The Night of the Shirts" to some basic questions ("Where is 'here'? What is 'it'? What is 'the same story'?"), concluding that "excessive transmutation of our 'modern dilemmas' has caused us to misinterpret them; what there should be more of at this time are critiques, poems that situate us in the world, or elaborate on real conditions" (p. 79).

Ironically, then, the very qualities in the poetry that were singled out for praise during what Bloom calls the "quasi-apocalyptic" sixties have been cited by certain articulate poet-critics, who came of age in just this period, as its defects. For Howard, Merwin's poetry embodies a quality "which used to be called visionary, and which must be characterized by its negatives, by what it is not, for what it is cannot be spoken." To which the student of Wittgenstein might retort: "Whereof one cannot speak, thereof one must be silent." A compelling case against Merwin's rhetoric—or, more accurately, against the rhetoric of "mysterious, bardic hush" as it appears in the poetry of Bly and Wright as well as that of Merwin—has been made by Robert Pinsky in *The Situation of Poetry* (1977). Here is Pinsky on "Whenever I Go There" from *The Lice:*

> Whenever I go there everything is changed
>
> The stamps on the bandages the titles
> Of the professors of water
>
> The portrait of Glare the reasons for
> The white mourning
>
> In new rocks new insects are sitting
>
> With the lights off
> And once more I remember that the beginning
>
> Is broken
>
> No wonder the addresses are torn
>
> To which I make my way eating the silence of animals
> Offering snow to the darkness
>
> Today belongs to few and tomorrow to no one.

(*L*, 24)

It is possible to think that this poem proceeds—elliptical, allusive, dark, introspective, abrupt, intimate—as a "contemporary" mode distinct from . . . more traditional method[s]. . . .
For that reason, some explicit exposition . . . may be helpful.
"There" seems to be an internal place and a region of the
mind which the poet chooses repeatedly to visit; knowledge of
that place seems necessary to his imaginative life. But "habit"
or expectation is useless in this place which never repeats
itself. If "there" is the starting place for one's poems, or more
valued perceptions, it is an absolute starting place: remembered categories and labels, if not quite discarded, must be
subjected to new learning. . . . To put it more simply, each time
the poet meditates upon—say—the fact that in some cultures
mourners wear white, his sense of the reasons must be new.

The life there is hidden in a nearly impenetrable darkness, and the effort even to describe it is awkward, somewhat
farcical, cruelly exposed.[13]

The voice that here, and in related poems, refuses the limitations of
the conscious mind is characterized by Laurence Lieberman as one
that "filters up to the reader like echoes from a very deep well, and
yet . . . strikes his ear with a raw energy—a sustained inner
urgency."[14] Richard Howard similarly observes that "all the poems
[in *The Lice*] appear to be written from one and the same place
where the poet has holed up, observant but withdrawn, compassionate but hopeless, isolated yet the more concerned . . . by the
events of a public world" (*AA*, 441–42). Pinsky is more skeptical:
"Whenever I Go There," he suggests, may well be *about* difficulty,
about the need to renounce habits and expectations, but Merwin's
"elliptically 'beautiful' phrases fall with a stylistic ease which we do
not question even while we are questioning whether those phrases
mean anything":

In a sense this poem embodies an extreme Romanticism: a
pursuit of darkness, of silence, of the soul moving in ways so
unlike abstract thought that it burrows into or "eats" its
immobile paradise. On the other hand, the Romanticism is
qualifed by the form of the last line

Today belongs to few and tomorrow to no one

which, despite the absence of end punctuation, is a summarizing abstract formula. You could nearly call it a moral. . . . in
fact the action of this poem, as with most of [Merwin's] best
poems, is to create a generic experience. (pp. 93–94)

Which is to say that the poem "moves in a resolutely elliptical way
from image to atomistic image, finally reaching a kind of generali-
zation-against-generalizing" (p. 164).

Cautiously stated as this is, Pinksy's charge is serious: he is saying that Merwin's rhetoric of vision is contradicted by a curiously nonvisionary penchant for summarizing moral statement, for the formulated abstract truth. Such questioning of the Merwinian mode is not an isolated case. A decade after Paul Carroll referred to Merwin as the "prince of poets," the British poet Andrew Waterman, reviewing *The Compass Flower* (1977) for the *Times Literary Supplement*, wrote, "Merwin . . . whose poetry has been admired in America for twenty-five years, offers a depressing case of extreme regression. . . . Merwin's is simply banal and devitalized writing . . . [its] enervation of language, sicklily ingenuous tone, and sentimentality are all self-consciously perpetrated."[15] If this dismissal sounds unduly harsh—and of course it is—we should remember that a critic as different in outlook from Pinsky and Waterman as Harold Bloom, who has declared himself to be "not unsympathetic to [Merwin's] work," concludes his discussion of the poetry with the statement "Merwin seems condemned to write a poetry that is as bare of true content as it is so elegantly bare in diction and design."[16]

It seems, then, that what was regarded a short decade ago as the epitome of "naked poetry," as "an Eliotic process of negative mysticism as the way to achieve a 'Poverty' beyond even love,"[17] now looks to many readers suspiciously like the Poetic Diction the "naked poets" were supposedly repudiating. How this process came about, how one generation's "prince of poets" could become, in the words of Turner Cassity, "a very talented practitioner in a very tired tradition,"[18] is my subject.

## II

Throughout the sixties and well into the early seventies, the debate between modernism and postmodernism in poetry (or "closed" versus "open" poetry, or poetry as "product" versus poetry as "process") revolved around two questions: the question of verse form ("fixed" versus "free") and the question of "transcendence" versus "immanence" or "presence." Thus, when in the last section of *The Drunk in the Furnace* (1960) Merwin turned from the traditional meters and stanzas of his first three books to the flexible blank verse of the final, more personal section, James Dickey hailed the change with the announcement that "with tools like these [an odd kind of roughed-up, clunking diction and meter] and with the discoveries about himself that this book shows him intent on making, Merwin should soar like a phoenix out of the neat ashes of his early work."[19] And soar like a phoenix Merwin did: by the time he published *The Moving Target* (1963), whose poems are written in short, abrupt free-verse units, critics like Richard Howard could speak of "an entirely different mastery of style." "On the page," said Howard, "the generally unpunctuated poems look as though they had been exploded, not written down, the images arranged so that the lines never enclose but instead *expose* them" (*AA*, 436). And in their introduction to *Naked Poetry,* Stephen Berg and Robert Mezey take it as a given that to break "the grip of traditional meters" is to "set out . . . into 'the wilderness of unopened life.' "[20] By such an account, Merwin, who had renounced the villanelle and sestina, the rondel and ballad stanza of his first books for the hushed and impassioned free verse of *The Moving Target,* could be nothing less than a creator of the New.

Two things were safely ignored at the time. First, Merwin's free verse, which may have seemed enormously innovative when read against the background of the formalism of the fifties—the mode, say, of Richard Wilbur or Allen Tate or Howard Nemerov—was nowhere as explosive as the free verse Pound and Williams were writing by 1916, a free-verse model carried on by Louis Zukofsky and George Oppen in the thirties, and by Charles Olson in the late forties and early fifties. Second, it should have struck the critics as slightly odd that a poetry so seemingly explosive—the poetry of "the wilderness of unopened life"—was routinely published in the *New Yorker, Poetry,* the *Hudson Review,* and *Harper's*—hardly the organs of the avant-garde. *The Moving Target* had gone through eight printings between 1963 and 1979; *The Lice,* eleven printings between 1967 and 1981. Eleven of the sixty-three poems in *The Lice* first appeared in the *New Yorker* and eighteen in *Poetry.* In the case of Merwin's subsequent volumes, this ratio has increased: in *The Compass Flower* (1977), eighteen out of sixty-one poems—almost one-third—were published in the *New Yorker.* How is it that readers of the *New Yorker,* coming across a poem like "The Asians Dying" on a glossy page between those gorgeous ads for fur coats and diamonds and resorts in St. Croix, were not put off by the newness of lines like

When the forests have been destroyed their darkness remains
The ash the great walker follows the possessors
Forever . . .

(*L,* 63)

and by their evident strangeness?

This is a question to which I shall return, but for the moment let me consider the more difficult question of Merwin's poetics of immanence. It has been argued, most notably by Charles Altieri in his important book *Enlarging the Temple,* that whereas the great modernists—Yeats, Eliot, Stevens—adopt the Coleridgean "commitment to the creative, form-giving imagination and its power to affect society, or at least personal needs for meaning, by constructing coherent, fully human forms out of the flux of experience," post-modern poets follow Wordsworth in developing "an essentially *immanentist* vision of the role of poetry": "Here poetic creation is conceived more as the discovery and the disclosure of numinous relationships within nature than as the creation of containing and structuring forms. Hence its basic commitment is to recovering familiar realities in such a way that they appear dynamically present and invigorate the mind with a sense of powers and objective values available to it" (*ET,* 17). And again, "In the symbolist aesthetic, especially in the enervated forms of it practiced in the 1950s, the central focus is on the mind's powers to balance opposites and to take up a perspective from which the mind can judge and interpret what it presents. In the aesthetics of presence, on the other hand, poems do not present direct experience but the direct aesthetic illusion of direct experience that depends on style and form as means of seeing the word freshly" (*ET,* 24). And Altieri quotes Robert Duncan's essay, "Toward an Open Universe": "Central to and defining the poetics I am trying to suggest here is the conviction that the order man may contrive or impose upon the things about him or upon his own language is trivial beside the divine order or natural order he may discover in them."[21]

Where does Merwin fit into this scheme? If a postmodern poet like Duncan can discover "natural order" in the "things about him," Merwin, so Altieri argues, is one of his "fallen counterparts" in that "at the very moment of intense awareness of presence there is produced a terrifying self-consciousness of all that cannot be made present or numinously 'here' " (*ET,* 19). This very sense of emptiness or "absence" now becomes "the source of more complex and satisfying modes of inhabiting the other side of despair, however bleak that territory might be. . . . Merwin makes loss itself the ground for numinous awareness that might suffice for the attentive imagination."

It is this sense of loss that accounts for Merwin's penchant for abstract language and surreal image. Altieri writes, "The illusory present is more insubstantial than the darkness or painful sense of absence it replaces. Moreoever, the language one uses to fix those particulars, or even to comfort oneself by lamenting their passing, eventually mocks one with its inadequacies and its absences" (*ET,* 194). Or, as Cary Nelson puts it, "The challenge Merwin sets himself in his best work . . . is to become the anonymous figure who announces the harmonizing dissolution of the language" (*MEOP,* 79). Such recurrent words as "silence," "emptiness," and "distance," already present in Merwin's earliest poems, are undercut in the later work, in which language is turned back on itself so as to measure "the loss of any real historical possibility" (*MEOP,* 90). Indeed,

Merwin's "formal self-subversions" mirror our own; they draw out the "inadequacies . . . of the language we share" (*MEOP*, 92).

My difficulty with these readings is that the sense of loss, of absence, of "the harmonizing dissolution of the language," so interestingly discussed by Altieri and Nelson, seems to me to be asserted rather than explored. Unlike Beckett, with whom he has frequently been compared,[22] Merwin rarely invents a fictional situation in which emptiness, darkness, the failure of the language to mirror "reality" are actually *experienced* by someone. It is time to look at a concrete example.

"For the Anniversary of My Death"

Every year without knowing it I have passed the day
When the last fires will wave to me
And the silence will set out
Tireless traveller
Like the beam of a lightless star

Then I will no longer
find myself in life as in a strange garment
Surprised at the earth
And the love of one woman
And the shamelessness of men
As today writing after three days of rain
Hearing the wren sing and the falling cease
And bowing not knowing to what.

(*L*, 58)

Karl Malkoff, who calls this "one of the most striking poems in the collection [*The Lice*]," provides an analysis that is worth pondering:

The central idea of the poem is simple: each year contains the date on which the poet will finally die, each year he unknowingly passes the anniversary of his death. But the implications of this premise are complex. They involve nothing less than the total breakdown of conventional modes of apprehending time. Viewing time *sub specie aeternitatis* . . . Merwin labels the linear sense of time—that is, time as inexorable, unfolding, continual movement—as illusory. The "beam of a lightless star" is in one sense a metaphor of Merwin's own language of silence, the silence of death, the silence of meaninglessness. A beam emanating from a lightless star also suggests that from a sufficiently detached perspective, a dead star can appear still alive. . . . This is a fine symbol of the poet's eternal longings. And it is a fine symbol of time as relative in a world of absolute being.

Merwin perceives that his death has already taken place in precisely the sense that the present exists eternally. The

temporal distinction is false. In the second stanza, however, he
sets up new distinctions to replace the old. He will no longer
"Find myself in life as in a strange garment." He will lose his
divisive perceptions that isolate him from the rest of being.
Merwin's response is characteristically ambivalent. He will no
longer be "surprised at the earth / And the love of one
woman." The uncomfortable world of time and change is also
the realm of specifically human satisfactions. It is finally to
this human universe that Merwin must return.[23]

I have cited this reading at such length because it strikes me
as wholly typical of what we might call a sixties reading of sixties
poetry. What Malkoff goes on to call "the hallmark of Merwin's 'new
style' " is that his images consist "not of detailed description, but
rather of actions and essential types." Indeed, the types become
"almost allegorical. . . . But like all modern allegory, it is not supported by an ordered universe; it is grounded in nothingness"
(p. 215). Here Malkoff unwittingly contradicts his own reading of
the text, for what he has just shown, painstakingly and convincingly,
is that Merwin's allegory, far from being "grounded in nothingness,"
is grounded in the familiar paradox that time is at once linear and
eternal. "Viewing time *sub specie aeternitatis,*" the linear view is
illusory, as the symbolic "beam" of the lightless star, shining millions
of miles from its dead source, suggests. On the other hand, to lose
one's linear sense of time is, as the poet says in the second stanza,
to lose one's humanity, one's ability to be "surprised at the earth /
And the love of one woman." A paradox as neat as any Cleanth
Brooks discovered in Wordworth's "It Is a Beauteous Evening," or
Yeats's "Among School Children." Yeats, for that matter, had pondered a similar time/eternity paradox as early as "The Stolen Child."

How, then, is the poem different from the late modernist lyric
of the fifties, including Merwin's own early work? For one thing, the
"I" is not a persona but quite simply the poet himself—here is a
point of departure that seemed much more striking to readers of
the sixties than it does to us today. For another, the imagery does
not have the texture of W. K. Wimsatt's "concrete universal," of the
metaphysical conceit dear to the New Critics. Merwin's language is,
in one sense, transparent: everyone knows what "day" means, or
"fire" or "silence" or "traveller" or "three days of rain." It is also
curiously abstract: most of the generic nouns are preceded by an
article but not by an adjectival modifier: "the day," "the silence,"
"the earth," "the beam," "the love," "the shamelessness." In the
rare cases when the noun does have a modifier, the adjective works
to increase the sense of abstraction—"the tireless traveller,"
"strange garment," "last fires," "lightless star." Accordingly, the
landscape of the poem seems to be mysterious; it has repeatedly
been called "dreamlike" or "surreal," even though both these terms

are probably misnomers: in a dream, one doesn't think in terms of "Every year" or "Then I will no longer / Find myself" or "today writing after three days of rain"; and "surreal" refers, not to something vaguely mysterious and blurred, but to a landscape, whether in the verbal or the visual arts, in which objects, people, actions, or situations that cannot conceivably coexist in the "real world" are brought together, as in Magritte's painting *Collective Invention* (in which a fish with the lower torso and legs of a woman—a sort of reverse mermaid—is seen lying on a naturalistically painted beach beside the ocean).

But whatever term we use to describe Merwin's images, it is true that they are unlike, say, John Crowe Ransom's metaphors in "The Equilibrists." If, for example, "Lemuel's Blessing" is, as Paul Carroll argues, a poem built around a single paradox ("one who is an archetype of civilized tribal values petitions in a traditionally communal form of prayer that he be allowed to exist outside of civilized communal values . . . and come to share as deeply as possible the nature and characteristics of the wolf"),[24] that paradox is nevertheless framed differently from Ransom's, an allegorical mode having replaced the symbolist mode of the moderns. This difference aside, the poems in *The Moving Target* and *The Lice* carry on the tradition of the well-made poem of the fifties. For what distinguishes a poem like "For the Anniversary of My Death" from the "undecidable" texts of a Beckett on the one hand, as from its modernist predecessors on the other, is the marked authorial control that runs counter to the lip service paid to "bowing not knowing to what." Far from being a poem of *dis-covery*, a test whose "echo repeats no sound," "For the Anniversary of My Death" is characterized by a strong sense of closure.

Consider, for example, the stanzaic division. The first stanza (five lines) describes what happens "Every year"; the second (eight lines) refers to "Then" (when I will be dead). The first concentrates on the silence of eternity, beyond "the last fires," the eternity symbolized by the beam of the lightless star. The second recalls, even as does the final stanza of Yeats's "The Stolen Child," what will be lost when death ends the inexorable forward movement of time, when the "strange garment" of life is shed: namely, the love of one woman, the shamelessness of men, the singing of the wren, the falling of rain, and, yes, the "bowing not knowing to what," which is to say, "bowing" to the premonition of death one has in moments of transition, as when a three-day rain comes to an end.

Does the language "mock the poet with its absences"? Not really, or at least the mockery seems to take place only on the surface. The first line quickly gives the game away: since there is obviously no way to know on what day of the year one will die, the phrase "without knowing it" strikes a rather self-important note.

This is the language, not of dream or of mysterious Otherness, but of calculation: the setting up of a hypothetical situation that brings the time/eternity paradox into sharp relief. Again, the reference to "death" as the moment when "the last fires will wave to me" seems to me the very opposite of "spare" (a word regularly applied to Merwin's poetry by his admirers); it is a gestural, a decorative metaphor reminiscent of, say, Dylan Thomas rather than of René Char.[25] Indeed, lines 2–5, with their heavy alliteration and assonance, their repetition and slow, stately movement, have the authentic Thomas ring:

> When the last fires will wave to me
> And the silence will set out
> Tireless traveller
> Like the beam of a lightless star.

The language of the second stanza is increasingly abstract, conceptual, and formulaic, recalling, as Bloom points out, the conservative rhetoric of poets like Longfellow or Archibald MacLeish. To call life "a strange garment," to define one's humanity in terms of "the love of one woman" and the need to wrestle with "the shamelessness of men"—such locutions have the accent of moral parable rather than surrealist lyric. Given this context, the "bowing not knowing to what" in the unpunctuated last line is a predictable closural device: it points us back to the title with its recognition that one of the days now lived through will, one year, be the day of the poet's death—a death that opens on the void beyond.

The poem's closure is reflected in its formal verse structure. Merwin's heavily end-stopped lines, each followed by a brief rest or hush, are lightly stressed, anapests predominating, as in

> Like the béam of a líghtless stár

or

> And bówing not knówing to whát

but in many lines the pattern is complicated by an initial trochee:

> Évery yéar without knówing it

> Tíreless tráveller

> Héaring the wrén síng.

Syntactic parallelism—"And the silence will set out," "And the love of one woman," "And the shamelessness of men"—provides a further ordering principle. And although the stress count ranges between two and five (and the syllable count between five and thirteen), the lines are organized tightly by qualitative sound repetition: Merwin's patterning is extremely intricate, as in the alliteration of *t*'s, *r*'s, and *l*'s in *"Tireless traveller,"* the assonance and consonance

in "Find myself in life," and the internal eye rhyme in "And bowing
not knowing to what."

"For the Anniversary of My Death" is thus a very elegant, well-
made poem; it has a finish that would be the envy of any number
of poets, and its theme is certainly universal—just mysterious
enough to arrest the reader's attention, yet just natural enough (this
is the way we all feel about death sometimes) to have broad appeal.
It is, I think, this blend of strangeness and a clear-sighted literalness
that makes a poem like "The Asians Dying" memorable. Consider
the lines

> Rain falls into the open eyes of the dead
> Again again with its pointless sound
> When the moon finds them they are the color of everything.
>
> (L, 63)

We don't usually think of rain falling precisely into open eyes, let
alone "the open eyes of the dead." The image is an odd one, and
yet the third line has a kind of photographic accuracy: in the moon-
light, the dead bodies, clothed in khaki, would indeed blend with
the colors of the forest ground, and so theirs is "the color of everything." Add to this the irony—a rather heavy-handed irony, I think—
of Merwin's implication that, in our world, the color of death has
become "everything," and you have an intricate enough layering of
meanings, which is not to say that Merwin's construction is in any
way radical or subversive. Indeed, I submit that nothing in "The
Asians Dying" has the startling modernity of

> I was neither at the hot gates
> Nor fought in the warm rain
> Nor knee deep in the salt marsh, heaving a cutlass,
> Bitten by flies, fought.

Cary Nelson has rightly noted Merwin's debt to Eliot (MEOP, 110),
but it is a good question whether "Gerontion" doesn't capture what
Lieberman calls "the peculiar spiritual agony of our time" at least
as well as do poems like "The Asians Dying."

In Merwin's poems of the early seventies, fragmentation of
syntax, abstraction, and ellipsis become, as the critics have noted,
more marked; these are "difficult" poems in that their nouns are
generic and their spatial and temporal adverbs usually have ambiguous referents. Of The Carrier of Ladders, Richard Howard writes:

> They are intimate poems, but not in the least personal—there
> are no persons here, nor even personifications. There are pres-
> ences, and they support processes which afford the speaking
> voice an access to prophecy, by which I mean the capacity not
> to predict the future but rather to release the present: "key /
> unlocking the presence / of the unlighted river / under the mountains."

For Merwin, for the poet who is the one voice raised in Merwin's book, anyone or anything can be the "key"—another person, his own body, an event, a landscape—the key to darkness, to unconditional life. (*AA*, 444)

Let us see how this "unconditional life" is released in a representative poem of this volume called "Beginning of the Plains":

On city bridges steep as hills I change countries
and this according to the promise
is the way home

where the cold has come from
with its secret baggage

in the white sky the light flickering
like the flight of a wing

nothing to be bought in the last
dim shops

before the plain begins
few shelves kept only by children
and relatives there for the holiday
who know nothing

wind without flags
marching into the city
to the rear

I recognize the first hunger
as the plains start
under my feet.[26]

"Beginning of the Plains" is the sort of Merwin poem often called Kafkaesque:[27] in a nightmare vision, the poet must climb city bridges "as steep as hills," must "change countries" in a journey that will paradoxically bring him "home," a home dreaded with the premonition that "the cold has come from [it] / with its secret baggage." As he sets out on his journey, the poet passes "dim shops / before the plain begins," but there is "nothing to be bought" in these, only a "few shelves kept only by children / and relatives there for the holiday / who know nothing." The nature of the holiday is not specified but it doesn't matter, for the holiday is, in any case, not destined for him. Rather, he must proceed on his lonely pilgrimage, driven "to the rear" by a "wind without flags," that is to say an empty air mass, one in which nothing flutters, nothing has life. As the poet is swept along by this wind, his exile begins: "I recognize the first hunger / as the plains start / under my feet."

It would be an interesting exercise to study how a poem like "Beginning of the Plains" "deconstructs," to use Cary Nelson's word, earlier journey poems like "Anabasis I," the opening poem of *A Mask for Janus*, which has passages like the following:

Silence about our silence grew;
Beached by the convenient stream

Night is familiar when it comes.
On dim gestures does the mind
Exorcise abandoned limbs,
Disbodied, of that other hand

Estranged almost beyond response.[28]

In the later poem Merwin has abandoned the complex modification
and inversion of his first experiments with poetic syntax; he has also
purged his language of recondite words like "disbodied." But the
journey into "silence" and "night" has not appreciably changed; it
is the journey of life, the eternal Pilgrim's Progress, even if the 1970
poem presents that journey in more abstract, more seemingly mysterious terms, the "I" now being overheard as if speaking in a trance:
"I see x, I do y, then I must do z. . . . ."

The Kafkaesque rhetoric of "Beginning of the Plains" does
not, for all the stress on absence, go very deep. In a Kafka journey,
as in a Beckett one, there are very concrete, specific signposts, signposts that yield particular meanings, even as those meanings are
undercut by other contradictory signs. But what is indeterminacy in
Kafka is mere vagueness here: we don't know *where* the poet must
journey or why or in what "city" he now finds himself, but the import
of the journey as rite of passage is clear enough. The traveler is
afraid, for the projected journey is fraught with danger, pain, and
hunger. Moreoever, this is not a journey for which one can prepare:
"nothing to be bought in the last / dim shops / before the plain
begins." One must simply go up those "bridges steep as hills"; there
is no choice. It is the familiar allegory of pilgrimage —*nel mezzo del
cammin di nostra vita.*

But the working out of this allegory involves Merwin in a certain contradiction between form and meaning. What Howard calls
the "key" to the "unconditional life" is found, formally speaking, all
too easily. We are told that the journey is difficult, that the beginning
of the plains marks a frightening threshold, but the poem unfolds
without struggle in what is a continuous narrative made up of simple
declarative sentences ("I change countries"; "I recognize the first
hunger") and noun phrases ("few shelves kept only by children";
"wind without flags"). Again, the sound structure is reassuring: the
nicely measured end-stopped lines with their lightly stressed anapests ("and rélatives thére for the hóliday") foreground intricate
patterns of sound repetition:

in the *whíte* ský the *líght flíckering*
*líke* the *flíght* of a *wíng.*

Here we have not only end rhyme but internal rhyme ("white"/
"light"/"flight"), assonance of both short and long *i*'s, and alliteration

of *f*'s, *l*'s, and *w*'s; the chiming recalls, say, Poe rather than Beckett. Interestingly, when Beckett does, in some of the late prose, use such sound patterns, it is for parodic effect, an effect quite unlike Merwin's solemn, low-key, evenly pitched speech. Indeed "Beginning of the Plains" presents a progress to a goal:

I recognize the first hunger
as the plains start
under my feet.

The "first hunger" marks the turn: the journey, we know, has begun. Punctuated or not, Merwin's last two lines, four syllables each, seem to close the box with a click of a spring on the off-rhyme "start"/ "feet."

"Beginning of the Plains" thus makes a series of statements about experience that are curiously at odds with what Howard calls "an access to prophecy," and Bloom, "the Native Strain, the American Orphic vision." Unlike Char or Beckett or Kafka, but like the three poets Bloom cites—Longfellow, MacLeish, and Wilbur (and I would add E. A. Robinson)—Merwin sets up his poems so that they press toward generalization even if the generalization to be made is only that we must recognize the nothing that is. Indeed, John Bayley, in a review of *Writings to an Unfinished Accompaniment* (1973), puts his finger on the problem when he says, referring to the book blurb, which reprints the previously cited statement by Richard Howard as well as an even more extravagant one by Adrienne Rich:

W. S. Merwin seems to me a poet of civility and civilisation, and as such a beautifully sensitive and accomplished one. What can Adrienne Rich mean by saying he "has been working more privately, profoundly and daringly than any other American poet of my generation"? . . . It was not *daring* of Gray to write "The curfew tolls the knell of parting day," though if he had written "The curfew strikes the hour of parting day," he would have failed to produce a line of good poetry. . . . Merwin's poetry, I would have thought, is of a kind not at all common today and decidedly interesting: it is the poetry of a kind of inner cultivation, requiring an audience with something of the same degree of experience and refinement, with expectations and pre-knowledge of what is going on.[29]

Precisely. That audience is the audience of the *New Yorker* and *Poetry,* of the *Hudson Review* and the *Virginia Quarterly Review,* and it is this audience that has kept Merwin's poems in print, unlike almost anyone else's poems one can cite today, going through countless editions in their elegant Atheneum jackets. It is an audience that recognizes that, like Gray, Merwin almost never writes a bad line of poetry: "wind without flags," for example, conveys precisely and economically the sense of emptiness Merwin wants to depict.

Merwin's poetry, Bayley suggests, "is both extremely solitary and extremely fastidious, and yet it seems to need and call for the presence of a roomful of invisible understanders in something of the same way . . . early Augustan poetry needed the presence of that receptive coffeehouse society . . . who were alert to their manifestations of intellectual fine breeding, and concerned to be pleased with it" (p. 117). I think this is a very telling point. From the time he won the Yale Younger Poets Award for *A Mask for Janus* in 1952 through the mid-seventies—that is to say, for a twenty-five-year span—Merwin could count on that "roomful of invisible understanders" who shared his fastidiousness, his good breeding, his elegant ways of distancing and yet bringing to mind the pain and emptiness of living in a bad time. It was an audience to whom the poet could say, as he does in "Avoiding News by the River," "Milky light flows through the branches / fills with blood / Men will be waking," and count on their instant response to his circumspect reference to the bloodshed in Vietnam.

But viewed more dispassionately, Merwin, as Bayley puts it, "is not strong meat," and it was inevitable that before long the younger generation, who had been in college and hence more or less on the barricades when the Vietnam War was coming to its climax, would be less well bred, less receptive to the measured abstractions and careful distancing in Merwin's poetry about war and suffering and loss. Two things happened. On the one hand, for poets like Robert Pinsky and Alan Williamson, Merwin's elegance came to represent a thinly disguised evasiveness, a turning of one's back on the real world. As Turner Cassity puts it, "I know of no poems from which the apparatuses of industrial revolution have been more rigidly excluded."[30] On the other hand, more experimental poets, writing in the wake of poststructural theory, have been creating a decentered and programmatically deconstructed universe—an undecidability—that exists on the other side of Merwin's "unduplicatable resonance."

In his recent work Merwin seems to be trying to meet this avant-garde on its own ground: he has, for instance, written a group of poems in long, prosaic lines, whose spacing is meant to mark the pauses in natural speech in what looks superficially like David Antin's "talk poems":

Something continues and      I don't know what to call it
though the language is full of suggestions
in the way of language
                              but they are all anonymous
and it's almost your birthday      music next to my bones.[31]

Surely this is writing against the grain, the flippant tone ("though the language is full of suggestions / in the way of language") not according with the more familiar Merwin locutions of lines 8–9:

> the leaks in the roof go on dripping     after the rain has passed
> smell of ginger flowers     slips through the dark house

locutions that would seem more at home in his usual free-verse stanzas:

> the leaks of the roof go dripping
> after the rain has passed
> smell of ginger flowers
> slips through the dark house.

Merwin's poetry has, in many ways, suffered at the hands of his admirers, who have championed it as a "testament of betrayals," a key prophetically unlocking the door of the present. But apocalypse has never been the métier of this fastidious poet, whose gift is perhaps less for revelation than for delicate resonance. Here is a short poem called "Dusk in Winter":

> The sun sets in the cold without friends
> Without reproaches after all it has done for us
> It goes down believing in nothing
> When it has gone I hear the stream running after it
> It has brought its flute it is a long way.

(L, 49)

Here in the compass of five lines, Merwin deftly debunks the pathetic fallacy, the human belief that the sun either does or does not have "friends," that it might "reproach" us for "all it has done for us." All one can do, Merwin implies, is to define how it feels to watch the sun go down—its look and its sound—for the sun has no importance beyond itself or, to quote Wallace Stevens, "beyond ourselves." "When it has gone I hear the stream running after it"—here Merwin defines a commonly experienced aural illusion, an intuition that in nature all things are related. That intuition is confirmed by the last line, which stands out both visually and aurally: a run-on sentence made up of ten monosyllables with a delicate echo structure of short *i*'s and *t*'s, the second clause trailing off at the line end—"long way"—thus crossing the basic iambic pentameter rhythm with anapest and spondee:

> *it* has bróught *it∫* flúte ‖ *ít i*s a lóng wáy.

The flute metaphor, precisely conveying the dying fall of stream and sun, reinforces this special sound effect. The poem thus ends on the carefully planned downbeat that we have come to recognize as the authentic Merwin signature. It is a signature ill at ease with phrases like "prophecy" or "negative mysticism" or "naked poetry" or "the opening of the field." As for being one of the "Barbarians inside the City Gates," surely Merwin himself knows better. As he puts it in "The Cold before the Moonrise":

> If there is a place where this is the language may
> It be my country.
>
> (L, 46)

# Chapter Twelve

# On the Other Side

# of the Field:

## The Collected Poems

## of Paul Blackburn

*L*ike Frank O'Hara, with whom he must inevitably be compared, Paul Blackburn died young (he was forty-four in
1971 when he succumbed to cancer) and left behind literally hundreds of unpublished poems. Like O'Hara, Blackburn had
in his lifetime published primarily chapbooks with minuscule print
runs and was known, if at all, through magazine publication in such
avant-garde journals as *Origin, Black Mountain Review, Trobar,
Evergreen Review, Yugen, Big Table,* and *Caterpillar.* Like O'Hara,
who published in many of the same journals, he was a prominent
figure on the sixties New York poetry scene, his own particular nexus
being less the art–ballet–new music world of O'Hara, John Ashbery,
Kenneth Koch, and their friends, than the Charles Olson–inspired
"open form" poetics as practiced by poets like Robert Creeley, Cid
Corman, Denise Levertov, Ed Dorn, Jonathan Williams, Gilbert Sorrentino, Robert Kelly, Jerome Rothenberg, George Economou,
Rochelle Owens, David Antin, Armand Schwerner, Clayton Eshleman, and Diane Wakoski.

O'Hara's blockbuster *Collected Poems,* edited by Donald Allen and with a concise and brilliant preface by Ashbery (still, for my money, the best single essay on O'Hara's work), appeared in 1971 and immediately changed the poetic landscape. Not that every poetic scrap preserved in its meticulously edited pages was worthwhile, but that O'Hara's jaunty and deliciously absurd "action poems" (in which the words became the actors) implicitly challenged the increasingly tedious confessionalism that dominated the early sixties, thus paving the way for a poetry in which, to paraphrase Lyn Hejinian, "vocabularies" would generate ideas, rather than ideas vocabularies.

The case of Paul Blackburn is very different. A faithful practitioner of Olsonian projective verse, of open form, of what M. L. Rosenthal calls, in his foreword to Blackburn's *Collected Poems,*[1] the "natural," his racy vernacular seems oddly out of step with the cool and mannered artifice of the late eighties. In 1969 Stephen Berg and Robert Mezey could declare, in the foreword to their popular anthology, *Naked Poetry,* "We began with the firm conviction that the strongest and most alive poetry in America had abandoned or at least broken the grip of traditional meters and had set out, once again, into 'the wilderness of unopened life.' "[2] Two decades later, young New Formalist poets like Brad Leithauser have reversed this doctrine in attacking precisely "the confinement of free verse" and declaring that "iambic pentameter—in the hands of a Richard Wilbur, anyway—thrives today in a form Chaucer would feel at home with."[3] As for "the wilderness of unopened life," this cornerstone of "naked poetry" is rejected not only by New Formalists like Leithauser but also by the poetic Left (Charles Bernstein, say, or Ron Silliman), which stands in opposition to what Joan Retallack has called, in an essay for *Parnassus,* the "theory of poetry" as "squeegeecleaned window on transcendent Truth," as "self-effacing medium to a world fully furnished and ready for inspection."[4] Free verse, open form, projectivism, oral poetics—these are as inimical to the poetic Left as they are to the Right, given the poststructuralist emphasis, all but inescapable these days, on writing as not just a reproduction of speech but as something radically other.

In this context the "natural" and "passionate" speech-based poetry of Paul Blackburn, now enshrined in Edith Jarolim's scholarly and monumental *Collected Poems,* appears as something of an anomaly. Blackburn is a poet I personally feel I *should* admire. He carried on the Pound-Williams tradition, which is to my mind the central tradition of postmodernism, and was the chief disseminator of Black Mountain poetics from Olson and Creeley to the younger New York poets I cited above. Indeed, many of his closest writer-friends—for example, Gilbert Sorrentino and David Antin—have gone on to transform "open-field" poetics into complicated performance stategies, intermedia works, and new narrative genres.

Blackburn's poems appeared in the most interesting little magazines and in the key anthologies, like Donald Allen's *New American Poetry* (1960). Perhaps most important, Blackburn was a superb translator, especially of Provençal poetry, as his posthumous anthology *Proensa*, recently edited by George Economou, testifies.[5]

Given all these admirable associations, why does the *Collected Poems* inspire the uneasy feeling that the whole is less than its parts? Perhaps because, unlike O'Hara, Blackburn was primarily a consolidator rather than an innovator—everyone's favorite poet and best friend precisely because he was not, after all, a very powerful rival. It is always interesting, in retrospect, to watch a so-called school or movement unravel. Imagism, Vorticism, Black Mountain, Beat poetry, the New York school, Deep Image—in hindsight, all these movements were meaningful entities only insofar as individuals have transcended them. Was H.D. primarily an "Imagiste," as Pound called her? Was John Cage, who organized the first happenings at Black Mountain College, "a Black Mountain artist"? Is John Ashbery a "New York poet"? And, conversely, does inclusion in Ron Padgett and David Shapiro's well-known *Anthology of New York Poets* (Random House, 1970) give importance to the work of, say, Joseph Ceravolo or Dick Gallup? The current controversy about the value of "language poetry," for that matter, will change its character once we stop talking about *the* language poets and look at the actual work of specific writers.

What kind of "New American Poet," then, was Paul Blackburn? Here is an early previously uncollected poem called "A Song":

Of sea and the taking of breath
and to match the impress of it, the
giving of breath :
of mercy, the true quality of,
and the rhythm of certain movements I
sing, lady

How heavy and soft
your flesh at morning
when we wake together
O lady, how heavy and soft
your eyes when I reach for you
the

        line of your back
half circumscribes our summer
           centers love, that
tall  sweet  mast to your vessel
        and we enact
how underneath the pleasure piers the seas
move.

(p. 22)[6]

From the first, it seems, Blackburn was drawn to Provençal love lyric, especially as that lyric had been "made new" by Pound. The short emphatic free-verse line, the inversion of the opening stanza played off against the no-nonsense monosyllables, the line cuts in quirky places, as in "I / sing, lady"—these are Poundian signatures. But the visual layout of the poem is less Pound's than Olson's: the stanza on the right side of the page balancing the one on the left, the lines ending on function words like "the," "of," and "that" and containing a relatively high degree of abstraction, as in the playful twist on Portia's words, "of mercy, the true quality of."

At the same time, this "Song" is much more openly erotic, more intimate than Pound's so-called love poems (exercises really) in *Personae,* and much less conceptually dense than Olson's. The rhythm of the sea paralleling the rhythm of love: the analogy is conventional enough, but Blackburn's rendition goes beyond the convention. Thus it is oddly the "line of your back," rather than, say, the lady's eyes or breasts, that leads to arousal, calling up the poet's own "tall sweet mast to your vessel." The enactment of love "underneath the pleasure piers" is conveyed visually through the repeated *ea* diphthong—"breath" (twice), "heavy" (twice), "reach," "underneath," "pleasure," "seas"—while the final line break of "seas" / "move" mimes the push/pull of the love act itself.

Here, then, is the Blackburn signature in embryo: the first person, present-tense mode, the intimate yet nonconfessional "I" (we don't know this speaker and his mistress in the way that we know, say, the couple of Lowell's "Man and Wife"), the direct address to a more or less archetypal feminine "you," the line as breath unit, likely to break off at odd intervals and arranged in pseudostanzas that reach no point of closure, the delicate sound echoes. "A Song" is on all counts a "lovely" poem, a charming expression of erotic desire.

Yet it is only fair to say that the poem is also a little thin, that its words do not markedly resonate. Compare Blackburn's poem with, say, William Carlos Williams's "Love Song" ("I lie here thinking of you . . .")[7] and the difference is clear. In reading Williams, we are immediately put to work: Why, to begin with, is "love" regarded as a "Yellow, yellow, yellow" "stain" "upon the world"? Or again, if this "honey-thick stain" is that of "love," why is it described as "spoiling the colors / of the whole world"? Different readers will have different responses. Whereas in Blackburn's "Song," such phrases as "the rhythm of certain movements" or "How heavy and soft / your flesh at morning / when we wake together" make no particular demands on us. Nice, we say, and go on to the next page.

It is not fair, of course, to judge Blackburn by such a relatively
slight early poem. To take a more challenging example, here is a
later "Love Song," this one from what Edith Jarolim calls Blackburn's best period (1958–63), and chosen by the poet for inclusion
in *The Cities* (1967) as well as by Michel Deguy and Jacques Roubaud for their Blackburn selection in *Vingt poètes américains* (Paris:
Gallimard, 1980):

> Upon returning home tonite
> and it is a home
> now
> surely,
> being the animal I am
> when I had undressed, I
> wrapped my hand around my
> balls, and their now-limp appendage.
> And afterward
> smelled my hand.
>
> It was you.
> As your perfume is still on my undershirt
> so this perfume also.
>
> (p. 127)

This vein of Blackburn's poetry has been highly praised for its naturalness, its candor, its ability to capture a particular aspect of sexual
(or rather postsexual) pleasure, its wry self-mockery. In such lyric,
as Gilbert Sorrentino has remarked of Blackburn's *Journals,* "The 'I'
. . . is as much artifice as the poem it speaks—and yet it can locate
itself with such immediacy that it looks like the vehicle for common
speech."[8] Certainly, the sound structure is highly wrought, the delay
of the single-word lines, "now" and "surely," building up to the
rhyming contentment of "animal I am," followed by the successive,
halting "I"s that are, so to speak, "now-limp" like the poet's "appen-
dage," and the delicate internal rhyme and consonance of "*And
afterword / smelled my hand.*"

Still, I would argue that this poem is more successful when
read than reread, especially since its coda, "It was you. / As your
perfume is still on my undershirt / so this perfume also," spells out
what the preceding stanza has already told us. Indeed, poems like
"Love Song" seem especially designed to be heard at poetry readings. Black Mountain was, of course, a movement heavily invested
in an oral poetics: the poet was to be, so Olson taught, a "man on
his feet talking" ("man" being by no means accidental, given the
inherently chauvinist character of Olsonian poetics); the line was to
image the "breath," so as to insure the speed and motion of the

"energy discharge" and to allow "composition by field" to take place. Picture Blackburn, by all accounts (and judging from recordings) an extraordinary reader, getting up in front of a receptive Village audience and reciting "Love Song," beating out the rhythm of the first six lines slowly so as to build up to the comic punch. Surely, given the context of the poetry reading, in which verbal subtlety and semantic complexity are inevitably less important than immediate impact, a poem like "Love Song" would have struck a responsive chord. More heat, we might say, than light.

But, it will be objected, wasn't Frank O'Hara's an equally casual, lighthearted, and purposely free-form poetry? And isn't it unfair to judge Blackburn by what seem to be New Critical standards of complexity and ambiguity, of double entendre, tropical discourse, and so on? Such questions raise the larger issue of what constitutes poetic language and how that language relates to the poet's culture. Consider, for example, the series of poems written in the "subgenre" that, according to Edith Jarolim, Blackburn "inaugurated" and "with which he is most often associated: the subway poem" (p. xxvii). One of the earliest of these is "The Yawn" (1957–58):

> The black-haired girl
> with the big
>            brown
>                   eyes
> on the Queens train coming
>        in to work, so
> opens her mouth so beautifully
>        wide
>              in a ya-aawn, that
> two stops after she has left the train
> I have only to think of her   and I
>                    o-oh-aaww-him
>                    wow!
>
>            (p. 104)

Immediacy, precision, vernacular accuracy, directness—it is these qualities that Blackburn's fellow poets evidently admired here. And sexual innuendo as well, the "mouth" opening "so beautifully / wide" to "ya-aawn" referring, of course, to that other "mouth" the thought of whose opening is enough to make the poet-observer "come" along with the Queens train. Then too, there's the witty lineation of lines 1–4, the "black-haired girl / with the big" producing the expectation that the word "breasts" will follow, only to be coyly deflated by the reference to "brown / eyes."

Twenty years and the feminist revolution later, Blackburn's "o-oh-aaww-him / wow!" seems less charming than irritatingly macho: here, and too frequently in Blackburn's poetry, woman (referred to as "girl") equals desirable body, period. It is not that the poet's response to this or that attractive woman, seen on a subway train, cannnot be a fit occasion for poetry but that Blackburn's language is mimetically reductive, providing no sense of the complex and confusing contexts within which desire actually occurs.

Consider, for example, a related and, in Jarolim's words, "deceptively simple" "subway poem" called "Clickety-Clack," which begins as follows:

                    I took
                    a coney island of the mind
        to the coney
        island of the flesh
                    the brighton local
        riding
        past church avenue, beverly, cortelyou, past
                    avenues h & j
        king's highway, neck road, sheepshead bay,
        brighton, all the way to stillwell
        avenue
                    that hotbed of assignation
                    clickety-clack

        I had started reading when I got on
        and somewhere down past newkirk reached
        number   29   and read aloud
                    The crowd
        in the train
        looked startled at first but settled down. . . .
                    (p. 123)

Jarolim comments, "We take a joy ride of the senses as we follow the poet through Brooklyn, listening to him read poetry aloud and watching him unsuccessfully attempt to engage the affections of a not-so-amused female passenger. Blackburn skillfully duplicates the lurching rhythms of the train, and anyone familiar with what is now New York City's 'D' line might observe that he eliminates those stations that don't fit into his rhythmic scheme" (pp. xxvii–iii). Certainly, the catalog of subway stops, with its internal rhymes ("avenue"/"cortelyou" [for Cortelue]; "h & j"/"king's highway"/ "sheepshead bay"/"all the way") and girl's names ("beverly"), is a delightful tour de force, preparing us for the "stillwell" (the last stop) of the mystery girl to come.

Still, the scene of sexual arousal is less than amusing:

        . . . when I reached the line   :   "the cock
        of flesh at last cries out and has his glory
                    moment God"
        some girl sitting opposite me with golden hair
        fresh from the bottle began to stare dis-
        approvingly and wiggle as tho she had ants
        somewhere where it counted.

Which is enough to make the subway troubadour forget all about his reading; rather, he mentally undresses the girl, "imagining / what she had inside those toreador pants besides / her bathing suit," "pants" rhyming with the "ants" of the previous passage. Getting off at the same stop ("well / we both got off at stillwell"), he can hardly wait to make a move on her. But desire outstrips bravery: "smitten, I / hadn't noticed her 2 brothers were behind me / clickety-clack." Under the circumstances he can only retreat: "Horseman," he tells himself, alluding to Yeats with mock-heroic self-deflation, "pass by."

In anticipating this final twist, Blackburn sketches in the sub-way-stop landscape, with its "tattoo artists," its "franks" that are phallically "12 inches long," its "wax museum" (an obvious death image) and "soft-drink stand with its white inside"—insides being, of course, what regularly interest this observer. Still, for all its doc-umentary realism, its edgy and nervous vernacular, "Clickety-Clack" is as flatly opaque as its title. It's fun, the poet seems to be saying, to pass the time on the dreary Brooklyn train reciting one's poetry and attracting the attention of "some girl . . . with golden hair / fresh from the bottle." Fun to watch "her high backside sway and swish down that / street," it being an object so much more desirable than the other objects in "the wax museum" and at the "soft-drink / stand." But for the contemporary reader, this image of a young girl as a piece of meat is surely problematic.

It is interesting to read Blackburn's "subway poems" against O'Hara's comparable "lunch poems," in which the poet-speaker (presented, like Blackburn's, in the first-person present tense) sim-ilarly makes his way around New York by subway or taxi or on foot, all the while thinking about the person (or persons) he loves. The obvious difference between Blackburn's aggressive heterosexuality and O'Hara's equally aggressive homosexuality aside, we find in these poems of the late fifties/early sixties a similar trajectory that makes their divergences all the more important.

Take "Poem (Khrushchev is coming on the right day!)," whose occasion is evidently a newspaper headline announcing the impending arrival in New York of the Soviet leader:

> Khrushchev is coming on the right day!
> the cool graced light
> is pushed off the enormous glass piers by hard wind
> and everything is tossing, hurrying on up
> this country
> has everything but *politesse,* a Puerto Rican cab driver says
> and five different girls I see
> look like Piedie Gimbel

with her blonde hair tossing too,
         as she looked when I pushed
her little daughter on the swing on the lawn it was also windy.[9]

At first the items rapidly presented for our contemplation here seem to be merely disparate. The poet, on his way to work in a cab in the early morning, finds it delightful that Khrushchev is about to arrive at Penn Station, but why? According to the absurd logic of O'Hara's poem, because it is a bright and windy day—"everything is tossing, hurrying on up"—and wind is the poet's own emblem for the intensity, speed, and exhilaration he wants from life. Here is the poem's climax:

New York seems blinding and my tie is blowing up the street
I wish it would blow off
         though it is cold and somewhat warms my neck
as the train bears Khrushchev on to Pennsylvania Station
and the light seems to be eternal
and joy seems to be inexorable
I am foolish enough always to find it in wind.

But what does Khrushchev have to do with the poet's mood? Nothing at all, except that, it being such a gorgeous September day, this must surely be the "right" day for anyone, even for such an unlikely person as Khrushchev, to come. The irony, of course, is that dour, single-minded Khrushchev, who "was probably being carped at / in Washington," couldn't care less what the weather is like since he obviously has other things on his mind. Indeed, there is no right day for Khrushchev to arrive—no *"politesse"*—which is precisely O'Hara's point, the poem comically dismissing anything that stands in the way of sheer momentary buoyancy: "where does the evil of the year go / when September takes New York / and turns it into ozone stalagmites / deposits of light."

Like Blackburn's "Clickety-Clack," O'Hara's is a process poem, charting the mental antics of the poet as he moves around the city. But whereas Blackburn's organizing principle is that of straightforward narrative (i.e., I did this and then this happened and then that), O'Hara's is a genuine energy construct in that words not only point to the words that follow them in a given phrase or clause but also, so to speak, signal to a whole network of others that are metonymically related. Thus "coming" (in "Khrushchev is coming on the right day") anticipates "graced," "pushed," "tossing," "blinding," and "blowing," whereas "cool graced light" modulates into "Grace Hartigan's painting *Sweden,*" and then into "ozone stalagmites," "New York seems blinding," and "the light seems to be eternal."

Further, these wind and light images dissolve the distinction between past and present even as the actual verb forms sustain it.

Blackburn's journey "to the coney / island of the flesh" on "the brighton local" catalogs place names that, as I noted above, provide documentary accuracy as well as a source for punning: for example, "cortelyou" ("courting you") or "neck road." But these puns constitute more or less local jokes, whereas O'Hara's seemingly random roll call of names is structured around the polarity that the poet takes to be the source of Manhattan's "cool graced light." Thus we are presented with North (Sweden) and South (the "Puerto Rican cab driver" who says that "this country / has everything but *politesse*"), East (Khrushchev, Ionesco) and West (Hans, Beckett), young (Piedie Gimbel's little daughter) and old (Vincent's mother), gentile (Purgatorio Merchado) and Jew (Gerhard Schwartz), poetry (François Villon) and painting (Grace Hartigan's painting *Sweden*), drama (Ionesco, Beckett) and film, in the shape of the "movie" to which "we went . . . and came out." But perhaps the most amusing polarity is that between the Soviet Russian Khrushchev and the one-time czarist Russian "blueberry blintzes" eaten with Vincent (the dancer Vincent Warren, who was O'Hara's lover at the time) the night before. The train bearing Khrushchev on his one-way journey to Pennsylvania Station is finally less "inexorable" than the "joy" of recurrence: "I go home to bed," "I get back up," "last night . . . Vincent said," "the early morning as I go to work." Indeed, Khrushchev's arrival never actually takes place: suspension, the arc of expectancy, the potential for action—these are the emotive notes that keep O'Hara's poem open, that make it impossible for closure to occur.

Black Mountain poetics, we recall, had as its cornerstone Olson's prescription in the "Projective Verse" essay to "USE, USE, USE the process at all points, in any given poem always, always one perception must must must MOVE, INSTANTER, ON ANOTHER!" What I hope the comparison between "Clickety-Clack" and "Khrushchev is coming on the right day!" makes clear is that, movement and speed aside, it is in the arena of "using everything," as Gertrude Stein put it, that Blackburn is deficient. In the Khrushchev poem, "USE, USE, USE the process" (an echo of Pound's Imagist credo, "Use no word that does not contribute to the presentation") means that every detail, no matter how small, turns out to be somehow relevant. But in the case of "Clickety-Clack," we can pull many threads out of the web without making a hole in the rug. Does it matter that the girl has on a bathing suit rather than, say, a bra and panties, "inside those toreador pants"? That "somewhere down past newkirk" the poet "reached / number 29" of his sequence? That "sorry to say / 5 lines later the poem finished," he "started to laugh

like hell"? Language is used here to provide narrative continuity, to
"keep it moving," but *textually* the poem goes increasingly limp.

Which is to say, I suppose, that we are now less excited than
we were in the sixties about the liberating potential of a speech-
based poetics. "Of the poets working in these past three decades,"
declared Robert Kelly in his introduction to *The Journals*, "I would
say Blackburn is the paradigm of the processual—the one who most
allowed his life and work to intertwine, who sought and found in
the happenstance of experience a mysterious beauty called music
when we hear it, that is, the Form made clear."[10] *Form*, it is implied
here, is something that will take care of itself, provided the poet is
true to his or her experience. "What I most value in *The Journals*,"
writes Kelly, "is the further transcendence of the closed poem (that
museum piece, that haunting but snake-like urn) his work had long
been moving from. And what gave his achievement of the open poem
its peculiar power is, in some awful and simple way, just how well
he could sing."

Surely this is the classic refrain of the late sixties and early
seventies, the late Romantic faith in an "idiolect in the written
language" that would quite simply reproduce the poet's "idiolect in
the spoken language." Was not form, after all, never more than the
extension of content? And wasn't the great American poet Walt
Whitman the father of open-field poetics?

Ironically, even as this doctrine was being disseminated in
poetry workshops around the country, Derrida's famous seminar
"Structure, Sign, and Language," held at Johns Hopkins in 1967, was
published in Richard Macksey and Eugenio Donato's *The Structur-
alist Controversy* (1972). For "composition by field," with its faith
in an aesthetic of presence, of immanence, of form as the natural
extension of content, and "writing" as the direct making present of
speech, Derrida substituted the notion of the decentered structure,
the absence of the transcendental signified, the treatment of text as
a system of differences, and the recognition that speech does not
necessarily have priority over writing.

One needn't be a Derridean to see that deconstruction has
forced us to question the very notion of "projective verse." For if
"content" can never be abstracted from the linguistic base itself, if
we take the materiality of the signifier seriously, then phonemics,
morphology, and especially syntax are not just ancillary "devices"
that flesh out the poet's meter-making argument, and "song" is
not just something that flows "naturally," given the right poetic
instincts.

Indeed, Blackburn's *Journals*, distinctive for their candor, their
clean simplicity, their willingness to bring so much of the poet's
actual life onto the page, may now strike us as barely distinguishable
from reportage, whereas it is, paradoxically, his more "formal"

poems that seem least dated. "Sirventes" of 1957–59 is a case in point. A *sirventes* is an Old Provençal genre, strophic in form, whose "main themes are personal abuse or (occasionally) praise. . . . The tone is mostly satiric, and gross vituperation is common."[11] Blackburn's *sirventes* is "made . . . against the city of Toulouse," where he spent his 1955 Fulbright lectureship year:

> Whole damn year teaching
> trifles to these trout with trousers
> tramping thru the damp
> with gout up to my gut
> taking all the guff, sweet
> > jesus crypt,
> > god of the he
> brews, she blows, it bawls, & Boses
> (by doze is stuffed)
> by the balls of the livid saviour, lead be
> back hindu eegypt-la-aad
> before I'b canned for indisciblidnary reasons.
>
> (p. 88)

Highly conventionalized as this is, the poem curiously has a more freewheeling, playful, and open-ended air than do Blackburn's subway poems or his "journals." The strophic unit becomes a kind of generative device, sound determining what comes next, as when we move from "trifles" to "trout," "trousers," and "tramping," and then, via rhyme, from "tramping" to "damp" and from "trout" to "gout." The elaborately punning lines splutter along, their sound play ("Boses," the cold victim's pronunciation for "Moses," as is "by doze" for "my nose"; "lead be / back hindu eegypt-la-aad" a wonderfully droll twist on the gospel song) culminating in the witty complexities of "indisciblidnary" which anagrammatically contains (or rather, cannot contain) the poet's *libido,* his *indiscretions,* his boredom with the *bible,* and so on. "Sirventes" may have no sensitive insight to convey, no larger meaning to divulge; it is simply good fun:

> in the street I piss
> on French politesse
> that has wracked all passion from the sound of speech.
> A leech that sucks the blood is less a lesion. Speech!
> this imposed imposing imported courtliness, that
> the more you hear it the more it's meaningless
> > & without feeling.
>
> (p. 89)

Like O'Hara, Blackburn claims to have little use for politesse, for bourgeois decorum, the joke here, as in the Khrushchev poem, being that the politesse rejected by the speaking voice everywhere informs the poem's language, O'Hara's "cool graced light" finding its coun-

terpart in Blackburn's formal rhythms, for example, "A leech that
sucks the blood is less a lesion. Speech!" whose alliterating and
rhyming iambic hexameter nicely offsets the more imitative speech
rhythms of "in the street I piss / on French politesse."

And it is the offset, of course, that matters. For the danger of
projectivism was what Charles Bernstein has wittily called "the *phal-
lacy* of the heroic stance, grounded as it is in the anthropomorphic
allegory of language as the stride of a man, with all the attendant
idealization of 'speech syntax' and a voice of authority."[12] I myself
would posit that Blackburn's best poems are those that sabotage,
whether consciously or not, the "heroic stance" of the poet-as-man
on his feet talking by heightening the system of contiguities in which
the "I" operates. "Pre-Lenten Gestures" (1963–65) is such a poem.

The setting is a bakery where "Aunt Ella" officiates while the
poet, sometimes bemused, sometimes attentive, sometimes bored,
observes the shoppers, listens to the radio, thinks of friends, and
tries as hard as he can not to think about a love that has ended. The
poem begins:

> Thank God one tone or
> one set of decibels is
> not all there is.      The
> *Dies Irae,* the radio behind me, is
> due to the mad programmer we never know, followed
> by a selection of military band music.
> How kind.      I
> can't help thinking of
> Ed Dorn, his line: *Why
> can't it be like this all the time?*
> "as my friend said"
> the band, the binding, the
> bound from one state to the next, and sometimes
> one is not even asked.
> What may be revealed, given.
> What?
> that it be revealed.
>
> (p. 239)

"One set of decibels is / not all there is." In "Pre-Lenten Gestures"
one perception immediately leads to a further perception. The radio
begins by playing *Dies Irae,* thanks to "the mad programmer we
never know," but quickly modulates into military band music. A line
from an Ed Dorn poem cuts to another by Robert Creeley, "as my
friend said." The "band" brings to mind "the binding" (of a book),
and then in a mock conjugation of the verb, "the bound from one
state to the next," with its memories of journeys the poet has made
but also the states of mind he has passed through. "Sometimes," he

comments, "one is not even asked." But we don't yet know what it
is that is asked or "What may be revealed, given."

Whatever the subject of the poet's meditation, it is now dis-
placed by the entrance of the "girl [who] comes in with her little fur
hat / and wants to buy T H A T / cake that looks like a group of
buns in the window. / Impulse buying." In a series of "pre-Lenten
gestures" that resemble comic film stills, we see the girl in the fur
hat, her young husband outside, Rudolph Valentino saying "Foolish
little girl," on the radio, and so on. It is all entertaining, both for us
and for the poet, but the camera soon zeros in on the "I":

> I AM BACK to an earlier question:
> someone had found it strange
> I should think of the concomitant physical cul-
> mination of love,
> fucking, in short, as a release, some
> times a relief from
> the pain of loving itself.
>
> Surcease of pain. The idea
> is medieval at least:
> "o lady, give me some relief,
> cure me of that sweet sickness
> I am subject to"
>
> (p. 241)

In the remainder of the poem, which is visually arranged on the
page so as to get a maximum of intensity from the successive juxtapositions and the use of white space, the anguish of the present is
seen through the prism of the troubadour love song, whether secular
or addressed to the Virgin, as well as through the lens of Yeats's
Crazy Jane poems, specifically "Her Anxiety" (no. 10), which begins
"Earth in beauty dressed / Awaits returning spring,"[13] the subsequent four lines being reproduced in Blackburn's poem:

> All true love must die
> Alter at the best
> Into some lesser thing.
> *Prove that I lie.*
>
> (p. 243)

Blackburn must have assumed his readers would know how
this particular poem continues:

> Such bodies lovers have,
> Such exacting breath,
> That they touch or sigh.
> Every touch they give,
> Love is nearer death.
> *Prove that I lie.*

Yeats's second stanza presents a chilling twist on the first. For it is one thing to say that "All true love must die" (a venerable cliché), but quite another to suggest that love itself is what moves us toward death. And it is this love-death equation that now preoccupies Blackburn's "I": "the act fore- / tells its own, what- / ever-breaking-now, its own / end . revealed (p. 243).

But the poem closes on a note of resignation, a "gesture" no longer "pre-Lenten" but of contrition, presented in a minimalist coda that is, to my mind, one of Blackburn's most moving passages:

> It always is,
> always was
> this way, Ed.
> all the time.

It is not that it does not happen.
It does,
> and there is no help for it.
> And
there is no end to it,
until there is .

(p. 244)

Here Blackburn picks up all the pieces: Dorn's *"Why can't it be like this all the time?"* now refers, not to pleasure, but to pain and death, and the Yeatsian refrain becomes the frightening "there is no end to it, / until there is." It is a somber conclusion to what began as a lighthearted poem about "radio days," shopping for buns in the bakery, the red Jaguar and "Robin's-egg Ford" seen through the "squeegee"-cleaned window, and the Provençal landscape ("the tower risen out of the olive grove"). At the end, the pre-Lenten "gestures" have given way to the season of repentance. And here poetry has made it happen.

Blackburn is not often as good as this. Seven-hundred pages of his poems may be more than all but a handful of former friends, disciples, or scholars of the period care to read. Again, the small-press collections of his poetry may well have been more user friendly, more intimate vehicles for Blackburn's particular sensibility, than is the heavy book under review. My own guess is that a *Selected Poems* of, say, one hundred pages would win this poet a more enthusiastic readership than the *Collected Poems* is likely to do. Still, we should not dismiss the importance of Jarolim's project or of Persea Books's production. For I know of no better place to learn what the sixties in American poetry were all about. Not the sixties of our most prominent poets—that would by now be familiar territory—but the sixties as represented by what is, so to speak, the decade's second string. As Blackburn puts it in "Bluegrass" (1966): "the work is only / what is not done."

*Chapter Thirteen*

# Barthes, Ashbery, and the

# Zero Degree of Genre

> J'aime le romanesque, mais je sais que le roman
> est mort.
> —Roland Barthes, interview, January 1975

> The prose [in *Three Poems*] is something quite
> new. . . . suddenly the idea of it occurred to me
> as something new in which the arbitrary divisions
> of poetry into lines would be abolished. One
> wouldn't have to have these interfering and scan-
> ning the processes of one's thought as one was
> writing; the poetic form would be dissolved, in
> solution. . . .
> —John Ashbery, interview, Winter 1972

## I

One of the anomalies of criticism in the late twentieth century is that the lyric poem, the great genre of the Romantics as of the high modernists, no longer seems central to
its discourse. Take the case of Roland Barthes, himself an extraordinarily "poetic" writer, if by "poetic" we mean that his writing
foregrounds the metaphoric, syntactic, and sound properties of language, exploiting these linguistic relationships at the expense of
"plot" or "character" or "thematics." Given Barthes's passion for
what he calls the "wounds" and "seductions" of language,[1] and given
his interest in such diverse texts as those of Racine and Balzac, Sade

*267*

and Fourier, Flaubert and the Goethe of *Werther,* and in such diverse media as photography and film, landscape design and architecture, it seems puzzling that he should have paid so little attention to poetry.

Or does it? Perhaps the difficulty is that discourse about poetry, for a writer of Barthes's generation, is inevitably colored by the image of The Poem laid down by the great modernist poets from Baudelaire to Valéry, whose claim it was, so Barthes argues in *Writing Degree Zero* (1953), that poetry is an autonomous language, arriving at truths that are above and beyond Nature:

> . . . under each Word in modern poetry there lies a sort of existential geology, in which is gathered the total content of the Name. . . . The word is no longer guided *in advance* by the socialized discourse; the consumer of poetry, deprived of the guide of selective connections, encounters the Word frontally, and receives it as an absolute quantity, accompanied by all its possible associations. The Word . . . therefore achieves a state which is possible only in the dictionary or in poetry—places where the noun can live without its article—and is reduced to a sort of zero degree. . . . This Hunger of the Word, common to the whole of modern poetry, makes poetic speech terrible and inhuman.[2]

Terrible and inhuman in its overdetermination of the sign. "Contemporary [i.e., modernist] poetry," writes Barthes in *Mythologies* (1957), "is *a regressive semiological system* . . . [in that] it attempts to regain an infra-signification, a pre-semiological state of language; in short, it tries to transform the sign back into meaning; its ideal, ultimately, would be to reach not the meaning of words, but the meaning of things themselves."[3]

To reach the meaning of things themselves—it is this desire to bypass the signifier that makes so much neo-Romantic and neo-Symbolist poetry written today seem, at least by Barthean standards, "regressive." But the "poetic" is not necessarily equivalent to the "poem," just as, for Barthes, the "novelistic" is to be distinguished from the "novel":

> The novelistic is a mode of discourse unstructured by a story [*une histoire*]; a mode of notation, investment, interest in daily reality, in people, in everything that happens in life. The transformation of this novelistic material into a novel seems very difficult to me because I can't imagine myself elaborating a narrative object where there would be a story, which to me means essentially verbs in the imperfect and past historic, characters who are psychologically believable—that's the sort of thing I could never do, that's why the novel seems impossible to me.[4]

And again, he tells Stephen Heath of his longing for "the novelistic without the novel, the novelistic without its characters: a writing of life, which could perhaps rejoin a certain moment of my own life" (*GV*, 130 [124]).

Why is Barthes, himself such a brilliant commentator on Balzacian "character" or Racinian "plot," so opposed to the very notion of *fictionality?* We can interpret his predilection for "work[ing] *in* the signifier" as the next step beyond the "nouveau roman," which had already posited a refusal to "invent" coherent psychological characters and plot structures. But whereas Alain Robbe-Grillet and Nathalie Sarraute still maintain the "fiction" that there is a story to be told and that this story involves invented persons, explicitly distinguished from the author himself or herself, Barthes wants to create a "novelistic" texture that is no longer "dominated by the superego of continuity, a superego of evolution, history, [and] filiation" (*GV*, 132 [126]).

When we turn to poetry, the "superego of continuity" clearly refers to such formal principles as meter and stanzaic structure. The Barthean paradox—and we will find analogies in Ashbery's work—is that, even as nonfictional narrative may be more "novelistic" than the novel, so prose has the capacity to be more "poetic" than poetry. Whereas modern poetry has the "essentialist ambitions" of trying to "actualize the potential of the signified in the hope of at last reaching something like the transcendent quality of the thing," it is *prose* that is the language of arbitrary rather than motivated signs, the language of what Barthes calls "open-work meaning" (*M*, 132). To put it another way: whereas poetry, in its modernist form, "wants to be an anti-language" (*M*, 133), "ordinary" prose—say, a fashion article in *Elle* or an advertisement for the new Citroën model—can provide the imaginative reader with any number of "poetic" possibilities.

But the aim is not, of course, to replace Balzac and Mallarmé with Citroën ads. To find the "poetic" outside the lyric poem, the novelistic outside the novel, Barthes turns to such models as Japan—a Japan, one should note, that is less a real country with such and such attributes than, in Barthes's own words, "my Japan, a system of signs I call Japan" (*GV*, 82 [82]), a locus that, as Barthes puts it in *The Empire of Signs* (1970), is characterized by "the ethic of the *empty sign*":

> Japan offers the example of a civilization where the articulation of the sign is extremely delicate, sophisticated, where nothing is left to the nonsign; but this semantic level, expressed in the extraordinary finesse with which the signifier is treated, in a way means nothing, says nothing: it doesn't refer to any signified, especially not to any ultimate signified,

and thus for me it expresses the utopia of a world both strictly semantic and strictly atheistic. (*GV,* 83 [82]).

The emblem of this utopia is the Japanese house, a dwelling that is "delightful" in that "it can be emptied-out, un-furnished, de-centered, dis-oriented, dis-originated" (*GV,* 87 [85]).

Such "dis-orienting" is central to Barthes's own verbal structures. Questioned about his fondness for the haiku, Barthes replies: "I have long had a taste for discontinuous writing, a tendency reactivated in *Roland Barthes. . . .* my mode of writing [is] never lengthy, always proceeding by fragments, miniatures, paragraphs with titles, or articles. . . . The implication from the point of view of an ideology or a counter-ideology of form is that the fragment breaks up what I would call the smooth finish, the composition, discourse constructed to give a final meaning to what one says" (*GV,* 209 [198]). And in the preface to the appropriately titled *Fragments d'un discours amoureux* (1977), Barthes explains that "no logic links the figures (i.e. the incidents or schema in the book), determines their contiguity: the figures are non-syntagmatic, non-narrative, they are Erinyes; they stir, collide, subside, return, vanish with no more order than the flight of mosquitoes."[5] The lover's discourse can only be horizontal: "No transcendence, no deliverance, no novel (though a great deal of the fictive)" (p. 7 [11]).

How does the nonfictional "fictive" manifest itself? In "the empire of signs," everything depends upon the processes of dis-ordering and dis-continuing—what Barthes calls *arthrology,* which is to say, the science of joints:

> At every moment of my life, wherever I go, even walking in the street, when I think, react, I constantly find myself on the side of thought that grapples with what is discontinuous and combinatory. Today, for example, I was reading a text by Brecht, admirable, as always, a text on Chinese painting, in which he says that Chinese painting puts things next to each other, side by side with each other. That's a very simple way of putting it, but very beautiful, and quite true, and what I want, after all, is precisely to feel the juxtaposition of things, the "next to" [*l'à côté de*]. (*GV,* 132 [125–26]).

Let us consider how this "next to," this *à côté de,* works in a text like *Roland Barthes par Roland Barthes* (1975).[6] In the unnumbered pages at the front of the text, we read, "It must all be considered as if spoken by a character in a novel." Yet this "novel" begins with a scrapbook of captioned family photographs, a series of childhood images that, as the author tells us, are at once disturbingly familiar and yet seem to portray an unfamiliar other, "whose units are teeth, hair, a nose, skinniness, long legs in knee-length socks which don't belong to me, though to no one else." What Barthes calls "the fissure in the subject" is thus immediately introduced. For who is Roland Barthes? Is he the little boy held by his mother in the first unnumbered photograph labeled "The demand for love"? Was his consciousness shaped by "Bayonne, the perfect city," by the two Proustian grandmothers, by the father, "dead very early in the war"?

The possibility of finding narrative or psychological continuity in these photographs is precluded by the introduction of a series of *dictées* (dictations), commentaries on given photographs that take the form of schoolboy exercises, written, says Barthes, "the way we were taught to write" (*GV*, 210). So the *dictée* called "The Three Gardens," facing the photograph of the family house (fig. 1), begins as follows: "That house was something of an ecological wonder: anything but large, set on one side of a considerable garden, it looked like a toy model (the faded gray of its shutters merely reinforced this impression). With the modesty of a chalet, yet there was one door after another, and French windows, and outside staircases, like a castle in a story." The effect of such *dictées* interspersed in the text is a kind Brechtian *Verfremdung* (and Brecht was, we know, one of Barthes's idols). For how can the reader identify with an autobiographer who writes (if indeed it is "he" who writes) such set dictations? Or with an autobiographer who provides us with a photograph of himself and a smiling young woman, seated in the grass (fig. 2), and captions it with the words, "Where does this expression come from? Nature? Code?"

With the coming of Barthes's adulthood the "image-repertoire," in any case, gives way to writing. And now the possibility of "understanding" Roland Barthes, as the child of such and such parents, growing up in such and such a place and attending a particular lycée, is called into question by the series of fragments that constitute the rest of the book. These fragments are introduced by short titles arranged in alphabetical order, from the *A* of "*Actif/réactif*" to the *T* of "*Le monstre de la totalité*," a fragment that ends with the passage: "Different discourse: this August 6, the countryside, the morning of a splendid day: sun, warmth, flowers, silence, calm, radiance. Nothing stirs, neither desire nor aggression; only the task is there, the work before me, like a kind of universal being: everything is full. Then that would be Nature? An absence . . . of the rest? Totality?" (*BBB*, 180). And of course the question is left open, the final page (fig. 3) containing a pictograph called "Doodling" ("La graphie pour rien"), and an illegible line of writing labeled ". . . or the signifier without the signified."

Between A and T (notice that Barthes does not give us the expected A to Z sequence with its inevitable move toward closure), the fragments are arranged so as to "be kept from 'taking,' from solidifying." Not that anarchy, Barthes is quick to point out, is the

**Figure 1.** Facing page to "The Three Gardens," *Roland Barthes by Roland Barthes* (New York: Hill & Wang, 1977), unpaginated.

*Where does this expression come from? Nature? Code?*

**Figure 2.** From *Barthes by Barthes*.

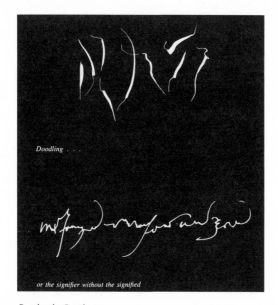

**Figure 3.** From *Barthes by Barthes*.

signified of the system. "The position," he explains, "is a bit paradoxical in relation to avant-garde style, but perhaps the best way to
prevent this solidification is to pretend to remain within an apparently classical code, to keep the appearance of a writing subject to
certain stylistic imperatives, and thus to attain the dissociation of an
ultimate meaning through a form that is not spectacularly disorganized" (*GV*, 210 [198]).

By "apparently classical code," Barthes refers, of course, to
the alphabetical order of the titles, each followed by a paragraph or
two of what seems to be commentary, as in a commonplace book.
But consider the choice of the thirteen "A" titles: *Actif/réactif; L'adjectif; L'aise; Le démon de l'analogie; Au tableau noir; L'argent; Le
vaisseau Argo; L'arrogance; Le geste de l'aruspice; L'assentiment,
non le choix; Vérité et assertion; L'atopie; L'autonymie.*[7] No two are
quite parallel: *Actif* is an adjective, *L'adjectif* a noun. In *Actif* the
*A* is the first letter, in *L'adjectif* it follows the article, in *L'aise* it isn't
sounded at all, and in the fourth title the *A* only appears in the
fourth word. Again, some of the titles are abstractions (*Vérité et
assertion*), while others designate a specific place (*Au tableau noir*)
or a proper name (*Le vaisseau Argo*). The seemingly orderly
sequence of parallel items is thus no more than a form of etiquette,
as if to say that once these codes are established, the author can
then do precisely as he pleases.

Consider what happens in a relatively long text under *F*,
(placed "next to" the tiny "Fourier ou Flaubert?") called "Le cercle
de fragments." It begins with an infinitive:

> Écrire par fragments; les fragments sont alors des pierres sur
> le pourtoir du cercle; je m'étale en rond: tout mon petit uni-
> vers en miettes; au centre, quoi?
>
> To write by fragments; the fragments are then so many stones
> on the perimeter of the circle: I spread myself around: my
> whole little universe in crumbs; at the center, what? (*BBB*,
> 92–93 [96–97])

But then the "I" whose universe is dispersed in little crumbs
(*miettes*) becomes a "he": "His first, or nearly first text (1942) consists of fragments." A little narrative of Barthes's career follows—
its Gidean beginnings, the lexias of *S/Z*, the fact that "he already
regarded the wrestling match as a series of fragments"—a narrative
interrupted as the author pauses to cite himself in *Mythologies*. Here
is the "novelistic" without the continuity of the "novel," the narrative
that presents its subject from different pronominal perspectives and
then, once removed, in his own earlier writings. But in the fourth
paragraph, narrative gives way to a rumination on the word:

> Not only is the fragment cut off from its neighbors, but
> even within each fragment parataxis reigns. This is clear if

you make an index of these little pieces; for each of them, the
assemblage of referents is heteroclite; it is like a parlor game:
"Take the words: *fragment, circle, Gide, wrestling match, asyndeton, painting, discourse, Zen, intermezzo;* make up a discourse
which can link them together." And that would quite simply
be this very fragment. The index of a text, then, is not only an
instrument of reference; it is itself a text, a second text which
is the *relief* (remainder and asperity) of the first: what is wandering (interrupted) in the rationality of the sentences.
(*BBB*, 93)

Here Barthes's "parlor game" ("Jeu de bouts rimés") links together
nine nouns that stand synecdochically for the whole: the "circle" of
"fragments," first learned from Gide and observed in the "wrestling
match"; the "figure of short-circuiting," which is "asyndeton" and
which operates in the picture Barthes tries to paint (paragraph 5)
in which the "naive" attempt to "connect detail to detail" leads to
the most "unexpected 'conclusions' "; the "abrupt, separated, broken openings" of Zen (paragraph 7; in Zen Buddhism, says Barthes,
"the fragment" [like the haiku] is *torin;* it implies an immediate
delight: it is a fantasy of discourse"). This fantasy of "discourse" (the
eighth term in Barthes's lyric string) can, he says, come to you anywhere: "in the cafe, on the train, talking to a friend (it arises laterally
to what he says or what I say); then you take out your notebook, to
jot down not a 'thought' but something like a strike, what would
once have been called a 'turn' [*un vers*]."

And, indeed, the whole "circle of fragments" has now taken a
lyric verse "turn." The last of Barthes's key terms is *intermezzo,* and
in paragraph 8 we read:

> . . . the fragment is like the musical idea of a song cycle . . .
> each piece is self-sufficient and yet it is never anything but the
> interstice of its neighbors. . . . The man who has best under-
> stood and practiced the aesthetic of the fragment (before
> Webern) is perhaps Schumann; he called the fragment an
> "intermezzo"; he increased the intermezzi within his works as
> he went on composing: everything he produced was ultimately
> *intercalated:* but between what and what? What is the meaning
> of a pure series of interruptions? (*BBB*, 94)

The musical analogy leads into the coda of what is surely a
poetic discourse, even if Barthes never allows it to "solidify" into
the prose poem that is its intertext: "The fragment has its ideal: a
high condensation, not of thought, or of wisdom, or of truth (as in
the Maxim), but of music: 'development' would be countered
by 'tone,' something articulated and sung, a diction: here it is *timbre*
which should reign. Webern's *small pieces:* no cadence: with what
sovereignty he *turns short!*" (*BBB*, 94–95). Note that the "small
pieces" bring us back to the "universe in crumbs" of the opening

paragraph, to the stones on the perimeter of the writer's circle. The "development" of the whole has been, as Barthes says of the Webern fragment, not one of thought or of wisdom or of truth, but of music; it is a "development" characterized by "a high condensation"—it "*turns short.*"

To reach the conclusion of this particular section of *Barthes par Barthes* is to realize that the "circle of fragments" of the title has been not so much described or talked about as enacted. Barthes invents no characters or plot and yet the fragment is surely fictive, if not fictional, in its development. The speaking subject is dispersed in the circle of fragments; pronouns and tenses shift, abstraction alternates with image, and bits of narrative are *intercalated* into the meditative structure. The form of the whole is what Barthes calls "discontinuous and combinatory": the "juxtaposition of things," the "next to," creates a postmodern analogue to the definition poem or riddle. The prose, highly condensed, alliterative and assonantal (e.g., "des pierres sur le pourtoir du cercle"), mimes "le cercle des fragments," moving, as it does, from writing to reading to wrestling, from parlor game to painting to Zen koan to the musical phrase. There are nine key words and nine paragraphs: in the ninth, we read that the musical fragment has a " 'tone,' something articulated and sung, a diction." And of course "diction" is Barthes's own domain.

## II

One of the later fragments in *Barthes par Barthes* is called "*On le sait.*" In the Farrar, Straus edition, Richard Howard translates this title as "*As we know.*" Barthes writes:

An apparently expletive expression ("as we know," "it is well known that . . .") is put at the start of certain developments: he ascribes to current opinion, to common knowledge, the proposition from which he will start out: his endeavor to react against a banality. And often what he must oppose is not the banality of common opinion but his own; the discourse which comes to him initially is banal, and it is only by struggling against the original banality that, gradually, he writes. Suppose he is to describe his situation in a Tangier bar—what he first manages to say is that the place is the site of an "interior language": a fine discovery! He then attempts to get rid of this importuning banality and to fish out of it some fragment of an idea with which he might have some relation of desire: the Sentence! Once this object is named, everything is saved; whatever he writes (this is not a question of performance), it will always be a vested discourse, in which the body will make its appearance (banality is discourse without body). In other words, what he writes proceeds from a *corrected* banality. (*BBB*, 137)

The title poem of John Ashbery's *As We Know*, published within four years of *Barthes by Barthes*, exemplifies precisely the struggl[e] against the original banality" of which Barthes speaks:

All that we see is penetrated by it—
The distant treetops with their steeple (so
Innocent), the stair, the windows' fixed flashing—
Pierced full of holes by the evil that is not evil,
The romance that is not mysterious, the life that is not life,
A present that is elsewhere.

And further in the small capitulations
Of the dance, you rub elbows with it,
Finger it. That day you did it
Was the day you had to stop, because the doing
Involved the whole fabric, there was no other way to appear.
You slid down on your knees
For those precious jewels of spring water
Planted on the moss, before they got soaked up
And you teetered on the edge of this
Calm street with its sidewalks, its traffic

As though they are coming to get you.
But there was no one in the noon glare,
Only birds like secrets to find out about
And a home to get to, one of these days.

The light that was shadowed then
Was seen to be our lives,
Everything about us that love might wish to examine,
Then put away for a certain length of time, until
The whole is to be reviewed, and we turned
Toward each other, to each other.
The way we had come was all we could see
And it crept up on us, embarrassed
That there is so much to tell now, really now.[8]

One's first impulse is to read this as a kind of riddle poem. Its rhetoric of paradox prompts us to try to name the mysterious "it" that penetrates the "distant treetops" and "the windows' fixed flashing," the "it" with which "you rub elbows" in the second stanza and which finally "crept up on us" in the fourth. But Ashbery's is not a Romantic longing for what Harold Bloom has called the "slight transcendence," nor do I take the speaking subject of the poem to be, in the Bloomian sense, a "spent seer."[9] On the contrary, Ashbery's "As we know" is the Barthean "On le sait," the "apparently expletive expression" that is the poet's given. And the "original banality" is, as in Barthes's case, not that of "common opinion" but the poet's own, in that his discourse cannot but intersect with the public discourses that surround it. "The distant treetops with their steeple (so / Innocent)," "the windows' fixed flashing," "those precious jewels of spring water / Planted on the moss"—these Romantic trappings constitute the "importuning banality" against which Ashbery's speaking subject struggles as he sets in motion his own "vested discourse."[10]

"Suppose," writes Barthes, "he [the author] is to describe his situation in a Tangier bar—what he first manages to say is that the place is the site of an 'interior language': a fine discovery! He then attempts to get rid of this importuning banality and to fish out of it some fragment of an idea with which he might have some relation of desire." Just so, the "I" of "As We Know" begins by referring to childhood settings as if they were stills in some old Hollywood movie: the "distant treetops with their steeple (so / Innocent)" of small-town America, a "stair" down which a "you" presumably "slid down on your knees" and who "teetered on the edge of this / Calm street with its sidewalks, its traffic, / As though they are coming to get you." And of course, just when you think "they are coming to get you," there is, mysteriously, "no one in the noon glare." No one, that is, except "birds like secrets to find out about."

Here is what Barthes calls "a *corrected* banality." For in the lexicon of childhood cliché, birds are not really "like secrets to find out about." Indeed, we cannot penetrate their "secrets" any more than we can determine whether the "home" of the following line is a place where the poet has already been or simply the projection of his desire. Indeed, the poem introduces clichés only to subvert them in its refusal to make the necessary connections. The "windows' fixed flashing" admits no possibility of seeing through the glass. We know neither what "That day you did it" refers to nor why this was also "the day you had to stop." The explanatory phrase "because the doing / Involved the whole fabric" is a proposition as emptied of signification as is the title, "As We Know." Throughout Ashbery's poem, the speaker's "present" continues to be, as he says, "elsewhere."

"At the center, what?" asks Barthes in "Le cercle des fragments." Ashbery's poem poses the same question. The final stanza opens with the proposition:

> The light that was shadowed then
> Was seen to be our lives. . . .

So reasonable, so relaxed is this statement, that we are all but persuaded by its "argument," until we stop to consider that the syntactic equation between "light" and "lives" is never justified semantically. The passive construction ("Was seen to be"), moreover, gives us no clue as to who it is that "sees" things this way. Indeed, the passage is dominated by what Barthes calls "the aesthetic of the empty sign." "Everything," "a certain length of time," "until," "The way we had come"—none of these pseudoconnectives construct a coherent story about "us." There is only the recognition that "there is so much to tell now, really now." And it is this urgent need to keep "telling" that is the poet's final "corrected banality." "There's so much to tell!"—it is a standard cliché of conversation when two people who have been separated for some time meet. And "really now" is a standard expletive of reinforcement. Yet, given the context, what can "really now" intensify but the poem's pervading stress on absence, on the intangibility of identity? Even such separate particles as the words "no one" in the third stanza coalesce into the glare of "noon."

"As We Know" is, as we know, a poem and hence, so the common wisdom would have it, quite different from a slice of Barthean prose. Or is it? "As a rule," writes Lawrence Kramer in *Music and Poetry: The Nineteenth Century and After,* "an Ashbery poem does not articulate a process, but simply lets a textured consciousness persist shimmeringly for a given duration, which is presented as something like an *objet trouvé.* Within that duration, the voices of the poem participate in the continuous flow of the present, without imposing any shape on it. . . . The nature of this flow is to be quirky, inconsistently coherent, and, contrary to conventional expectations, non-linear."[11] To put it another way, lineation, stanzaic structure, indeed the whole visual arrangement of the poem constitute one aspect of the "original banality" against which the postmodern poem must struggle. The lineation is, for that matter, purposely unobtrusive, the lines ranging from six to sixteen syllables and seeming to succeed one another as best they can. No sooner is an iambic flow established, as in "the way we had come was all we could see," than Ashbery, so to speak, "makes it ugly":

> And it crept up on us, embarrassed
> That there is so much to tell now, really now.

Ashbery's sound structure is almost willfully antilyric even as his images refuse to be anchored in any kind of coherent system. "The continuity of the ego," as Kramer says, "dissolves experience instead of integrating it. The mind becomes the only constant presence, and it presides over a continuous recession of objects into absence, some of which it is reluctant to let go" (p. 219).

The same thing could be said of the Barthes fragment. Lineation aside, we are dealing with two very similar modes of writing. In both cases, the fragmentary, discontinuous form breaks up what Barthes calls "the smooth finish, the composition, discourse constructed to give a final meaning to what one says, which is the general rule of all past rhetoric" (*GV,* 209 [198]). Again, in both cases,

the personal pronoun is unstable, the author representing himself
sometimes as "I," sometimes as "he" or "you." " 'I,' " says Barthes,
"is the pronoun of the image-repertoire; 'he' . . . is the pronoun of
distance. . . . 'You' can be taken as the pronoun of accusation . . .
but also as the 'you' of the writing operator, who puts himself . . .
in position to disengage the scriptor from the subject" (*GV*, 216).
Similarly, Ashbery says:

> The personal pronouns in my work very often seem to be like
> variables in an equation. "You" can be myself or it can be
> another person, someone whom I'm addressing, and so can
> "he" and "she" for that matter and "we." . . . my point is that
> it doesn't really matter very much, that we are somehow all
> aspects of a consciousness giving rise to the poem. . . . I find
> it very easy to move from one person in the sense of a pro-
> noun to another and this again helps to produce a kind of
> polyphony in my poetry. . . .[12]

Polyphony, in such writing, replaces the pattern of crisis and resolution to which we are accustomed in nineteenth-century writing.
The conflict between self and other that animates such Romantic
poems as Keats's "Ode to a Nightingale" gives way to the fluidity of
consciousness, a loosening of syntactical connections that allows
experience to *happen* rather than to make sense.

The same process of discovery, this time in more radical form,
occurs in *Three Poems*, Ashbery's pivotal text of the early seventies,
a text that could easily have as its epigraph Barthes's "On le sait."
Here is the opening of the first "poem," "The New Spirit":

> I thought that if I could put it all down, that would be one
> way. And next the thought came to me that to leave all out
> would be another, and truer, way.
>
>> clean-washed sea
>>
>>> The flowers were.
>
> These are examples of leaving out. But, forget as we will,
> something soon comes to stand in their place. Not the truth,
> perhaps, but—yourself. It is you who made this, therefore you
> are true. But the truth has passed on
>
>> to divide all.
>
> Have I awakened? Or is this sleep again? Another form of
> sleep? There is no profile in the massed days ahead. They are
> impersonal as mountains whose tops are hidden in cloud. The
> middle of the journey, before the sands are reversed: a place
> of ideal quiet.
>
> You are my calm world. This is my happiness. To stand, to go
> forward into it. The cost is enormous. Too much for one life.
>
> There are some old photographs which show the event. It
> makes sense to stand there, passing. The people who are

there—few, against this side of the air. They made a sign,
were making a sign. Turning on yourself as a leaf, you miss
the third and last chance. They don't suffer the way people
do. True. But it is your last chance, this time, the last chance
to escape the ball

of contradictions, that is heavier than gravity bringing all
down to the level. And nothing to be undone.[13]

It is customary to read "The New Spirit" as a prose poem that
charts a difficult rebirth process set in motion by a mid-life crisis.
Harold Bloom, in what is the classic statement of this position,
argues that the poem is "addressed by *I*, John Ashbery writing to
*You*, Ashbery as he is in process of becoming"; *I*, that is to say, as
what Yeats called the "antithetical" self addressing the "primary"
*You*. Bloom further finds a "beautiful and simple design" in the text:
"First, self-acceptance of the minimal anomalies we have become. . . . Second, [the necessity of] the wintry reduction of that
conferred self," and third, "a movement to the *you* and to reimagining of the *I*, with a realization that the *you* has been transformed
already, through the soul's experience as a builder of the art of
love."[14]

But the Yeatsian dialectic of primary and antithetical, the Ste-
vensian reimagining of the First Idea, become, in Ashbery's text, a
springboard to something quite different. For, when we look closely
at the language of "The New Spirit," we cannot help being struck
by what we might call its "background noise" or static—the constant
interruption or undercutting of "beautiful and simple design[s]" by
parody, pastiche, and the lampooning of the self, whether that self
is designated as "I," "you," "we," or "he."

The poem opens by positing an all-but-impossible choice—"to
put it all down" or "to leave all out"—and then equivocates by putting down a great deal that is nevertheless not the confessional or
revelatory "it" we might have expected. It is an irony not unchar-
acteristic of Wallace Stevens—one thinks, for example, of "Le Mon-
ocle de Mon Oncle"—but here the irony is itself called into question
by the curious use of allusion. For the very positing of the choice, as
Ashbery presents it, is a pastiche of Robert Frost's already ironic
treatment of the rationalization of one's choices in "The Road Not
Taken," a poem to which Ashbery specifically alludes in "The System," where we read: "You discovered that there was a fork in the
road, so first you followed what seemed to be the less promising, or
at any rate the more obvious of the two branches until you felt you
had a good idea of where it led. Then you returned to investigate
the more tangled way . . ." (*TP*, 90).

"Leaving all out," as Ashbery presents it, provides us with two
imagistic fragments—"clean-washed sea" and "The flowers were"—

"examples," not so much of "leaving out," as of banality, as if to say that the mere mention of "sea" and "flowers" should put us in a poetic frame of mind. And, sure enough, the poet now announces that "forget as we will, something soon comes to stand in their place." Here the substitution of "forget as we will" for "try as we will" inverts the meaning of the homely adage: obviously, if we "forget" the images, they will be replaced by something else. And "It is you who made this, therefore you are true" has a faint Tin Pan Alley echo, as in "They asked me how I knew/My true love was true"—an absurdity not resolved by the subsequent information that "the truth has passed on / to divide all."

In the consciousness of the postmodern poet, fragments of earlier poetry float to the surface, not to be satirized as in, say, Eliot's work, or to make the past contemporaneous with the present as in Pound, but as the "blank parody" Fredric Jameson has defined as pastiche, which is to say, the neutral mimicry that takes place when there is no longer a norm to satirize or parodize.[15] When Ashbery's speaker asks, "Have I awakened? Or is this sleep again?" he is not satirizing Keats's "Ode to a Nightingale" ("Was it a vision? Do I wake or sleep?"). Rather, the question is latent in his poetic discourse as a central question about imagination and reality that haunts our culture. But because the terms are no longer Keats's, because Ashbery cannot quite believe in a magic realm where "I cannot see what flowers are at my feet / Or what soft incense hangs upon the boughs," the Keats motif is just a faint echo—"Have I awakened? Or is this sleep again? Another form of sleep?"—leading to the recognition that "There is no profile in the massed days ahead." Those "massed days" are, in an allusion now to Wordsworth rather than Keats, "impersonal as mountains whose tops are hidden in cloud," but the metaphor is dropped just as abruptly as it is introduced. The speaking voice clings to the assurance of clichés: "The middle of the journey, before the sands are reversed." *Il mezzo del cammin* is traditionally a dramatic turning point, a moment of crisis, but here it is "a place of ideal quiet," a "calm world." And when the poet contemplates the journey ahead, he takes refuge in clichés: "The cost is enormous." "Too much for one life."

Indeed, there is no access to the "event" itself but only to "some old photographs which show the event." And these old photographs don't, in fact, "show the event" but only the image of an event. "It makes sense," the poet says, "to stand there, passing." But since we don't know where "there" is, and since when one "stands," one cannot be "passing," except, say, on an escalator, in which case "the event" is no longer present, "It" does not, in fact, "make sense." Where, for that matter, is "this side of the air"? It is a question we don't stop to ask because what is foregrounded is the rhyme:

> The people who are there—
> few, against this side of the air.

The faceless and nameless "people" now make "a sign" (correction, "were making a sign") because that's what we expect in stories about "The middle of the journey," stories in which choices must be made between putting it all down and leaving it out, stories in which "The cost is enormous," and where the hero, "Turning on [himself] as a leaf" (note the fairy-tale motif here) "miss[es] the third and last chance."

All the banalities of popular romance are here: the middle of the journey, mountains whose tops are hidden by cloud, the reversal of the sands of time, the enormous cost ("Too much for one life"), the proffering of "a sign," the "third and last chance," the cliché that there are those (animals) who "don't suffer the way people do." And when, as in this sentence, rhyme is introduced—

> They don't suffer the way people do.
> True—

it is the rhyming refrain of pop song rather than the semantically charged rhyme of a Yeats or Blake. "The third and last chance" is, oddly, not a chance to hit the ball, as in baseball, but a chance to escape it, and this "ball / of contradictions, that is heavier than gravity" recalls, again without quite parodying it, Marvell's "Let us roll all / Our sweetness up into one ball / And tear our pleasures with rough strife / Through the iron gate of life." There is, in any case, as the final twist of the cliché has it, "nothing to be undone." The archaism of this phrase, with its ambiguous syntax (it can be either a declarative sentence fragment or an imperative) further calls attention to the vast storehouse of stock images—a kind of bogus Spiritus Mundi—which we draw upon in our own speech and writing.

The great feat of "The New Spirit" is not, I think, its "beautiful and simple" tripartite design but Ashbery's ability to modulate the linguistic units just discussed into repeated new and startling juxtapositions, even as his text gradually moves out of the realm of cliché to what Barthes calls "a corrected banality." "Nothing to be undone" becomes "There is nothing to be done" (*TP*, 6): the mountains, "whose tops are hidden in cloud," begin to "stand forth in a relief all their own" (*TP*, 9). The verse pastiche of Eliot's *Four Quartets* ("We must remember to keep asking it the same question / Until the repeated question and the same silence become answer," *TP*, 6–7) gives way to the recognition that "there is no way or rather . . . everything is a way," that "Today is cooler or warmer than yesterday" (*TP*, 17–18).

Throughout *Three Poems,* as most readers have remarked, Ashbery alludes to the loss of love, more specifically to the failure of a love relationship and the gradual acceptance of that failure. To "correct" the banality of one's language is thus, in a larger sense, to abandon the self-pity and self-regard that accompanies the breakup of an affair. It is in this sense that we must understand the conclusion of *Three Poems*. The last paragraph reads:

> A vast wetness as of sea and air combined, a single smooth, anonymous matrix without surface or depth was the product of these new changes. It no longer mattered very much whether prayers were answered with concrete events or the oracle gave a convincing reply, for there was no longer anyone to care in the old sense of caring. There were new people watching and waiting, conjugating in this way the distance and emptiness, transforming the scarcely noticeable bleakness into something both intimate and noble. The performance had ended, the audience streamed out; the applause still echoed in the empty hall. But the idea of the spectacle as something to be acted out and absorbed still hung in the air long after the last spectator had gone home to sleep. (*TP*, 118)

Ashbery does nothing so simple as to avoid his earlier use of clichés altogether in the interest of an "original" private language. There is, the poet knows, no purely original language. As in the opening of Goethe's *Wilhelm Meister,* when the performance ended, "the audience streamed out; the applause still echoed in the empty hall," and "the idea of the spectacle still hung in the air." These locutions are only too familiar. But the spectacle now belongs to "the last spectator," which is to say to the poet himself as well as to his reader, and it has become "a single smooth, anonymous matrix without surface or depth."

Literature, Barthes suggests, can no longer coincide with the function of *mathesis,* which is his word for "a complete field of knowledge." We live "in a profuse world, and what we learn about it is made known immediately, but we are bombarded by fragmentary, controlled bits of information. . . . For centuries, literature was both a *mathesis* and a *mimesis,* with its correlative metalanguage: reflection. Today the text is a *semiosis*"; that is to say, "a *mise en scène of signifiance*" (*GV,* 237–38 [225]).

It is precisely such *mise en scène* that we witness in a work like Ashbery's *Three Poems.* A "fictive" narrative that is not quite fictional, a poetic text that is not, strictly speaking, a poem, Ashbery's "prose" text marks a decisive swerve away from the mathesis of its modernist precursors. Eliot's "fragments" "shored against" the poet's "ruin" here give way to a delight in the very discontinuity and *mise en scène* of fragmentation. As in Barthes's *Empire of Signs,* it is *l'à côté de,* the *next to,* that provides the pleasure of the text. As we know . . .

*Chapter Fourteen*

# "Voice Whisht Through

# Thither Flood":

## *Steve McCaffery's* Panopticon

## *and* North of Intention

**P**anopticon" was the name given by Jeremy Bentham in 1791 to a proposed form of prison "of circular shape having cells built round and fully exposed toward a central 'well,' whence the warders could at all times observe the prisoners" (*OED*). "In a Panopticon prison," wrote Bentham, "there ought not any where be a single foot square, on which man or boy shall be able to plant himself . . . under any assurance of not being observed." Further: not only is the inmate visible to the supervisor, he is visible *only* to the supervisor, cut off, as he is by the prison design, from any contact with those in adjoining cells. This frightening image—and real prisons, for example, the penitentiary at Millbank, London, were originally constructed according to Bentham's plan—furnished Michel Foucault with one of his central paradigms for the operation of power in post-Enlightenment society. "The Panopticon," observed Foucault in *Discipline and Punish* (1975), is "a generalizable model of functioning; a way of defining power relations in terms of the everyday life of men. . . . It is the diagram of a mechanism of power reduced to its ideal form. . . . It is in fact a figure of political technology that may and must be detached from any specific use."[1]

Powerful as this paradigm of "enlightened" surveillance is, its applicability to our postmodern media age may be questionable. The "ideology of power," Jean Baudrillard suggests in *Simulations* (1983), has itself been replaced by the "*scenario* of power," there being no "reality" behind the simulacra that confront us. "The territory no longer precedes the map, nor survives it. Henceforth, it is the map that precedes the territory."[2] In the case, for instance, of a "TV-verité" spectacle like the much publicized saga of the Loud family of California, watched by twenty million Americans in 1971, "the eye of TV is no longer the source of an absolute gaze, and the ideal of control is no longer that of transparency. The latter still presupposes an objective space (that of the Renaissance) and the omnipotence of a despotic gaze," whereas the TV model abolishes any imperative to submit to that gaze or model since, as Baudrillard puts it, " 'YOU are the model!' . . . the event is you" (p. 53). Thus, "No more violence or surveillance: only 'information,' " which is to say, "The End of the Panopticon" (p. 49).

It is this "generation by models of a real without origin or reality: a hyperreal" (p. 2) that provides the context for the astonishing verbal works—sound poems, fictions, manifestos, essays—of the Canadian writer Steve McCaffery. McCaffery's own *Panopticon* turns the Benthamite model inside out: the "place where everything is visible" (*OED*) becomes, on the contrary, the place where nothing is.[3] The very layout of this unpaginated book—with its paste-up cancels and overprints, its mixed type fonts, horizontal black and white bands of "simultaneous" verbal material, its partial and equivocal replicas of Vesalius's anatomical drawings, and its titles that do little to shed light on the material they introduce—suggests that the time of central "wells," from which all "individuals" are to be "observed," has long since passed.

The first long prose section of *Panopticon* opens with the sentence "The focus moves to a woman writing." But we soon come to see that there is no focus. Is this middle-aged "woman writing" the same as the woman of the frontispiece who "EMERGES FROM HER BATH TOWELS HERSELF DRY AND COMMENCES DRESSING"? Is she the "woman reading" who is next introduced? As McCaffery puts it, in the account of the film script that this first narrative purports to represent, "The reception is weak and the conversation frequently fades. There is a pause in the reading. Some words get lost."

In a 1976 essay called "The Death of the Subject" (heavily revised and reprinted in *North of Intention* under the title "Diminished Reference and the Model Reader"), McCaffery refers to the poet's task as that of "demystify[ing] the referential fallacy of language," and he adds, "Reference, I take it, is that kind of blindness a window makes of the pane it is."[4] Blindness, in the sense that a window pane, being transparent, is not "seen" at all by the viewer who looks through it at the "reality" on the other side. It is this view of language as mere transom that McCaffery, like the "language" poets of the United States with whom he has been closely associated, wants to explode. The aim is "to let the word receive your sight. . . . To let the direct, empirical experience of a grapheme replace what the signifier in a word will always try to discharge: its signified and referent."

Which is by no means to argue that signification doesn't matter. The phrase "referential fallacy" has been so widely misunderstood by detractors of the "language" movement that in the revised version of "The Death of the Subject" McCaffery has avoided it altogether, the point being that, however inevitably "reference enters the flow of language to become immanent within the very thing it structures" (*NI*, 17), it is possible to produce a discourse that does not merely "reproduce a world according to the *logic* of the referent"—the window theory—but that foregrounds the materiality of the signifier, thus preventing the word from becoming primarily a "textual commodity to be ideally consumed by a 'comprehending' reader" (*NI*, 21). The writing, that is to say, "is less the exclusive code of the author, theologically transmitted *down* to a reader recipient than a productive field which a reader can enter to mobilize significations" (*NI*, 14). A useful analogy for this "shift from sign consumption to sign production" is the biotopological form known as the Klein worm, "a form which differs from conventional geometric forms in its characteristic absence of both inner and outer surfaces" (*NI*, 20). Like the Klein worm, the new literary text "is without 'walls' with milieu and constellation replacing syntax." Such a text "demands a reading 'on' rather than a reading 'through' " (*NI*, 21).

What this means in the case of McCaffery's own *Panopticon* is that the familiar narrative elements of pop fiction or film—a woman toweling herself dry in front of a mirror, a woman reaching for a silver (or gold) object, the image of a typewriter carriage with a note in it, the appearance of a man with a gun who reads the note—are subjected to a kind of metaphoric "typeover," to use a term found on the word-processor key board. The narrative bits, that is to say, remain intact, the text returning to them at specific points, but "complication" is introduced, not at the level of plot, but at the level of language event:

> Again and again. And so on. And so forth. And back again.
> And once more. And one more time. Again and again and
> through and through. Over and over again and again.

Moments anticipatory of. Then cancelled. And then again.
And again and again. And over and over. . . . And even more.
And yet again. And still further. And further to that. And
that. And more than that. And even more and
nonetheless. . . .

Modulating such temporal and spatial markers, McCaffery gradually
turns his "Klein worm" into what might more accurately be called
a (Gertrude) Stein worm, for example:

Supposing that. Then again. Supposing that. But then again.
Then a why. Then a meanwhile. Then a during. Supposing
that. Then a there. Supposing that. And as well. Supposing
that. Then as well. Supposing that. And as well. Supposing
that. Then as well. Supposing that. Then again and then and
why and where they go and why truth and why woman. Supposing that.

And this prose unit ends with two pages of "and on and on and on,"
the two words forming a kind of concrete poem made of successive
columns.

"A TEXTUAL SYSTEM," as McCaffery puts it in the section
called "Summer Alibi," "UNDERLIES EVERY TEXTUAL EVENT
THAT CONSTITUTES THIS STORY." In "Summer Alibi," a first-
person narrator recounts his stay in a psychiatric hospital whose
mindless regimentation is, so to speak, reinscribed in the series of
inserted sentence fragments (printed in caps) that refer to the comparable regimentation syntax imposes upon language: "THE MEAN-
ING OF THE MARK RESIDES IN LANGUAGE AS AN
INSTITUTION." But, neither at the level of story nor within the
capitalized word blocks is such institutionalization allowed full sway:
at every turn, *Panopticon* shifts registers, alternates viewing "chan-
nels," and disrupts whatever linear mechanisms we might expect.

The high point, at least for me, comes in the section near the
end which splices two "plots," the first, again in caps, written in the
style of what we might call, to paraphrase an Ashbery title, the
Deconstruction Manual, the second a Harlequin romance–cum–
morality-play plot in which all the proper names refer to ethical or
philosophical abstractions:

THE TEXTUAL INTENTION PRESUPPOSES READERS WHO KNOW THE
It was a very hot day and her name was Ambiguity. She
LANGUAGE CONSPIRACY IN OPERATION. THE MARK IS NOT IN-
never did know anyone else. When she got on the boat to go
ITSELF BUT IN-RELATION-TO-OTHER-MARKS. THE MARK SEEKS
to Clarity her elder brother stayed at home. This is his
THE SEEKER OF THE SYSTEM BEHIND THE EVENTS. THE MARK
story. Sitting in a darkroom in Potential with the bottle
INSCRIBES THE I WHICH IS THE HER IN THE IT WHICH MEANING

always open by his bed side. When I get older i'm going to
MOVES THROUGH. A TEXTUAL SYSTEM UNDERLIES EVERY TEXTUAL
write and what i'm going to write is the story of my sister.
EVENT THAT CONSTITUTES "THIS STORY." HOWEVER THE TEXTUAL
Everyone coughed. The day was hot. As she moved towards
HERMENEUSIS OF "THIS STORY" DOES NOT NECESSARILY COMPRISE A
the river the sheets fell from her hands. Someone picked
TOTAL TEXTUAL READING. THE TELEOLOGY OF "THIS PHRASE BEFORE
them up. After she thanked him she decided that was the
YOU" DOES NOT SIGNIFY PER SE BUT RATHER MOVES TOWARD A
time to change her name. After she changed her name she

"Voice
Whisht
through
Thither
Flood"

and so on. Most readers, I suspect, will read the two print bands separately rather than follow the text consecutively from line to line. But interestingly, "theory" (the A band) and "praxis" (B) don't quite travel on parallel tracks: five pages into the section, the former begins to borrow plot elements and linguistic analogues from the latter:

she had six months at the most to live. They talked a
ONE SHOWS THE SKELETAL FORM OF A YOUNG WOMAN. THE WOMAN
lot about sincerity. She really liked his shoes. Every
PREVIOUS TO THIS HAD RETIRED TO HER STUDY AFTER A BRIEF
christmas she bought him new ones. He always got her
VISIT TO THE BATHROOM WHERE SHE REPLACED A CAKE OF PALE
chocolates. Sometimes she felt hurt. It grew to be a
AND METHOL FLAVOURED SOAP UPON THE BATH EDGE. THE FIGURE

Here indeed is "THE LANGUAGE CONSPIRACY IN OPERATION," the text implying that the pure banality of the dislocated "story," with its muffled and illogical references to love, sex, family trauma, alcoholism, and death, exerts so strong a pull on conceptual statement that the latter becomes a parasite of the former. But then again the "theory" line also exerts a counterpull on the original story, the A and B threads finally coming together in the reference to "A SEQUENCE OF WORDS TO FORM AS MISSIVE LOOPS AND SPOOLS WITH A CURIOUS ANALOGY TO A WIRED CIRCUIT OR A GATHERING OF PUBIC HAIR."

By this time the reader has been made aware that in McCaffery's anti-Panopticon, the traditional distance between subject and object has undergone a curious implosion. Where, that is to say, do we locate the central gaze of surveillance, the authorial voice? Is it the narrator of the horizontal gray band of the final section, which relates such items as "HER BODY REMAINED MOTIONLESS AND A COLD LUMP CAME INTO HIS THROAT"? Or is it the voice of the caption underneath that band, which reads,

"The word. The word read. The writing of the word read. The quotation of the writing of the word write. The removal of the quotation of the writing of the word write. The writing of the word word"? In this "multi-panel language environment,"[5] the reader may choose whether to foreground the "readerly" or the "writerly," the discourse of the signified or that of the signifier. "WHEREVER A BOOK CLOSES," as McCaffery puts it, "A WRITING BEGINS."

*North of Intention* takes up the same questions from a more overtly discursive perspective. Like Charles Bernstein's *Content's Dream,*[6] McCaffery's book is not adequately described as a collection of critical essays, including, as it does, lineated texts like "(Immanent) (Critique)" and "Lyric's Larynx," collage writings ("Anti-Phonies: Fred Wah's *Pictograms from the Interior of B.C.*"), mock-catalogs ("Blood. Rust. Capital. Bloodstream"), and interviews ("Nothing Is Forgotten but the Talk of How to Talk"). Again like *Content's Dream, North of Intention* must be understood as a set of *working papers,* that is to say, as an exploratory text in which the poet tries to deal with the problems that haunt his own practice.

The notion of working paper is closely related to the question of style. Like many of the poets loosely associated with the "language" movement (here Susan Howe is the great exception), McCaffery writes a critical prose that seems, on a first reading, irritatingly jargon ridden—indeed, downright ugly:

> The cipheral text involves the replacement of a traditionally "readerly" function . . . by a first order experience of graphemes, their material tension and relationships and their *sign potentiality* as substance, hypo-verbal units simultaneously pushing towards, yet resisting, contextual significations. The cipher thus offers a strategic method for motivating non-commodital productivities that cast both writer and reader into an identical work process. (*NI,* 19–20)

A "first order experience of graphemes," "hypo-verbal units," "non-commodital productivities"—is this way of putting things, one wonders, the way to reform the debased and cliché-ridden language of the dominant culture? Or is it, as the vociferous detractors of the "language" movement would have it, merely one jargon replacing another?

These are not easy questions to answer but I think contextualization may help. The "ugliness," the intentional ungainliness of much of the prose written by McCaffery, as by Charles Bernstein or Bruce Andrews or Lyn Hejinian or Johanna Drucker, must be understood as a reaction against two currents. The first is the "genteel," gentlemanly (or ladylike), graciously tactful and elegant style of what is still called "the man of letters," as that style—British Oxbridge in origin—is carried on in, say, the pages of the *Sewanee Review* or in Hilton Kramer's *New Criterion*. Laymen and -women, which is to say predominantly well-educated Ivy League men and women who are not "narrow specialists" in English literature or philosophy, can read Edmund Wilson or Randall Jarrell or Mary McCarthy or, more recently, Joseph Epstein or Annie Dillard with pleasure and relative ease. At the same time, or so it seems to a writer like McCaffery, to privilege such prose is equivalent to paying homage to a world in which "style" remains largely a function of class.

"Voice Whisht through Thither Flood"

The second and less overt object of attack is the casual speech-based, notebook- or diary-style poetics of the Beats and New York poets: "First thought, best thought" (Allen Ginsberg), or "I don't even like rhythm, assonance, all that stuff" (Frank O'Hara). The casual approach to poetry ("Nobody," remarks a tongue-in-cheek O'Hara in "Personism: A Manifesto," "should experience anything they don't need to, if they don't need poetry bully for them. I like the movies too")[7] of the upbeat "hot" sixties is oddly out of step with the ethos of our own cool and analytic fin de siècle. The renewed Marxist emphasis on poetry as material production, circulation, and distribution implies that the text should exhibit signs of the *work* that produced it, a work that has less to do with individual intention than with the general economy within which it functions. "If they don't like poetry bully for them. I like the movies too" is thus replaced by questions like, What is "poetry" that "they" should or should not like it? What conditions "liking"? Who are "they"? Why do "they" prefer "movies," or, for that matter, TV? And what do all these sign systems have in common?

I don't mean to imply, however, that McCaffery's essays (or Bernstein's or Ron Silliman's) are dry, intellectual, philosophical, or political tracts. On the contrary: despite the proliferation of Marxist and poststructuralist buzz words, the constant references to French theory (Derrida, Barthes, Lacan, Deleuze and Guattari, Kristeva, Baudrillard) and to the Frankfurt school (Benjamin, Adorno, Horkheimer, Habermas), *North of Intention* comes across primarily—and paradoxically—as a work of the imagination. Indeed, what McCaffery has in common with such precursors as O'Hara or Ginsberg, Creeley or Rothenberg, is best defined as *passion:* a rhetorical and verbal energy that won't let its subject go, a determination to use every available resource—pun, metaphor, epigraph, pictogram, aphorism, and especially example—to keep the reader on the edge of his or her seat.

Take, for example, "*The Martyrology* as Paragram," McCaffery's reading of his fellow poet b. p. nichol's [Barry Nichol's] ongoing long poem by that name. The "normal" way for McCaffery to proceed would be to relate Nichol's work to that of other avant-garde poets, to the Olson tradition, and so on. But McCaffery does no such thing: he begins with three epigraphs from "classical" writers: Dryden, Addison, and Novalis. The Dryden epigraph comes from *Mac Flecknoe:*

> Chuse for thy command
> Some peaceful province in Acrostic land;
> There may'st thou *Wings* display, and *Altars* raise,
> And torture one poor word a thousand ways.
>
> (*NI,* 58)

For Dryden, banishment to Acrostic land is, of course, the deserved fate of dunces like Shadwell, to whom the words above are addressed by the "high priest" of bogus poets, Flecknoe. But McCaffery inverts Dryden's mock heroic, artfully making the belittled "torture [of] one poor word a thousand ways" the linchpin of his analysis. "We will," he begins matter-of-factly, "focus on the ludic features of *The Martyrology,* those varieties of wordplay (pun, homophony palindrome anagram, paragram, charade) which relate writing to the limits of intentionality and the Subject's own relation to meaning" (*NI,* 58). Note that these "ludic features" are precisely those Dryden so blithely relegated to the likes of Shadwell. And indeed, in the next paragraph, McCaffery proposes a "rather perverse genealogy" for Nichol's poem, "a genealogy to carry us not through *The Martyrology*'s 'natural and obvious' antecedents (Olson, Zukofsky, the Utaniki or Japanese poetic journal and Gertrude Stein) but through the Plato of the *Cratylus,* Peter Ramus, Edmund Spenser, the German Romanticism and *witz* theoreticians of the Jena School (the Schlegels, Novalis, J. P. Richter), Freud, Lacan and M. M. Bakhtin" (*NI,* 59).

Having set this pseudoscholastic scene, McCaffery pulls out all stops, conducting his tour through "The Scene of Witz" (the German Romantic version of *wit*), "The Paragram" ("A text is paragrammatic . . . in the sense that its organization of words . . . grammar, and syntax is challenged by the infinite possibilities provided by letters or phonemes combining to form networks of signification not accessible through conventional reading habits"), "The Unconscious As a Lettered Production," "Cratylean Linguistics through Ramus," and "Michael Bakhtin: The Dialogic Utterance." Along the way, Nichol's poetry is presented and re-presented as a kind of encyclopedia of *witz,* paragram, charade, etymology, and heteroglossia. Here, for example, is McCaffery's reading of the following Nichol charade:

> vision
> riddle we are all well rid of
> the dull pass of wisdom
>
> w is d
> o ma

i'n h and
the me's restated
at the pen's tip's ink
at the tongue's noise
w in d

"Voice
Whisht
through
Thither
Flood"

> In line 2 "riddle" announces its own homophonic split: "rid"
> "dull" which, thus motivated as a duality, generate a phrasing
> around themselves ("we are well rid of / the dull pass of wis-
> dom"). The homophonic play results in "wisdom" which is
> then submitted to a charade: "wisdom / w is d / o ma." At the
> same time meanings coagulate through a sort of back-forma-
> tion or reverse charade. In line 7, for instance, "the me's re-
> stated" suggests a centripetal motivation that would draw the
> letters into a space that would generate "themes restated" . . .
> the paragrammatic function in *The Martyrology* is clearly that
> of remotivation of the single letter as an agent of semantic dis-
> tribution. (*NI*, 65–66)

Here McCaffery's analysis is reminiscent of Khlebnikov and Kru-
chenykh's famous manifesto, *Bukva kak takovya* (The letter as such)
of 1913. And the link is not just coincidental. Just as Khlebnikov
used *zaum* (transrational or "beyondsense" language) to bypass the
"ideological Realism" (*NI*, 39) of the late nineteenth century, so
McCaffery's focus on the letter (or phoneme) itself, far from being
motivated by a narrow formalism, has a political thrust. "The paragram," he writes, "as the 'other' region of sign economy forms part
of language's *unconscious* dimension where meanings exist as lettered proliferations and escape the closure of an aggregate intention" (*NI*, 66).

It is this "eruption through fissures," this "casting off of
compression," this "abrupt emergence of plurality through ruptures
in the transmissions of the poem's semantic order" (*NI*, 69) that is,
for McCaffery, the key to poetic innovation in our time. In the interview with Andrew Payne ("Nothing Is Forgotten but the Talk of How
to Talk"), McCaffery argues that it is naively romantic to think of
*sound poetry* as the Dadaesque "privileging of the pre-linguistic,
child-sound, the Rousseauist dream of immediate-intuitive communication, all of which tended to a reinscription of a supposed presymbolic order in a present, self-authenticating instant" (*NI*, 111–
12). On the contrary, he suggests, sound poetry must be understood
"through the economic notion of outlay," which is to say "particular
lines of obliteration in an economy in which 'profit' necessarily
entails 'loss.' " Sound devices, anagrams, paragrams—these, far
from constituting a textual recuperation and self-presence, work
toward the "utter dismantling of the notion of TRUTH as anything
exterior to the signifying practice" (*NI*, 125). The pronoun, for example, can be treated as "a locus for a simultaneous break-down and

recomposition (without prediction) of the Subject" (*NI*, 112). Or again, the pun can be—and here McCaffery paraphrases Marshall McLuhan—"the most disarming fusion of language and music, the chordal resonance of a contradiction, a linguistic push beyond choice and the logic of exclusion towards the polyphony of indecision" (*NI*, 87).

*The polyphony of indecision*—again and again, McCaffery stresses the need to free poetic language from the co-option by what he calls the "media model" (*NI*, 42), the model of "linguistic transparency" and grammatical rule:

> Grammar is a repressive mechanism designed to regulate the free flow of language. Imposing its constraints upon non-gravitational circulation, it realizes a centred (and centralized) meaning through a specific mode of temporalization. Grammatically realized meaning is a postponed reward attained by arrival at the end of a horizontal, linearized sequence of words. Grammar precludes the possibility of meaning being an active, local agent functioning within a polymorphous, polysemous space of parts and sub-particles; it commands hierarchy, subordination, and postponement. (*NI*, 97–98)

This is the core of McCaffery's poetics, and it needs, I think, to be taken very seriously at a time when the Anglo-American poetry establishment seems once again to be working on the philistine assumption (an assumption one would think I. A. Richards and the New Criticism had dispelled half a century ago) that "subject matter" is something evidently separable from "formal" concerns. In a recent essay for the *New Criterion* called "The Confinement of Free Verse," for example, the poet-novelist Brad Leithauser writes:

> Whether the formal poet chooses to uphold the prosodic contract, or to break it, or initially to conceal its terms, his or her poem addresses the reader on two levels. The underlying reassurance and occasional trickeries that the poem's prosody engineers are related to, but ultimately detachable from, the poem's content. Prosody is a game played with the reader's legitimate expectations, and the more firmly these are established, the more fruitfully can the game's designer meet or upset them.[8]

The implication of Leithauser's statement is that the poet first chooses *what to say* and only then determines what form might be the appropriate vehicle. The container and the thing contained—bifurcation theories, it seems, are once again with us, partly, no doubt, in keeping with the nostalgia for a lost "gentility" (oh, for the good old days of sonnets and blank verse!) that characterizes the late eighties, but also perhaps because the new wave of "protest poetry," whether written by women or blacks or Chicanos or Asian-

Americans, is judged, in the middlebrow press and in special-interest journals, by its message rather than its medium. X's poem "about" rape, Y's "about" Nicaragua—to thus characterize poems trivializes the whole poetic process.

Indeed, this is one of the lessons *North of Intention* teaches us. Language, as McCaffery argues so passionately, is itself always already politically and ideologically motivated. The positioning of the subject as panoptic and controlling "I," for example, is itself a political statement that calls into question whatever professedly "radical" content is expressed in that I's monologue. Grammar, after all, is not just some sort of outer shell, protecting and embellishing an inner core of "meaning"; on the contrary, as McCaffery puts it, "It commands hierarchy, subordination, and postponement"—the delayed gratification incumbent upon the completion of meaning.

In articulating his "new poetics," McCaffery draws not only on Baudrillard's theory of the *simulacrum* and the Lacanian view of the unconscious as itself a structured language but, closer to home, on the work of John Cage and especially on the writings of his fellow Canadian Marshall McLuhan. Both, McCaffery suggests, are often misrepresented as optimists, as technocrats suspiciously enthusiastic about our electronic age. But, as McLuhan once put it, "The new environment shaped by electronic technology is a cannibalistic one that eats people. To survive one must study the habits of cannibals" (*NI*, 87).

Precisely. It is McCaffery's great merit that he takes the issues of mediaspeak head on, that he has studied "the habits of the cannibals" and made "Writing Degree Xerox" his own. His is a prolegomena to the dispersal of the Panopticon's inmates, the release of the "imprisoned" words and letters from their cells. I conclude with a brief example of such release: here is the opening of the poetic charade called "(Immanent) (Critique)," written in 1983:

> It should even then have still appeared
> where this is. Notby me ans of an a-
> ppropriation but as a sampl e question
> -ing which space this was. If one choo
> sesto elimina te suspicion or suspen
> d (not by a thread but in aliquid) a
> certain break implicit in the sign. Th
> -en what mar ksar e thes e?
> (*NI*, 165)

What marks are these? The investigation has just begun.

*Chapter Fifteen*

# "Collision or Collusion

# with History":

## *Susan Howe's* Articulation

## of Sound Forms in Time

Flocks roost before dark
Coveys nestle and settle

Meditation of a world's vast Memory

Predominance pitched across history
Collision or collusion with history
— Howe, *Articulation*

*T*he two words are identical except for a single letter: according to the *OED, collision* means "1. The action of colliding or forcibly striking or dashing together; violent encounter of a moving body with another. 2a. The coming together of sounds with harsh effect. 3. *fig.* Encounter of opposed ideas, interests, etc. clashing, hostile encounter." Whereas *collusion* means "Secret agreement or understanding for purposes of trickery or fraud; underhand scheming or working with another; deceit, fraud, trickery."

What a difference a phoneme makes! One's *collision* with history may be accidental, an encounter of opposed ideas neither planned nor anticipated. One's *collusion,* on the other hand, is by definition premeditated. Attentiveness to such difference (/*i*/ versus /*uw*/) has always distinguished Susan Howe's "history poems" from those of her contemporaries. The opening page of the early chapbook, *The Western Borders,* for example, looks like this:

IRELAND

sandycove
keel

a snicker hugged this face that lay in sand cliffs are cruel yes
cruel rock and rook of cloud past all    and Ireland a place
circled round by the sea    and Ibex a creature with horns like
a goat    and Ibis a bird that in Egypt I've read was worshipped while living and honored when dead    galloped
across the laugh of it all    for a light sand floor am told to go
down    while hills hem dawn into

SONG

o

name my cottage Merlin
shutter it in trees
Merlin of the Dark Gate,
deep calling into Sleep[1]

*Ireland, sandycove:* one thinks immediately of James Joyce's *Ulysses* as well as of Samuel Beckett's Irish novels, but what about *keel?* The apposition suggests that keel is another place in Ireland (there is, of course, a city called Keele in England), but in fact it's not on the map. Rather, the keel of a boat appears just where one would expect it—at Sandycove beach, and the block of words that now follows opens with reference to a "face that lay in sand / cliffs." We don't know whose face, but it doesn't matter, the poem's aim being to anchor that face in the Irish shorescape of *rock* and *rook, Ibex* ("a creature with / horns like a goat") and *Ibis* ("a bird that / in Egypt I've read was worshipped while living / and honored when dead"). Like *collision/collusion, rock/rook* and *Ibex/Ibis* are look-alike and sound-alike pairs whose meanings are divergent. "I've read," "am told to go down": these are the only references to a first-person speaker and they do little to make the "I" present, the first being parenthetical, the second omitting both pronoun and agent (the construction is passive) and subordinating individual selfhood to proverbial action ("go down" to the ships, "go down" to the sea, etc.). This is the Ireland, not of Susan Howe observer/traveler/poet (at least not overtly), but of myth and legend, a place where "hills hem dawn into / SONG" and Merlin of the Dark Gate shares the space with the alien ibis and ibex.

From the first, Howe has been interested in such mythic/historical configurations of "sound forms." Untypically, she seems to have had no apprentice period during which she wrote derivatively "in the style" of X or Y. No doubt her relatively late start as a poet had something to do with this: she began as a visual artist and was in her late thirties by the time her first book appeared. Her visual sense is reflected everywhere in her attention to page design—how the whole page is going to *look* is central to her poetics. Concrete poetry may well have been an influence; there is not, in any case, so much as a trace in Howe's work of the "I-centered" mode so ubiquitous in the poetry of the early seventies. Except for "Buffalo. 12.7.41" in *Pythagorean Silence*[2] (and this only in part), I know of no Howe poem that is directly autobiographical or personal. I don't mean to suggest that the work isn't emotive, but its emotive contours depend upon the collisions (and sometimes, it may be, collusions) of three codes—the historical, the mythic, the linguistic—all three, it should be added, as informed by an urgent, if highly individual, feminist perspective.

Perhaps the best place to show how this process works is in Howe's most recent book, *Articulation of Sound Forms in Time*.[3] On the first and otherwise blank page of this long poem, we read:

from seaweed said nor repossess rest
scape esaid

*From seaweed said:* the story to be told here, if not quite "Spelt from Sybil's Leaves" (Hopkins), evidently consists of fragments shored from the ocean of our American subconscious. Yet one cannot "respossess [the] rest"; or, since what is said from seaweed cannot be repossessed, one must rest one's case. Or just rest. "Scape" may refer either to the seascape or to the landscape or, most plausibly, it may be an abridged version of *escape:* "there is, no escape, he said," or "let it be said from what the seaweed said" (cf. Eliot's "What the Thunder Said"), no escape, moreover, from the desire to repossess the rest.

Obviously there are many ways of interpreting the eight words in these two lines, which is not to say that they can mean anything we want them to mean. We know from this introduction that an attempt will be made to "repossess" something lost, something primordial. The sound structure of the passage, with its slant rhyme of *sea/weed* and *repossess/rest,* its consonance of *weed/said/esaid,* and its alliteration of *s*'s (nine out of forty-one characters) and assonance of *e*'s and *o*'s, enacts a ritual of repossession we can hear and see. And so small are the individual morphemes—*from, said, scape, esaid*—that we process them one by one, with difficulty. This "saying" "from seaweed" will evidently not be easy.

Who speaks these opening lines? The voice is impersonal, part bardic, part comic—a voice akin to Beckett's in *Ping* or *Lessness*. But the abrupt opening is immediately juxtaposed to a document, a text taken from the "real" world, namely, an *"EXTRACT from a LETTER (dated June 8th, 1781,) of Stephen Williams to President Styles"*:

"In looking over my papers I found a copy of a paper left by the Rev. Hope Atherton, the first minister of Hatfield, who was ordained May 10th, 1670. This Mr. Atherton went out with the forces (commanded by Capt. Turner, captain of the garrison soldiers, and Capt. Holyoke of the county militia) against the Indians at the falls above Deerfield, in May, 1676. In the fight, upon their retreat, Mr. Atherton was unhorsed and separated from the company, wandered in the woods some days and then got into Hadley, which is on the east side of the Connecticut River. But the fight was on the west side. Mr. Atherton gave account that he had offered to surrender himself to the enemy, but they would not receive him. Many people were not willing to give credit to this account, suggesting he was beside himself. This occasioned him to publish to his congregation and leave in writing the account I enclose to you. I had the paper from which this is copied, from his only son Jonathan Wells, Esq., who was in the fight and lived afterward at Deerfield and was intimately acquainted with the *Indians* after the war, did himself inform *me* that the *Indians* told *him* that after the fall fight, a little man with a black coat and without any hat, came toward them, but they were afraid and ran from him, thinking it was the Englishman's God, etc., etc."

I reproduce this document in its entirety so that we can see what Howe does with her *donnée*. For *Articulation of Sound Forms in Time* is by no means a retelling of the Hope Atherton story or the invention of an up-to-date analogue that points to the "relevance" of the Indian Wars to our own time. Still, the story, as gleaned from the letter above and from a number of old chronicles of New England towns, is inscribed everywhere in Howe's poem. It draws, for example, upon the basic paradox that the Reverend Hope Atherton, ostensibly a Man of God, would accompany the Colonial militia on an Indian raid. And further, that having somehow gotten separated "from the company," this "little man with a black coat and without a hat," as one chronicle calls him, would surrender himself to the Indians, only to be rejected by them as suspect, indeed perhaps the "Englishman's God." Suspect as well to his own people, who, upon his return to Hatfield, refused to believe his story. Atherton, in the words of the chronicle, "never recovered from the exposure" and died within the year, an isolated figure, indeed something of a pariah.[4]

Such "untraceable wandering" culminating in the "nimbus of extinction" is, so Howe believes, a ubiquitous fact of early New England history, and its burden continues to haunt our language. *Artic-*

*ulations of Sound Forms in Time* draws upon, not only Hope Atherton's story, but also the captivity narratives Howe has been studying, specifically the 1682 *Narrative of the Captivity and Restoration of Mrs. Mary Rowlandson,* which is the subject of a Howe essay published in *Temblor,* an essay more accurately described as a poetic collage-text, creating meanings, as it does, from its stark juxtapositions of seemingly disparate materials: Colonial documents, biblical extracts, historical records, quotations from Mary Rowlandson's own narrative, poems by Anne Bradstreet, snatches of Algonquin speech, Howe's own poetic response to the "events" recorded by Rowlandson, and so on.[5]

The text begins with the words *"Nawwatuck note-shem/I came from farre,"* immediately followed by Rowlandson's eloquent opening:

> *Come, behold the works of the Lord, what dissolations he has made in the Earth.* Of thirty-seven persons who were in this one House, none escaped either present death, or a bitter captivity, save only one, who might say as he. *Job* 1.15. *And I only am escaped alone to tell the News.* (CMR, 113)

Rowlandson's narrative, Howe tells us, "is both a microcosm of colonial imperialist history, and a prophecy of our contemporary repudiation of alterity, anonymity, darkness" (CMR, 113).

Taken out of context, this claim may sound bombastic, but, remarkably, Howe makes us believe that this "first narrative written by a white American woman" really functions as such a microcosm. As in the case of Atherton, it is the seeming contradictions of Mary Rowlandson's story that interest the poet. On the one hand, there is Rowlandson's "thoroughly reactionary figuralism," her obsessive orthodoxy, her view of her Indian captors, who actually never touched her, as " 'murderous wretches,' 'bloody heathen,' 'hellhounds,' 'ravenous bears,' and 'wolves' "; she recalls " 'the roaring, and singing, and dancing, and yelling of those black creatures in the night, which made the place a lively resemblance of hell' " (CMR, 115). Yet, as Howe puts it, "The idiosyncratic syntax of Mary Rowlandson's closed structure refuses closure": the white woman captured by these "wolves" also remembers incidents like the following: " 'Now must we pack up and be gone from this Thicket.' . . . As we went along they killed a *Deer,* with a young one in her. They gave me a piece of the *Fawn,* and it was so young and tender, that one might eat the bones as well as the flesh, and yet I thought it very good" (CMR, 119). Indeed, Rowlandson's "risky retrospective narrative" (CMR, 117) everywhere exceeds its author's intentions: She "saw what she did not see said what she did not say" (CMR, 121).

Here, as in *My Emily Dickinson,*[6] Howe displays an uncanny ability to enter the experience of an actual historical woman and to make that experience her own. It is not, of course, a question of accuracy: who knows what went through the mind of the "real" Mary Rowlandson? The "real" Emily Dickinson? Rather, the seeming authenticity, the credibility of Howe's documentary collage, depends upon the positioning of the language field, the juxtaposition, for example, of flat narrative ("Mary White Rowlandson, one of the seven children of John and Joane White, was born in England. The date of her birth is uncertain, but the Whites crossed to Salem, Massachusetts in 1638") with extracts from Deuteronomy and Psalms, from Increase Mather's *Brief History of King Philip's War,* and so on. Howe's is never the reductive capsule biography that trivializes so many of the sonnets in Robert Lowell's *History:* for instance, "Margaret Fuller Drowned":

> You had everything to rattle the men who wrote.
> The first American woman? Margaret Fuller . . .
> In a white nightgown, your hair fallen long
> at the foot of the foremast, you just forty,
> your husband Angelo thirty, your Angelino one—
> all drowned with brief anguish together. . . . Your fire-call,
> your voice, was like thorns crackling under a pot,
> you knew the Church burdens and infects as all dead forms,
> however gallant and lovely in their life;
> progress is not by renunciation.[7]

Here the poet positions himself securely outside his character's consciousness, condescendingly addressing her as "you" and telling her about the "brief anguish" she must have felt; he wraps up Fuller's complex philosophical position in phrases like "you knew the Church burdens and infects as all dead forms." Indeed, Fuller serves Lowell primarily as a vehicle for his own clear-eyed recognition that "progress is not by renunciation"; he endows her with the stereotypical rebellious spirit that wants out from under: "your fire-call, / your voice, was like thorns crackling under a pot."

Howe, on the other hand, forces us to see and smell and take part in Mary Rowlandson's eleven weeks and five days in the wilderness, even as she examines her subject's words from the vantage point of a sophisticated poet writing in the late twentieth century: "This is a crime story in a large and violent place. Too large for subject and object. Only a few of her captors have names. Nearly all of their names are wrong" (CMR, 120).

The wrongness of names in the old chronicles of New England provides the poet with an opportunity to call the very act of naming into question. In a sermon of 28 May 1670, reproduced in one of Howe's sources for *Articulation of Sound Forms in Time,* the Reverend Hope Atherton recalls that when, in his forest wanderings, he came face to face with the Indians, "I spake such language as I thought they understood." But evidently "they" did not understand, and this failure-to-understand what the other is saying becomes Howe's point of departure in *Articulation*. Here is the opening poem of part 1, "Hope Atherton's Wanderings":

Prest try to set after grandmother
revived by and laid down left ly
little distant each other and fro
Saw digression hobbling driftwood
forage two rotted beans & etc.
Redy to faint slaughter story so
Gone and signal through deep water
Mr. Atherton's story Hope Atherton

We note right away that in this poem Hope Atherton is not a "character," with such and such traits and a definable history. The "Wanderings" of Howe's title (there are sixteen sections in part 1, ranging in length from two to fifteen lines)[8] are presented, not as articulations *of* time—not, that is to say, as accounts of what happened— but *in* time, in the time it takes to articulate the "sound forms" themselves. Thus poem #1 is a deceptive square (eight lines of predominantly eight- and nine-syllable lines), which tries to contain, both visually and aurally, the linguistic displacements produced by a faulty memory.

The first word, *Prest,* may refer to Atherton's condition: he was pressed by the Indians to "try to set after" his own people, perhaps after he was revived by a grandmother and left to lie ("ly") in the forest. But the absence of the subject or object of "Prest" brings other meanings into play: "oppressed," "impressed," "presto." We cannot be sure whom "he" (if there is a he here) was "revived by," or whose "grandmother" is involved. As for "left ly," the tiny suffix makes it possible to bring to bear a whole host of *-ly* words: "left mercilessly," "left unkindly," "left ruthlessly," "left carelessly." The reader is given all these options; he or she can construct any number of scenarios in which two people are lying a "little distant [from] each other" and moving to and "fro." It is only dimly, after all, that we can reconstruct the Colonial/Indian conflict, with the colonists' "hobbling driftwood" and "forag[ing] two rotted beans & etc."—"& etc." suggests that it is what comes after speech ceases that matters—as well as the militia's "Redy to faint slaughter story," a story, "Mr. Atherton's story," now "so gone" that it can only come to us as a "signal through deep water."

Not only does Howe frequently decompose, transpose, and refigure the word (as in *ly*); she consistently breaks down or, as John Cage would put it, "demilitarizes" the syntax of her verbal units. Reading the poem above, one is never sure what subject pronoun goes with what verb, what object follows a given preposition, which of two nouns a participle is modifying, what phrases a conjunction connects, and so on. An extraordinarily taut sound structure—e.g., "revived *by* and *l*aid down *left ly*"—holds in check a syntax that all but breaks down into babble. Indeed, by poem #8 all the connectives that make up "normal" syntax have been abandoned:

> rest chrondriacal lunacy
>
> velc cello viable toil
>
> quench conch uncannunc
>
> drumm amonoosuck ythian

Is "rest" a noun or a verb and how does it relate to "chondriacal" (hyperchondriacal?) "lunacy"? In line 2, "velc" may be an abridgment of "velocity," which doesn't help us make sense of the intricately sounded catalog "velc cello viable toil"; in line 3, "uncannunc" contains both "uncanny" and "annunciation" (the prophecy, perhaps of the "conch" shell which cannot "quench" our thirst); in line 4, the Anglo-Saxon ("drumm"), Indian ("amonoosuck"), and Greek ("ythian") come together in a "collusion" that makes us wonder if the "rest" isn't some sort of hyperchondriacal lunacy on Atherton's part. Or, some would say, a "lunacy" on the poet's part as well.

What justifies such extreme verbal and syntactic deconstruction, a decomposition that has become something of a Howe signature? Is the obscurity of *Articulation* merely pretentious? Confronted by lines like "velc cello viable toil," many readers have closed the book, concluding that the poet is talking only to herself. The charges leveled against "language poetry" in general—obscurity, abstraction, lack of emotion, the absence of lyric selfhood—all these can easily be leveled at Susan Howe. Yet even readers unsympathetic to her work, readers who claim a book like *Articulation* is too private, that it isn't really "about" anything, will, I submit, find themselves repeating lines like "velc cello viable toil," if for no other apparent value than their complex music, the way *e, l,* and *c* in the first word reappear as *cel* in the second, or the way the *v, e, l* in *velc* reappear in the very different sounding word *viable,* the latter also containing the *l* of *cello* and *toil.*

Is this then jabberwocky, nonsense verse? If Howe wants to talk about Hope Atherton's mission to the Indians or apply the "themes" implicit in the tale—Colonial greed, Puritan zeal, the fruits of imperialism, the loneliness of exile, the inability to communicate with the Other—to the contemporary situation, why doesn't she just get on with it? Even a prose piece like the Mary Rowlandson essay is, after all, by and large comprehensible.

It would be easy to counter that the breakdown of articulation, which is the poem's subject, is embodied in the actual breakdown of the language, that the fragmentation of the universe is somehow mirrored in the fragmentary nature of the text. But the fact is that in Howe's work, as in Charles Bernstein's or Lyn Hejinian's, demilitarization of syntax may well function in precisely the opposite way—namely, as a response to the all-too-ordered, indeed formulaic, syntax that characterizes the typical "workshop" poem. Thus a recent poem called "Thoreau" by Rodney Jones begins:

> It is when I work on the old Volvo,
> lying on my back among the sockets,
> wrenches, nuts, and bolts,
> with the asphalt grinding the skin
> over my shoulderblades and with the cold grease
> dripping onto my eyeglasses,
> that I think of Thoreau
> on his morning walks around the pond
> dreaming of self-sufficiency.[9]

This is certainly more accessible, more "natural" than the opening of Howe's "Thorow":

> Go on the Scout they say
> They will go near Swegachey
>
> I have snow shoes and Indian shoes
>
> Idea of my present
> not my silence[10]

But if emotion can be thus neatly packaged ("It is when I work on the old Volvo . . . that I think of Thoreau"), if "poetry" is really no more than such reportage, the straight-but-sensitive "nuts and bolts" talk broken arbitrarily into line segments so as to remind us that, yes, this is a poem, why read in the first place rather than turning on the TV? The Phil Donahue show, for instance, where the Reverend Hope Atherton would no doubt be a popular guest: his decision to leave his congregation and accompany the militia on a war raid might well prompt some heated debate, caller A telling Phil that the minister should have stayed home and minded his own business, caller B insisting that, on the contrary, Atherton's action was "compassionate" and "caring."

How, then, to give life to a "poem including history"? There is Ezra Pound's way: the documentary collage with its "repeats" and "subject rhymes," but, except in prose pieces like the Mary Rowlandson essay, this way is not Howe's. Emily Dickinson's punning, wordplay, and syntactic ambiguity are closer:

> The Zeros taught Us—Phosporus—
> We learned to like the Fire
> By handling Glaciers—when a Boy—
> And Tinder—guessed—by power[11]

but Dickinson provides no direct models for the history poem. In this regard, Hart Crane, one of Howe's favorite poets, provides a kind of bridge (no pun on his "epic of America" intended) between Dickinson and Howe:

> Often beneath the wave, wide from this ledge
> The dice of drowned men's bones he saw bequeathed
> An embassy. Their numbers as he watched,
> Beat on the dusty shore and were obscured.
>
> —"At Melville's Tomb"[12]

How, Harriet Monroe wanted to know about these lines, could "dice" have "bequeathed / An embassy"? How could "numbers" "Beat on the dusty shore"? And as for line 8, "The portent wound in corridors of shells," is "wound" a verb or a noun?[13]

Crane's syntax looks ahead to Howe's, as does, to some extent, his "myth of America." But Howe's austere, condensed "articulation of sound forms" does not really resemble Crane's oracular, apocalyptic vision; indeed, the missing link in the Dickinson-Crane-Howe chain is surely the late Beckett. Here is the opening paragraph of "Lessness":

> Ruins true refuge long last towards which so many false time out of mind. All sides endlessness earth sky as one no sound no stir. Grey face two pale blue little body heart beating only upright. Blacked out fallen open four walls over backwards true refuge issueless.[14]

If we lineate and scan Beckett's last sentence:

> Blácked oút fállen ópen fóur wálls óver báckwârds trúe réfuge
> íssuelêss

we are close to Howe's structures of apposition, for example:

> Pósit gáze lével dimínish lámp and asléep(sélv)cánnot sée

In both cases, there seems to be a felt need to remake a language that in its ordinary, which is to say formulaic, state (see Rodney Jones's "Thoreau" or, for that matter, Robert Lowell's "Margaret Fuller Drowned") cannot approximate the difficulties of what the postmodern poet and her/his readers perceive to be a multitrack experience.

Poem #5, for example, articulates a "sound form" that refers to Hope Atherton's journey home:

> Two blew bird eggs plat
> Habitants before dark
> Little way went mistook awake
> abt again Clay Gully

espied bounds to leop over
Selah cithera Opynne be
5 rails high houselot Cow
Kinsmen I pray you hasten
Furious Nipnet Ninep Ninap
Little Pansett fence with ditch
Clear stumps grubbing ploughing
Clearing the land

"Two blew bird eggs plat": "blew" is a pun on "blue" and "plat" means "flat" as well as the truncated "plate." The image of the "Two blew bird eggs plat" gives a fairy-tale aura to this segment of the journey, as does "Little way went mistook" with its Hansel and Gretel echo. Again, the "bounds to leop over" ["leop" is OE for "leap"] are more than "houselot" divisions, for the real crossing of the poem is over the borders into another language where the "babble-babel" (LMP) is formed from words and sounds taken from Hebrew ("Selah"), Indian ("Nipnet Ninep Ninap"), and English ("Clay Gully"), with the mythological reference to Venus's isle "Cythera" thrown in.

The poems now become increasingly fragmented, gnomic, enigmatic, as if the breakdown depicted is not so much Hope's as that of language itself. Regression sets in, poem #9 going back to Anglo-Saxon origins:

scow aback din

flicker skaeg ne

barge quagg peat

~~sieve catacomb~~

stint chisel sect

and then in #13 to a kind of aphasia, words, now without any modification or relationship, being laid out on the page as follows:

chaotic architect repudiate line Q confine lie link realm
circle a euclidean curtail theme theme toll function coda
severity whey crayon so distant grain scalp gnat carol
omen Cur cornice zed primitive shad sac stone fur bray
tub epoch too tall fum alter rude recess emblem sixty key

Epithets young in a box told as you fly

By this time, Hope's search has become the poet's search. It is the poet who must deal with the "chaotic," must "repudiate" the "line" that "confine[s]," the "euclidean" "circle" too neat in its resolution of "theme theme," and the "severity" of its "coda." But one can also read this poem as dealing with any form of making, of "architect[ure]," the placement of "cornice" and "stone" so as to "alter rude" appearances. And the Indian motif never quite disappears, here found in the reference to "scalp," "gnat," "primitive," and "rude."

In #13, words are spread out insistently on the white ground of the page; in #15, by contrast, words run together:

MoheganToForceImmanenceShotStepSeeShowerFiftyTree
UpConcatenationLessonLittleAKantianEmpiricalMaoris
HumTemporal-spatioLostAreLifeAbstractSoRemotePossess
ReddenBorderViewHaloPastApparitionOpenMostNotion *is*

The "collusion" that forces words into this particular "collision" is oddly painful: the text is, so to speak, wounded, as if to say that the nightmare war with the Savage Other has come back to haunt Hope/ Howe with its "AKantian Empirical" "Force" or "Immanence" of "Mohegan" or "Maori" presence, its reference to "Shot," "Shower," "Fifty Tree," "ReddenBorderView." This particular lyric concludes with a refrain already articulated in #14, a couplet producing a verbal mirror image:

blue glare(essence)cow bed leg extinct draw scribe    sideup
even blue(A)ash-tree fleece comfort (B)draw scribe    upside

"Sideup"/"upside" is a breaking point; after this particular collision, the sequence suddenly shifts to the formal and coherent monologue (#17) of Hope Atherton himself:

Loving Friends and Kindred: —

When I look back

So short in charity and good works

We are a small remnant

Of signal escapes wonderful in themselves

We march from our camp a little

and come home

Lost the beaten track and so

River section dark all this time

We must not worry

how few we are and fall from each other

More than language can express

Hope for the artist in America & etc

This is my birthday

These are the old home trees

On a first reading, this lyric coda seems excessively sentimental as well as unwarranted. Having wandered with great difficulty through the forest of the preceding lyrics, one is, of course, relieved

to come into this clearing, to hear the sermonlike address to "Loving
Friends and Kindred." But the resolution here provided—"We must
not worry / how few we are and fall from each other / More than
language can express / Hope for the artist in America & etc"—is a
shade too easy, given the intractability of the material that has been
put before us. How and why, after all, does Hope become Howe?
How and why is there "Hope for the artist in America"? And finally,
what do we do once we reach the birthday when we settle down
under "the old home trees"?

But perhaps we are meant to feel slightly queasy at this point.
The "old home trees" turn out to be no more than a brief point of
rest en route to the "Corruptible first figure" of part 2, "Taking the
Forest." In the twenty-five meditations that follow, "Hope for the
artist" once again grows dim, in the face of "Collision and impul-
sion," "Lives to be seen pressing and alien." But increasingly, the
focus is now on "Girl with forest shoulder / Girl stuttering out mask
or trick," and the penultimate poem brings us to a vision of "Lost
fact dim outline / Little figure of mother," a "Face seen in a landscape once," with the assurance that "She is and the way She was."

Of this lyric, Howe writes, "It would have been easy to end on
the second to last poem as I have done in readings of it and which
makes it more overtly feminist. It's too easy that way. There are no
answers and life is hard. Hart Crane leaped off the boat to his death;
Hope Atherton was treated like a fool—like Pip in *Moby*. Melville
and Dickinson died in obscurity." And she cites line 9 of the final
poem: "Far flung North Atlantic littorals" (LMP). Indeed, the final
poem is essential:

To kin I call in the Iron-Woods
Turn I to dark Fells last alway

Theirs was an archheathen theme
Soon seen stumbled in lag Clock

Still we call bitterly bitterly
Stern norse terse ethical pathos

Archaic presentiment of rupture
Voicing desire no more from here

Far flung North Atlantic littorals

Lif sails off longing for life
Baldr soars on Alfather's path

Rubble couple on pedestal
Rubble couple Rhythm and Pedestal

Room of dim portraits here there
Wade waist deep maidsworn men

Crumbled masonry windwept hickory

A dark conclusion but nevertheless triumphant. Over against the "Far flung North Atlantic littorals" of Melville, Crane, and Olson—littorals that are also the borders that open the verbal signifier to the possibilities of meaning—the poet sets the "Stern norse terse ethical pathos" of traditional myth, the myths of Lif and Baldr, of the "Rubble couple on pedestal" and the "Room of dim portraits here there." At the end, Old Hickory still triumphs, "Crumbled" though the masonry may be. But Howe's *Articulation of Sound Forms in Time* has opened up the possibilities for difference, for the "presentiment of rupture / Voicing desire no more from here."

"No more from here" because the voicing of desire in *Articulation,* as is Howe's other poems, avoids the personal "I," so pervasive in contemporary lyric. Ostensibly absent and calling no attention to the problems and desires of the "real" Susan Howe, the poet's self is nevertheless inscribed in the linguistic interstices of her poetic text. Howe has been called impersonal, but one could argue that the "muffled discourse from distance," the "collusion with history" in her poetry, is everywhere charged with her presence. She is not, after all, a chronicler, telling us some Indian story from the New England past, but a poet trying to come to terms with *her* New England past, *her* sense of herself vis-à-vis the Colonial settlers' actions, *her* re-creation of the Hope Atherton story in relation to Norse myth as well as to contemporary feminist theory.

Most contemporary feminist poetry takes as emblematic its author's own experience of power relations, her personal struggle with patriarchy, her sense of marginalization, her view of social justice. There are Howe's subjects as well, but in substituting "impersonal" narrative—a narrative made of collage fragments realigned and recharged—for the more usual lyric "I," Howe is suggesting that the personal is always already political, specifically, that the contemporary Irish-American New England woman who is Susan Howe cannot be understood apart from her history. But history also teaches the poet that, however marginalized women have been in American culture and however much men have been the purveyors of power, those who have suffered the loss of the Word are by no means only women. Indeed, what Howe calls the "Occult ferocity of origin" is an obstacle that only a persistent "edging and dodging" will displace if we are serious about "Taking the Forest."

# Notes

**Chapter One:** *Can(n)on to the Right of Us, Can(n)on to the Left of Us: A Plea for Difference*

1.  The sources of these texts are as follows: (1) Lyn Hejinian, *The Guard* (Berkeley, Calif.: Tuumba Press, 1984), unpaginated; (2) John Cage, "Writing through Howl" (1984), forthcoming in a festschrift for Allen Ginsberg's sixtieth birthday, courtesy of John Cage; (3) Michel Leiris, "Le Sceptre miroitant," in "Glossaire," *Mots sans mémoire* (Paris: Gallimard, 1969), p. 111; reprinted in "Special Section: New Translations of Michel Leiris," ed. James Clifford, *Sulfur,* no. 15 (1986): 4—125, on p. 29; (4) Brad Leithauser, "In a Bonsai Nursery," Part 3 of "Dainties: A Suite," *Cats of the Temple* (New York: Alfred A. Knopf, 1986), p. 14; (5) Charles Bernstein, "Dysraphism," in *The Sophist* (Los Angeles: Sun & Moon Press, 1987), p. 44; (6) Jacques Derrida, *Glas,* 2 vols. (Paris: Denoël, 1981), 2:221.

2.  Paul de Man, "Lyrical Voice in Contemporary Theory: Riffaterre and Jauss," in *Lyric Poetry: Beyond the New Criticism,* ed. Chaviva Hosek and Patricia Parker (Ithaca and London: Cornell University Press, 1985), p. 55. This collection is subsequently cited in the text as *LP.*

3.  Charles Bernstein, headnote to "Dysraphism," *Sulfur,* no. 8 (1983): 39. This headnote is omitted in the version of the poem printed in *The Sophist.*

4.  Michel Leiris, "Glossaire: J'y serre mes gloses," in *La Révolution surréaliste* (1925); translated as "Glossary: My Glosses' Ossuary," by Lydia Davis, *Sulfur,* no. 15 (1986): 27.

5.  Geoffrey Hartman, *Saving the Text: Literature/Derrida/Philosophy* (Baltimore and London: Johns Hopkins University Press, 1981), pp. 33–66. "Epiphony in Echoland" is the title of Hartman's second chapter.

6.  See, on this point, the article "Lyric" by James William Johnson in the *Princeton Encyclopedia of Poetry and Poetics,* ed. Alex Preminger et al., enl. ed. (Princeton, N.J.: Princeton University Press, 1974), pp. 460–70, esp. pp. 460–61.

7.  Edward Said, "Opponents, Audiences, Constituencies, and Community," *Critical Inquiry* 9 (September 1982): 4–5.

8. See chap. 13, "Barthes, Ashbery, and the Zero Degree of Genre," below, and my "Introduction," in *Postmodern Genres*, ed. Marjorie Perloff, *Genre* 20, nos. 3–4 (Fall–Winter 1987): 233–40; Cf. Ralph Cohen, "History and Genre," *New Literary History* 17 (Winter 1986): 203–18. Cohen writes, "What acts and assumptions are concealed in the infinitive to *identify?* After all, classifications are undertaken for specific purposes. . . . different authors, readers, critics have different reasons for identifying texts as they do" (p. 205).

9. Roland Barthes, *Le Grain de la voix: Entretiens 1962–1980* (Paris: Editions du Seuil, 1981), p. 210. For an English translation, see *The Grain of the Voice: Interviews 1962–1980*, trans. Linda Coverdale (New York: Hill & Wang, 1985), p. 222.

10. The one exception is David Bromwich's brief (4 pp.) discussion of the Canadian poet Jay Macpherson.

11. Jerome J. McGann, "Tennyson and the Histories of Criticism" (1982), in *The Beauties of Inflections: Literary Investigations in Historical Method and Theory* (Oxford: Clarendon Press, 1985), p. 222. Subsequently cited in the text as *BI*.

12. David Antin, "George Oppen and Poetic Thinking," panel discussion at the Oppen Symposium, University of California, San Diego, 16 May 1986.

13. On this point see Gregory L. Ulmer, *Applied Grammatology: Post(e)-Pedagogy from Jacques Derrida to Joseph Beuys* (Baltimore and London: Johns Hopkins University Press, 1985), chap. 1, passim, esp. pp. 8–9.

14. Charles Bernstein, "Three or Four Things I Know about Him" (1975), in *Content's Dream, Essays 1975–84* (Los Angeles: Sun & Moon Press, 1986), p. 26.

15. Susan Howe, *My Emily Dickinson* (Berkeley, Calif.: North Atlantic Books, 1985), pp. 11–12.

16. Ulmer, *Applied Grammatology*, p. 13.

### Chapter Two: Canon and Loaded Gun: Feminist Poetics and the Avant-Garde

1. Alicia Ostriker, "American Poetry, Now Shaped by Women," *New York Times Book Review*, 9 March 1986, p. 1.

2. Cleanth Brooks, *Modern Poetry and the Tradition*, 2d ed. (New York: Oxford University Press, 1965), pp. xiv–xxiii. Cf. Babette Deutsch, *Poetry in Our Time*, rev. and enl. ed. (New York: Doubleday, Anchor Books, 1963). Deutsch treats Williams more sympathetically than does Brooks and devotes a whole chapter to Pound; nevertheless, she follows New Critics like Brooks in regarding modernism as essentially the creation of Hardy, Yeats, and Frost.

3. See, for example, the admiring essays by Pound, Eliot, Williams, Stevens, R. P. Blackmur, Kenneth Burke, and John Crowe Ransom in *Marianne Moore: A Collection of Critical Essays,* ed. Charles Tomlinson (Englewood Cliffs, N.J.: Prentice-Hall, 1969). Men were, of course, inclined to be somewhat patronizing to Moore; one thinks of Eliot's "compliment" that "Miss Moore's poetry is as feminine as Christina Rossetti's, one never forgets that it is written by a woman; but with both one never thinks of this particularly as anything but a positive virtue" (p. 50). The fact remains that she was one of the few poets praised by her fellow poets as well as by leading critics.

4. Herbert Leibowitz, "Introduction," in *A Celebration of Women & Poetry,* ed. Leibowitz, *Parnassus: Poetry in Review* 12 (Spring–Summer 1985)–13 (Fall–Winter 1985): 6, 15.

5. Alicia Ostriker, *Stealing the Language: The Emergence of Women's Poetry in America* (Boston: Beacon Press, 1986), p. 7. Subsequently cited in the text as *SL.*

6. In *Poetry as Discourse* (London and New York: Methuen, 1983), Anthony Easthope argues that iambic pentameter is "not a neutral form of poetic necessity but a specific historical form producing certain meanings and acting to exclude others. . . . Pentameter comes to power as a neo-classical form and this is inscribed into its defining feature of counterpoint" (pp. 64–65). See Easthope's bibliography for related studies.

7. Susan Howe, *My Emily Dickinson* (Berkeley, Calif.: North Atlantic Books, 1985), pp. 7, 13. Subsequently cited in the text as *MED.*

8. Susan Howe, *Defenestration of Prague* (New York: Kulchur Foundation, 1983), pp. 10, 11.

9. Since this essay was first published (1986), I am happy to report that the latest edition of the *Norton Anthology of American Literature* (1989) does include a series of poems by Lorine Niedecker. Essays on her work are also beginning to appear.

10. In his controversial essay "The Sorrows of American-Jewish Poetry," in *Figures of Capable Imagination* (New York: Seabury Press, 1976), Harold Bloom argues that no American-Jewish poet "of undoubted major status has established himself in a century now more than two-thirds gone" (p. 247). Zukofsky, who is named only to be dismissed, is thus declared ineligible for a canon that includes, aside from the major modernists, Hart Crane, John Crowe Ransom, R. P. Warren, e. e. cummings, Theodore Roethke, and Elizabeth Bishop.

11. My account of Niedecker's life is based on Robert J. Bertholf's introduction to *From This Condensery: The Complete Writings of Lorine Niedecker,* ed. Bertholf (Highlands, N.C.: The Jargon Society, 1985), pp. xxiii–xxx; subsequently cited in the text as *FTC.* See also George Butterick's "Ain't Those the Berries?: The Writings of Lorine Niedecker," *Conjunctions* 8 (1985): 224–38. Butterick is reviewing Bertholf's edition together with that of Cid

Corman, *The Granite Pail: The Selected Poems of Lorine Nie-*
*decker* (Berkeley, Calif.: North Point Press, 1985), subsequently
cited in the text as *GP*.

We are fortunate to have both these editions of Niedecker's
poetry published in one year. But it is only fair to point out that
Bertholf's *Complete Writings* has come in for a good deal of criticism. See Elliot Weinberger, "The New Niedeckers," *Sulfur,* no. 16
(1986): 148–54, for an acute discussion of Bertholf's problematic
handling of the variants of the long poems, as well as of the inadequacy of the notes and cross-referencing.

*12.*  See Jenny Penberthy, review of *The Full Note: Lorine Niedecker*
(London: Interim Press, 1983), in *Sulfur,* no. 12 (1985): 150–52;
Michael Heller, *Conviction's Net of Branches: Essays on the Objec-
tivist Poets and Poetry* (Carbondale and Edwardsville: Southern
Illinois University Press, 1985), pp. 48–57.

*13.*  See Lisa Pater Faranda, ed., *"Between Your House and Mine":*
*The Letters of Lorine Niedecker to Cid Corman, 1960 to 1970*
(Durham, N.C.: Duke University Press, 1986). Faranda's annotations provide much useful—and astonishing—information. See, for
example, the discussion of Niedecker's relationship to Emily Dickinson, pp. 210–12.

*14.*  There have been some recent exceptions. A version of Bertholf's
introduction to *From This Condensery* appears in the *Parnassus*
special issue *Celebration of Women & Poetry. Parnassus,* for that
matter, published a piece on Niedecker as early as 1977: see
Thomas Meyer's "Chapter's Partner" (review of *Blue Chicory*),
*Parnassus: Poetry in Review* 5 (Spring–Summer 1977): 84–91.
See also Jane Augustine, "The Evolution of Matter: Lorine
Niedecker's Aesthetic," *Sagetrieb* 1, no. 2 (Fall 1981): 277–84;
Douglas Crase, "Free and Clean" (review of Niedecker, *From
This Condensery* and *The Granite Pail), Nation,* 15 March 1986,
pp. 309–31. At this writing, Jenny Penberthy's edition of
Niedecker's letters to Zukofsky, with a very full critical and bio-
graphical apparatus, is forthcoming from Duke University Press.
An extract, with important biographical information, is pub-
lished as "Poems from Letters: The Lorine Niedecker–Louis
Zukofsky Correspondence," *Line* 6 (Fall 1985): 3–20.

*15.*  "The Friend" appeared in Marge Piercy, *Circles of Water:
Selected Poems* (New York: Alfred A. Knopf, 1982), p. 39;
reprinted in Ostriker, *SL,* p. 91.

**Chapter Three: Traduit de l'américain: *French Representations***
**of the "New American Poetry"**

*1.*  *L'Espace Amérique,* special issue of *Change* 41 (March 1981): 9.
Subsequently cited in the text as *EA*. Unless otherwise noted, the
translations in this essay are my own.

> The navigation of the ocean which to us signifies
> A M E R I C A
> will cross, successively
> and synchronically

the mountain peak of the *cut up*
the peninsula of the *New York School*
the active space of the *Performing Arts*
the dispersed archipelago of the
*Language Poetry Movement*
the incessant influx of
A F R O A M E R I C A
Our vision unites them and takes them apart.

2. Ezra Pound, "Paris," *Poetry* 1 (1913): 27.

3. *Po&sie*, no. 27 (1983): 57. The first issue of *Po&sie* (1977) is the Olson issue, with translations by Michel Deguy, Jacques Roubaud, and Kenneth White; no. 3 has Pound's "Ecrits sur la musique" and Stein's "Deux textes de *Comment écrire*," both translated by Jacques Roubaud; no. 22 (1982) has Pound's Canto 85, translated by Ghislain Sartoris; and no. 25 features David Antin, Jerome Rothenberg, and Clayton Eshleman in an Ethnopoetics number.
It should be pointed out that *Po&sie* tends to have a wider range of translations from the American than do *Change* or *Action poétique.* Stevens is translated by Linda Orr and Claude Mouchard for no. 12 (1980), an issue that also carries Claude Minière and Margaret Tunstill's translations of Frank O'Hara. Elizabeth Bishop appears in no. 24, Sylvia Plath in no. 22 and again in no. 24, Denise Levertov together with William Carlos Williams in no. 30, Louise Gluck in no. 34. Issue 31 carries a new translation of T. S. Eliot's *Waste Land (La Terre vague)* by Michel Vinaver.

4. *Vingts poètes américains,* bilingual edition, ed. Michel Deguy and Jacques Roubaud, introduction by Jacques Roubaud (Paris: Gallimard-NRF, 1980), p. 9.

5. Emmanuel Hocquard and Claude Royet-Journoud, eds., *21 + 1,* vol. 1: *Poètes américains d'aujourd'hui,* trans. Marc Chénetier, Philippe Jaworski, and Claude Richard; Vol. 2: *American Poets Today* (Montpellier: Delta, 1986).

6. Helen Vendler, ed., *The Harvard Book of Contemporary American Poetry* (Cambridge, Mass.: Harvard University Press, 1984; published in the U.K. as *The Faber Book of Contemporary American Poetry* [London: Faber & Faber, 1986]), p. 16. Subsequently cited in the text as *HB*.

7. There is also the special case of Sylvia Plath. *Ariel* was published by the Gallerie des Femmes in 1978, in a translation by Laure Vernière, and the novel *The Bell Jar* has been translated a number of times. But such commentary as exists on Plath in the poetry journals suggests that this is a case of interest in the melodramatic life and suicide of the poet rather than in her work as such.

8. Dave Smith and David Bottom, eds., *The Morrow Anthology of Younger American Poets* (New York: William R. Morrow, Quill Books, 1985). Subsequently cited in the text as *MA*.

9. Ron Silliman, ed., *In the American Tree* (Orono, Maine: National Poetry Foundation, 1986).

10. Robert Lowell, "Harriet" ("Summer," part 5), in *For Lizzie and Harriet* (New York: Farrar, Straus & Giroux, 1973), p. 15.

11. Mark Strand, "A Morning," in *HB*, p. 327.

12. Harold Bloom, "Dark and Radiant Peripheries: Mark Strand and A. R. Ammons," in *Figures of Capable Imagination* (New York: Seabury Press, 1976), pp. 150–68.

13. Issue after issue of *Change* contains discussion of Mallarmé's language and syntax: see, for example, Mitsou Ronat, "Mallarmé, visible syntaxe," *Change* 26–27 (February 1976): 171–77.

14. For these statistics see the annual compilation in *Les Livres disponibles* (Paris, 1980–). See also *Action poétique, Change,* and *Po&sie* for bibliographical information. Another important anthology is Serge Fauc</br>hereau's *41 poètes américains d'aujourd'hui* (Paris: Les Lettres Nouvelles, 1970). Faucjereau has a section on Objectivists, on Black Mountain poets and the New York school, as well as one entitled "La Nouvelle subjectivité," which does include poetry by James Wright, Galway Kinnell, Louis Simpson, W. S. Merwin, and Robert Bly, and another section called "Nouvelles tendances," with poems by James Merrill, Robert Creeley, and Tom Clark, among others.

15. Jacques Darras, ed., *Arpentage de la poésie contemporaine: 14 portraits-entretiens suivis d'un essai* (Amiens: in 'hui, Trois Cailloux, 1987). Subsequently cited in the text as JD.

16. Pierre Joris is technically also an American. Born in Belgium, he grew up in the United States and has lived both there and abroad.

*Chapter Four: The Pursuit of Number: Yeats, Khlebnikov, and the Mathematics of Modernism*

1. Harold Bloom, *Yeats* (New York: Oxford University Press, 1970), p. 65. Subsequently cited in the text as Bloom.

2. *Collected Works of Velimir Khlebnikov,* vol. 1: *Letters and Theoretical Writings,* trans. Paul Schmidt, ed. Charlotte Douglas (Cambridge, Mass., and London: Harvard University Press, 1987), p. 119. Subsequently cited in the text as *VKCW*.

3. In William Butler Yeats, *Autobiographies* (London: Macmillan, 1955), p. 188.

4. *Letters on Poetry from W. B. Yeats to Dorothy Wellesley* (London and New York: Oxford University Press, 1964), p. 173.

5. William Blake, *Jerusalem, Selected Poems and Prose,* ed. Hazard Adams (New York: Holt, Rinehart & Winston, 1970), p. 126. Subsequently cited in the text as Blake.

6. Ironically, this pull between the mechanism of "mathematical system" and the appeal of numerology is prefigured in Blake's own

writings. In the later prophecies, human history from Adam to Milton is divided into 28 periods or "Churches," and in *Jerusalem*, "Albion" (England) comprises 28 cathedral cities. And so on. For Blake, however, these numbers mark the progressive steps in the movement toward Apocalypse, with its final separation of human redemption from human misery; they are not, as in the case of Yeats and Khlebnikov, variables in the equations that chart the recurrent moments of history. On this point see Northrop Frye, "The Rising of the Moon: A Study of 'A Vision,' " in *An Honoured Guest: New Essays on W. B. Yeats*, ed. Denis Donoghue and J. R. Mulryne (New York: St. Martin's Press, 1966), pp. 8–33, esp. pp. 11–12; Frye, *Fearful Symmetry: A Study of William Blake* (Princeton, N.J.: Princeton University Press, 1969), pp. 256–68; and Bloom, *Yeats*, pp. 52–63.

7.   Alfred North Whitehead, *Science and the Modern World: Lowell Lectures, 1925* (New York: Macmillan, 1946). Subsequently cited in the text as ANW.

8.   Leo Steinberg, *Other Criteria: Confrontations with Twentieth-Century Art* (New York: Oxford University Press, 1972), p. 28.

9.   Samuel Taylor Coleridge, MS 195, in *Inquiring Spirit: A Coleridge Reader*, ed. Kathleen Coburn (New York: Minerva Press, 1968), pp. 251–52.

10.  Henry James, "Preface to *The Ambassadors* (1909)," in *The Art of the Novel: Critical Prefaces by Henry James*, ed. Richard P. Blackmur (New York: Charles Scribner's Sons, 1934), p. 321.

11.  See Raymond Cooke, *Velimir Khlebnikov: A Critical Study* (Cambridge: Cambridge University Press, 1987), p. 99.

12.  W. H. Auden, "Yeats as an Example" (1948), in *The Permanence of Yeats*, ed. James Hall and Martin Steinmann (New York: Collier Books, 1961), p. 309: "However diverse our fundamental beliefs may be, the reaction of most of us to all that occult is, I fancy, the same: How on earth, we wonder, could a man of Yeats's gifts take such nonsense seriously? I have a further bewilderment, which may be due to my English upbringing, one of snobbery. How *could* Yeats, with his great aesthetic appreciation of aristocracy, ancestral houses, ceremonious tradition, take up something so essentially lower-middle class—or should I say Southern Californian—so ineluctably associated with suburban villas and clearly unattractive faces?"

13.  In *Vladimir Tatlin and the Russian Avant-Garde* (New Haven, Conn., and London: Yale University Press, 1983), John Milner explains that Tatlin related the revolutions of the Tower's various halls about their axis to the movements of the planets, as if to say that there is a harmony of rhythm between the processes of human social development and the movement of heavenly bodies. Further, just as Zodiacal Man "relates the stars to the anatomy of the individual human being, Tatlin's tower, seen as an image of collective man, relates celestial rhythms to the anatomy of the social body" (pp. 164–65). Note in fig. 6 that the Tower's deployment

of a circle (the perfect form), sitting on top of a triangle, which signifies the aspiration toward the celestial, the triangle in its turn resting on the solidity of the rectangle beneath it, is a standard figure from astrological-alchemical charts (figs. 7, 8.)

*14.* See Douglas, "Introduction," *VKCW*, pp. 26–27.

*15.* William Butler Yeats, *A Vision* (1937); New York: Macmillan, 1962), p. 8. Subsequently cited in the text as *AV*.

*16.* Frye, "The Rising of the Moon," pp. 28–29.

*17.* Christopher Butler, *Number Symbolism* (London: Routledge & Kegan Paul, 1970), p. 162.

*18.* See Richard Ellmann, *The Identity of Yeats* (New York: Oxford University Press, 1954), chaps. 2 and 4, passim; Bloom, *Yeats,* chaps. 14–15; Allen Grossman, *Poetic Knowledge in the Early Yeats: A Study of "The Wind among the Reeds"* (Charlottesville: University of Virginia Press, 1969).

*19.* *The Letters of W. B. Yeats,* ed. Allan Wade (New York: Macmillan, 1955), pp. 712–14.

*20.* Although Whitehead's opposition of *organic* and *materialistic* recalls the Romantic poets, his use of the word *organic* refers, not to natural unimpeded growth, but to interrelationship, system— or, to use his own word, *prehension.*

*21.* *The Variorum Edition of the Poems of W. B. Yeats,* ed. Peter Allt and Russell K. Alspach (New York: Macmillan, 1957), p. 427. Subsequently cited in the text as *VP.*

*22.* The reference is to the familial bond between Pound and Yeats, Yeats's wife, Georgie Hyde-Lees, being a cousin of Dorothy Shakespear's and Dorothy being the daughter of Olivia Shakespear, Yeats's former mistress and lifelong close friend.

*23.* Yeats scholarship has paid very little attention to this issue. In his recent review essay "To 'Beat Upon the Wall': Reading *A Vision,"* in *Yeats Annual,* no. 4, ed. Warwick Gould (London: Macmillan, 1986), pp. 219–30, Colin MacDowell comments that *A Vision* (1937) "is complete enough for detailed exposition to be undertaken" (p. 222), but then says nothing of *A Packet for Ezra Pound.*

*24.* Ezra Pound, *Gaudier-Brzeska* (1916; New York: New Directions, 1970), p. 91.

*25.* *Letters of Yeats,* ed. Wade, p. 825.

*26.* William Butler Yeats, *Essays and Introductions* (London and New York: Macmillan, 1961), p. 522. Subsequently cited in the text as *E & I.*

*27.* See A. Norman Jeffares, *A Commentary on the Collected Poems of W. B. Yeats* (Stanford, Calif.: Stanford University Press, 1968), p. 350.

**28.** Bloom writes, "Where the shells kept Newton from the larger vision they prophesied for Yeats the 'more substantial joy' of his mature poethood. That is the meaning of the poet's powerful and inspiring confidence in the last stanza of this deeply satisfying meditation upon death. . . . the reply, for once, is confidently in the power of the imagination" (pp. 383–84). But this interpretation skirts the issue of the poem's increasing abstraction, the third stanza's refusal to define its terms.

**29.** "Introduction," *The Oxford Book of Modern Verse, 1892–1935*, chosen by W. B. Yeats (Oxford: Clarendon Press, 1936), p. xxvi.

**30.** Georges Perec, *La Vie mode d'emploi* (Paris: Hachette, 1978); *Life: A User's Manual*, trans. David Bellos (Boston: David R. Godine, 1987). I refer to the English text, subsequently cited as Perec.

**31.** See Georges Perec, "Quatres figures pour *La Vie mode d'emploi*," in *OULIPO: Atlas de littérature potentielle* (Paris: Gallimard, 1981), pp. 387–95. A good explanation of the workings of Perec's grid (with a slightly different explanatory chart) is found in Gabriel Josipovici, "George Perec's Homage to Joyce (and Tradition)," *Yearbook of English Studies* 15 (1985): 179–200.

**32.** David Bellos, "George Perec's Puzzling Style," *Scripsi* 5, no. 1 (1988): 66–67. Subsequently cited in the text as Bellos.

**33.** I owe this notion in part to Kent Johnson, letter to me of 16 March 1989.

### Chapter Five: *Lawrence's Lyric Theater:* Birds, Beasts and Flowers

**1.** See D. H. Lawrence, letter to Curtis Brown, 10 February 1923, in *The Collected Letters of D. H. Lawrence*, ed. Harry T. Moore, 2 vols. (New York: Viking Press, 1962), 2:737. For the dates of composition of Lawrence's writings as well as much useful contextual information, see Keith Sagar, *D. H. Lawrence: A Calendar of His Works* (Manchester: Manchester University Press, 1979).

**2.** See Sandra M. Gilbert, *Acts of Attention: The Poems of D. H. Lawrence* (Ithaca, N.Y.: Cornell University Press, 1972), pp. 131–89; and Gilbert, "D. H. Lawrence's Uncommon Prayers," in *D. H. Lawrence: The Man Who Lived*, ed. Robert B. Partlow, Jr., and Harry T. Moore (Carbondale: Southern Illinois University Press, 1980), pp. 73–93; Harold Bloom, "Lawrence, Eliot, Blackmur, and the Tortoise" (1959), in *The Ringers in the Tower: Studies in the Romantic Tradition* (Chicago: University of Chicago Press, 1971), pp. 197–206; Joyce Carol Oates, *The Hostile Sun: The Poetry of D. H. Lawrence* (Los Angeles: Black Sparrow Press, 1974), pp. 7–8, 37–57. The place of Lawrence's poetry in the English Romantic tradition is the subject of Ross C. Murfin's *The Poetry of D. H. Lawrence: Texts and Contexts* (Lincoln: University of Nebraska Press, 1983).

3.  D. H. Lawrence, *Aaron's Rod* (1922; reprint, New York: Viking, Compass Books, 1967), pp. 255–56. Subsequently cited in the text as *AR*.

4.  *The Complete Poems of D. H. Lawrence*, ed. Vivian de Sola Pinto and F. Warren Roberts (New York: Viking Press, 1971), p. 296. Subsequently cited in the text as *CP*. See also the first edition published by Thomas Seltzer in New York (1923).

5.  D. H. Lawrence, *Etruscan Places* (1932; reprint, New York: Viking Press, 1966), pp. 28–29.

6.  Oates, *Hostile Sun*, p. 37.

7.  W. H. Auden, "D. H. Lawrence" (1948), in *The Dyer's Hand and Other Essays* (New York: Random House, Vintage Books, 1968), p. 289.

8.  Lawrence to Edward Marsh, 18[–20] August 1913, in *The Letters of D. H. Lawrence*, vol. 2, ed. George J. Zytaruk and James T. Boulton (Cambridge: Cambridge University Press, 1981), p. 61. I shall subsequently cite the Cambridge edition of the collected letters, of which the first three volumes, covering the years to 1921, have been published at this writing, as *CL*.

9.  A. Alvarez, "D. H. Lawrence: The Single State of Man" (1958), in *Modern Poetry: Essays in Criticism*, ed. John Hollander (New York: Oxford University Press, 1968), p. 285. Lawrence's poetry, says Alvarez, is notable for its "complete truth to feeling." Furthermore, "The real material of poetry . . . depends on getting close to the real feelings and presenting them without formulae and without avoidance, in all their newness, disturbance, and ugliness" (p. 300).

10. See especially Gilbert, "Lawrence's Uncommon Prayers," pp. 81–82. Gilbert argues that the whole volume is "held together by the covert story of a trip underground, a voyage of death and resurrection. . . . But in the *Birds, Beasts and Flowers* narrative . . . , [the poet's] fall is fortunate not because it will enable him, like Milton's Adam, to rise again by his own efforts, but because it is a fall into a hell that he knows is really a darkly radiant heaven, and he may be lucky enough to fall even further, deeper, into the center of all energy" (p. 80).

11. In their notes to the poems Pinto and Roberts state that "the little prose prefaces to the various sections of the collection were first printed in the illustrated edition of *BBF* [*Birds, Beasts and Flowers*] published by the Cresset Press in June 1930. . . . These prefaces contain a number of quotations, chiefly from John Burnet's *Early Greek Philosophy* (3rd Edition, 1920). Lawrence seems to have first read Burnet's book (which was given to him by Bertrand Russell) when he was in Cornwall in 1916" (*CP*, p. 993).

12. See Robert Graves, *The Greek Myths* (Baltimore: Penguin Books, 1952), 2:103–11.

13. D. H. Lawrence, *Sea and Sardinia* (New York: Viking Press, 1948), pp. 1–2.

14. Here Lawrence evidently conflates Pentheus and Dionysus. In the myth (see esp. Euripides' *The Bacchae*), Pentheus is, of course, Dionysus's victim: the maenads kill and dismember the king at Dionysus's command. For Lawrence's purposes, however, both represent the male victimized by the devouring female goddess, and hence they can be used interchangeably, just as Syracuse replaces Thebes in his allusion to the maenads.

15. Compare Lawrence's letter to Cynthia Asquith, 23 October 1913, *CL*, 2:89: "Did you make your dash to Venice—and did it stink?" And to the same correspondent, he writes a few weeks later, "I am sorry you've got a cold. But what do you expect, after purpling in Venice" (*CL*, 2:107).

16. Murfin, *Poetry of Lawrence*, p. 197.

17. D. H. Lawrence, "The Nightingale," in *Selected Literary Criticism*, ed. Anthony Beal (New York: Viking Press, 1966), pp. 98–101, on p. 99. "Poetry of the Present" was the introduction to the American edition of *New Poems* (1918); it is reprinted in *CP*, pp. 181–86.

18. Elizabeth Bishop, *The Complete Poems* (New York: Farrar, Straus & Giroux, 1969), p. 49.

19. For an important discussion of this central distinction, see J. Hillis Miller, *Poets of Reality: Six Twentieth-Century Writers* (1965; reprint, New York: Atheneum, 1969), pp. 1–2, and chap. 7 ("William Carlos Williams"). Lawrence is not one of the six writers (Conrad, Yeats, Eliot, Thomas, Stevens, and Williams) discussed here, but Miller's thesis about the "new region of copresence," the new space in which "mind is dispersed everywhere in things and forms one with them" (pp. 8–9) seems especially applicable to Lawrence.

20. M. L. Rosenthal and Sally M. Gall, *The Modern Poetic Sequence: The Genius of Modern Poetry* (New York: Oxford University Press, 1983). Yeats's sequence-poems are given approximately forty pages, as are Pound's and William's. Charles Olson's *Maximus* gets eighteen, Ted Hughes's *Crow*, sixteen.

21. In "Lawrence's Uncommon Prayers," Gilbert perceptively remarks that Lawrence is finally a poet's poet. But whereas Gilbert cites Joyce Carol Oates, Robert Bly, Denise Levertov, Ted Hughes, and Adrienne Rich as poets who have followed the Lawrentian model, no doubt because she is primarily concerned with the mythic structure and Orphic symbolism of the poems in *Birds, Beasts and Flowers,* I would argue that, as a rhetorician, Lawrence is closer to such poets as Charles Olson, Robert Duncan, Robert Creeley, and Allen Ginsberg—all, incidentally, poets who have written admiringly of his lyric.

*1.*   Basil Bunting in conversation with Eric Mottram, 1975; see William S. Milne, "Basil Bunting's Prose and Criticism," in *Basil Bunting, Man and Poet,* ed. Carroll F. Terrell (Orono, Maine: National Poetry Foundation, 1980), p. 286; subsequently cited in the text as *BBMP.*

*2.*   Charles Wright in conversation with Stuart Friebert and David Young, 1976, "Charles Wright at Oberlin," *Field, Contemporary Poetry and Poetics* 17 (Fall 1977): 48.

*3.*   Guy Davenport, "Ezra Pound, 1885–1972," in *The Geography of the Imagination: Forty Essays* (San Francisco: North Point Press, 1981), pp. 175–76; subsequently cited as *GOI.*

*4.*   Allen Ginsberg, "The Death of Ezra Pound" (radio interview, 1972), in *Allen Verbatim: Lectures on Poetry, Politics, Consciousness,* ed. Gordon Hall (New York: McGraw-Hill, 1974), p. 179.

*5.*   In Keith Sagar's standard work *The Art of Ted Hughes* (Cambridge: Cambridge University Press, 1975), for example, Pound's name does not so much as appear in the index.

*6.*   Ted Hughes, "The Swifts," in *Season's Songs* (1975); reprinted in *New Selected Poems* (New York: Harper & Row, 1982), p. 144.

*7.*   See Donald Sheehan, "An Interview with James Merrill," *Contemporary Literature* 9 (Winter 1967): 3.

*8.*   Hugh Kenner, *The Pound Era* (Berkeley and Los Angeles: University of California Press, 1971), pp. 557–58.

*9.*   Under the editorship of Carroll F. Terrell and Burton Hatlen, the National Poetry Foundation at the University of Maine, Orono, has brought out a series of volumes that contain seminal materials, both critical and bibliographical, on Louis Zukofsky, Basil Bunting, and George Oppen. The Pound relationship is central to all three: *Louis Zukofsky, Man and Poet,* ed. Carroll F. Terrell (1979); *Basil Bunting, Man and Poet,* ed. Carroll F. Terrell (1980); *George Oppen, Man and Poet,* ed. Burton Hatlen (1981). See especially, in the last volume, Rachel Blau du Plessis, "Objectivist Poetics and Political Vision: A Study of Oppen and Pound," pp. 123–48.
        On Pound and Olson, see especially Catherine Seelye, ed., *Charles Olson and Ezra Pound: An Encounter at St. Elizabeths* (New York: Grossman Publishers, 1975); Robert von Hallberg, *Charles Olson: The Scholar's Art* (Cambridge, Mass.: Harvard University Press, 1978), pp. 44–63. On Pound and Duncan, see especially Don Byrd, "The Question of Wisdom as Such," in *Robert Duncan: Scales of the Marvelous* (New York: New Directions, 1979), pp. 38–55; Ekbert Faas, "An Interview with Robert Duncan," *Boundary 2* 8 (Winter 1980): 1–20. On Pound and Creeley, see two special Creeley issues: *Boundary 2* 6–7 (Spring–Fall 1978); *Sagetrieb* 1, no. 3 (Winter 1982).
        In *The Influence of Ezra Pound* (London: Oxford University

Press, 1966), K. L. Goodwin is concerned mainly with Pound's relationship to his contemporaries, especially Yeats and Eliot. The influence on Olson, Bunting, and H.D. is minimized because Goodwin considers them only minor poets. Conversely, the influence on such Pound contemporaries as Archibald MacLeish and Hart Crane now seems curiously exaggerated.

10. Denise Levertov, "Grass Seed and Cherry Stones," in *The Poet in the World* (New York: New Directions, 1973), pp. 251–52.

11. Robert Creeley, "A Note on Ezra Pound" (1965), in *A Quick Graph* (San Francisco: Four Seasons Foundation, 1970), p. 196. See also "I'm given to write poems," ibid., pp. 68–69; David Ossman, "Interview with Robert Creeley" (1961), in *Contexts of Poetry: Interviews, 1961–1971* (Bolinas, Calif.: Four Seasons Foundation, 1973), pp. 3–12; "Robert Creeley in Conversation with Charles Tomlinson," ibid., pp. 15, 19.

12. L. S. Dembo, "An Interview with Carl Rakosi," *Contemporary Literature* 10 (Spring 1969): 180.

13. Donald Davie, *Ezra Pound: Poet as Sculptor* (New York: Oxford University Press, 1964), chaps. 3 and 4; and cf. Davie, *Pound* (London: Fontana/Collins, 1975), chap. 2.

14. "A Retrospect" (1918), in *The Literary Essays of Ezra Pound* (New York: New Directions, 1968), pp. 4–5; *Gaudier-Brzeska* (1916; New York: New Directions, 1970), p. 92; *ABC of Reading* (New York: New Directions, 1960), pp. 30, 32, subsequently cited in the text as *ABCR*.

15. Theodore Weiss's fascinating love-hate essay on Pound, "E.P.: The Man Who Cared Too Much," first appeared in *Parnassus: Poetry in Review* 5 (Fall–Winter 1976); it is reprinted in *The Man from Porlock: Engagements, 1944–81* (Princeton, N.J.: Princeton University Press, 1982), pp. 17–57.

16. See John Ashbery, "Tradition and Talent" (review essay on Philip Booth, Adrienne Rich, Stanley Moss), *New York Herald Tribune Book Week*, 4 September 1966, p. 14. In "The Mind's Own Place," *Kulchur* 10 (1963), reprinted in *Montemora* 1 (Fall 1975): 132–33, George Oppen writes: "Modern American poetry begins with the determination to find the image of the thing encountered, the thing seen each day whose meaning has become the meaning and color of our lives." Frank O'Hara's equivalent of this "image of the thing encountered" is "presence"; see Edward Lucie-Smith, "An Interview with Frank O'Hara," *Studio International* (September 1966), reprinted in *Standing Still and Walking in New York*, ed. Donald Allen (Bolinas, Calif.: Grey Fox Press, 1975); and "Larry Rivers," ibid., p. 96.

17. Basil Bunting, "Open Letter to Louis Zukofsky" (1932), in *BBMP*, p. 242.

18. Allen Ginsberg, "Encounters with Ezra Pound: Journal Notes," in *City Lights Anthology* (1974), reprinted in *Composed on the Tongue* (Bolinas, Calif.: Grey Fox Press, 1980), pp. 4–5.

**19.** Ibid., p. 12.

**20.** Louis Zukofsky, "An Objective," in *Prepositions,* expanded ed. (Berkeley and Los Angeles: University of California Press, 1981), pp. 16, 13. This section on Louis Zukofsky appeared in slightly different form in my "Postmodernism and the Impasse of Lyric" in *The Dance of the Intellect: Studies in the Poetry of the Pound Tradition* (Cambridge and New York: Cambridge University Press, 1985), pp. 184–86.

**21.** Ibid., p. 13.

**22.** Louis Zukofsky, *All: The Collected Short Poems, 1923–1964* (New York: W. W. Norton, 1971), p. 52. By permission of W. W. Norton and Company, Inc. Copyright © 1971, 1966, 1965 by Louis Zukofsky.

**23.** Burton Hatlen, "Zukofsky, Wittgenstein, and the Poetics of Absence," *Sagetrieb* 1, no. 1 (Spring 1982): 92.

**24.** On this point, see my *Poetics of Indeterminacy: Rimbaud to Cage* (Princeton: N.J.: Princeton University Press, 1981), esp. chap. 1.

**25.** Hatlen, "Zukofsky," p. 73.

**26.** "Robert Creeley in Conversation with Charles Tomlinson," pp. 15–16.

**27.** Davie, *Ezra Pound,* p. 181. Also, p. 43: "It still needs to be stressed that the momentousness of Imagism as Pound conceived of it lies just in its being not a variant of *symbolisme* nor a development out of it, but a radical alternative to it."

**28.** Donald Davie, *Events and Wisdoms* (Middletown, Conn.: Wesleyan University Press, 1965), p. 26.

**29.** "Provincia Deserta," in *Personae: The Collected Shorter Poems of Ezra Pound* (New York: New Directions, 1971), p. 121.

**30.** James Merrill, *The Changing Light at Sandover* (New York: Atheneum, 1982), p. 97.

**31.** John Berryman, "The Poetry of Ezra Pound," in *The Freedom of the Poet* (New York: Farrar, Straus & Giroux, 1976), p. 264.

**32.** Charles Tomlinson, *Some Americans: A Personal Record* (Berkeley and Los Angeles: University of California Press, Quantum Books, 1981), pp. 1–2.

**33.** Davie, *Ezra Pound,* pp. 44–45.

**34.** Walt Whitman, "Song of Myself," in *Leaves of Grass,* ed. Scully Bradley and Harold W. Blodgett, Norton Critical Edition (New York: W. W. Norton, 1973), p. 59.
    The notation used here and elsewhere in this book is a modified version of Trager-Smith. A primary stress is marked (´), secondary (ˆ), tertiary (ˋ), caesura with a double bar (‖), a shorter pause with a single bar (|). An arrow at the end of a line means the line is enjambed.

35. *The Cantos of Ezra Pound* (New York: New Directions, 1975), p. 15.

36. Basil Bunting, "Chomei at Toyama," in *Collected Poems* (Oxford and New York: Oxford University Press, 1978), p. 63.

37. H.D., "Sea Heroes," in *Selected Poems* (New York: New Directions, 1957), p. 11.

38. H.D., "Winter Love," in *Hermetic Definition* (New York: New Directions, 1972), p. 109.

39. Charles Wright, "White," in *Hard Freight* (1973); reprinted in *Country Music: Selected Early Poems* (Middletown, Conn.: Wesleyan University Press, 1982), p. 21.

40. Larry Eigner, *Selected Poems*, ed. Samuel Charters and Andrea Wyatt (Berkeley: Oyez, 1972), p. 66.

41. Robert Duncan, *The Opening of the Field* (1960; reprint, New York: New Directions, 1973), p. 62.

42. Louis Zukofsky, *"A"* (Berkeley, Los Angeles, and London: University of California Press, 1978), p. 189.

43. Ginsberg, *Allen Verbatim*, pp. 172, 180.

44. Allen Ginsberg, *Howl and Other Poems*, (1959; San Francisco: City Lights, 1982), p. 14.

45. Bunting, *Collected Poems*, p. 129.

46. Guy Davenport, "The Symbol of the Archaic," in *GOI*, p. 21.

47. See Guy Davenport, "The House That Jack Built," in *GOI*, pp. 57–58: "The essence of daedalian art is that it conceals what it most wishes to show."

48. Jerome Rothenberg, "A Dialogue on Oral Poetry with William Spanos" (1975), in *Pre-Faces and Other Writings* (New York: New Directions, 1981), p. 27.

49. Robert Lowell, *Imitations* (New York: Farrar, Straus & Giroux, 1961), p. xi.

50. Letter to the Editor of the *English Journal*, 24 January 1931, in *The Selected Letters of Ezra Pound, 1907–1941*, ed. D. D. Paige (New York: New Directions, 1971), p. 231.

51. Frederick Seidel, "An Interview with Robert Lowell," in *Robert Lowell: A Portrait of the Artist in His Time*, ed. Michael London and Robert Boyers (New York: David Lewis, 1970), p. 279; subsequently cited as London and Boyers.

52. John Simon, "Abuse of Privilege: Lowell as Translator," *Hudson Review* 20 (1967–68); reprinted in London and Boyers, pp. 143–44.

**53.** Heinrich Heine, *Sämtliche Werke*, ed. Oskar Walzel et al. (Leipzig: Insel, 1911), 3:404.

**54.** The translation is John Simon's in London and Boyers, p. 142. Cf. Hal Draper, *The Complete Poems of Heinrich Heine, a Modern English Version* (Boston: Suhrkamp/Insel, 1982), p. 88.

**55.** Lowell, *Imitations,* p. 39.

**56.** John Simon makes a similar point: see London and Boyers, p. 142.

**57.** Michael A. Bernstein, *The Tale of the Tribe: Ezra Pound and the Modern Verse Epic* (Princeton, N.J.: Princeton University Press, 1980), pp. 39–40.

**58.** See, for example, Joel Conarroe, *John Berryman: An Introduction to the Poetry* (New York: Columbia University Press, 1977), p. 97: "*The Dream Songs,* in spite of crucial differences in intention and poetic strategy, resembles the *Cantos* more than any other modern sequence, with the possible exception of Lowell's *Notebooks.* . . . Each is a poem in progress, composed over a long period of time, that develops in concert with the life-in-progress of a protean poet. Each introduces an enormous cast of characters. . . . Each is thickly allusive, and each constantly alludes to itself, building up an elaborate network of cross references, repeated images, recurring motifs, and thematic variations."

**59.** Don Byrd, "The Shape of Zukofsky's Canon," Louis Zukofsky Issue, *Paideuma 7* (1978): 464.

**60.** In "The Transfigured Prose," ibid., pp. 447–53, Cid Corman gives an interesting account of the reworking of a passage in Reznikoff's *The Manner Music* into the poetic version found in "*A*"-12.

**61.** Bernstein, *Tale of the Tribe,* pp. 170–72.

**62.** I have discussed Davenport's collage mode in "Between Verse and Prose: Beckett and the New Poetry," in *The Dance of the Intellect,* pp. 148–52.

**63.** Guy Davenport, "Persephone's Ezra," in *GOI,* pp. 150–51.

**64.** Ron Silliman, "Louis Zukofsky," *Paideuma 7* (1978): 405.

**65.** Rothenberg, "Dialogue on Oral Poetry," p. 27; Rothenberg, "Deep Image and Mode: An Exchange with Robert Creeley" (1960), in *Pre-Faces,* p. 58.

**66.** Rothenberg, *Pre-Faces,* p. 105.

**67.** Ibid., p. 139.

**68.** Ibid., p. 143.

**69.** Bernstein, *Tale of the Tribe,* p. 172.

70. George Quasha and Jerome Rothenberg, eds., *America a Prophecy: A New Reading of American Poetry from Pre-Columbian Times to the Present* (New York: Random House, 1973), pp. xxix, xxxiii.

71. *Hypnologue* is Eugene Jolas's term for "a verbal replica of the experiences between waking and sleeping" (ibid., p. 428); *mudra* is Chogyam Trungpa's term for "a symbol, in the sense of gesture or action. It arises spontaneously as an expression of the inspiring color of phenomena. Also it is a symbol expressed with the hands to state for oneself and others the quality of different moments of meditation" (ibid., p. 437). Each term on Rothenberg's list is explained and exemplified somewhere in the section.

72. Hugh Kenner, "More on the 'Seven Lakes Canto,' " *Paideuma* 2 (1971); reprinted in part in Carroll F. Terrell, ed., *A Companion to the Cantos of Ezra Pound,* vol. 1 (Berkeley, Los Angeles, and London: University of California Press, 1980), p. 190.

73. Sanehide Kodama, "The Eight Scenes of Sho-Sho," *Paideuma* 6 (1977); reprinted in part in *Companion to the Cantos,* pp. 190–91.

*Chapter Seven: "A Fine New Kind of Realism": Six Stein Styles in Search of a Reader*

1. See, for example, Richard Bridgman, *Gertrude Stein in Pieces* (New York: Oxford University Press, 1970); Marianne DeKoven, *A Different Language: Gertrude Stein's Experimental Writing* (Madison: University of Wisconsin Press, 1983), pp. xiii–xvi; Randa Dubnick, *The Structure of Obscurity: Gertrude Stein, Language, and Cubism* (Urbana and Chicago: University of Illinois Press, 1984), chap. 4; Ulla E. Dydo, "*Stanzas in Meditation:* The Other Autobiography," *Chicago Review* 35 (Winter 1985): 4–32. When Bridgman writes of *The Autobiography of Alice B. Toklas* that "after twenty years of enigmatic utterances, Gertrude Stein at last chose to speak in a voice of singular clarity" (p. 206), he is voicing what is still the prevalent view. But whether we take the clarity/enigma distinction to be diachronic (Bridgman, DeKoven) or synchronic (Dubnick, Dydo) is less important than that the "straight" and the "experimental" tend to be placed in binary opposition.

2. Gertrude Stein, "Sentences," in *How to Write* (1931; New York: Dover, 1975), p. 167. Subsequently cited in the text as *HTW*.

3. Gertrude Stein, *Paris France* (1940; New York: Liveright, 1970), p. 1. Subsequently cited in the text as *PF*.

4. Lyn Hejinian, "Two Stein Talks: (1) Language and Realism, (2) Grammar and Landscape," *Temblor* 3 (1986): 137.

5. Bridgman, *Stein in Pieces,* p. 298.

6. See Donald Gallup, ed., *The Flowers of Friendship: Letters Written to Gertrude Stein* (New York: Alfred A. Knopf, 1953), p. 50. James made this characterization of Stein's work more or less in spite of himself. Stein had sent him a copy of *Three Lives* when it was published in 1909 and asked her former teacher what he thought. James responded: "You know how hard it is for me to read novels. Well, I read 30 or 40 pages, and said 'this is a fine new kind of realism—Gertrude Stein is great!' I will go at it carefully when just the right mood comes" (p. 50). Since James died in August 1910, we may assume that the "right mood" never did come.

7. Gertrude Stein, "A Transatlantic Interview—1946," in *A Primer for the Gradual Understanding of Gertrude Stein*, ed. Robert Bartlett Haas (Santa Barbara, Calif.: Black Sparrow Press, 1946), p. 15.

8. Gertrude Stein, *The Autobiography of Alice B. Toklas* (1933), in *Selected Writings of Gertrude Stein*, ed. Carl Van Vechten (New York: Vintage Books, 1972), pp. 128–29. Subsequently cited in the text as *SW*.

9. Gertrude Stein, "One," in *Geography and Plays* (Boston: The Four Seas Co., 1922), pp. 199–200.

10. Gertrude Stein, "Composition as Explanation" (1926), in *SW*, pp. 511–33, on p. 518.

11. Stein, "Transatlantic Interview," p. 26.

12. John Ashbery, "The Impossible" (review of *Stanzas in Meditation*), *Poetry* 90 (1957): 251.

13. Ulla E. Dydo, who is currently completing what will be the most comprehensive scholarly book on Stein so far, based on close study of the MSS in the Beineke Library at Yale, informs me that she has been able to find no evidence of "gay" meaning "homosexual" at the time of Stein's short story and the related "A Long Gay Book" (1909–12). Cf. Bruce Kellner, "Ex Libris: The Published Writings of Gertrude Stein," in *A Gertrude Stein Companion: Content with the Example*, ed. Kellner (New York: Greenwood Press, 1988), p. 34. Kellner points out that in Stein's short story, published in *Geography and Plays* (1922), the "gay" life recounted is "perhaps the first use of that appellation in print to refer to a homosexual alliance."

14. Gertrude Stein, *Writings and Lectures 1909–1945*, ed. Patricia Meyerowitz (Baltimore: Penguin Books, 1967), p. 285.

15. DeKoven, *Different Language*, p. 106.

16. Hejinian, "Two Stein Talks," p. 129.

17. Gertrude Stein, *Portraits and Prayers* (New York: Random House, 1934), p. 80.

18. Wendy Steiner, *Exact Resemblance to Exact Resemblance: The Literary Portraiture of Gertrude Stein* (New Haven, Conn., and London: Yale University Press, 1978), p. 120.

19. For this terminology, see Julia Kristeva, *Revolution in Poetic Language*, trans. Margaret Waller, with an introduction by Leon S. Roudiez (New York: Columbia University Press, 1984), pp. 19–106. The advantages and difficulties of the recent adaptations, in feminist studies of Stein, of Kristeva's distinction between the semiotic and the symbolic are very interestingly discussed in Harriet Scott Chessman's recent study, *The Public Is Invited to Dance: Representation, the Body, and Dialogue in Gertrude Stein* (Stanford, Calif.: Stanford University Press, 1989), esp. pp. 3–8, 71–76.

*Chapter Eight: "Une Voix pas la mienne": French/English Beckett and the French/English Reader*

1. Richard Coe, *Samuel Beckett* (New York: Grove Press, 1969), p. 14.

2. Samuel Beckett, *Enough*, in *First Love and Other Shorts* (New York: Grove Press, 1974), p. 56. Cf. Beckett, *Assez*, in *Têtes-mortes* (Paris: Editions de Minuit, 1967), p. 44. For Beckett bibliography and chronology I am indebted to *No Symbols Where None Intended: A Catalogue of Books, Manuscripts, and Other Materials Relating to Samuel Beckett in the Collections of the Humanities Research Center*, selected and described by Carlton Lake (Austin: Humanities Research Center, University of Texas, 1984).

3. See Coe, *Beckett*, p. 14. Cf. A. Alvarez, *Samuel Beckett* (New York: Viking Press, 1973), pp. 40–41; John Fletcher, "Ecrivain bilingue," in *Samuel Beckett*, special issue of *Cahier de l'Herne*, ed. Tom Bishop and Raymond Federman (Paris: Editions de l'Herne, 1976), pp. 212–18; Harry Cockerman, "Bilingual Playwright," in *Beckett the Shape Changer*, ed. Katharine Worth (London and Boston: Routledge & Kegan Paul, 1975), pp. 139–59. For an interesting analysis from the linguist's point of view, see Ekundayo Simpson, *Samuel Beckett: Traducteur de lui-même: Aspects de bilingualisme littéraire* (Quebec: International Center for Research on Bilingualism, 1978).

4. Letter, in German, to Axel Kaun, 7 September 1937; reprinted in Samuel Beckett, *Disjecta: Miscellaneous Writings and a Dramatic Fragment*, ed. Ruby Cohn (New York: Grove Press, 1984), pp. 52–53. I cite here an English translation by Martin Esslin provided in the notes, pp. 170–73.

5. Cited in Vivian Mercier, *Beckett/Beckett* (New York: Oxford University Press, 1977), pp. 26–27.

6. Worth, *Beckett the Shape Changer*, pp. 6–7.

7. Cited in Mercier, *Beckett/Beckett*, p. 23. The references are, respectively, to W. B. Yeats's *At the Hawk's Well*, John Synge's *The Well of Saints*, and Sean O'Casey's *Juno and the Paycock*.

8. Samuel Beckett, *Mal vu mal dit* (Paris: Editions de Minuit, 1953); *Ill Seen Ill Said* (New York: Grove Press, 1981). Subsequent

citations in the text give page numbers to these editions in parentheses.

**9.** The case of Beckett's plays is somewhat different. From the radio play *All That Fall* (1957) and *Krapp's Last Tape* (1958) to the present, Beckett has composed many of his plays first in English, and their language and rhythms frequently allude to English literature, to proverbs, and the King James Bible. The most allusive of the plays is *Happy Days* (1962). In his bilingual edition of *Happy Days/Oh les beaux jours* (London and Boston: Faber & Faber, 1978), James Knowlson catalogs the literary references and finds that Winnie's speeches are tissues of quotations from Shakespeare, Milton, Gray, Browning, etc. In some cases, the French version matches the English in that Beckett substitutes, say, Ronsard for Shakespeare or Verlaine for a British ballad, and so on.

Winnie's allusions are, however, rather different from those of *Ill Seen Ill Said*. The dramatic character is always trying to remember a particular "poetic" quotation and announces that she will quote a passage, thus displaying her conventionality, her constant need to resort to authorized ways of saying things. As such, Winnie's citations are more obviously comic than the complex allusions made by the narrators themselves in Beckett's fictions.

**10.** Samuel Beckett, *Company* (New York: Grove Press, 1980), p. 19.

**11.** Samuel Beckett, *Compagnie* (Paris: Editions de Minuit, 1980), p. 24.

**12.** Brian T. Fitch, "The Relation Between *Compagnie* and *Company:* One Work, Two Texts, Two Fictive Universes," in *Beckett Translating/Translating Beckett,* ed. Alan Warren Friedman, Charles Rossman, and Dina Sherzer (University Park and London: Pennsylvania State University Press, 1987), pp. 25–35.

**13.** Raymond Federman has pointed out to me that some of the French phrases cited above similarly allude to the French Romantic and Symbolist tradition. Thus "choses et chimères" (example 7) may allude to Mallarmé's lines, "Quelle soie aux baumes de temps / Ou la chimère s'extenue," and the "charogne" of example 20 points back to Baudelaire's great poem by that name. But such allusions constitute at best a minor chord in the French text and their parodic implications remain undeveloped.

**14.** See Robert Taubman, "Beckett's Buttonhook," *London Review of Books,* 21 October–3 November 1982, p. 16.

**15.** For early discussions, see Ruby Cohn, "Samuel Beckett Self-Translator," *PMLA* 76 (December 1961): 613–21; Martin Esslin, *The Theatre of the Absurd* (New York: Doubleday, Anchor Books, 1961), pp. 8–9; Ludovic Janvier, *Pour Samuel Beckett* (Paris: Editions de Minuit, 1966), pp. 224–30; Hugh Kenner, "Beckett Translating Beckett: *Comment c'est,*" *Delos* 5 (1970): 194–210; and Fletcher, "Ecrivain bilingue."

Most British and American essays on Beckett's fictions written over the past decade simply accept the English text at face value, without considering its relationship to the French original. See, for example, John Pilling's otherwise very helpful *Samuel Beckett* (London: Routledge & Kegan Paul, 1966), pp. 25–66; and his "Ends and Odds in Prose," in *Frescoes of the Skull: The Later Prose and Drama of Samuel Beckett,* ed. James Knowlson and John Pilling (London: John Calder, 1979), pp. 132–94. For a short but notable exception, see George Craig, "The Voice of Childhood and Great Age," *Times Literary Supplement,* 27 August 1982, p. 921. Comparing *Mal vu mal dit* to *Ill Seen Ill Said,* Craig talks of the "verbal no-man's land where neither French nor English holds sway."

*16.* David Read, "Beckett's Search for Unseeable and Unmakeable: *Company* and *Ill Seen Ill Said," Modern Fiction Studies* 29 (Summer 1983): 111–26.

*17.* Judith E. Dearlove, *Accommodating the Chaos: Samuel Beckett's Nonrelational Art* (Durham, N.C.: Duke University Press, 1982), p. 113.

*18.* Jude Stephan, *Nouvelle revue française* 344 (1981): 126.

*19.* Maurice Nadeau, review of *Molloy, Combat,* 12 April 1951; reprinted in *Samuel Beckett: The Critical Heritage,* ed. Lawrence Graver and Raymond Federman (London and Boston: Routledge & Kegan Paul, 1979), p. 53; subsequently cited as Graver and Federman.

*20.* Georges Bataille, Review of *Molloy, Critique,* 15 May 1951; reprinted in Graver and Federman, pp. 55–64, see pp. 57, 59; cf. Jean Pouillon, *Temps modernes,* July 1951; reprinted in ibid., pp. 64–67.

*21.* Maurice Blanchot, review of *L'Innommable, Nouvelle revue française,* October 1953; reprinted in Graver and Federman, pp. 116–20, see p. 119.

*22.* Donald Davie, *Spectrum,* Winter 1958; reprinted in Graver and Federman, pp. 154–55.

*23.* Hugh Kenner, *Samuel Beckett: A Critical Study,* rev. ed. (Berkeley and Los Angeles: University of California Press, 1968), p. 13.

*24.* For example, Jacques Lemarchand, reviewing *En attendant Godot* for *Figaro littéraire* 17 (January 1953): 10, calls the play a "resolutely comic" work and comments on its "circus" quality; see Beckett issue of *Cahier de l'Herne,* p. 92; the translation is Ruby Cohn's. Examples of the converse (English and American interpretations that take Beckett as the voice of angst, of existential despair, of the failure of language to signify, and so on) are too numerous to list.

*25.* Samuel Beckett, *Molloy* (Paris: Editions de Minuit, 1951), pp. 40–41; *Molloy,* in *Three Novels (Molloy/Malone Dies/The Unnamable)* (New York: Grove Press, 1965), p. 31. Subsequent citations in the text give page numbers to these editions in parentheses.

**Chapter Nine: The Two** Ariel**s: The (Re)Making of the Sylvia Plath Canon**

1. Sylvia Plath, *Ariel* (London: Faber & Faber, 1965); *Ariel* (New York: Harper & Row, 1966). The New York edition includes one poem, "The Swarm," not in the London edition. All further references to *Ariel* will be to the Harper & Row edition, subsequently cited in the text as *A*.

2. These early reviews are cited in Mary Kinzie, "An Informal Check List of Criticism," in *The Art of Sylvia Plath, a Symposium,* ed. Charles Newman (London: Faber & Faber, 1970), pp. 293–303; subsequently cited as Newman. See also A. Alvarez, "Sylvia Plath," ibid., pp. 56–69; and his *The Savage God: A Study in Suicide* (New York: Random House, 1972), pp. 5–34.

3. George Steiner, "Dying Is an Art," *Reporter* 33 (7 October 1965); reprinted in Newman, pp. 211–18. Plath, says Steiner, was "one of a number of young contemporary poets, novelists, themselves in no way implicated in the actual holocaust, who have done most to counter the general inclination to forget the death camps," and he calls "Daddy" "the 'Guernica' of modern poetry" (p. 218).

4. Stephen Spender, "Warnings from the Grave," reprinted in Newman, pp. 199–203.

5. Kinzie writes, "Whether they are pedantic, musing, miffed, or so obviously confused that they can't find cover, most reviewers become 'adjectival' to a fault," and she provides us with a revealing catalog; see Newman, p. 289.

6. Marjorie Perloff, "*Angst* and Animism in the Poetry of Sylvia Plath," *Journal of Modern Literature* 1 (1970): 57–74.

7. See M. L. Rosenthal, "Sylvia Plath and Confessional Poetry," in Newman, pp. 69–76; Rosenthal, *The New Poets: American and British Poetry since World War II* (New York: Oxford University Press, 1967), pp. 79–89; Judith Kroll, *Chapters in a Mythology: The Poetry of Sylvia Plath* (New York: Harper & Row, 1976).

8. See, for example, John Frederick Nims, "The Poetry of Sylvia Plath—a Technical Analysis," in Newman, pp. 136–52; Hugh Kenner, "Sincerity Kills," in *Sylvia Plath: New Views on the Poetry,* ed. Gary Lane (Baltimore and London: Johns Hopkins University Press, 1979), pp. 33–44. This collection of essays is subsequently cited in the text as GL.

9. See especially Sandra M. Gilbert, " 'A Fine White Flying Myth': The Life/Work of Sylvia Plath," in *Shakespeare's Sisters: Feminist Essays on Women Poets,* ed. Sandra M. Gilbert and Susan Gubar (Bloomington: Indiana University Press, 1979), pp. 245–60; Gilbert, "In Yeats' House: The Death and Resurrection of Sylvia Plath," in *Critical Essays on Sylvia Plath,* ed. Linda W. Wagner (Boston: G. K. Hall, 1984), pp. 204–22; this volume subsequently cited as Wagner. See also Lynda K. Bundtzen, *Plath's Incarnations: Woman and the Creative Process* (Ann Arbor: University of Michigan Press, 1983).

10. Bundtzen's view is typical: "There is a strong continuity between the early and late work in terms of content, and the new choices [Plath] makes in *Ariel* are primarily those of style and presentation." Bundtzen, *Plath's Incarnations,* p. 163.

11. *The Journals of Sylvia Plath, 1950–1962,* ed. Frances McCullough; Ted Hughes, consulting editor; foreword by Ted Hughes (New York: Dial Press, 1982), p. xiii; subsequently cited in the text as *J.* Sylvia Plath, *The Collected Poems,* ed. Ted Hughes (New York: Harper & Row, 1981) is subsequently cited in the text as *CP.*

12. Nancy Milford, "From Gladness to Madness," *New York Times Book Review,* 2 May 1982; reprinted in Wagner, pp. 77–83, on p. 83.

13. On the contrary, Hughes's editing was generally praised. In a review for *Encounter* 58 (January 1982): 53–54, reprinted in Wagner, pp. 64–67, Laurence Lerner writes: "Now at last everything has been gathered together, and edited with care and tact by Ted Hughes. All good things are worth waiting for" (p. 65). And in a review for the *New Republic,* 30 December 1981, pp. 32–35, reprinted in Wagner, pp. 72–77, William H. Pritchard remarks that "Ted Hughes has done an exemplary job in editing these poems, writing notes to them year by year. . . . And he strikes the right note in his introduction" (p. 73).

    In her review for the *Nation,* 16 January 1982, pp. 52–55, reprinted in Wagner, pp. 67–72, Katha Pollitt does note that "*Ariel* itself, as printed, was not the manuscript of that name completed by Plath three months before her death but a selection put together by her executors in an order of their choosing. . . . the published *Ariel* destroyed the artistic pattern of Plath's manuscript" (p. 68). Even so, Pollitt praises the *CP,* "a handsome edition chronologically arranged, introduced and annotated by Ted Hughes. It is a beautiful book, prepared with seriousness and love. Every poet should be so well served" (pp. 68–69).

14. Murray M. Schwartz and Christopher Bollas, "The Absence at the Center: Sylvia Plath and Suicide," *Criticism* 18 (Spring 1976): 147–72; reprinted in GL, pp. 179–202.

15. Marjorie Perloff, "Sylvia Plath's 'Sivvy' Poems: A Portrait of the Poet as Daughter," in GL, pp. 155–78.

16. *Crossing the Water* was published in London by Faber & Faber and in New York by Harper & Row in 1971; *Winter Trees,* in London by Faber & Faber in 1971 and in New York by Harper & Row in 1972. I discuss the contents of these two volumes and the editing problems involved in "On the Road to *Ariel*: The 'Transitional' Poetry of Sylvia Plath," *Iowa Review* 4 (Spring 1973): 94–110; reprinted in *Sylvia Plath: The Woman and the Work,* ed. Edward Butscher (New York: Dodd, Mead, 1975), pp. 125–42.

    *Letters Home: Correspondence 1950–63,* selected and edited with commentary by Aurelia Schober Plath, was published in 1975 in New York by Harper & Row. Edward Butscher's biography, *Sylvia Plath, Method and Madness* was published in 1976 in New York by Seabury Press. Both of these volumes, although somewhat unreliable owing to crucial lacunae in the texts, provide essential clues for reading the poems.

17. The discovery clearly comes some time between the writing of "Elm" (19 April 1962) and "The Rabbit Catcher" (21 May 1962): see *CP*, pp. 192–94; and Linda W. Wagner-Martin, *Sylvia Plath: A Biography* (New York: Simon & Schuster, 1987), pp. 205–8.

In *Plath's Incarnations*, Bundtzen cites some unpublished letters, written a few months later; these are in the Plath Manuscript Collection, Lilly Library, Indiana University, and are labeled Box 6, MSS II. On 9 October 1962, for example, Plath complains to her mother of "the foulness I have lived, his wanting to kill all I have lived for six years by saying he was just waiting for a chance to get out, that he was bored & stifled by me, a hag in a world of beautiful women just waiting for him." And on October 21, "It is as if, out of revenge, for my brain and creative power, he wanted to stick me where I would have no chance to use it. I think now my creating babies and a novel frightened him—for he wants barren women like his sister and this woman" (pp. 26–27).

18. Cited by Buntzen, *Plath's Incarnations*, p. 11.

19. See Butscher, *Method and Madness*, pp. 320–22; Wagner-Martin, *Sylvia Plath*, pp. 218–20; Plath, *Letters Home*, pp. 459–61.

20. Perloff, "On the Road to *Ariel*," pp. 127–29.

21. Wagner-Martin, *Sylvia Plath*, p. 205.

22. Richard Allen Blessing, "The Shape of the Psyche: Vision and Technique in the Late Poems of Sylvia Plath," in *GL*, p. 68.

23. I discuss this poem in some detail in "On Sylvia Plath's 'Tulips,' " *Paunch* 42–43 (December 1975): 105–9; see also Perloff, "Sylvia Plath's 'Sivvy' Poems," pp. 170–73.

24. See Perloff, "*Angst* and Animism," pp. 70–72.

25. For the background of these poems, see Butscher, *Method and Madness*, pp. 322–24; Plath, *Letters Home*, p. 469.

26. Margaret Dickie Uroff, *Sylvia Plath and Ted Hughes* (Urbana: University of Illinois Press, 1979), pp. 164–65.

27. See Ted Hughes, notes to *CP*, p. 293.

28. See A. R. Jones, "On Daddy," in Newman, p. 234.

29. See n. 3.

30. See Irving Howe, "Sylvia Plath: A Partial Disagreement," *Harper's Magazine*, January 1972, p. 90; Kenner, "Sincerity Kills," in *GL*, p. 43.

31. Charles Newman, "Candor Is the Only Wile: The Art of Sylvia Plath," in Newman, p. 24.

1. Allen Ginsberg, *Collected Poems, 1947–1980* (New York: Harper & Row, 1985), p. 126. Subsequently cited as *CP.*

2. See Charles Altieri, *Enlarging the Temple: New Directions in American Poetry during the 1960s* (Lewisburg, Pa.: Bucknell University Press, 1979); Altieri, *Self and Sensibility in Contemporary American Poetry* (Cambridge and New York: Cambridge University Press, 1984); Hugh Kenner, *A Homemade World: The American Modernist Writers* (New York: Alfred A. Knopf, 1975); Robert von Hallberg, *American Poetry and Culture, 1945–1980* (Cambridge, Mass., and London: Harvard University Press, 1985); Marjorie Perloff, *The Poetics of Indeterminacy: Rimbaud to Cage* (Princeton, N.J.: Princeton University Press, 1981).
   The exception is James E. B. Breslin's *From Modern to Contemporary: American Poetry, 1945–1965* (Chicago: University of Chicago Press, 1984). Breslin's chapter on Ginsberg remains the best all-round treatment of the poet. Another important—though highly critical—essay, which appeared after my own had been completed, is that of Paul Breslin in *The Psycho-Political Muse: American Poetry since the Fifties* (Chicago: University of Chicago Press, 1987).

3. Denis Donoghue, *Connoisseurs of Chaos: Ideas of Order in Modern American Poetry* (New York: Macmillan, 1965), p. 49.

4. Harold Bloom, *Figures of Capable Imagination* (New York: Seabury Press, 1976), p. 260.

5. Interview with Allen Ginsberg in *Writers at Work: The Paris Review Interviews, Third Series,* ed. George Plimpton (New York: Viking Press, 1968), pp. 287–88.

6. See John Tytell, "The Broken Circuit," in Jack Kerouac, *On the Road: Text and Criticism,* ed. Scott Donaldson (New York: Viking Penguin, 1979), pp. 327–28.

7. See William Carlos Williams, *Paterson* (New York: New Directions, 1963), p. 174. The letter is reprinted as the preface to *The Gates of Wrath: Rhymed Poems 1948–1951* (Bolinas, Calif.: Grey Fox Press, 1972).

8. On this point, see James Breslin, *Modern to Contemporary,* pp. 88–92.

9. Allen Ginsberg, "Notes for *Howl and Other Poems,*" in *The Poetics of the New American Poetry,* ed. Donald Allen and Warren Tallman (New York: Grove Press, 1973), p. 319.

10. For a discussion of the function of stress, syllable count, breath units, and stanza forms, both in his own poetry and in that of poets ranging from Charles-Michel Campion and Milton to Williams, Marianne Moore, and Robert Creeley, see Ginsberg's "Improvised Poetics" (1971) and "An Exposition of William Carlos Williams'

Poetic Practice" (1976), both in *Composed on the Tongue*, ed. Donald Allen (Bolinas, Calif.: Grey Fox Press, 1980), pp. 18–62, 118–53.

11. Ezra Pound, "Vers Libre and Arnold Dolmetsch" (1918), in *Literary Essays of Ezra Pound*, ed. T. S. Eliot (London: Faber & Faber, 1954), p. 437. Ginsberg quotes this passage in "Improvised Poetics," p. 59.

12. Walt Whitman, "Song of Myself," in *Leaves of Grass*, ed. Scully Bradley and Harold W. Blodgett, Norton Critical Edition (New York: W. W. Norton, 1973), p. 62.

13. In a 1956 letter cited by James Breslin, *Modern to Contemporary*, pp. 104–5, Louis Ginsberg writes his son: "["Howl"] has violence; it has life, it has *vitality*. In my opinion, it is a one-sided neurotic view of life; it has not enough glad, Whitmanian affirmations."

14. The former point of view is best represented by Paul Portuges, *The Visionary Poetics of Allen Ginsberg* (Santa Barbara, Calif.: Ross-Erikson, 1978); the latter by Paul Breslin, *The Psycho-Political Muse*, pp. 22–41.

15. See Allen Ginsberg and Anne Waldman, *Beauty and the Beast, Naropa Institute Recordings* (Boulder, Colo., 1976).

16. Quoted in Portuges, *Visionary Poetics*, p. 162.

17. See John Cage, "Writing through Howl" (1984), MS.

18. See Cage, "Foreword," *M, Writings '67–72* (Middletown, Conn., 1973).

19. Richard Howard, *Boston Review* 9 (September 1984): 33.

20. John Hollander, "Review of *Howl and Other Poems*," *Partisan Review*, Spring 1957; reprinted in Lewis Hyde, ed., *On the Poetry of Allen Ginsberg* (Ann Arbor: University of Michigan Press, 1984), pp. 26–27.

21. There are some notable exceptions to what follows. See James Atlas, "A Modern Whitman," *Atlantic* 254 (December 1984): 132–36; Terence Diggory, "Ginsberg's Voice," *American Book Review* 7 (September–October 1985): 13–14; Lewis Hyde, "States of Altering Consciousness," *New York Times Book Review*, 30 December 1984, pp. 5–6; Charles Molesworth, "Language, and Sweet Music Too," *Nation*, 23 February 1985, pp. 213–15; Helen Vendler, "A Lifelong Poem Including History," *New Yorker* 61 (13 January 1986): 77–84.

22. Bruce Bawer, "The Phenomenon of Allen Ginsberg," *New Criterion* 3 (February 1985): 1–14, on p. 10. Cf. Robert Richman, "Allen Ginsberg Then and Now," *Commentary* 80 (July 1985): 50–55. Ginsberg's poetry, Richman remarks, is best characterized as "sleaze."

23. Roger Rosenblatt, "A Major Minor Poet," *New Republic* 192 (4 March 1985): 33–35.

24. Lachlan Mackinnon, "A Loss of Beat," *Times Literary Supplement,* 24 May 1985, p. 574.

25. Mark Jarman, "Generations and Contemporaries," *Hudson Review* 38 (1985–86): 327–40, on p. 330. Subsequent citations to this work are in the text.

26. R. Z. Sheppard, "Mainstreaming Allen Ginsberg," *Time,* 4 February 1985, p. 72.

27. Christopher Buckley and Paul Slansky, "Yowl: For Jay McInerny," *New Republic* 195 (8 December 1986): 48–49.

28. Allen Ginsberg, *Howl: Original Draft Facsimile, Transcript & Variant Versions, Fully Annotated by Author, with Contemporaneous Correspondence, Account of First Public Reading, Legal Skirmishes, Precursor Texts & Bibliography,* ed. Barry Miles (New York: Harper & Row, 1986), p. 124. Subsequently cited in the text as *HODF.*

It was the publication of Miles's edition that prompted the MLA session *"Howl* Twenty Years Later" at which these remarks were first delivered.

29. Hollander, "Review of *Howl,"* p. 26.

30. In the first draft (*HODF,* pp. 12–13), this line read:
      who poverty and tatters and fantastic minds
         sat up all night in lofts
               contemplating jazz
   which lacks the interesting juxtaposition of natural and supernatural ("floating across the tops of cities") in the final version.


*Chapter Eleven: Apocalypse Then: W. S. Merwin and the Sorrows of Literary History*

1. Laurence Lieberman, "Recent Poetry in Review: Risks and Faiths," *Yale Review,* Summer 1968, pp. 597–601; reprinted in Lieberman, *Unassigned Frequencies* (Urbana: University of Illinois Press, 1977), p. 257.

2. For a good overview of the difference between mainstream sixties and seventies poetry, see Charles Altieri, *Self and Sensibility in Contemporary American Poetry* (Cambridge and New York: Cambridge University Press, 1984); cf. Stanley Plumly's two-part article, "Chapter and Verse," part 1: "Rhetoric and Emotion," part 2: "Image and Emblem," *American Poetry Review* 7 (January–February 1978): 21–42, (May–June 1978): 21–32.

3. See Charles Altieri, *Enlarging the Temple: New Directions in American Poetry during the 1960s* (Lewisburg, Pa.: Bucknell

University Press, 1979), p. 19. Subsequently cited in the text as *ET.* The section on Merwin is reprinted in revised form as "Situating Merwin's Poetry since 1970," in *W. S. Merwin: Essays on the Poetry,* ed. Cary Nelson and Ed Folsom (Urbana: University of Illinois Press, 1987), pp. 159–97. This collection, in which my own essay first appeared, is subsequently cited in the text as *MEOP.*

4.  Stephen Berg and Robert Mezey, eds., *Naked Poetry: Recent American Poetry in Open Forms* (Indianapolis and New York: Bobbs-Merrill, 1969), p. xi.

5.  Richard Howard, *Alone with America: Essays on the Art of Poetry in the United States since 1950* (New York: Atheneum, 1969; enl. ed. 1980), p. 444. All references are to the second edition, subsequently cited in the text as *AA.* In the first edition Merwin gets thirty-two pages, followed closely by John Hollander (thirty-one) and James Dickey (twenty-three). Some other figures to measure against these: John Ashbery (nineteen), Frank O'Hara (sixteen), Denise Levertov (thirteen), Robert Creeley (nine), Allen Ginsberg (seven).

6.  Paul Carroll, *The Poem in Its Skin* (Chicago: Big Table, 1968), pp. 219–20.

7.  Karl Malkoff, *Crowell's Handbook of Contemporary American Poetry* (New York: Thomas Y. Crowell, 1973), p. 208.

8.  Cary Nelson, "The Resources of Failure: W. S. Merwin's Deconstructive Career," *Boundary 2* 5 (Winter 1977): 573–98; reprinted in a revised version in *Our Last First Poets* (Urbana: University of Illinois Press, 1981), pp. 179–215; and revised again in *MEOP,* pp. 78–121, see p. 80.

9.  Harold Bloom, "The New Transcendentalism: The Visionary Strain in Merwin, Ashbery, and Ammons," in *Figures of Capable Imagination* (New York: Seabury Press, 1976), pp. 124–27.

10. Alan Williamson, "Language against Itself: The Middle Generation of Contemporary Poets," in *American Poetry since 1960: Some Critical Perspectives,* ed. Robert Shaw (Cheadle Hulme: Carcanet Press, 1973), p. 56.

11. W. S. Merwin, *The Lice* (New York: Atheneum, 1967), p. 30. Subsequently cited in the text as *L.*

12. James Atlas, "Diminishing Returns: The Writings of W. S. Merwin," in Shaw, *American Poetry since 1960,* p. 76.

13. Robert Pinsky, *The Situation of Poetry: Contemporary Poetry and Its Traditions* (Princeton, N.J.: Princeton University Press, 1977), pp. 92–93.

14. Lieberman, *Unassigned Frequencies,* p. 260.

15. Andrew Waterman, "The Illusions of Immediacy," *Times Literary Supplement,* 29 July 1977, p. 836.

**16.** Bloom, "New Transcendentalism," pp. 128, 129.

**17.** Altieri, "Situating Merwin's Poetry," p. 172.

**18.** Turner Cassity, "Dresden Milkmaids: The Pitfalls of Tradition," *Parnassus: Poetry in Review* 5 (Fall–Winter 1976): 300. There are, of course, notable exceptions to this generational schema. In *MEOP,* William H. Rueckert ("Rereading *The Lice:* A Journal") and Charles Molesworth ("W. S. Merwin: Style, Vision, Influence"), among others, testify to Merwin's continuing appeal for some very acute critics. Still, if we compare the nonpartisan book reviews of the sixties and early seventies to their more recent counterparts, the difference is clear.

**19.** James Dickey, *Babel to Byzantium* (New York: Farrar, Staus & Giroux, 1968), p. 143.

**20.** Berg and Mezey, *Naked Poetry,* p. xi.

**21.** Altieri, *ET,* pp. 38–39, quoting Robert Duncan, "Toward an Open Universe," in *Poets on Poetry,* ed. Howard Nemerov (New York: Basic Books, 1966), p. 139.

**22.** See Nelson, "Merwin's Deconstructive Career," in *MEOP,* pp. 89–90; Robert Scholes, "Reading Merwin Semiotically," ibid., p. 77; Walter Kalaidjian, "Linguistic Mirages: Language and Landscape in Merwin's Later Poetry," ibid., p. 211; Robert Peters, *The Great American Poetry Bake-Off* (Metuchen, N.J.: Scarecrow Press, 1979), pp. 259, 267.

**23.** Malkoff, *Crowell's Handbook,* pp. 214–15.

**24.** Carroll, *Poem in Its Skin,* pp. 146–47.

**25.** For the Char connection, see Howard, *AA,* p. 435; and cf. Altieri, *ET,* p. 196: "Merwin is so disturbing in large measure because his roots are European—in poets like Rilke and Follain who have developed numerous variations on the *via negativa* as the way of enduring presence." It should be noted that Altieri's discussion of Merwin, although first published in *ET* (1979), was framed, as are the other chapters in that book, before 1970.

**26.** W. S. Merwin, "Beginning of the Plains," in *The Carrier of Ladders* (New York: Atheneum, 1970), p. 80.

**27.** See, for example, Harvey Gross, "The Writing on the Void: The Poetry of W. S. Merwin," *Iowa Review* 1 (Summer 1970): 105.

**28.** W. S. Merwin, *A Mask for Janus* (New Haven, Conn.: Yale University Press, 1952), p. 3.

**29.** John Bayley, "How to Be Intimate without Being Personal," *Parnassus: Poetry in Review* 2 (Fall–Winter 1973): 116–17.

**30.** Cassity, "Dresden Milkmaids," p. 295.

**31.** W. S. Merwin, "A Birthday," in *Opening the Hand* (New York: Atheneum, 1983), p. 67. But for a defense of the "variable caesura" as "dramatic interruption," see Edward Brunner, *"Opening*

*the Hand:* The Variable Caesura and the Family Poems," in
*MEOP,* pp. 276–95.

### *Chapter Twelve: On the Other Side of the Field:* The Collected Poems of Paul Blackburn

1. *The Collected Poems of Paul Blackburn,* ed. Edith Jarolim (New York: Persea Books, 1985). All parenthetical references in the text are to this edition.

2. Stephen Berg and Robert Mezey, eds., *Naked Poetry: Recent American Poetry in Open Forms* (Indianapolis and New York: Bobbs-Merrill, 1969), p. xi.

3. Brad Leithauser, "The Confinement of Free Verse," *New Criterion* 5 (May 1987): 11.

4. Joan Retallack, "The Meta-Physik of Play: *L-A-N-G-U-A-G-E* U. S. A.," *Parnassus: Poetry in Review* 12 (Fall–Winter 1984): 218.

5. Paul Blackburn, comp. and trans., *Proensa: An Anthology of Troubadour Poetry,* ed. George Economou (New York: Paragon House, 1986).

6. Jarolim's text follows Blackburn's own lineation, spacing, and layout. Some poems are single-spaced, others double-spaced. For convenience, all poems quoted in this chapter are single-spaced.

7. *The Collected Poems of William Carlos Williams,* vol. 1: *1909–1939,* ed. A. Walton Litz and Christopher MacGowan (New York: New Directions, 1986), p. 107.

8. Gilbert Sorrentino, "Singing, Virtuoso," *Parnassus: Poetry in Review* 4 (Spring–Summer 1976); reprinted in Sorrentino, *Something Said: Essays* (Berkeley, Calif.: North Point Press, 1984), p. 109.

9. *The Collected Poems of Frank O'Hara,* ed. Donald Allen (New York: Alfred A. Knopf, 1971), p. 340.

10. Robert Kelly, "Introduction," in *The Journals of Paul Blackburn,* ed. Kelly (Santa Barbara, Calif.: Black Sparrow Press, 1975), unpaginated.

11. Alex Preminger, Frank J. Warnke, and O. B. Hardison, Jr., eds., *Princeton Encyclopedia of Poetry and Poetics,* enl. ed. (Princeton, N.J.: Princeton University Press, 1974), p. 770.

12. Charles Bernstein, "Undone Business," in *Content's Dream, Essays 1975–84* (Los Angeles: Sun & Moon Press, 1986), p. 332.

13. *The Collected Works of W. B. Yeats,* vol. 1: *The Poems,* ed. Richard J. Finneran (New York: Macmillan, 1989), p. 262.

*1.* Roland Barthes, *The Pleasure of the Text,* trans. Richard Miller (New York: Hill & Wang, 1975), p. 38. For the French original, see *Le Plaisir du texte* (Paris: Editions du Seuil, 1973), p. 62.

*2.* Roland Barthes, *Writing Degree Zero,* trans. Annette Lavers and Colin Smith (New York: Hill & Wang, 1967), p. 48. For the French original, see *Le Degré zero de l'écriture* (Paris: Editions du Seuil, 1953), pp. 37–38.

*3.* Roland Barthes, *Mythologies,* trans. Annette Lavers (New York: Hill & Wang, 1972), pp. 133–34; subsequently cited in the text as *M.* For the French original, see *Mythologies* (Paris: Editions du Seuil, 1957), pp. 219–220.

*4.* "Twenty Key Words for Roland Barthes," interview conducted by Jean-Jacques Brochier in *Magazine littéraire,* February 1975; reprinted in Roland Barthes, *Le Grain de la voix: Entretiens 1962–1980* (Paris: Editions du Seuil, 1981), p. 210. The citations in this essay are primarily from the English translation: *The Grain of the Voice: Interviews 1962–1980,* trans. Linda Coverdale (New York: Hill & Wang, 1985), p. 222; subsequently cited as *GV,* with references to the French version in brackets.

*5.* Roland Barthes, *A Lover's Discourse: Fragments,* trans. Richard Howard (New York: Hill & Wang, 1978), pp. 6–7. For the French original, see *Fragments d'un discours amoureux* (Paris: Editions du Seuil, 1977), p. 10. Subsequent citation in the text has the French page number in brackets.

*6.* *Roland Barthes by Roland Barthes,* trans. Richard Howard (New York: Hill & Wang, 1978), pp. 6–7. For the French original, see *Roland Barthes par Roland Barthes* (Paris: Editions du Seuil, 1975). Subsequent citations ae primarily to the English version, cited as *BBB;* when included, French page numbers are in brackets. In the Hill and Wang edition, the opening forty-two pages of photographs and captions are unnumbered; the first page of the text is thus p. 43.

*7.* In the Richard Howard translation, the original French titles are used so as to maintain the alphabetical sequence; each title is then followed by an English translation: see pp. 43–49.

*8.* John Ashbery, *As We Know* (New York: Viking Press, 1979), p. 74.

*9.* See Harold Bloom, "John Ashbery: The Charity of the Hard Moments," in *Figures of Capable Imagination* (New York: Seabury Press, 1976), pp. 169–208.

*10.* For a related treatment of Ashbery's mediation of "cliché and assertion," see Charles Altieri, "John Ashbery and the Challenge of Postmodernism in the Visual Arts," *Critical Inquiry* 14 (Summer 1988): 805–30. This essay appeared after I had completed my own.

11. Lawrence Kramer, *Music and Poetry: The Nineteenth Century and After* (Berkeley, Los Angeles, and London: University of California Press, 1984), p. 218.

12. Janet Bloom and Robert Losada, "Craft Interview with John Ashbery," *New York Quarterly* 9 (Winter 1972): 24–25.

13. John Ashbery, *Three Poems* (New York: Viking Press, 1972), pp. 3–4. Subsequently cited in the text as *TP*.

14. See Bloom, "Charity of Hard Moments," pp. 200–203; cf. Stephen Fredman, *Poet's Prose: The Crisis in American Verse* (Cambridge and New York: Cambridge University Press, 1983), pp. 115–24.

15. Fredric Jameson, "Postmodernism and Consumer Society," in *The Anti-Aesthetic: Essays on Postmodern Culture*, ed. Hal Foster (Port Townsend, Wash.: Bay Press, 1983), pp. 113–14. Jameson argues that pastiche replaces parody in the late twentieth-century culture of corporate capitalism because there is no longer a fixed set of "Establishment" norms to react against, as there was for the High Modernists. "Pastiche is, like parody, the imitation of a peculiar or unique style . . . but it is a neutral practice of such mimicry, without parody's ulterior motive, without the satirical impulse, without laughter, without that still latent feeling that there exists something *normal* compared to which what is being imitated is rather comic. Pastiche is blank parody" (p. 114). Pastiche is further related to "the end of individualism," to "the conception of a unique self and private identity."

**Chapter Fourteen: "Voice Whisht through Thither Flood": Steve McCaffery's Panopticon and North of Intention**

1. Michel Foucault, *Discipline and Punish: The Birth of the Prison*, trans. Alan Sheridan (New York: Random House, Vintage Books, 1979), p. 205.

2. Jean Baudrillard, *Simulations*, trans. Paul Foss, Paul Patton, and Philip Beichtman (New York: Semiotext(e), 1983), p. 2.

3. Steve McCaffery, *Panopticon* (Toronto: Blew Ointment Press, 1984), unpaginated.

4. Steve McCaffery, "The Death of the Subject: The Implications of Counter-Communication in Recent Language-Centered Writing," $L=A=N=G=U=A=G=E$ (June 1980): Supplement Number One: Symposium on "The Politics of the Referent," unpaginated. For the revised version, see McCaffery, *North of Intention: Critical Essays, 1978–85* (New York: Roof Books, 1986), pp. 13–29. In a footnote on p. 13 McCaffery explains the process of revision. *North of Intention* is subsequently cited in the text as *NI*.

5. See McCaffery, "Carnival," $L=A=N=G=U=A=G=E$, February 1978, unpaginated.

6. Charles Bernstein, *Content's Dream, Essays 1978–84* (Los Angeles: Sun & Moon Press, 1986). I discuss this book in "Essaying Hot and Cool," *Michigan Quarterly Review* 26 (Spring 1987): 404–12.

7. Frank O'Hara, "Personism: A Manifesto," in *Collected Poems,* ed. Donald Allen (New York: Alfred A. Knopf, 1971), p. 498.

8. Brad Leithauser, "The Confinement of Free Verse," *New Criterion* 5 (May 1987): 6.

*Chapter Fifteen: "Collision or Collusion with History": Susan Howe's*
Articulation of Sound Forms in Time

1. Susan Howe, *The Western Borders* (Willits, Calif.: Tuumba Press, 1976), unpaginated.

2. Susan Howe, *Pythagorean Silence* (New York: The Montemora Foundation, 1982), unpaginated.

3. Susan Howe, *Articulation of Sound Forms in Time* (Windsor, Vt.: Awede, 1987), unpaginated.

4. In a letter to me of 15 June 1987 (subsequently cited, with her permission, as LMP), Susan Howe explains that, while reading about captivity narratives in the library, she happened upon a *History of Hatfield* (author unknown) that related the story of Hope Atherton. This and various other histories entered her poem: "I also love in these old histories and used," she writes, "the strict boundaries and fences, lots, and row numbers etc. against the unmapped wilderness they were interrupting." They became "metaphors for grammar." The quotes in this paragraph are from pp. 87, 85 of *History of Hatfield,* sent to me by Howe.

5. Susan Howe, "The Captivity and Restoration of Mrs. Mary Rowlandson," *Temblor* 2 (1985): 113–21. Subsequently cited in the text as CMR.

6. Susan Howe, *My Emily Dickinson* (Berkeley, Calif.: North Atlantic Books, 1985), discussed above in chap. 2, "Canon and Loaded Gun."

7. Robert Lowell, "Margaret Fuller Drowned," in *History* (New York: Farrar, Straus & Giroux, 1973), p. 87.

8. Since the pages of the Awede edition are unnumbered, I shall refer to the sections by number.

9. Rodney Jones, "Thoreau," in *The Morrow Anthology of Younger American Poets,* ed. Dave Smith and David Bottoms (New York: William R. Morrow, Quill Books, 1985), pp. 346–47.

10. Susan Howe, "Thorow," *Temblor* 6 (1987): 3–21.

11. Howe cites this stanza in *My Emily Dickinson,* p. 135.

12. Hart Crane, *The Complete Poems and Selected Letters* (New York: Doubleday, Anchor Books, 1966), p. 34.

13. See Crane, letter to Harriet Monroe (1926), ibid., pp. 234–40.

14. Samuel Beckett, "Lessness," in *I Can't Go On, I'll Go On, a Selection from Samuel Beckett's Work,* ed. Richard Seaver (New York: Grove Press, 1966), p. 555.

# Index